Mountford John Byrde Baddeley, Charles Slegg Ward

South Devon, Including W. Dorset Coast, and South Cornwall

With a Full Description of Dartmoor and the Scilly Isles

Mountford John Byrde Baddeley, Charles Slegg Ward

South Devon, including W. Dorset Coast, and South Cornwall
With a Full Description of Dartmoor and the Scilly Isles

ISBN/EAN: 9783337033729

Printed in Europe, USA, Canada, Australia, Japan

Cover: Foto ©Andreas Hilbeck / pixelio.de

More available books at **www.hansebooks.com**

Thorough Guide Series.

SOUTH DEVON
[INCLUDING W. DORSET COAST]

AND

SOUTH CORNWALL

WITH A FULL DESCRIPTION OF

DARTMOOR AND THE SCILLY ISLES.

BY

C. S. WARD, M.A.,
AUTHOR OF "NORTH DEVON AND NORTH CORNWALL," ETC.

AND

M. J. B. BADDELEY, B.A.,
AUTHOR OF "THE ENGLISH LAKES," ETC.

17 MAPS AND PLANS
By BARTHOLOMEW.

THIRD EDITION, REVISED.

"The foam-laced margin of the western sea."

LONDON:
DULAU & CO., 37, SOHO SQUARE, W.
1889.

MAP INDEX.

※ The inch Ordnance Survey of South Devon and South Cornwall is about 80 years old, and, except for the addition of the railways, the maps are issued to the public unrevised. In two directions revision is specially needed, viz., the neighbourhood of towns, *e.g.*, Torquay and Falmouth, and of Dartmoor. In the former case many new roads have been made, and much ground that at the date of the survey was out in the country has been covered with buildings; in the latter many tracks are retained, which, if they ever existed, have long ceased to show more than intermittent vestiges of their former course. The map of Dartmoor is indeed free from the glaring errors which mark the survey or rather non-survey of parts of Exmoor, and, as a whole, it is trustworthy. Our half-inch maps of the Lizard and Land's End districts are from the new inch Ordnance maps, and sections II., III., IV., and V. have been much improved for this edition, though we still await the publication of the inch survey of Dartmoor to render them complete. The Gidleigh and Merrivale plans are reduced from the new six-inch survey.

As far as possible the maps are inserted so as to face the portions of the volume they illustrate.

Index Map	. . . .	inside cover
Sections.		To face Page
I.	Seaton, Sidmouth, Exmouth, Exeter, &c. . .	3
	Plan of Exeter Cathedral	27
	Plan of Exeter	30
IA.	Exeter, Exe Valley	32
II.	Dawlish, Torquay, Dartmouth, &c . . .	39
III.	Kingsbridge Slapton, Salcombe, &c. . .	70
IV.	Ivybridge, Totnes, and South Dartmoor . .	75
	Plans of Gidleigh and Merrivale Antiquities .	93
V.	Princetown, Okehampton, and North Dartmoor .	122
	Plans of Plymouth, &c.	133
VI.	Plymouth, Tamar and Tavy valleys . . .	146
VII.	Looe, Fowey, Truro, &c.	149
VIII.	Falmouth, Lizard, Land's End, and Scilly Isles .	167
IX.	Lizard	181
X.	Land's End	193

CONTENTS.

	Page
Introduction	x
Approaches	1
London to Bridport or Exeter, G.W.R.	2
Bridport to Charmouth and Lyme Regis	3
Charmouth	4
Lyme Regis	5
Lyme Regis by the Landslip to Seaton	6
Bristol	9
Tiverton Junction to Tiverton or Hemyock	11
London to Exeter, &c., L. & S.W.R.	12
Axminster to Lyme Regis	13
Seaton Junction to Seaton	13
Sidmouth Junction to Sidmouth	14
North and Midlands to Bristol or Bath and Templecombe	15
Seaton	17
Excursions from Seaton :	
Axmouth, Bindon, &c.	17
Landslip, Lyme Regis, &c.	17
Seaton to Sidmouth	18
Sidmouth	21
Excursions from Sidmouth :	
Ladram Bay, Sidbury Castle, &c.	22
Sidmouth to Ottery St. Mary	23
,, ,, Seaton	25
,, ,, Budleigh Salterton	25
Exeter	26
Exeter to Tiverton and Dulverton	31
,, ,, Exmouth and Budleigh Salterton . . .	33
Exmouth	34
Exeter to Dawlish or Teignmouth (over Haldon) . .	36
Exeter to Chagford	37
Exeter to Plymouth	38
Dawlish	39
Dawlish to Teignmouth (over Holcombe Down) . .	40
Teignmouth	41
Teignmouth to Torquay (by road)	41

CONTENTS.

	Page
Newton Abbot	42
Newton Abbot to Ipplepen, &c.	43
,, Torquay and Dartmouth	43
Kingsbridge Road to Kingsbridge	44
Torquay	46
Excursions from Torquay:	
Anstey's Cove, Babbicombe, &c.	50
Compton Castle, &c.	51
Berry Pomeroy Castle and Totnes (by road)	52
Torquay to Dartmouth or Brixham	53
Brixham to Kingswear (by coast)	55
Dartmouth	57
Dartmouth to Totnes (by river)	58
Totnes	60
Totnes to Dartmouth (by river)	62
Dartmouth to Kingsbridge (by road)	62
Torcross to Salcombe	63
Kingsbridge	66
Kingsbridge to Kingsbridge Road	66
,, ,, Dartmouth	66
,, ,, Plymouth (by road)	67
,, ,, Salcombe, Bolt Head, &c.	68
Salcombe to Torcross	69
,, ,, Bolt Head	70
Dartmoor	72
Totnes to Ashburton	74
Ashburton	75
Excursions from Ashburton:	
Buckland Drives, Holne Chase, &c.	76
Rippon Tor, Heytor, &c.	77
Ashburton to Widdecombe and Chagford	78
,, ,, Tavistock (by road)	81
Two Bridges to Okehampton	82
Newton Abbot to Chagford (by Dunsford)	84
,, ,, ,, (by Moreton Hampstead)	87
Bovey Tracey	87
Bovey to Heytor and Ashburton	88
Lustleigh	89
Chagford	92
Excursions from Chagford:	
Holy Street Mill, Rushford Mill	93
Gidleigh, Fingle Bridge, &c.	94
Castor, Cranmere, &c.	96
Cranmere to Lidford	99
Cawsand Beacon	100
Chagford or Moreton to Widdecombe, Tavistock	101
Widdecombe to Ashburton	102
Princetown to Yelverton	103
Exeter to Okehampton L. & S.W.R.	104

CONTENTS

	Page
Okehampton	105
Excursions from Okehampton:	
Cawsand Beacon, Two Bridges	106
Yes Tor	107
Yes Tor to Lidford	107
Okehampton to Tavistock	108
Bridestowe to Mary Tavy (over the Moor)	108
Lidford	108
Lidford to Chagford	109
" " Okehampton	110
" " Tavistock and Plymouth	110
Tavistock	111
Excursions from Tavistock:	
Brentor, Lidford	112
" to Mary Tavy	113
Mary Tavy, Bridestowe (over the Moor)	113
Princetown	115
Princetown to Ivybridge (over the Moor)	117
Ivybridge	118
" to Plymouth (by coast)	119
" " Princetown	121
Tavistock to Moreton Hampstead or Ashburton	122
Two Bridges to Ashburton	123
Tavistock to Ivybridge by Cadover Bridge	123
" " Liskeard (by road)	124
" " Plymouth	126
Plymouth to Princetown	127
" " Ivybridge (by rail)	129
" " " (by coast)	130
Plymouth & Devonport	133
Excursions from Plymouth	
Saltram, Mount Edgcumbe, &c.	139
Trematon, Antony, &c.	140
River Tamar, &c.	141
Eddystone Lighthouse	143
Rame Head, &c.	145
Plymouth to Truro (by rail)	147
Liskeard	148
Excursions from Liskeard:	
Looe	148
St. Cleer, Cheesewring, &c.	149
Tavistock, &c.	150
St. Neot	152
Lostwithiel	154
Par to Fowey and Luxulion	155
St. Austell	157
Truro	159
Truro to Falmouth	161

CONTENTS.

	Page
Plymouth to Falmouth (by coast)	161
Plymouth to Looe	162
Looe to Liskeard	163
„ „ Fowey	163
St. Austell to Mevagissey	166
Mevagissey to Portlscatho	167
Portlscatho to Falmouth	170
Falmouth	171
Excursions from Falmouth:	
Pendennis Castle, Truro (by water)	172
St. Mawes, St. Anthony, Portlscatho, &c.	173
Helford Passage, &c.	174
Roscrow, &c.	176
Penjerrick	177
The Lizard (road and coast)	177
Truro to Penzance	178
The Lizard	180
Approaches to Helston	181
Helston to Lizard Town	181
Coast-walk round the Lizard Peninsula	182
Helston, Gunwalloe, Mullion, &c.	182
Mullion to Lizard Town (by Kynance)	183
Lizard Town to Cadgwith	187
Helston to Penzance (by coast)	188
Marazion	190
St. Michael's Mount	190
Penzance	192
Excursions from Penzance:	
Gulval, Castle-an-Dinas, &c.	194
Madron, Lanyon Quoit, &c.	195
St. Just (direct)	197
„ (by Sancreed)	197
„ to Land's End	197
Land's End (direct)	198
„ to the Logan	200
Land's End (by the Logan)	203
Lamorna	204
„ to the Logan	205
St. Ives to St. Just	205
Helston (by coast)	206
Scilly Isles	208
Index	218

INTRODUCTION.

Our aim in this book is to complete, from a tourist's standpoint, the description of that beautiful south-western portion of England which was begun in our Guide to North Devon and North Cornwall. The kindly reception accorded to that volume has encouraged us in our endeavours to render the present one as correct and complete as possible, and we venture to hope that the traveller, who decides on exploring some of the less frequented and comparatively remote portions of the southern coast-line, will here find assistance not hitherto provided for him.

District described.—Taking as our starting-points Bridport and Axminster, as far as which towns we have briefly treated the approaches from London, and—as a focus of the Midlands—Birmingham, we furnish guidance along the whole coast-route to the Land's End. Inland we trace the course of the Great Western and South Western Railways through the two counties. Exeter and its delightful environs are described at some length, and of Dartmoor we treat as fully as we did of Exmoor in the companion book. The Cornish Moors culminating in Brown Willy belong to the northern district, but the lower and navigable portion of the Tamar, and the Liskeard region, extending to the Cheesewring, are included in the area covered by this volume. The peninsula about Penzance is debatable ground and is described in detail in both volumes, and as the Scilly Islands may be made the terminus of a tour along either seaboard, they, too, find a place in each book.

The Scenery.—On this head few words need be added to what has been written in the body of the book. Extent and varied formation of coast-line, beauty or quaintness, as the case may be, of the towns and villages upon it, silvan luxuriance in deep and fertile valleys—these are the distinguishing features of the scenery of South Devon and South Cornwall. The coast presents a succession of abrupt changes, interesting alike to the geologist and the lover of unsullied natural beauty. First we have the exquisite confusion of the Landslip, flanked eastward by the singular, flat-topped range of hills abutting on the coast between Lyme Regis and Bridport. Then come the chalk cliffs of Seaton and Beer, followed by the blood-red ones of Sidmouth, the sandstone of which, with an interval of depression about the estuary of the Exe, is continued past Dawlish almost to Teignmouth. The next noticeable feature is the magnesian limestone about Babbicombe, Anstey's Cove and Hope's Nose, beyond which, round the inner part of Tor Bay, green meadows, broken only by a crumbling cliff or two of sandstone, slope gently to the shore. To these succeed the towering limestone bluff of Berry Head and the cliffs onward to the mouth of the Dart, beyond which the metamorphosed slates are represented by the Start and the rugged weather-worn promontories of Prawle Point, Bolt Head, Bolt Tail and Stoke Point—the boldest and most picturesque headlands along the South Devon coast. Thence to Plymouth, cultivation with a few breaks again approaches the water's edge. At and about Plymouth limestone once more crops out, and beyond that town the green wooded slopes of Mount Edgcumbe quickly give place to an almost continuous line of lofty cliffs which, interrupted by narrow rivermouths and still narrower V-shaped ravines, extend the whole length of the Cornish coast. The only considerable breaks in this bold sea-front are at Tywardreath Bay and at the head of Mount's Bay, where, for some five or six miles, owing to the comparatively low level of the country thereabouts, there is an interval of sandy shore. Beyond Penzance, granite, which so far has only now and again appeared, forms the magnificent cliff-rampart of which the Logan, Tol-pedn-Penwith and the Land's End are only the most prominent features. In these last few miles we have undoubtedly the wildest and grandest bit of English coast scenery, and happily the nature of the cliff-top is such that it can be fully seen without overtaxing the endurance or the nerves of the least valiant pedestrian.

Additional beauty and interest is imparted to the coastline by the number and variety of the estuaries which indent it. Of the larger ones, the Fal and the Tamar are the finest. Both admit of a delightful sail up them for

12 or 15 miles. The Salcombe opening, a blue and almost land-locked expanse, branching into numberless creeks, and flanked by gently sloping acclivities, offers, at high tide, a similar excursion as far as Kingsbridge. The Teign and the Exe, with their picturesque surroundings of green hill and woody glade, as seen from some of the neighbouring heights, atone, in a measure, for the absence of fresh-water inland lakes, and the full length view of the former from Buckland Beacon and other heights about Ashburton, may recall to the memory of the Westmorland tourist the exquisite vista of the lower reach of Windermere, as seen from the High Street range.

Among the narrower estuaries the Dart carries off the palm, and the sail up it from Dartmouth to Totnes has a well-earned reputation for beauty. Next to it in attractiveness come the Fowey and the Looe Water, while the mouths of the Yealm, the Erme, and the Avon, have one and all their particular charms. The little towns of Fowey and East and West Looe at the entrance to their respective estuaries are almost unique in their situation and appearance, but quaintest and most extraordinary of all Cornish places of habitation is the village of Polperro four miles west of Looe. How a population numbering some hundreds has contrived to squeeze itself into the bottom of a valley hardly wide enough to accommodate a tiny stream, may be seen, but not imagined.

Of the numerous, more or less, fashionable watering places which line this favoured coast, it is unnecessary to say more than is said in the body of the book. Torquay, Teignmouth, Dawlish, Exmouth, Sidmouth, Seaton, Budleigh Salterton, Paignton, Dartmouth, Falmouth, and Penzance have all special claims on the seaside sojourner, and are all described as fully as their importance as tourist-resorts seems to require.

We have treated the physical character of Dartmoor so fully in our section devoted to that wide upland, that we need only here make a passing comment on its featurelessness as a mountain region, its genuine interest to the antiquarian, and the charming bird's-eye views of the surrounding country which are presented from its frontier heights. The only other hills worth mention in the district we describe are the Haldon range, from the backbone of which the prospect is on both sides singularly rich and diversified. The Cornish uplands are barren in themselves and afford comparatively poor views, though the environment of sea about the westernmost hills is a pleasant feature.

The valley scenery of South Devon and South Cornwall, lying between the source of the rivers and the commencement of their estuaries, though lacking equally the powerful contrasts imparted to the valleys of the Lake District and of Wales by the crags and screes which rise above their cultivated parts, and the impressiveness which the limestone dales of Derbyshire obtain from their narrowness and the broken precipitous character of their sides, is beautiful and seldom monotonous. The streams are bright, clear and winding, alternating between shallow rock-strewn bed and tranquil pool. There are few bare or dull shore-lines, and the lower hills are mostly luxuriant with leafy honours. Taken throughout, perhaps, the most beautiful river-valley is that of the Teign from above Chagford to Chudleigh; the Dart from Holne Chase to Totnes follows close in its wake, and the other Dartmoor streams run sparkling down combes in which the angler and the lover of nature equally delight to linger. In Cornwall the Fowey distances all competitors, and it cannot be better seen than from the railway between Doublebois and Bodmin Road. All this river scenery is at its best in the late autumn, when the varied tints of the foliage are as delightful as are the delicate colours of the sea-pink and wild squill with which many of the Cornish sea-slopes are decked in spring. The Luxulion valley (*p.* 155) is as beautiful as it is geologically interesting.

Accommodation.—In all the recognised watering-places hotels and lodgings abound, and except during August, the passing traveller will find no difficulty in obtaining quarters to suit his taste and his purse. During that month, however, he will do well to secure his bed beforehand, and it need scarcely be said that no familly party should at that time arrive unannounced on the chance of being able to find lodgings. We should not give this obvious warning had we not listened, in the course of our westward wanderings, to more than one direful tale from paterfamilias at his wits' end. The hotel charges and the rents of apartments call for no special comment. Compared with those of other holiday resorts they are, perhaps, somewhat below the average, and the thrifty traveller will find that the whole district may be traversed at a very moderate outlay, if he makes his journey either before or after the time of the summer rush of visitors. Along the less frequented portions of the seaboard, the inns are humble and proportionately cheap. Cyclists' inns (H.Q. and Q.) and Temperance houses have been given throughout.

The season for a tour.—The majority of visitors to our holiday resorts appear to have little or no alternative as to the time when they shall leave home, but it may be worth while to point out to those who are free to choose that neither Devon nor Cornwall is seen at its best during the often sultry days of August. Devonshire, from the end of May and on into the early weeks of summer, has a freshness of colouring that lends to its loveliest scenes a charm which is lost when its woods and lanes have put on a deeper and maturer shade of green, and the angler need not be reminded that August is the one summer month when the trout of the west rise worst to the fly. The latter part of the autumn brings the rich colouring of changing foliage and, in spite of shorter days and possibly unsettled weather, may well be preferred, by the rambling traveller, to days when the narrow Devon lanes are often as close and stifling as they are steep. The Cornish scenery is less dependent on the seasons for its attractiveness than that of Devon, and much of it even in mid-winter shows to full advantage. There are few combinations of beauty and grandeur more impressive than that of a mighty ground-sea rolling in, under a bright sky, against the gorgeously lichen-coloured cliffs between the Logan and the Land's End. Of course, the average weather in summer is the more favourable for travelling, but if our own experience of these western shores may be taken as a sample, there is no time of the year in which the properly equipped pedestrian may not, with small risk of being seriously weather-bound, explore the Cornish coast. More than once we have ourselves followed the cliffs afoot from Falmouth round to Hartland during the month of January and met with no inconvenience to detract from the enjoyment of the walk.

Fishing.—Fresh-water angling is, except in the Fowey, for which Lostwithiel is the best head-quarters, scarce in South Cornwall. In South Devon it abounds, and small trout, a good many peel, with sea-trout or truff, and salmon are the rewards of the skilful fly or minnow-fisher. The fishing is preserved by fishery boards, and tickets can be obtained for a nominal sum either of agents in the principal towns or at the hotels and inns on or near the banks of the several streams. The lower parts of the rivers are generally wooded, while their upper courses traverse the open moor. As a natural consequence, the largest and best fed fish are to be found where they are most difficult to capture, and if the angler desires to catch many fish he will have to content himself with the smaller fry, with which the moorland waters are well stocked. The remarkable " Leas " or " Leys " at Slapton and Tor Cross afford excellent sport of its kind.

The following details have been kindly supplied to us by the secretaries of the several associations and by others interested. Anglers new to the district will find useful the "Guide to Sea-fishing and the Rivers of South Devon," and the "Fisherman's Map" of the district, both published by Hearder & Sons, Union St., Plymouth, who also issue fishing-tickets for all the streams, and will give any information.

The AXE [Seaton, Colyton, Axminster]. *Season* : Mch. 1 to Oct. 1. Artificial flies only. No wading. No trout less than 7 inches long to be kept. *Tickets* (including license) : season, 30s.; month, 10s. 6d. to 15s. of Sec. Upper Axe Association, Axminster. "Riverlands," [Axminster]. *Season*, as above. *Tickets :* season, 21s.; month, 10s. 6d.

The DART [Totnes, Buckfastleigh, (Ashburton), Post Bridge]. *Season :* Mch. 1 to Sept. 30 (trout), to Oct. 30 (salmon). *Tickets :* (salmon) season only, 20s.; (trout) season, 10s.; day, 2s., of the Sec. to the conservators, Bridgetown, Totnes. Tickets are also issued at the *Seymour* and *Seven Sisters'* Hotels, Totnes, &c.

The ERME [Ivybridge]. Apply to Hearder & Sons, Union St., Plymouth.

The FOWEY [Lostwithiel]. Best months, July to Sept. Salmon-peel and trout, salmon. *Licenses :* (trout) 3s.; (peel and salmon) 10s., to be had of the agent, Lostwithiel.

The PLYM, with tributaries *Meavy* and *Cadover* [Plymouth to Bickleigh or Dowsland Station]; and the TAVY, with tributary *Walkham* [Tavistock, Horrabridge] are under the Tavy and Plym Fishery Board (apply to the Clerk to the Board, Tavistock). *Season :* Mch. 1 to Oct. 1 (trout), Nov. 1 (salmon). *License*, 7s. 6d. *Tickets :* season (all the preserved water), 12s. 6d.; Cadover, 5s.; Walkham, 2s. 6d.; Tavy above junction with Walkham, 5s. Day tickets, 1s.

Artificial fly only below Denham Bridge. No wading in
Tavy. The Plym between Bickleigh and Shaugh Bridges
may not be fished.

THE TEIGN. (i.) *Upper Teign Association*, Hon. Sec. at
Chagford. *Season:* March 3 to Sept. 30. No wading above
Clifford Bridge. *License:* 2s. 6d. *Tickets:* season, 21s.;
month, 10s. 6d.; week, 5s.; day, 1s. of the Hon. Sec. Day-
tickets only are issued at Chagford, Exeter (12 & 20
North St., 251, High St.), Moreton Hampstead (White
Hart), Drewsteignton (New Inn), and Dunsford (Royal Oak).

(ii.) *Lower Teign Association*, Hon. Sec. at Chudleigh.
Season: March 3 to Sept. 30 (trout), Nov. 20 (salmon). No
wading before June 1. *License and ticket:* (salmon) season,
22s. 6d.; day, 3s.; (trout) season, 13s.; month, 7s. 6d.;
week, 5s.; day, 3s. 6d. N.B.—The trout license (2s. 6d.)
included in foregoing charges holds good for the season.
Tickets can be obtained of the Hon. Sec., and also at
Chudleigh (Clifford Arms), Moreton Hampstead (White
Hart), Lustleigh (Cleave Hotel), Bovey Tracey (Dolphin),
Christow (Teign House Inn), and at Teignmouth, Newton
and Torquay.

Of other waters in South Devon the following are the
chief :—

AVON [South Brent, Kingsbridge Road].
EXE [Exeter, Tiverton].
OKEMENT, East and West Okehampton].
OTTER [Ottery St. Mary, Honiton].
YEALM [Cornwood].
SLAPTON LEA [Slapton Sands Hotel].
TORCROSS LEA [Torcross Hotel].

Visitors at the hotels have the privilege of fishing the
respective Leas, both of which abound in pike, perch, and
rudd. Boat and man, 4s. per day.

NOTE TO THE THIRD EDITION.—For this edition many of
the routes have been again travelled by the authors and a
good deal of the book re-written. Some routes have been
added, and the number of maps increased.

To the many travellers who have kindly made sugges-
tions, founded on experience, for the improvement of the
volume, we are much indebted and we hope for similar
communications in the future. As far as possible all
matter liable to alteration has been brought up to date.—
May, 1888.

ERRATA &c.

p. 34, under **Post**, cancel the word "Sunday" after *Del*.
p. 51, l. 9, read Phillpotts.
p. 111, l. 13 from foot, read *Nabarr*.
p. 196, l. 26, read *Kolumbethra*.
p. 218, under Beesands read [Kingsbridge].

At Ivybridge (*p.* 118), the *King's Arms* (also known as *Tom's*) is the C.T.C. house.

---

* 1st and 2nd Class only, 3rd Class as far as Plymouth, ½ hr. longer. All trains on the Midland and L. & S. W. lines carry third-class passengers and S. Devon.

Approaches.

GENERAL REMARKS.

As we have already remarked in our volume on North Devon and North Cornwall, the south-western counties of England can be reached by some of the best train services in the kingdom, both from London and from the central and northern counties. Tourist tickets, of which particulars will be found in the yellow sheet at the commencement of this volume, are issued from all parts. The best points for beginning a tour are:— Bridport (*G.W.R.*) or Axminster (*L.&S.W.R.*) for the whole length of the south coast of Devon and Cornwall; Exeter or Exmouth for the western part of Devon and the whole of Cornwall; Plymouth for Cornwall only; Liskeard, St. Austell, Falmouth, or Penzance for West Cornwall. Appended is a summary of the distances and time occupied on the journey from London, and (as a focus of the Midland Counties) from Birmingham to these starting points:—

		Miles.	Time (approx.) hrs. min.
London to Bridport (*G.W.*)		154	5.30
,, ,, Axminster (*S.W.*)		145	4.0
,, ,, Exeter (*S.W.*)		172	4.15
,, ,, ,, (*G.W.*)		194	4.15*
,, ,, Exmouth (*S.W.*)		182	5.0
,, ,, Plymouth (*G.W.*)		247	6.0*
,, ,, ,, (*S.W.*)		230	6.15
,, ,, Liskeard (*G.W.*)		265	7.0*
,, ,, Fowey		285	8.0
,, ,, St. Austell (*G.W.*)		286	7.50*
,, ,, Falmouth (*G.W.*)		314	8.50*
,, ,, Penzance (*G.W.*)		327	9.15*
Birmingham to Axminster (*Mid. and S.W.*)		168	6.0
,, ,, Exeter (*Mid. and G.W.*)		169	4.0*
,, ,, Plymouth (*Mid. and G.W.*)		221	5.45*
,, ,, Liskeard (*Mid. and G.W.*)		239	7.0*
,, ,, Fowey (*Mid. and G.W.*)		260	8.5*
,, ,, St. Austell (*Mid. and G.W.*)		260	7.50*
,, ,, Falmouth (*Mid. and G.W.*)		288	9.0*
,, ,, Penzance (*Mid. and G.W.*)		301	9.20*

* 1st and 2nd Class only, 3rd Class as far as Plymouth, ½ hr. longer.
All trains on the Midland and L. & S. W. lines carry third-class passengers and

There is now an excellent alternative route from the North *via* Crewe and the Severn Tunnel, worked with through carriages by the L. & N. W. and the G. W. conjointly.

London to Bridport (for Lyme Regis and Seaton) or Exeter by the Great Western Railway.

London to Swindon, 77 *m*; *Chippenham*, 94 *m*; *Bath*, 106½ *m*; *Bristol*, 118½ *m*; *Taunton*, 163½ *m*; *Exeter*, 194 *m*.

Chippenham to Bridport, 60 *m*. *Bridport to Charmouth (coach)*, 8 *m*; *Lyme Regis*, 10 *m*; *Seaton (road or footpath)*, 18 *m*.

The best scenery on the line, between London and Bristol, is that in the Thames valley between Slough and Reading, in the neighbourhood of Chippenham, and along the Avon and its tributaries from the Box tunnel to Bristol. After leaving London, the first objects of interest are, the Asylum and Cemetery of *Hanwell* (8 *m*.) on the left hand of the line. Near *Slough* (18½ *m*.), Windsor Castle comes into view on the left hand. Then we catch a glimpse of a singularly picturesque reach of the Thames, when the line crosses that river, a little short of *Maidenhead* (24 *m*.). Very pretty views of the Thames valley are also obtained to the north of the line near *Reading* [36 *m*.; Ref. Rms.; Hotels: *Great Western*; *Vastern* Temp., close to G.W., S.W. and S.E.R.; *George*, (H.Q.), King St.], between which town and Swindon we get a pretty view of the Thames at *Pangbourne* (41¼ *m*.; *Elephant and Castle*) and then pass no object of greater natural interest than the undulating chalk downs of Berkshire and Wilts. At **Swindon** (77 *m*.; *Ref. Rms.*) trains stop ten minutes, except the 9 a.m. from Paddington. *Chippenham* is the junction for Bridport.

For continuation of rail to Exeter, see p. 9.

Chippenham to Bridport (60 *m*.) **and Lyme Regis** (70 *m*.). Soon after leaving Chippenham, we see on the left the luxuriantly wooded hills in the midst of which stands Bowood, the noble mansion and park of the Marquess of Lansdowne. Then *Melskham* and its church are passed on the same side. Just short of *Trowbridge*, the lines from Devizes and Bath converge from the left and right respectively. At *Westbury*, the junction of the G.W.R. Salisbury Section, the north-western limit of Salisbury Plain appears close at hand on the left, and attracts special attention, by reason of its famous White Horse. This colossal design is formed

---

all on the G.W., except the 11.45 a.m. from Paddington and the corresponding up train.

From Bridport Station a well-appointed coach or omnibus starts about 4 p.m. (in connection with trains from Paddington, Bristol and Bath), *vid* Charmouth, 8 *m*., for Lyme Regis, 10 *m*.

From Axminster to Lyme there is an Omnibus 3 times a day, as well as a mail-cart that is allowed to convey passengers.

by the cutting away of the sward to show the chalk. It is of unknown antiquity, but has in recent years been cleared out afresh.

At **Frome** (Hotels: *Crown, George*, H.Q.), where some tourists will halt awhile to visit the beautiful *church* and the Bennett Memorial Cross, the North Somerset line from Bristol and Radstock comes in on the right, and then passing Marston House, the seat of the Earl of Cork and Orrery, on the same side, we reach *Witham*, the junction for Wells. *Alfred's Tower*, marking the spot where King Alfred raised his standard against the Danes, is soon conspicuous on the left, and then at *Bruton*, the next station, close to the line on the right is a magnificent Perpendicular church, with a tower worthy to rank with the best in Somersetshire. On the other side of the line appears, shortly afterwards, the ruined tower of a large dovecote, and then we pass under the Somerset and Dorset railway, just west of *Cole*. After leaving *Yeovil* (Pen Mills) *Station*, the town is passed on the right, and then threading a richly wooded valley, we go under the main line of the L. & S.W.R.

The succeeding country for some miles is particularly green, though somewhat flat. Just before reaching *Maiden Newton*, the fine and striking church of Cattistock is close by on the left. **Maiden Newton** (*Refreshment Room*) is the junction for Weymouth, and here passengers for Bridport change carriages. From it our route ascends one of the chief tributary valleys of the River Froom, and then passes through a half cultivated district, with a good deal of wood and common, which forms the watershed dividing this branch of the Froom from a tributary of the Brit, the stream that gives its name to Bridport. Eggardon Hill is the eminence above the line on the left. As we near our destination, the pretty and prettily situated village and church of Bradpole are seen on the right.

Bridport [Hotels: *Bull* (H.Q.); *Greyhound*; Coffee Tav.: *Three Cups. Pop.* 6,790] is a bright and clean town, with a broad main street. It is chiefly occupied with the manufacture of rope and twine and sea-fishing gear, and is only remarkable for the large number of its inns, said to number more than a hundred. The sea is about 1½ m. distant at Bridport Harbour [*George* (Q.)], to which point the railway is now extended—an uninteresting spot.

The pedestrian can begin his walk westward from Bridport Harbour by the cliffs, and in this way pass over the summit of *Golden Cup*, 615 ft., and *Stonebarrow* to *Charmouth* and *Lyme*, but the road from Bridport to these places is very picturesque.

Bridport to Charmouth, 7 m; **Lyme Regis**, 9 m. *Coach takes* 1½ *hrs.* These distances are from the western side of the town. From the station a good ¾-m. must be added. The route is a succession of ups and downs, and owing to high banks and hedges the views are best seen from the outside of the coach. The bridge over the Brit is crossed, and a long steady climb begins. Soon a roadside house, the *London Inn*, is passed, and *Symondsbury*, with a good church, is on the right in a well timbered valley. Over the hill on the left is *Eype Down*, whence the unfortunate Mr. Powell, M.P., was carried out to sea in his balloon. *Golden Cap* is the prominent table-topped hill on the same side. As we ascend, the view behind and to the right gradually widens, and then we pass round the southern slopes of *Haddon Hill*, crowned with an entrenchment, and having a few fragments of masonry, including an arched doorway. Then *The Vale* extends away on the right to Pillesdon Pen (910 *ft.*), locally reputed to be the highest Dorsetshire hill. **Chideock** (Inn : *Castle*, 1 bed), is a well-kempt village, about 3 m. from Bridport, with an interesting and well-restored church. Hence a road leads to *Seatown*, a fishing village under Golden Cap.

From Chideock our road becomes steep, and opens up a correspondingly extensive and beautiful view as we ascend.

The pedestrian by taking a path on the left may from the top of the ascent reach the summit of *Golden Cap*, a stiff little climb, worth making on account of the glorious view thence obtainable. He can then follow the cliffs to Charmouth and will pass on the sea-slopes of Stonebarrow Hill, the remains of an old chapel. An obelisk in a field nearer Charmouth has an inscription which tells its own tale.

The next village is *Morcombelake*, where are three roadside inns, of which the *Ship* is, perhaps, the best. We are now about half way to Lyme Regis, and begin the descent to the valley of the Char. The *Vale of Marshwood*, very beautiful, stretches far away to the right, and is bounded northwards by a succession of hills. The points on the skyline, reckoning from E. to W., are, Lewsdon, Pillesdon, 3 groups of firs called the Devil's Jumps, Marshwood Church and Lambert's Castle (trees on its east slope). Charmouth, backed by Black Ven, is due west, and further off still we catch sight of one or two of the houses in the upper part of Lyme Regis.

Charmouth.

Approaches : *vid* Axminster, *p.* 13 ; *vid* Bridport, *p.* 3.
Hotel : *Coach and Horses* (Q.) ; **Inn** : *George*.
Post : *Del.* *8 *a.m.*, 3.30 *p.m.* ; *desp.* *6.10 *p.m.* [*Sundays also.]

This is a singularly prettily placed little town. It is half-a-mile inland from the mouth of the Char and two miles east of Lyme Regis. Besides the inns above-named there are a good many lodgings, and few pleasanter places of a quiet sort are to be found along this coast. In itself the town possesses no features calling for special notice, but the many shapely hills which rise about it afford a variety of glorious views within easy walking distance. Among the pleasantest of such walks is that by *Conig's Castle*, an entrenched camp on the ridge bounding Marshwood Vale on the west, to *Lambert's Castle*, an important earthwork. Charmouth was made a borough by grant of the Abbot of Ford in 1320, but is chiefly known to history as the spot whence Charles II. tried to escape to the Continent after the battle of Worcester. He slept at the George Inn, then situated opposite to the present house of that name.

Whitchurch Canonicorum, 3 m. by road, has an interesting cruciform church, restored in 1888-9. The tower is Perpendicular, but the nave arcades are late Norman and Transitional-Norman. There is also some Early English work. In the north transept is a very early plain altar tomb, shown as that of St. Candida, to whom the church is dedicated. Notice also a curious painted wooden monument to one of the Floyers.

From Charmouth to Lyme Regis by road involves a sharp climb and descent. At low water the pedestrian can make his way by the shore. The road passes through a deep cutting at the top of the hill, and a large crack on both sides shows that, as on the cliffs between Lyme and Seaton, the treacherous "fox-mould" is still preparing further landslips. The view of Lyme from the high ground is pleasant but not to be compared with that from the west which we shall obtain on the way to Seaton.

Lyme Regis.

Approaches: *vid* Axminster, *p.* 13; *vid* Bridport, *p.* 3.
Hotels: *Cups* (H.Q.); *Lion*. **Inn**: *New*.
Post: del. *7.45 a.m., 12.45 p.m.; desp. 9.20 a.m., 12.20 and *5.40 p.m.
[* Sundays also.]

This little port and watering-place was once a town of some importance. It is first mentioned in 774, when Cenwulf, of Wessex, granted land near the mouth of Lyme Brook for salt boiling for the church at Sherborne. In Domesday fourteen saltmen are recorded as trading here, and in 1279 Edward I. made Lyme a borough. From 1295 to 1832 it returned two members to Parliament. The Cobb or quay was first built in 1347 and for a time the port was a flourishing one. It sent four ships to the siege of Calais, and two against the Armada, and its shipping in the days of Elizabeth was estimated as one-sixth that of London. During the Civil War it was fortified and favoured the side of the Parliament. The Royal troops vainly besieged it from April to June, 1644. The Duke of Monmouth landed here June 11, 1685, when Daniel Defoe, author of Robinson Crusoe, enlisted under him. Judge Jeffreys marked the demerits of the town by hanging twelve of its burgesses. Thomas Coram, the founder of the Foundling Hospital in London, was born here in 1668. Monmouth made his head-quarters at the "George Inn," but this and many other houses were destroyed by a great fire in 1844. Miss Mary Anning (*b.* 1800, *d.* 1847) was a native of Lyme, and she it was who first discovered the *ichthyosaurus* and *pleiosaurus* in its fossil-beds. She is buried in the church-yard and there is a window to her memory in the church, which was restored in 1885.

The town is situated in a steep and narrow valley close to the shore at the head of a large bay. Its main thoroughfare, *Broad Street*, contains the inns given on *p.* 5. Like Bridport, it is remarkable for the large number of its small inns, there being some two dozen in addition to those already named. The chief trade of the place is in stone. Along the shore west of the town runs the *Marine Parade*, the only level promenade about the place. It is furnished with shaded seats, and extends to a group of dwellings adjoining the Cobb—or quay—which forms a small harbour. The view of the town from the end of the Cobb and of the coast eastward is delightful. Black Ven and Hardown are close at hand. Next rises abruptly the level-topped Golden Cap, and beyond it the bright-coloured cliffs at Bridport Harbour. Then the green slopes about Abbotsbury, and the long low bank of the Chesil Beach, over which (on a clear day) rises the church of Wyke Regis, near Weymouth. The Isle of Portland, with its quarries is the outmost land. Of excursions from Lyme, Charmouth and the hills about it need not to be further noticed (*p.* 4). A pleasant inland walk is to *Uplyme*, *p.* 13. This may be reached by Silon Street and the Axminster road, and Hay Lane, but a pleasanter way is by the fields, "Middle Mill." From Silver Street, after two fields, cross the road to Colway lane and the Charmouth Road. We get a glimpse of the old manor house of Colway and its yews. A path goes by Hay Farm to Mill, and thence a lane to Uplyme, or from Mill we may go through meadows by Lovers' Walk Copse, and so to Uplyme Church with its aged yew tree. Close by is an old farm-house known as *Court Hall*, and by taking the road opposite the "Talbot Arms," we can proceed to *Holcombe*, where are the remains of a Roman villa. The return to Lyme may be varied by taking Gore Lane from Holcombe back to Uplyme.

Lyme Regis by the Landslip to Seaton.

(i.) *By the shore* (on a falling tide, starting not later than 2 hours after high water) to Whitlands, and there taking a cart-road that runs inland to the main road from Lyme to Exeter. This route involves a somewhat rough scramble. It has less to recommend it than either of those that follow. From the point where the main road is joined it is described under (iii.)

(ii.) "*Through the cliff*" to Whitlands, thence to the main road. This is a very picturesque walk. Ascend the hill by the road turning west at the top of Broad Street, and pass through a gate to a railed-off path on the left. This leads "through the cliff" as the local expression has it, *i.e.*, it traverses the undercliff which for so large a portion of the distance from Lyme to Seaton forms an irregular terrace between the higher ground and the shore. It is the result of a landslip more or less ancient. The view of the shore-line, eastward, is one of the most beautiful on the south coast, and is similar to, but finer than, that from the Cobb. The undercliff is not a level terrace, but delightfully irregular, and everywhere beautified by rich wild growth of underwood and climbing plants, and in the spring carpeted with wild flowers. It is, we believe, permissible to go by it all the way to the Landslip at Dowlands, but the tourist had better turn inland by the cart track to Whitlands and the main-road. For the route onward, see below under (iii.)

(iii.) *By road through Rowsedown and Dowlands to the Landslip and Seaton, about 8 m.*

Climb out of Lyme by the western road and, where this turns sharply to the right, look back for the exquisite view up the coast. We then in another half-mile or so enter Devonshire. At the cross-roads, beyond the second mile stone, turn to the left, and at the next junction to the right through Charton to **Rowsedown.** Here a modern Jacobean Lodge spans the road, and we enter the domain of Sir Henry Peek. All around is model and æsthetic, mansion, church and farm-buildings. The little church is worth inspection, and so is the fine hall of the mansion, if permission can be obtained. Its windows, by Lavers, depict events connected with the Duke of Monmouth and the history of Lyme. Leaving the domain by another lodge, in a few yards, Dowlands farm is reached. Here a fee of 6d. is payable, and then the visitor is free of the whole of the beauties and wonders of the Landslip, which is reached by passing through the farm-yard and then by a lane. The **Landslip** (*p.* 8) consists of a huge horse-shoe ravine, that has been caused by the slipping forward and downward of the land that previously filled up the inside of the shoe. The shifted mass, of many acres, has been projected on to the previously existing undercliff and in the process many curious shapes and contortions of the land have resulted. The view from the cliffs at the east end of the ravine affords the best idea of the appearance of things immediately after the subsidence in 1839, because there many isolated masses still preserve their covering of greensward, and seem to have weathered but little. The tourist is advised to follow the cliff westward till a track descends to the east end of the ravine, and then to ascend to its opposite side. There is no danger, but a little care is needed to hit off the way up. He should then walk round the inner margin of the ravine to its west end. Here it is occupied by huge edges and pillars of chalk, and seamed by long roof-like ridges. Bearing a little eastward again and seaward he can descend to the undercliff. As seen from above this undercliff is beautiful, but it can only be really appreciated by a leisurely ramble along its devious tracks. The finest part is just west of the west end of the ravine. There from below it is easy to fancy oneself gazing at some huge ivy-mantled castle. We seem to occupy the outside of the deep moat, neglected and well-nigh filled by a tangled growth of underwood and creepers. Across it rises a many-bastioned wall festooned and almost hidden in ivy. Along the top of that we see the main platform, whence tower, stern and abrupt, the walls of the fortress. This is really no fancy description, as the tourist will himself realise, if he views this grand confusion of nature from below. He will find, too, that the depth of the "moat," and the height of the "ramparts" forbid any attempt to ascend direct from the lower ground to the cliff-top. He should return by the way he came, or, better, pick his way westward, until the beautiful tangle of greenery and flowers gives place to a much fissured and broken slope, by which he can regain the higher ground, and make his way in the direction of **Seaton** (*p.* 17). A path presently leads obliquely inland, and he will descend past the Coast-guard station, getting a fine view of the chalk cliffs of White Cliff and Beer Head, to the Axmouth and Seaton road, and by crossing the bridge (*toll* 1*d.*) over the Axe reach the latter place.

The undercliff was formed by subsidence long ages back, but the ravine of the Dowlands Landslip in December, 1839. On the 23rd cracks were noticed along the cliff, and on the 24th the occupants of some cottages quitted their houses, which were felt to be sinking. On the night of the 24th the Coast-guard men found that large fissures had formed, and daylight on Christmas Day revealed the fact of the great slip. The surface remained comparatively undisturbed, and the cottages and their gardens and orchard were little injured. Since then the isolated masses about the ravine have many of them fallen, and most of them been much altered, especially at the west end, by weathering. This convulsion had, doubtless, long been preparing. The chalk and greensand here rest on the impervious lias, and water, especially in the wet summer of 1839, having gradually washed out the loose intervening sand, locally called "fox mould," the upper layers crushed down where they were undermined, and where that was not the case heaved and contorted the adjacent ground. The ravine resulted from a general movement seaward of the disturbed mass. The process is still going on, and the road between Lyme and Charmouth during the winter of 1882-3 was considerably injured in this way. The great landslip at Crich, in Derbyshire, which occurred in the summer of 1882, was brought about in the same manner—a stratum of hard limestone slipping away from an impervious lower one—locally known as "t'clee bed."

Chippenham to Bristol (*main route continued from p. 2*).

At *Chippenham* we cross the Avon, and 5 miles further enter the famous *Box tunnel* (16½ m. beyond *Swindon*) 1¾ m. long. Hence to within a mile of Bristol, we thread a narrow valley, flanked by graceful slopes and abundantly enriched with wood. A third of the way down, after re-entering the valley of the Avon between Box and *Bathampton*, just where the river issues from the beautiful Warleigh valley on the left hand, we reach **Bath** [107 m.; *Ref. Rms.* The Midland Station, Manvers St., is ¾ m. from G.W. Sta. Hotels: *Grand Pump Room*; *York House*; *White Lion* (H.Q.); *Christopher*, commercial; *Fernley's* Temp.] the handsome terraces and crescents of which are seen to very fair advantage from the railway on both sides of the station.

Between Bath and Bristol the railway, running parallel for some distance with the road, the river, and the Bath extension of the Midland system, affords a succession of very pleasing views, especially in the neighbourhood of *Kelston Park* on the right hand, where the beautifully timbered lower slopes of Lansdown descend to the riverside. Then, after quitting the river for a while, between Saltford and Keynsham, we rejoin it in a narrow ravine, of which very pretty glimpses are obtained from the short intervals between a succession of tunnels which mark the approach to Bristol. *Rail continued to Exeter, p.* 10.

Bristol.

Ref. Rms. **Hotels**: *George*, opposite station; *Royal Talbot* (H.Q), ½ m. from Sta., in Victoria St., on tram-route to the centre of the city; *Royal*, 1 m. from Sta., in College Green, close to Cathedral, also on tram-route.

Cabs: 1s. first mile, 6d. per ¼ m. addit.; 2s. 6d. first hour, 6d. per ¼ hr. addit.

The old city of Bristol, at one time second to London only in importance, is far away from the district described in this book. As, however, many travellers, especially 3rd class passengers by the "West of England" expresses of the Midland Company from the north, may choose to break their journey there, a brief notice of the chief objects of interest is here given.

St. Mary Redcliffe (6 *min.* from sta.) is reached by turning to the left from the railway bridge (which crosses the main street close to the station) into Pile St. It is one of the most beautiful parish churches in England.

The **Cathedral**, a mile from the station, is reached (tram-route) by Victoria St. and Bristol Bridge. When over the latter turn, left, along Baldwin St. to the Draw Bridge and beyond that left again, following the tram-line to College Green. The present building is mainly Decorated (nave rebuilt in 1868), but the *Chapter House* is late Norman; the *Elder Lady Chapel*, Early English; the *Cloisters* and *Tower*, Perpendicular. Notice the E. window of the Choir. Bp. Butler of the *Analogy*, is buried in the Choir. To the W. of the Cathedral is **College Gate**, Norman, part of the original abbey.

The **Clifton Suspension Bridge** is two miles from the station and one mile beyond the Cathedral, and the pleasantest way to it is up the steep hill called Park-street, which connects Bristol and Clifton. In returning, tram-cars running along the low level of the river are available.

Bristol to Exeter, *rail continued from p. 9.*—Issuing from Bristol and its suburb Bedminster, we obtain almost at once a distant view of the Suspension Bridge on the right hand. Nothing further of interest is encountered till we reach *Yatton* (130½ m.), where the Clevedon Branch diverges on the right, and that to Cheddar and Wells on the left. The Mendip Hills now come into view on the latter side, and a few miles onward we pass almost within a stone's throw of the popular and increasing seaside resort of **Weston-super-Mare** [Hotels: *Royal*; *Imperial*; *York*; *Pier*; *Railway* (H.Q.)]. The town, spreading over the plain south of Worle Down, is in full view. South of it Brean Down projects far into the sea, continued at a few miles' interval by the singular rock-circled islet called the Steep Holm. The sea itself is not visible.

As we proceed, if the day be clear, a sudden break in the line of the Mendips is noticeable far away to the left. This marks the position of the famous Cheddar cliffs, the most abrupt face of limestone rock in the kingdom. Then we continue over the wide alluvial strath of the Parrot for several miles, the only variation from the dead level being produced by *Brent Knoll*, which rises green and isolated close at hand on the left. Beneath it is East Brent, the benefice of Archdeacon Denison. At *Highbridge Station* we cross the Somerset and Dorset railway, on its way from the unaccountably popular watering-place of Burnham, which is only a mile or so west of our route. Then after passing *Bridgwater* the Quantock Hills relieve the monotony of the scene on the same side, coming nearer and nearer to us as we approach **Taunton** (163¼ m.; Hotels: *London* (H.Q.); *Castle*). The fine Perpendicular church-towers of the latter town, among the handsomest of a county remarkable for its achievements in that style of architecture, are well seen from the railway.

Beyond Taunton the line passes through a pleasant and fertile country of which the most noteworthy feature is the *Quantock Hills* on the right hand, to *Norton Fitzwarren*, where the branches to Minehead and Barnstaple diverge on the same side. The next station is *Wellington*, a little beyond which, on the left hand, the *Wellington Monument* is seen crowning the northwestern abutment of the Black Down Hills.

The highest point on the line between Taunton and Exeter is reached in *Burlescombe Tunnel*, nearly a mile long, on the boundary line between Somerset and Devon. Beyond it we descend to **Tiverton Junction.** (*Inn at the Station.*)

Tiverton Junction to Tiverton, 5 *m*. For Tiverton and the Exe Valley line, *see pp.* 31, 32.

Tiverton Junction to Hemyock, 7 *m*. This little branch line threads the valley of the Culm, passing in 3 *m.*, *Uffculme*, which enjoys a good local reputation for its ales, and in 5 *m.*, *Culmstock*. **Hemyock** (Inns : *Culm Valley*, near station ; *Star*, in village) or "Hemmick," as it is called, is situated at the foot of the Black Down Hills. It has the remains of a *castle*, once utilised by the Roundheads as a prison, and affords fair trout fishing. From it a walk affording extensive views, including Dartmoor, may be taken by the *Wellington Monument* to the town of *Wellington*, 7 *m*. distant ; or the country may be crossed to Honiton by *Dempeswell Abbey*, a characteristically secluded retreat, of which very slight fragments remain, or by *Hembury Fort* (*p.* 14*) or by both places to **Honiton** (*p*. 13). The distance is about 10 miles, and much of the intermediate ground is on a high level.

Two miles beyond Tiverton Junction, we pass on the right hand the small town of **Cullompton** (*White Hart*, Q.), noteworthy only for its fine Perpendicular *church*, the tower of which is a conspicuous object from the railway. As in the case of Tiverton, the former prosperity of the town is shown by a splendid addition to the church made early in the sixteenth century by a local merchant. It forms part of the south side, and is called after its donor, the *Lane Chapel*. The chief feature is the beautiful fan tracery of its roof. There is also a finely carved screen.

From Cullompton we follow the valley of the Culm, passing on the left the woods of *Killerton* (Sir T. Dyke Acland), till it joins the Exe a few miles short of Exeter. The red house on the right, about a mile beyond the meeting of the two rivers, and just short of the convergence of the South Western line from North Devon, is *Pynes* (Earl of Iddesleigh). Then the red, loamy hills which give such richness and warmth to the scenery of Mid-Devon close in upon us, and we enter *St. David's Station* at **Exeter**, *p*. 26 ; *rail continued to Plymouth p.* 38.

London (Waterloo) to Seaton, Sidmouth, Exeter, Exmouth, Okehampton, Tavistock, and Plymouth, by the London and South Western Railway.

London to Salisbury, 84 m; Axminster, 144½ m; Seaton Junction, 148 m; Sidmouth Junction, 159 m; Exeter, 172 m.
Axminster to Lyme Regis (omnibus), 5 m.
Seaton Junction to Seaton (rail), 4 m.
Sidmouth Junction to Sidmouth, 8½ m.
Quickest Times: London to Seaton, 4 hrs. 30 min.; Sidmouth, 5 hrs.; Exeter (Queen Street), 4 hrs. 12 min. 3rd class by all trains.

The London and South-Western route to Exeter is shorter than the Great Western by 23 miles, and to Plymouth by 18 miles. The time however is about the same.

The scenery along this route presents considerable variety, and is in parts of a very interesting character. Between London and Exeter no single river-valley is followed for more than a few miles. After leaving London the line passes for many miles through one of the most favourite suburban districts, including *Wimbledon* and *Surbiton*, after which a wide area of common land, overgrown with fir-woods, heather, and gorse, but in rapid process of reclamation, is traversed. Nearing *Basingstoke*, after noticing the fine Perpendicular church of Basing on the left hand, we enter the undulating chalk country, which extends past *Andover Junc.*, and along the southern boundary of Salisbury plain to Salisbury itself, a little short of which city we have an excellent view, on the right hand, of the extensive and still clearly defined earthworks of *Old Sarum*, which was the original site of the city itself, and which retained the privilege of returning two members to Parliament till the number of electors was reduced to one.

Passing through a tunnel the railway enters **Salisbury** (*Ref. Rms.*; Hotels: *White Hart*; *Angel*, near station; *Red Lion*, H.Q., Milford St.). From both sides of the station the exquisitely beautiful spire of the Cathedral is well seen. Passengers who leave London by the morning express about 11 o'clock may spend upwards of 3 hours in the city, and proceed by the afternoon express. Those bound by either train for Lyme, Seaton, or Sidmouth, will probably have to change carriages here or at Yeovil Junction.

Beyond Salisbury the scenery becomes richer. We pass along a succession of valleys, threaded by streams and flanked by wooded hills. The picturesque thatched cottages are a feature in this part of the journey, and past *Templecombe Junc.* (112 m.) we soon come in sight, right, of the fine minster-church of **Sherborne** (*Digby*; *Half Moon*, H.Q.). The near view is particularly pleasing in the neighbourhood of *Yeovil Junction*, where the line crosses the Weymouth branch of the Great Western Railway, but it attains its greatest interest when, passing close at hand, on the left, the old

Cistercian monastery of *Ford Abbey*, now converted into a dwelling-house, we reach the valley of the Axe.

Axminster (Inns: *George* H.Q., *Three Cups. Pop. abt.* 2,500.). Beyond its pleasant position this town has little to interest the tourist. It is slumberous to a degree. The church or minster displays a little of every style from Norman to churchwarden Gothic. A great battle is traditionally reported to have been fought here in the days of Æthelstan, and, as a matter of real history, the town was seized by the Cavaliers in 1644, and fifty years afterwards served William III. as a halting place on his march to London. The carpet manufacture is a thing of the past.

Axminster to Lyme Regis by omnibus (*abt.* 3 *times a day*) 5 *m*. This is a pleasant drive, but presents no remarkable features. It passes, rather more than 2 miles on the way, *Hunter's Lodge Inn*, and then goes through *Uplyme* whence it descends to Lyme itself. *For Lyme Regis, see p. 5.*

Two miles beyond Axminster, on the far side of the river, is a farmhouse called *Ashe*, the birthplace of the great Duke of Marlborough, and then, leaving the verdure-fringed stream to pursue its peaceful course between graceful hills to the sea, we reach **Seaton Junction.**

A little north of Seaton Junction is *Shute*, occupied for several centuries by the Pole family. Of the old mansion only an ivy-clad Tudor gateway remains. The churchyard hard by contains a fine old yew.

Seaton Junction to Seaton 4 *m*. This little branch line strikes southward, and in 2 miles reaches **Colyton** (Inn : *Colcombe Castle*, H.Q. *Pop. about* 2,400), another quiet old-fashioned town, with nothing noteworthy about it but the Early English and Perpendicular *Church*, which has a fine tower, octagonal in its upper part, and an altar tomb said to be in memory of Margaret Courtenay, daughter of the 9th Earl of Devon by Katherine, daughter of Edward IV. On the left of the line are the remains of Colcombe Castle, a former possession of the Courtenays. From Colyton the line continues along the valley of the Axe, and passing Axmouth, on the far side of the stream, enters Seaton Station. *For Seaton see p. 17.*

The country between Axminster and Honiton is the most pleasing on the S.W. route from London to Exeter, and Honiton is without doubt, in respect of situation, the most attractive-looking town upon it. From Seaton Junction the railway winds upwards through a narrowing and verdant valley, and then passes through a tunnel, a little beyond which the town comes into view on the right.

Honiton (Hotels: *Dolphin*, H.Q.; *Angel. Pop. abt.* 3,300) extends nearly a mile east and west along a rich undulating country at the base of hills, well timbered and of varied shapes, which attain a height of over 800 feet. Beautiful though its situation is, the town has no features of special interest. The famous Honiton lace is made in the villages around. The old parish church is on the south of the railway, some way from the station and from the town. It is worth visiting for the sake of the view from the churchyard along the valley of the Otter, in which the town lies.

The church contains an elegant oak screen, and the marble tomb of Thomas Marwood, who was physician to Queen Elizabeth, and lived to the age of 105. *Marwood House*, in the town, gave a night's shelter to Charles I., in the year 1644.

There are several ancient forts in the neighbourhood of Honiton. *Hembury Fort*, 4 m. N.W. to the right of the Cullompton Road, stands on high ground, and commands a fine view westwards over the estuary of the Exe to Great and Little Haldon and Dartmoor. It is oval in shape, and nearly a quarter of a mile long. *Sidbury Castle* (*p.* 22) may be included in the pleasant walk over the hill and down the valley of the Sid to Sidmouth.

After quitting the valley of the Otter near Sidmouth Junction, the route onward to Exeter traverses a flat and fertile district destitute of special features.

Sidmouth Junction (*Inn close to the Station*) **to Ottery St. Mary**, 3 m.; **and Sidmouth**, 8½ m. This branch continues for some miles down the Otter valley. Ottery St. Mary occupies a hill-side on the left of it. The towers of the church, which is fully described on page 23, are seen very picturesquely above the trees a little short of Ottery Station. From the next station, *Tipton*, the line ascends out of the Otter valley and crossing the leafy little hollows of *Harpford Wood*, drops gently into that of the Sid, reaching its terminus a mile short of the beach at Sidmouth. Omnibuses meet the trains. *For Sidmouth, see p.* 21.

For **Exeter**, *see p.* 26.

From the Midlands.

From the Northern and Midland Counties by Bristol, or by Bath and Templecombe.

Birmingham to Bristol (Midland), 93 m ; *Taunton (G.W.)*, 138 m ; *Exeter*, 169 m.
Birmingham to Mangotsfield, 88 m ; *Bath*, 98 m ; *Templecombe Junction*, 134 m ; *Axminster (for Lyme Regis)*, 165 m.
Third-class by all trains to Bristol and to Axminster, and by all trains from Bristol to Exeter except the 2.26 p.m. from Bristol.

The great majority of travellers from the Northern and Midland counties to South Devon adopt the direct route *viá* Bristol. Those, however, who wish to commence their tour at the eastern end of the county, or at the watering-places of Seaton or Sidmouth, may, with advantage, travel by Bath and Templecombe. As will be seen from the Midland bills, there are two excellent express trains a day by which through-carriages are run from York, Bradford, Leeds, and Birmingham as far as Templecombe, where a change of carriage is made on to the South-Western system. The line—called the Somerset and Dorset—between Bath and Templecombe is the joint property of the Midland and South-Western companies. Tourists from Great-Western stations in the Midlands may also travel by Didcot and Chippenham, and so on to Bridport, for a description of which route *see* p. 2.

With regard to the country north of Bristol along this route we shall only say here that the Midland line passes through that rich and pleasant scenery which is characteristic of the western counties almost all the way from Birmingham to Bristol. The most striking natural feature is the eminently graceful outline of the Malvern Hills, which are well seen after passing Worcester—the West of England expresses travel over the old line nearly five miles east of the "faithful city"—and again between Cheltenham and Gloucester. After passing Cheltenham, the long ridge of the Cotswold, varied by several sharply outlined green acclivities, commences and continues a great part of the way to Bristol. The tourist may, by breaking his journey, visit the cathedrals of Worcester and Gloucester, and—by a slight divergence—that of Hereford on the way.

The G. W. R. route beyond Bristol is described on *page* 10.

BATH TO TEMPLECOMBE.

From Mangotsfield Junction, where the route *via* Bath and Templecombe leaves the main line, it is 10 miles to Bath. At *Bitton*, 4 miles on the way, the valley of the Avon is entered, and the scenery is more or less interesting all the rest of the way. On the left, *Kelston Round Hill* (800 *ft.*), an outlier of Lansdown is distinguished by its crowning clump of fir and other trees, and from it, after we have passed *Kelston Station*, the beautiful glades of Kelston Park descend to the line, which is closely skirted on the other side by the Avon. From this point the main line of the Great Western runs parallel with our route all the way to Bath, the crescents and terraces of which city soon appear before us.

Bath (*Maurers St. Sta.*; *Ref. Rm.*; *for Hotels see p.* 9). is as commodious and pleasant a station as a long-distance traveller can wish to alight at for a few minutes. It is a terminus, and the route onward retraces about half-a-mile of its previous course. Then it sweeps round abruptly to the left, and after crossing the Great Western line, affords from the hill-side which it is steeply climbing, a very fine view of the city with its crescents and terraces rising tier above tier to the summit-ridge of Lansdown. A short tunnel is succeeded by a beautiful little peep on the left, and then a long tunnel introduces us to a romantic valley, up which the line passes by viaduct and embankment for several miles. One branch of this valley is crossed at *Midford*, and 2 miles further the Perpendicular tower of *Wellow Church* arrests attention on the right. The next station—*Radstock*—is the outlet of a small coal-mining district, and the scenery is correspondingly marred. Here the Great Western branch from Bristol to Frome is crossed, and the long ascent of the Mendip Hills commenced. *Midsomer Norton* shows a handsome church rising above rich foliage, and the line beyond passes, by intermittent cuttings of magnesian limestone, the village of Chilcompton in a hollow on the right. The summit of the Mendip range is reached at *Maesbury*, a short distance to the left of which the earthworks of an ancient stronghold may be detected. Then, as we wind down to Shepton Mallett, a charming prospect reveals itself on the right, including the towers of Wells Cathedral and the conspicuous cone of Glastonbury Tor. On the same side the town of *Shepton Mallett* is passed as we cross a viaduct some little distance short of its station. Hence the line, pursuing a level course, presents little that is noteworthy until we reach the junction with the South Western at *Templecombe* (refreshment room). *For the route onward to Axminster and Exeter, see p.* 12.

Seaton.

Approaches: *via* Seaton Junction, *p.* 13; from Lyme Regis, *p.* 6; from Sidmouth, *p.* 25.
Hotels: *Royal Clarence, Pole Arms, Lion* (Q.) from ¼—½ m. from the station; *Coffee Tavern* (beds) on the Esplanade.
Post: *del.* 8.20 *a.m.*, 4.10 *p.m.*; *desp.* 12.55 and 5.45 *p.m.* Sundays, *del.* 8.20 *a.m.*; *desp.* 1.18 *p.m.*

Seaton is a pleasant little watering-place with a resident population somewhat exceeding a thousand. Since the opening of the branch line from Axminster gave it communication by rail with the country at large it has grown in size and popular esteem. Like many other little towns which guard the entrance of our southern streams, it appears at one time, in conjunction with Axmouth on the opposite side of the River Axe, to have possessed considerable commercial importance, but the alluvial tract which once formed a delta has now been reclaimed. *Moridunum*, the ancient name of the place, is inscribed in huge letters on the esplanade front.

As a bathing place Seaton is safe and good. It has little sea frontage, the main street running inland, but there is a pleasant promenade along the old bar of the Axe. The cliff rises somewhat abruptly on the western side, and on the east the ascent commences at once from the far side of the Axe, the intervening space of half-a-mile or so being quite level. Consequently the site is as much more open and airy as it is less rich and luxuriant than that of Sidmouth. The hotel accommodation is good, and there are plenty of lodgings. The bay on which the town stands is bounded by Beer Head (426 *ft.*) on the west, and Culverhole Point on the east.

A pleasant walk may be taken across the river to **Axmouth** (1½ *m.* Inn: *Kings' Head.*). The church here, an old one, has a Norman doorway. Behind the village is *Hawksdown* surmounted by a Roman Camp. About a mile south-east from Axmouth is **Bindon Farm**, a small but very interesting 15th century house with good details. From the old oak staircase a small chapel is entered. This is no longer used for worship but retains its screen. Bindon can also be reached direct from Seaton by the road to Lyme.

To Lyme Regis by the Landslip, *about* 8 *m.* This walk, a very pleasant one, is described the reverse way on page 6. The cliff-road is entered a little beyond the bridge (*toll* 1*d.*) and rises at once past the coast-guard station to the flag staff on *Culverhole Point*, passing *Haven Cliff* on the way. A fee of 6d. is payable

S. Devon.   c

for a ticket, which frees the whole cliff to Dowlands. The seaward slopes soon become broken up by cracks and fissures, and these shortly give place to an exquisite tangle of brushwood and climbing plants everywhere beautified by abundant wild flowers. It is now and again somewhat difficult to find one's way, but there are many little paths, any of which bearing westward will do. A little black hut is seen ahead, and a path beyond it. These give the general direction that should be taken. It is worth while to take some trouble to discover the point whence the "moat" and bastioned "rampart" that, with the upper cliff, form a veritable natural stronghold, may best be seen. The finest bits are certainly just west of the western end of the ravine. When the path past the hut is gained, ascend by it to the upper ground landwards, and bear a little to the west, so as to approach the edge of the ravine which should be followed throughout its circuit eastward. When the eastern end is reached, a path is seen ascending its opposite side, and this can be easily reached. At its top those who are disposed to be giddy should bear a little to the left, as the cliff is somewhat high pretty close on the right. The west end of the ravine and the thickly-wooded undercliff below present a strange but beautiful picture from the meadow just onward along the cliff. Note, where a cart-track descends to the undercliff, how strangely the earth has been heaved into long parallel ridges. The shore, as seen from this point, is bounded by a long sharp point. High up above the cliff is a low group of buildings within a boundary wall. This is not a prison or asylum, but Sir Henry Peek's mansion, of *Rowsedown*. Persons are not allowed to pass along the cliffs through his property, and we, therefore, take a foot-path that strikes diagonally inland to a lane which almost immediately brings us to *Dowlands Farm*, where we turn eastwards through the model and modern buildings of the Rowsedown domain. The *church* is worth a visit, and the hall of the mansion too, if permission can be obtained. The tourist will probably wonder to see such expensive buildings on so bleak and bare a site. The lane from the east lodge leads into the main road and thence onward there is nothing of note except the fine view just as we descend into Lyme, which would recompense even a toilsome journey. *For a description of it see p. 6, and for the "through the cliff" route p. 6.*

Seaton to Beer, $1\frac{1}{2}$ *m*; **Branscombe,** $4\frac{1}{2}$ *m*; **Sidmouth,** 9 to 10 *m.*

This route is of a very up-and-down character, whether by road or by the coast. The latter alternative makes little difference in respect of distance, and is decidedly to be preferred. Both routes are in reality pedestrian, as the carriage-road misses most of the coast scenery, and is deficient in interest. Pedestrians will, in any case, leave the road about three-quarters of a mile on the way, and take the path that, after cresting *White Cliff*, an ivy-clad escarpment of chalk, drops abruptly to the village of **Beer** which the carriage-road also passes through. Beer consists mainly of a long straggling street threading a narrow valley upwards from the sea, and containing two or three fair inns. Beer is now a centre of the Honiton lace trade. A feature of the place is the large and handsome modern church.

From Beer to Sidmouth the pedestrian may either follow the more direct route, by road almost all the way, or hug the cliff by a fairly marked footpath.

1. *The Road Route.* This ascends again at once and passes on the left hand, opposite an exposed limestone quarry about a mile on the way, the tunneled entrance to a hidden one. The portals are festooned with shrubs and ferns, and the tourist may grope his way inward through the various workings for several hundred yards, and even beneath the sea. This quarry is said to be in part of Roman origin.

From the quarry you may descend by lane and path to the romantic village of **Branscombe** (2 *Inns*), which is seen scattered all about the convergence of three narrow combes about a quarter of a mile from the sea. The church, an ancient one, remarkable for its massive tower, is at the far end of the village; the 17th cent. altar rails are interesting. Those who wish to cling to the coast will climb the green hill from the churchyard (*see p.* 20). The road route continues up the combe and passes nothing noteworthy for several miles. Then it joins the carriage route from Seaton, and runs a little to the right of the village of **Salcombe Regis**, the last Royalist town in Devon to surrender to the Parliamentarians. Hence to Sidmouth the road falls abruptly, making a descent of 500 feet in 1½ miles. The view down into the deep, richly coloured and cultivated valley is very beautiful.

2. *By Beer Head and the coast.* From Beer, instead of following the road up the village and combe, take the lane that ascends to the top of the cliff from the lower end of the village. This leads up to the common called *South Down*, where are a flagstaff and a coast-guard station. The view from this point is magnificent, especially eastward, and on a fairly clear day the coast from Portland Bill to Start Point is distinctly seen. **Beer Head** is marked by two natural towers of chalk, and the walk to the actual Head is rather rough, owing to the irregular nature of the ground. It is, however, worth the trouble, and is included in the longer estimate given (*p.* 18) of the distance. From the Head keep westward along the Down until the end of the cliff overlooking *Branscombe Mouth* is reached. Hence a steep path goes down to the Mouth, and on the opposite side another of somewhat easier gradient leads up again to the cliff-top westward. If these be taken, then **Branscombe**, in one of the sweetest combes on the coast, is missed. To reach it, instead of descending to the Mouth, we bear to the right along the hillside, and with little descent, owing to the

rapid rise of the level of the combe from the shore, arrive at the principal part of the village (Inn : *Mason's Arms*), situated in the mouth of a little branch combe. Then through the straggling village, beautiful with greenery and brook and shapely enclosing hills, it is a charming half-mile to the church, dedicated to St. Winifred, and well worth notice. We then take the path from the churchyard up the wooded steep of *Littlecomb Hill*. The sea only comes into sight again when the top of the ascent is reached, but then the view all round is delightful. Heytor, between Ashburton and Moreton Hampstead, is prominent on the western horizon. The cliff is now close at hand, curiously broken up along its margin by pyramidal masses, and with a narrow undercliff below. Little further direction is needed in our course westward, except to say hug the cliffs. *Weston Mouth*, the next combe-outlet involves a steep descent to the shore, and thence, over the pebbles, Sidmouth can be reached in about $2\frac{1}{2}m.$, but the walking is detestable, and only to be endured by the most ardent geologist who perhaps may find compensation in being thus enabled to scan the cliff-sections. The fine cliff west of the mouth is *Dunscombe*, and the pedestrian here minded to turn inland can ascend its eastern slope obliquely, and strike the road to Sidmouth at **Salcombe Regis** (*p.* 19). If rejecting both the pebbles and the inland route, he wisely determines to keep to the cliff, he can ascend once more to their summit by a track up the combe on its western slope, doubling back as he reaches the higher ground. In the course of the next mile he will again have to cross a dip, at *Salcombe Mouth*, and then he can either continue still along the cliffs and take a zigzag track down to Sidmouth, which is by far the best course, or striking about half-a-mile inland gain the road named above. The view in either case is very beautiful. Just beyond Sidmouth is High Peake, and to the north of it Peake Hill and Beacon Hill, which separate the valley of the Sid from that of the Otter. **Sidmouth** lies immediately below, and gives promise of being the almost model little watering-place that nearer acquaintance proves it to be. Its situation at the mouth of a densely-wooded combe, only open to breezes from the south, accounts for its being at times in the height of summer close and sultry.

Sidmouth.

Approaches: *vid* Sidmouth Junction, *p.* 14 ; by coast *pp.* 18 and 36.
Hotels: *Knowle* (good grounds), between the station and the town ; *York, Bedford*, on the Esplanade ; *London* (H.Q.) in High St. near the Esplanade ; *Coffee Tavern* (beds) in Fore St.
Boarding House: *The Glen* (*p.* 22).
Post: del. *7 a.m. 12.20 ; desp. 2.10 and *7 p.m. [* Sundays also.]

₊ The station is a mile from the beach ; 'bus and cabs meet the trains.

Sidmouth (pop. 3500) is one of the most compact and, of its kind, beautiful watering-places in England. Those who love warmth and to loiter along a pleasant shore, and to climb green hill-sides almost from their doorstep, will hardly find a sea-side resort more to their taste, while the more actively inclined will obtain as much healthy fatigue as they can well desire in the up and down cliff-rambles to Beer and Seaton eastwards, and to Budleigh Salterton, and Exmouth westwards. Of the wilder and sterner features of nature, such as lie within the reach of visitors to Llandudno, Barmouth, Lynton, and many other favourite places of resort on the western shores of England and Wales, the neighbourhood of Sidmouth has none. The hills around rise to an almost uniform height of 500 feet. Their slopes, though steep, are green to the summit, and in many instances, where there is any shelter from the sea breezes, more or less wooded throughout. The abrupt cliffs which they present to the sea are of a deep and rich red colour contrasting finely with the green of their slopes.

The *town* occupies a valley about half-a-mile in width between two such hills, and watered by the tiny rivulet which lends its name to the place. The hill to the east is Salcombe Down ; that to the west, Peake Hill. The ascent of both by road or path is long and steep. The general direction of the town is northwards from the shore along the valley, but there is a terrace of lodging-houses facing the sea. The place has a thoroughly Devonian aspect of prosperity and sufficiency, there being a marked absence of that ragged and unfinished appearance which so often characterizes the modern watering-place. Indeed, at the beginning of the present century Sidmouth was the most fashionable sea-side resort in Devon, and now, though it has lost its preeminence, and indeed for a while seemed likely to lapse into insignificance, its natural attractions, and the establishment of communication by rail, effected in 1874, have enabled it to re-assert its position as one of Devon's chief watering-places, however slow its later growth may have been compared with that of its neighbours. Besides the lodging houses, a large number of well-to-do villas testify to the favour in which Sidmouth is regarded by people who are free to choose their place of residence.

Several years of the infancy of Queen Victoria were spent at *The Glen* (p. 21), the house at which her father, the Duke of Kent, died in 1820. In his memory the west window of the parish church, *St. Nicholas*, was presented by her Majesty. This church is picturesquely situated on a bowery sward near the shore. Since its restoration, in 1860, the interior has been enriched by a handsome reredos and a pulpit of Devonshire marble. Almost all the windows are of coloured glass. The other church, *All Saints*', on the way to the station, has nothing remarkable about it, beyond its complete covering of ivy.

The *Sid*, which is crossed by a foot-bridge at the east end of the esplanade, almost disappears in the shingle as it enters the sea, on the shore of which calcedonies, jaspers, and agates may be found.

The hotel accommodation of Sidmouth is good, and has been considerably improved by the opening of the Knowle Hotel. There are abundant facilities for bathing.

The Neighbourhood of Sidmouth.

The favourite boating excursion is to **Ladram Bay**, 3 *m. to the west*. Occasionally this may be reached by walking along the shore under the cliffs. The attractions are the caverns which the sea has bored into the red sandstone, and a natural archway through a detached part of the cliff. A path forming part of the coast-walk to Budleigh Salterton, and described on *p.* 25, leads to the same place.

Eastwards, from Sidmouth, the cliff-path leads up Salcombe Hill, forming the first part of the walk to Beer and Seaton. **Salcombe Regis**, not to be confused with the larger Salcombe near Kingsbridge, lies a little beyond the brow of the hill, in a wooded and sequestered depression. The addition of "Regis" is due to the fact that there was once a small fort hard by, which was the last to hold out for Charles I. From Salcombe you may drop through Dunscombe to Weston Mouth.

Inland an interesting walk may be taken, starting by Alexandra Road,* which strikes to the right of the station, to **Sidbury Castle**, 3 *m*. from Sidmouth, and S.W. of the village of Sidbury,

---

* Or along the main street from the town.

a little short of which a lane turns up on the left to the castle. This is in shape somewhat like a kite, and is one of several earthworks hereabouts. The walk may agreeably be continued to *Honiton* (10½ *m. see p.* 13). There is a fine view of the valley of the Sid, Sidmouth itself, and the sea beyond, from the bare and lofty down which rises between Sidbury and the railway at Harpford Wood.

Ottery St. Mary (6 *m. by road or rail*; Inns: *King's Arms*, Q.; *London*). No lover of church architecture should omit this excursion. The *road* passes to the left of Sidmouth station, and crosses the line about a mile further near a roadside inn, and to the right of *Harpford Wood*, pursuing for the rest of the way an undulating course unmarked by any special feature. The *railway*, after going under the road, affords pleasant peeps into the verdant dells of *Harpford Wood*, and then descends to the side of the Otter, passing *Tipton Station* (*small inn*) and reaching Ottery a little to the left of the town, which occupies a slight acclivity on the far side of the river. The towers of the church are seen from the station, but are too low to be conspicuous. The town, the focus of an agricultural district, is at a standstill in regard to population, about 4,000. It is a companion in misfortune with Chudleigh, upwards of a hundred of its houses having been burnt down in 1866. Historically, it is interesting as having been the residence for a time of Sir Walter Ralegh, the headquarters of Fairfax for a month, and the birth-place, in 1772, of S. T. Coleridge, whose father was vicar and master of the grammar school, a building close to the church, but no longer used. On the west side of the churchyard is the house of Lord Coleridge, a red brick mansion, rebuilt in 1882, the only part of the old building retained being the south-west front, which has been raised, and is said to have once been occupied by Cromwell.

Church of Sts. Mary and Edward.

Sexton's house behind the street skirting east end of churchyard.

On entering the churchyard we notice along its south side two parallel rows of elms trained, some of them, literally to death, so as to form an avenue; also a remnant of the stocks, and an elegant monument consisting of a slender granite shaft surmounted by a Celtic Cross, in memory of J. T. Coleridge.

The first thing which strikes the visitor about the church is the different periods of architecture which it represents. There are two transeptal towers—the northern one surmounted by a short leaded spire. These towers occupy the same relative positions as those of Exeter Cathedral, of which other parts of the fabric, notably the west front, are miniature reproductions—a circumstance attributable to the part taken by Bishop Grandisson in the erection of both. In the west front we have a noticeable instance, externally, of the mixture of styles already commented on, a Perpendicular north aisle called the *Dorset Aisle*, from its donor, Cicely, Countess of Dorset, having been added at the beginning of the sixteenth century, and made to form a continuation of the Decorated west end of the nave. As to the rest of the exterior, the other aisles and the towers are Early English, the chancel and Lady Chapel Decorated. In a niche in the gable of the west end is a mutilated figure of the Virgin.

Entering by the porch, we have, over the doorway, the arms of Henry VIII., and on the left hand side the record of a singular bequest, a portion of which was to be assigned to " some man or woman of exemplary life and some skill in physick" for the purpose of helping the sick poor gratis until they could get proper medical attendance. Among the females preference is given to the testator's kin, the clerk's wife, the minister's wife, and the vicar's wife in the order named, the only provision being that the recipient should be "very fit—or as fit as Mrs. Alford, the late vicar's wife."

The north aisle has a richly groined roof like those of Henry VII.'s Chapel at Westminster, and King's College Chapel at Cambridge, while that of the nave has been painted blue with gold stars, and by reason of the juxta-position, has a somewhat tawdry appearance. The roof of the chancel is also painted, but in more subdued colours and better taste. Two large crayon drawings of St. Matthew and St. John introduced at the west end in 1879, seem out of place. The north aisle has a large window representing the twelve apostles, and placed there in the memory of the mother of Bishop Patteson (*see p.* 28). The bench-ends, with fifteenth century linen panels, are good. The new *Font*, on the north side of the nave, was the gift of the late Mr. Beresford Hope. It is of Devon and Cornwall and white Italian marbles, the supporting pillars being serpentine, and the cover of carved oak. The raised tombs and effigies of Sir Otho Grandisson, brother of the bishop, and his wife, placed on either side of the nave, are more characteristic of their period than beautiful in themselves. In striking contrast to them is the modern tomb of Lady Coleridge, in the south transept—the work of Frederick Thrupp, sculptor. This is a beautiful piece of sculpture, especially noticeable for its good and delicately worked drapery. The whole south transept has been tastefully restored by the Coleridge family. It contains a *Wooden Gallery*, from which the chimes are now rung, and a clock like that in Exeter Cathedral (*p.* 28), which is not, however, at present in working order.

The oak pulpit was carved by a native in 1722. The *Reredos*, of stone with mosaic work, has been restored, and behind it is the *Lady Chapel*, which possesses a *Minstrels' Gallery*. Notice the oak seats and misereres, also the carving generally in the church and Lady Chapel.

On either side of the chancel is an Early English Chapel, the northern dedicated to St. Lawrence, the southern to St. Stephen. The latter has a piscina, and in its vestibule are three well preserved brasses, the oldest of which bears date 1542. The windows contain much stained glass by Hardman, Warrington, Wailes, &c. The restoration of the church was commenced in 1849.

⁎ Visitors to Ottery often extend their excursion to *Cadhay*, a fine ivy-covered Elizabethan house. For directions enquire of the sexton.

Sidmouth to Beer (7½ to 8½ m.) and **Seaton** (9½ to 10 m.). This is a very hilly route, and the road misses a great deal of the best scenery. Pedestrians may either cross Salcombe Hill to Salcombe and thence drop to Weston Mouth, or they may reach the latter place by the shore at low tide—a tiresome walk. The route we would recommend to those who are going the whole distance is to ascend Salcombe Hill to *Salcombe*; thence to drop through *Dunscombe* to *Weston Mouth*; then to ascend again and follow the cliff till the path descends to *Branscombe Church* (*p.* 19). At Branscombe there are two inns, from the further of which a direct route, beginning with a footpath and continuing by a road, may be followed past the quarries (*p.* 19) to *Beer*, or a circuitous one, worth the extra time, round the rugged promontory of *Beer Head*.
From **Beer** (*p.* 19) ascend the cliff again by path from the seaward end of the village. This takes you over *White Cliff* and into the carriage road just above **Seaton** (*p.* 17).

Sidmouth to Budleigh Salterton, 6½ m. *on foot.* (The road goes considerably inland and is dull.) The coast part of this excursion extends to *Ladram Bay*, 3 m. (*p.* 22) from Sidmouth, beyond which a descent is made by a rough lane to Otterton, and the sea again reached at Budleigh Salterton.

Cliff-Route all the way. Continue from Ladram Bay over *High Peake Hill* to *Otterton Point*, where a boat may sometimes be hailed, failing which turn inland by the green bank of the Otter to a plank-bridge, whence Budleigh is reached in about a mile. The whole distance is 7 miles.

From the west end of Sidmouth the road strikes upwards at once between high walls till a little past a fantastic cottage, a path strikes to the left and makes straight for the top of *Peake Hill*, whence the view is fine, stretching as far west as Dartmoor and the Heytor Rocks. Then we descend through cultivated fields close to the edge of the cliff to *Ladram Bay* (*p.* 22). A little beyond we leave High Peake to the left and enter a lane which, presenting a view over Bicton Park and the lower ground beyond, drops to the long village of *Otterton (Inn).* Many of the cottages are built of " cob." A low cliff, on which stands the church, overhangs the river Otter. Hard by are a few remnants of *Otterton Priory.* The grounds of *Bicton Lodge*, a seat of the Rolle family, are across the river from Otterton.

The Budleigh Salterton road bends to the left a little beyond Otterton Bridge, and soon reaches the picturesque village of *East Budleigh* (Inn: the *Rolle Arms*). The church here contains the pew of the Ralegh family, dated 1537. Sir Walter was born at Hayes Barton, a long mile west of the village. Onward to **Budleigh Salterton** (*p.* 35) the road is devoid of special interest.

Exeter.

Railway Stations: *St. David's*, G.W.R. and L. & S.W.R., to the N.W. of the city, 20 to 25 min. walk from the Cathedral. Take footpath opposite station (see plan) and then turn to the right and keep straight on to the centre of the city. *Queen Street*, L. & S.W.R. only, close to the Castle, and the walks of Northernhay. From it Queen St. (in which on left is the Museum) leads direct to High St. and the Cathedral, 7 to 8 min. *St. Thomas* (local S. Devon traffic) across the Exe, on the S.W. of the city.

N.B. —Passengers from the East by the South Western line, who wish to spend a few hours *en route* for South Devon by the G. W. R., should leave the train at *St. David's Sta.*; those going West by the L. & S. W. R. at *Queen Street Sta.*

Hotels: (see plan) *Rougemont*, first-class (table d'hote, 5s.); *Clarence*, facing the Cathedral; *Queen's, New London, Half Moon, Globe, Bude* (H.Q.). The *Elmfield* and *Railway*, both close to St. David's Station, are smaller second-class houses. *Carnall's Coffee Tavern* (beds) Fore St.

Post Office (see plan): del. abt. 7.15a.m. (London, &c.); 10.15 a.m.(North); desp. 4.10 p.m. (North); 9.15 p.m. (London, &c.).

Population: abt. 38,000.

Exeter, though exceeded in population by Plymouth, still keeps its ancient position as capital of the shire. The city proper stands on a peninsular hill rising sharply from the left bank of the Exe, nearly ten miles from its mouth. Since the 16th cent., such sea-traffic as it has has reached the city by a canal which runs from near Starcross to just below Exe Bridge. To the E., S.E., and N.W. the modern city has extended beyond the walls, which still exist in parts, but all the city gates have disappeared. The thick line on the plan shows approximately the course of the walls.

History of the City. Exeter, "the Camp on the Exe" or "water," is confessedly the capital of the West, a distinction that has belonged to it from very early times. That it was a British stronghold before the Roman Conquest is certain, and under the Romans it was strengthened, and became an important depot of trade. Æthelstan rebuilt its walls with "square stones" about 926, and the course of these differed little, probably, from that of the existing walls.

Of its long and eventful history since then, the briefest outline must suffice. In 1003 the Danes successfully attacked the city, and did serious damage (they failed in their efforts two years previously), but the walls were soon increased in strength, and about 1050 the Bishop's see, which had hitherto been at Crediton, was removed for safety's sake to Exeter. Gytha, Harold's mother, for two years after the battle of Hastings held the city, but in 1068 it submitted to William, who built the Castle on Rougemount. In 1112 the Norman Cathedral, of which the transept-towers are still standing, was begun. Stephen, in 1137, besieged and took the castle from the partisans of Matilda, who, however, avenged themselves by burning a great part of the Cathedral. Thence onward, except a visitation of the "Black Death," in 1349, and the erection of the present

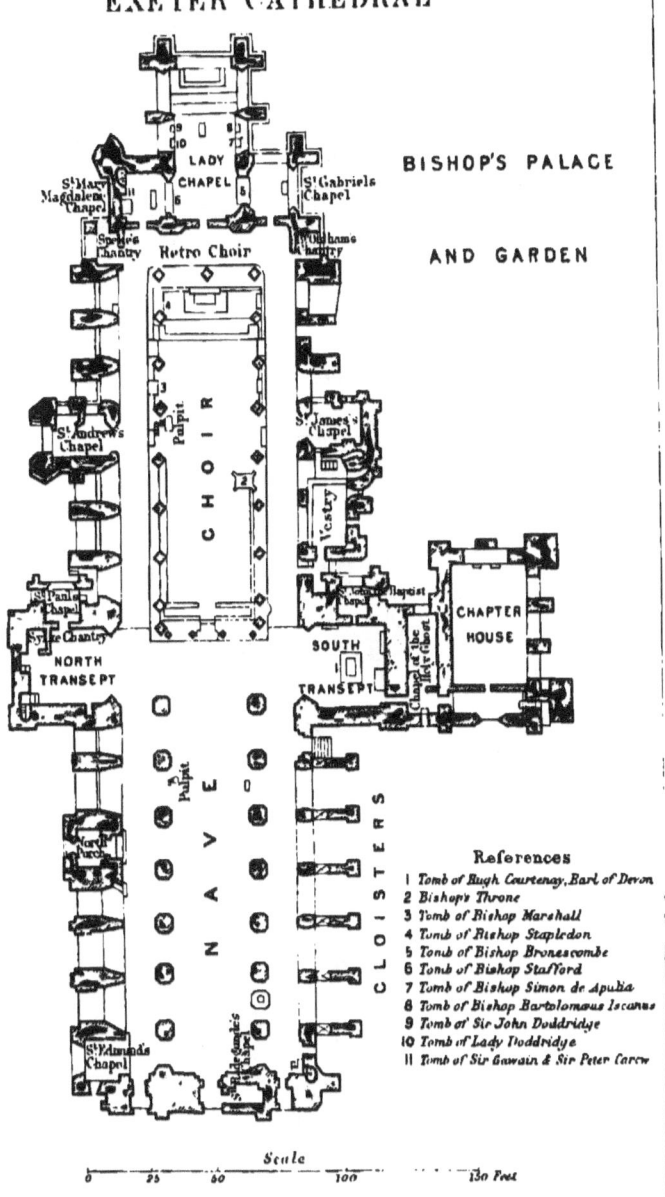

EXETER C.

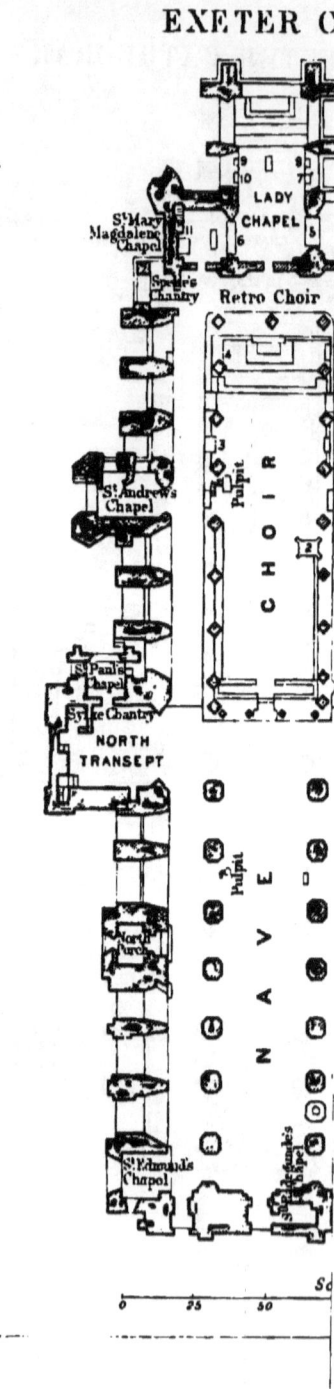

Cathedral at intervals during the 14th century, nothing calls for notice till the period of the dreary struggle between the houses of York and Lancaster. Exeter adhered to the latter party, and in 1649 underwent a short and unsuccessful siege. In 1497 it was attacked by Perkin Warbeck with a like result. At the "Rising of the West" against the introduction of the English Liturgy (first used on Whit Sunday, 1549), Blackaller, the Mayor, in spite of divided counsels, gallantly held out against the rebels until relieved by Lord Russel. Twice during the Civil War did the city, which favoured the side of the Parliament, change hands. In 1643 it was taken by Prince Maurice, and in 1646 retaken by Fairfax. Since this, the last of its many sieges, the history of the city has been uneventful.

The Cathedral.

Services: 10.30 a.m.; 3 p.m. *Admission to choir at other times*, 6d.

Dimensions: total length, 408 ft.; width, 76 ft., including transeptal towers, 140 ft. Height of nave, 66 ft., towers, 166 ft.

This stands just off the High Street, in the quarter between that thoroughfare and South Street. The Close, known as Cathedral Yard, can be entered from either of these.

Down to 1050, when it was transferred by Edward the Confessor to Exeter, the Devon see was at Crediton. Of the monastic church that at first did duty as a Cathedral, nothing remains, and the transept-towers (Norman) are the only portions preserved of the building which early in the 12th century began to succeed it. Next in age (late 13th century) to these towers, are parts of the Lady Chapel, but the rest of the Cathedral with the exception of the West Screen was erected from the designs of Bishop Quivil (*d.* 1291) by his successors. The style, Geometrical, is nowhere seen to better advantage. The west front, "not the last part finished, is the least satisfactory ... the gable is thrown into insignificance by the battlement carried in front of it, and continued along the *sloping* tops of a piece of wall on each side of it." *E.A.F.* The screen with its sixty-eight statues was added by Bp. Brantingham (*d.* 1394). The niches on either side of the west window contain statues of Æthelstan and Edward the Confessor. The rest are too weather-worn to be identified. The best general view of the Cathedral is from the north side of the Yard near the Clarence Hotel.

The Interior. As we enter by the north-west door, the delicate lines of the clustered pillars and many-membered arches, together with the rich vaulting of the long and unbroken roof, are very beautiful. There is no triforium, but a lofty clerestory, underneath which is a small arcade, but no passage. The corbels of the vaulting shafts, though somewhat shapeless, are exquisitely carved. On the north side of the nave projects the *Minstrels' Gallery*, a fine example of an unusual feature in English churches. Notice the sculptures on its front. The windows of the nave aisles (opposite ones alike) show great variety of tracery, and that of the great west window is magnificent (execrable glass). At the west end of the north aisle is the *Chapel of St. Edmund*, used as the Consistory court, and a font originally provided for the baptism of Henrietta, daughter of Charles I., born at Exeter in 1644. Within the Western screen on the south of the principal doorway is the small *Chapel of St. Radegunde*, converted into a chantry by Bishop Grandisson (*d*. 1369). The east end of the **Nave** has been fitted up for service, and the carved stone *pulpit*, a memorial of Bishop Patteson, killed on an island in the South Pacific in 1871, is a work worthy of the saintly hero it commemorates and of the church in which it stands. The front panel represents friendly savages caring for his corpse, and the side panels, scenes in the lives of St. Alban and St. Boniface. The Transepts were formed by Bishop Quivil out of the Norman towers. Notice the projecting galleries and the beautiful windows (1294-95). In the **North Transept** is the *Sylke Chantry*, a statue of James Northcote (*d*. 1831) by Chantry, and a curious 13th century *clock*. [The N. tower, which can be ascended from here, contains the bell Great Peter, 6 tons; the view from the tower is worth seeing.] Opening from the east side of this transept is *St. Paul's Chapel*. In the **South Transept** the principal item of interest is the restored monument of Hugh Courtenay, Earl of Devon (*d*. 1377), and his wife. It was removed to its present position from a chantry in the second bay, from the east, of the south side of the nave, close by the site of which there still remains on the floor the brass of the earl's son, Sir Peter Courtenay. Entered from the S.W. corner of this transept is the Early English, but much altered, *Chapter House*, in which is kept the Cathedral library. Between the transept and the Chapter House is the small *Chapel of the Holy Ghost*. The *choir* is divided from the nave by a stone screen of three arches, the work of Bishop Stapledon (*d*. 1326). It carries the organ, a fine instrument, originally built in 1665, but enlarged early in the present century, and very noticeable on account of its bright silver-like pipes.

The **Choir** (like most of the church, from Bishop Quivil's designs) was built by Bishop Bitton, 1292-1307. Notice the arch next the screen on either side, inserted apparently in the original Norman masonry. The roof and the corbels of the vaulting shafts are like those of the nave, but of more elaborate workmanship. The new *Stalls*, with which the Early English misereres, the work of Bishop Bruere (*d*. 1244), have been incorporated, are excellent and not unworthy to keep company with the *Bishop's Throne* (abt. 1470), which is about 50 feet in height and magnificently carved. This throne is put together without nails, and owes its preservation from the iconoclastic fury of the Puritans to this peculiarity which enabled it to be readily taken down and removed to a place of safety. The stone *sedilia*, also the work of Bishop Stapledon, are exceedingly fine; notice the head of a bishop over the middle seat, and those of a king and queen over those on either side. The *Reredos* is a very rich modern work in alabaster, with its central portion representing the Ascension. It was this that some years ago gave rise to litigation, happily unsuccessful in effecting its removal or mutilation. The **East Window**, the only one in the Cathedral not Decorated, had Perpendicular tracery inserted in 1391. The glass in part belonged to the earlier window—viz.: the three central figures in the top row, and the three outermost at each end of the bottom row, which are assigned to Bishop Grandisson (*d.* 1369). The only **monuments in the choir** that need be mentioned are those of Bishop Marshall and Bishop Stapledon. Both are on the north side. Bishop Marshall (*d.* 1206) completed the Norman Cathedral begun by Bishop Warelwast in 1112, Bishop Stapledon, some of whose work has already been mentioned, and of which we shall see more immediately, was murdered in London, in 1326, by the partisans of Queen Isabella. The alabaster pulpit in the choir is modern.

The **Choir-aisles, Chapels, Retro-choir** and **Lady Chapel**. Entering the south choir aisle from the south transept, opposite the effigy of a cross-legged knight, is *St. James' Chapel*, with a chamber over it. In its present state it is Early Geometrical, Bishop Marshall's work having been altered by Bishop Brantingham. Passing another nameless effigy, on the left, we come to *Bishop Oldham's Chantry*, containing the bishop's tomb with effigy, and close by, at the end of the aisle, to *St. Gabriel's Chapel*, built by Bishop Bronescombe (*d.* 1280). The **Lady Chapel**, of three bays, was begun by Bishop Bronescombe, and finished by Bishop Quivil, whose grave is marked by a slab. No part of the Cathedral has benefited more by the recent restoration. Under the arches, communicating with the chapels of St. Gabriel and St. Mary Magdalene, are the tombs (S.) of Bishop Bronescombe, and (N.) of Bishop Stafford (*d.* 1419). Other monuments are, *on the south side*, Bishop Simon of Apulia (*d.* 1223), Bishop Bartholomew (*d.* 1184), both of which are of much interest. *On the north side* are those of Sir John Dodderidge (*d.* 1628) and Lady Dodderidge. The beautiful east window, as well as the side ones, have been filled with good modern glass. The **Chapel** of **St. Mary Magdalene** is of the same date as the Lady Chapel, with the exception of the Perpendicular screen dividing it from the north aisle. It contains the monuments of Sir Gawain Carew, his wife, and his nephew, Sir Peter Carew (*d.* 1575), and on the floor is a brass, 1413. Adjoining this chapel on the north-west is the *Speke Chantry*, an enriched Late Perpendicular work. Just beyond it, on the right hand, is the effigy of Richard de Stapledon, brother of the bishop; and then, on the same side, corresponding to the chapel of St. James already described, is that of *St. Andrew*, now the muniment room of the Cathedral.

St. Pancras Church—from High Street take the street just W. of the Guildhall, cross Waterbeer Street and from the Police Courts (1888) go up St. Pancras Lane—perhaps the oldest foundation in Exeter. After years of neglect the church was re-opened, after restoration by Pearson, in June 1889.

The oldest windows are Early English, one corbel is possibly Saxon. At the E. end is a pointed 3-light window under a Norman arch. In the S.E. corner is an early 13th cent. piscina. Part of a Roman pavement was found close to the Church in digging the foundation for the Courts. The Roman prætorium is supposed to have been hereabouts.

Of the other noteworthy buildings of Exeter :—

The **Guildhall** (*open daily, free*), in High Street, is a picturesque object in a very picturesque street. Its front, built in 1593, is " a confusion of styles, English windows between Italian columns." The hall (1464) 62 feet long and 25 feet broad, and terribly dark, has an interesting roof, and contains, amongst others, portraits of General Monk and the Princess Henrietta (born at Exeter, 1644), by Lely, and several by Hudson (*d*. 1779), one of Sir Joshua Reynolds' masters. Above the hall is the *Council Chamber*, which is of little interest.

The **Albert Memorial Museum** (*open daily, exc. Thurs., free; Catalogue, 3d.*) is in Queen Street, and externally is a building of some merit, though still too new to be very interesting. Within, its rooms lack the dignity which size alone can give. There is on the left of the entrance, on the ground floor, a reading room ; and other rooms contain a fair library and natural history, geological, antiquarian, and economic collections. A prominent feature in the natural history section, is the skeleton head of a fin-whale, cast ashore on the coast below Exeter. Of local lace manufactures, old and modern, there are several interesting frames. The ornithological collection is excellent.

Rougemont Castle, with the adjacent promenade called **Northernhay**, rises from the city just above the L. & S.W.R. Station. It may be entered either from High Street or Queen Street. The *Castle* dates from the days of William the Conqueror. Very little remains, and that little has no special interest, while the modern additions could not well be surpassed in ugliness. There are some interesting ruins, however, in the grounds of *Rougemont Lodge*, entered from Castle Street, and the tourist is allowed to examine them on presentation of his card.

The *Northernhay Promenade* is between the Castle and the railway station, and commands pleasant views, somewhat obstructed by the trees, which form an avenue. Here are statues of Sir Thomas Acland, Mr. John Dinham, and the late Earl of Iddesleigh, and one entitled the "Deer Stalker," by E. B. Stephens, A.R.A.

Mount Dinham is close to the Exe on the west side of the city. It is best reached by turning west from Ironbridge. It is a slight eminence on the left bank of the river, and affords a fine view. Here St. Michael's Church (modern ; built for the late Mr. Gibbs, of Tyntesfield, the munificent benefactor of Keble College, Oxford) has a tower, and a fine though somewhat heavy-looking spire, and many beautiful details within and without. The style is Early English. Adjoining are the *Episcopal Charity*

RAILWAY STATIONS.

G.W.R.—St David's   Aa.
    St Thomas's   Bf.
L. & S.W.R.—Queen St.   Db.

HOTELS.

Bude   Fc
Clarence   Ed.
Globe   Dd.
Half Moon   Ec.
New London   Fb.
Queen's   Dc.
Rougemont   Db.

Albert Museum   Dc.
Castle   Eb
Cathedral   Ed.
Guildhall   Dc.
Mt. Dinham   Bc.
Northernhay   Eb.
Post Office   Ec.
St Pancras Church   Dc.
Theatre   Fc.
Training College   Bd.
Vicars' College   Dd.

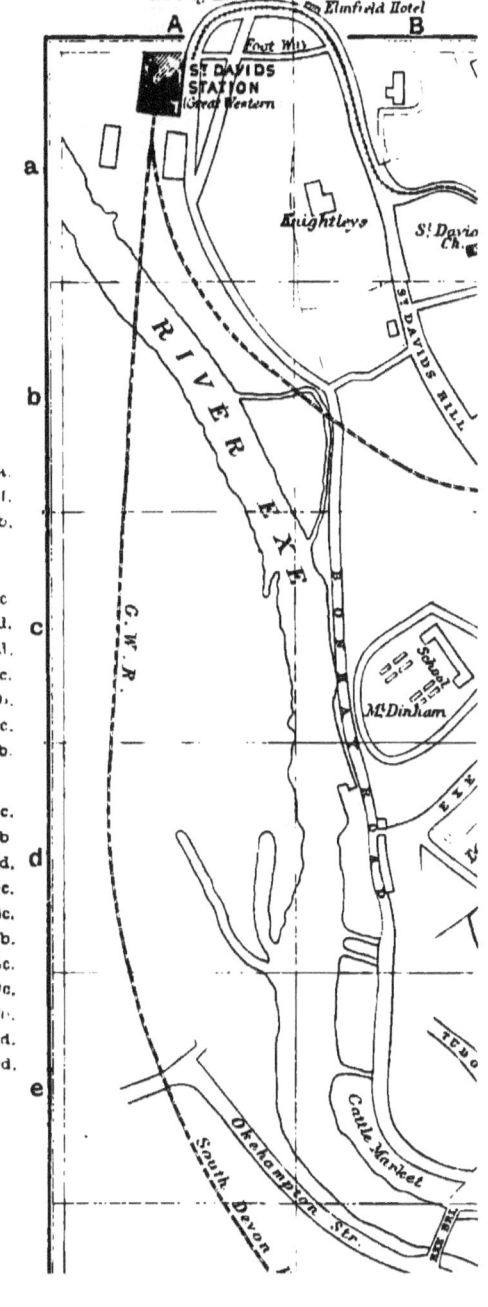

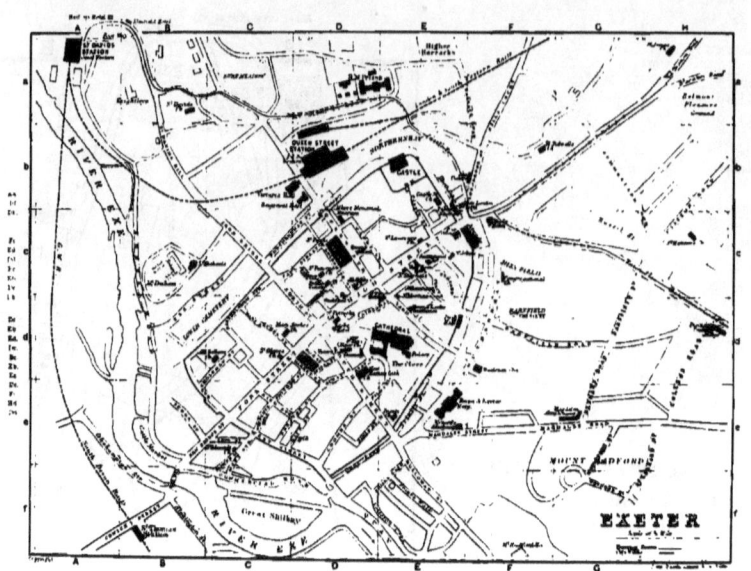

Schools and the *Free Cottages*, 40 in number, with tastefully laid out grounds. The place is named after the gentleman who originated the free-cottage scheme and built 24 of them.

The *College of Priest Vicars*, in South Street, containing the collections of the Architectural Society, and the 15th century *Chapel of Wynard's Almshouse*, in Magdalen Street, are worth a visit.

Pennsylvania. Tourists who wish to obtain the best and most commanding **view of the city** should turn out of High Street at the New London Hotel by Longbrook Street, which descends to and crosses the S.W. railway, and is thence continued by a long hill which leads up through Pennsylvania, the pleasantest suburb of the city. By turning to the right at one or two unmistakable points along proprietary roads they will gain a bird's eye view, which includes not only the city itself but the country beyond as far as the sea, the estuary of the Exe, and the richly-wooded Haldon range to the right of it. On the top of the hill, left of the road, is a small *reservoir* ($\frac{1}{2}hr.$), whence the prospect is still more extensive; ask leave at the cottage close by. Then, on the same side, a little beyond the old toll-gate, and about $\frac{3}{4}$ m. from the reservoir, is the entrance to the **Duryard Park Estate** (1d. each on foot or in carriage). Through this, two drives, of which the farther one, *Argyll Road*, is the best, lead down to the valley of the Exe, entering the high-road about half-a-mile north of St. David's Station. The entire round is about 4 miles.

Exeter (St. David's) to Tiverton and Dulverton by the Exe Valley line. For the road, see p. 32.

This is a beautiful route, and offers pleasant rambles from several intermediate stations. In 4 m. the main line of the G. W. R. is followed towards London. At first the Exe is seen on the left and presently a 3-arch bridge over it. Just beyond this the South-Western (N. Devon branch) diverges on the left, and then *Pynes* (Earl of Iddesleigh) is well seen on that side. After crossing the Exe twice our line diverges to the left from the main line, a little short of Stoke Cannon, and reaches *Brampford Speke* ($4\frac{1}{4}$ m.) where the station is on the E. of the river, beyond which the church appears above the trees.

In 1849-51, this parish became famous in connection with the lawsuit, Gorham v. Bp. of Exeter (Phillpotts).

Beyond Bramford Speke we again cross the Exe, and see on its E. bank the small dilapidated church of Nether Exe. Then through a deep-red sandstone cutting, we arrive at *Thorverton* (6 m.).

Thorverton village, $\frac{1}{2}$ m, N.W. has a good (restored) church. It is a pleasant walk of $2\frac{1}{4}$ m. up a tributary valley to *Cadbury Castle*, an ancient earthwork on the hill at its head. This was occupied by Fairfax in 1645. On the N. side of the hill runs the road from Crediton to Tiverton and by that it is $2\frac{1}{2}$ m. N.E. down to the Exe valley at Bickleigh (*Cadeleigh and Bickleigh*) see *p.* 32.

Once more our line crosses the Exe, and, passing the hamlet of Up Exe, left, reaches *Up Exe and Silverton* (6½ m.). Beyond this the hillside, left, is prettily dotted with white little farmsteads and cottages, and Bickleigh Court, an ivied farm-house, once a seat of the Carew family, is seen, left, as we near *Cadeleigh and Bickleigh* (10¼ m.), where the road crosses the Exe by a picturesque old bridge of 5 arches.

Bickleigh (*New Inn*) village is about ½ m. S. from the station on the E. bank of the Exe. In the churchyard is buried the "King of the Gipsies," Bamfylde Moore Carew (1693-1770) who was born at Bickleigh Court (*above*). The neighbourhood of Bickleigh is very picturesque, and the valley of the Dart, which joins the Exe (for fishing see Tiverton, *below*) on the W. bank about ½ m. below Bickleigh, is worth exploring. It is about 2½ m. up it to Worthy Bridge and thence 3 m. N.E. by road to Tiverton.

North of Cadeleigh the Exe valley, flanked by wooded and steep hills, is beautiful. The mansion, right, about 3 m. on the way is Collipriest House. After that Tiverton Bridge is seen on the left, and we skirt the E. side of the town of *Tiverton*, 14 m.

Tiverton (Hotels: *Palmerston* H.Q.; *Angel*) connected with the main G.W.R. at Tiverton Junction (5 m.), is a pleasantly situated town of 10,000 inhab., in a richly wooded part of the Exe valley. The river-fishing is preserved by the Tiverton Fishing Association (apply to the Secretary). The **Church**, in great part rebuilt in 1853, is fine. The *tower* is Perpendicular, and the *Greenway Chapel* (1517) is richly carved. It takes its name from its merchant-founder, John Greenway (*d*. 1529), to whom and his wife there are brasses. Here too is an altar-piece "St. Peter in Prison," by Richard Conway (*d*. 1821), the miniature painter who was a native of Tiverton. Of the **Castle**, the chief portion left—it was "slighted" by Fairfax, 1645—is the fine gateway. The **Greenway Almshouses**, in Gold Street, were founded about the same date as the chapel (*above*). **Blundell's School**, familiar to the readers of *Lorna Doone*, was founded by Peter Blundell (*d*. 1601), a clothier. Tiverton has a considerable lace manufacture and is an important agricultural centre. Lord Palmerston was M.P. for the town from 1835-65. *For rail to Hemyock see p.* 11.

North of Tiverton we still follow the Exe valley for 5 m., and beyond Cow Bridge, a single arch, left, cross the river twice. Then the line ascends the tributary valley of the Batham to **Bampton** (19½ m., *White Horse*, Q.), a dull little place, with a humble church close to the station. Beyond this the scenery is commonplace, and we join the Barnstaple branch just under Morebath village, whose ridge-roofed church tower is conspicuous on the hillside. For **Dulverton** (23¼ m.; *Carnarvon Arms* at station; *Red Lion*, 'bus, in the town), see our *North Devon and North Cornwall, p.* 5.

Exeter to Tiverton and Dulverton, by road. This is a beautiful route nearly identical with the rail route, *above*. It keeps E. of the Exe as far as Bickleigh, then follows the W. bank to Tiverton, where it returns to the E. bank and keeps to it all the way to Exe Bridge. Crossing this it ascends the W. bank of the Barle, past Dulverton station, to Dulverton. The **distances** are: Exeter to Stoke Cannon, 3½ m.; Silverton, 7 m.; Bickleigh, 10½ m.; Bickleigh Bridge, 11 m.; Tiverton (bridge), 15 m.; *Exeter Inn*, and bridge over the Batham, above its junction with the Exe, 21¼ m.; *Foxford Hotel* (Post Town: Bampton) 24 m.; Exe Bridge (*Inn*), 26 m.; Dulverton Station, 26¾ m.; Dulverton (*town*), 27½ m. *see above*.

N.B. The bridge over the Batham (*see above*) is ¾ m. short of Bampton, for which you do not cross the bridge. You cross it for Dulverton.

The return can be varied by returning by *St. John-in-the-Wilderness*, where is a ruined church, now used only for funerals in the surrounding grave-yard. The whole round is between 9 and 10 miles.

Exmouth to Budleigh Salterton, 5 *m.* Sojourners at Exmouth will enjoy exploring the coast-line between these places. The rocks about Straight Point—half-way, abt. 3 *m.*—afford good scrambling and a fine view up and down the coast. An alternative route is to pursue the high road for about $1\frac{1}{2}$ miles, and then to branch off to the right along the road to Littleham, whence a path leads to Beacon Hill, overlooking Budleigh. Those, however, who intend walking along the coast further east are advised to take the 'bus to Budleigh, and after climbing Beacon Hill from thence, to pursue their course through Otterton, or over the plank bridge nearer the mouth of the Otter, to Sidmouth. The view from the Budleigh Beacon comprises all that is especially interesting between Exmouth and Budleigh, and the 'bus route is pretty.

The high-road ascends slightly out of Exmouth, and presents, looking back, fine views over the Exe estuary to the Haldon range and along the blood-red coast, in the midst of which Dawlish lies in its little combe. To the left rise heights on which the old church of St. John-in-the-Wilderness stands. Then from the crest of the hill we descend a pleasantly wooded slope, past villas whose walls and surrounding gardens testify to the genial climate, down the length of the main street, till we are landed at the pleasantly-placed *Rolle Arms Hotel.*

Budleigh Salterton [Hotels: *Rolle Arms* (H.Q.), *Feathers, Coffee Tavern* (beds) in Fore St. *Post*: 2 deliveries and 2 despatches. Pop. abt. 2,000] is as pleasant a little retreat as can be imagined for those who desire, without making hermits of themselves, a temporary respite from the hum-drum of every-day life. A long street sloping gently to the sea, fringed by houses which allow plenty of breathing space between them, and intersected in its lower part by a limpid stream, which is crossed by several rustic bridges; a pleasant beach, a cliff-walk of gentle slope, culminating in a lovely view-point, a wealth of blossom and foliage, including myrtle and hydrangea—these are the charms of Budleigh. The tourist should walk westward along the coast—for by so doing and by descending from the Beacon through Littleham to the high-road to Exmouth, he may greatly improve upon the through road-route to that place—or, if he incline to pebble-hunting, then he may spend hours between the mouth of the Otter on the east, and the Beacon on the west. The stones, which are flat and oval in shape, are composed of quartzite, and present a variety of charming colours, especially when they are still wet.

The stroll from Budleigh is up the gravel walk west of the village, to the flagstaff on the *Beacon*, from which there is a lovely coast-view extending from Berry Head, south of Torquay, past Teignmouth and the red cliffs of Dawlish to Otterton Point and High Peake Hill eastwards.

Budleigh Salterton to **Otterton** (2¼ *m.*), and **Sidmouth**, 6½ *m.*

This route is described the reverse way on *p.* 25. The best way for the pedestrian is by road through East Budleigh and Otterton, whence first a lane and then a path leads to the cliff above Ladram Bay, and proceeds over *Peake Hill*, joining the road-route about half-a-mile short of *Sidmouth*.

*** The coast may be more closely followed by crossing the Otter by a plank bridge, half-a-mile from its mouth, going over *High Peake Hill*, and joining the above route above *Ladram Bay*.

Great and Little Haldon.

The two heights thus named form a long ridge of an almost uniform height of about 800 feet, between the valleys of the Exe and the Teign, and are crossed at almost their highest points by the high roads from Exeter to Newton Abbot and to Chudleigh. One spur of them drops upon Dawlish, whence the walk over their ridge may be accomplished by a variety of intricate lanes climbing to the summit-ridge. The drive or walk from any of the places we have named, as well as from Teignmouth, is well worth taking, both for the sake of the bracing character of a great part of it, and for the glorious views which it commands over two of the richest valleys of Devon to the hills beyond and the sea. Those who simply cross the ridge by one of the high-roads need no guidance beyond that which sign-posts afford, and we think that our duty will be best performed by a description of a walk or drive along the backbone of the ridge, and a few hints as to the road up to it from the various places of popular resort near its foot, as we arrive at each in our account of the country. There is no better starting point than Exeter, and our route is:

Exeter to **Newton Abbot, Teignmouth,** or **Dawlish,** *by road.*

The distances by high-road, across the ridge, to these places are—to Newton Abbot, 15 *m*; to Teignmouth, 14 *m*; and to Dawlish 12 *m.* (the last 6 being by cross-country lanes). The following route adds from 3 to 5 miles to each distance.

Leave Exeter by New Bridge Street, cross Exe Bridge, and beyond St. Thomas' Station (*G.W.R.*) follow the Moreton Hampstead and Plymouth road for about 3 miles. This part of the journey is very up-and-down, and is best got over in a carriage. A third of a mile beyond a little inn, right, proceed almost straight on along a lane on the left, instead of bending to the right with the highroad.

HALDON HILLS.

To Dunsford Bridge and Chagford. The main road descends from here to *Dunsford Bridge* on the Teign - Dunsford (*Inn*; 7 m. from Exeter) is high up on the left bank. From the bridge, pedestrians may follow the river, upwards by a track on the right bank to *Clifford Bridge* and thence proceed direct to Chagford; *see p.* 86.

A tower, seen on the left when we reach the high ground, is one point that we are making for. In about a quarter of a mile, where the lane forks, take the right-hand branch, and then avoid turnings on either hand till you reach the tower, about 3 miles distant. During the walk there are lovely views on the right across the Teign valley to Dartmoor.

The **Belvedere Tower** (*key at Haldon Farm*, ¼ m. E.) lies a little to the left of the road in the midst of a wood so thick that only from the top is there any view. This is remarkable for the richness and silvan character of its foreground, the wide expanse of sea visible, and the environment of distant hills, which include Dartmoor to the west, Exmoor to the north, and the Blackdown Hills between Devon and Somerset to the north-east. Crowning the last named, the Wellington Monument, near the town of the same name, is distinctly seen. Immediately below, on the same side, are the grounds and tower of Powderham and the estuary of the Exe, with Exmouth at its southern, and Exeter a little beyond its northern extremity. The intervening country towards Dartmoor is occupied by the Teign valley, as lovely an expanse of wooded, undulating scenery as is to be found in England. The twin rocks of Heytor are conspicuous outliers of the moor. Southwards the long and level ridge of Haldon itself hides the coast.

Quitting the Belvedere we may descend at once to *Ashton* (*p.* 86) in the Teign valley, nearly 2 miles distant, and the present terminus of the Teign valley railway. Those, however, who enjoy an opportunity of easy walking or driving over high ground will continue south-eastwards along the ridge. A good road goes in this direction, crossing in 2 miles the high-road from Exeter to Chudleigh.

From the crossing-point the right-hand road leads to Chudleigh in 3½ miles. Keeping straight on at the crossing the road soon reaches the old *Exeter Racecourse*—a successful rival in point of situation to the famous "Lansdown" of Bath. Beyond it we join the Exeter and Newton Abbot road. From this point there is a lovely view eastward down to Exmouth and the sea beyond it.

Hence there is a choice of routes, see map. (1) *Exeter* may be reached in 6¼ miles by the high-road ; *Inn* at *Kennford*, 2¼ m. (2) The same road may be followed in the opposite direction to *Newton Abbot* (8½ m.), or to *Teignmouth*, over Little Haldon (8 m.) or you may reach *Dawlish* in between 6 and 7 miles, the road passing near an obelisk (*p.* 39) in the centre of a wood above Mamhead, and descending thence into the little valley whose waters flow through the centre of Dawlish. The *Obelisk*, erected as a sea-mark, is a useful guide post, but affords no view whatever. The intricacy of the lanes about and beyond it makes it difficult to find the way after dark.

Exeter to Plymouth—with the branches to Torquay and Kingswear—by the Great Western Railway.

Exeter to Dawlish, 12 m; *Teignmouth*, 15 m; *Newton Abbot*, 20 m; *Totnes*, 29 m; *Ivybridge*, 42 m; *Plymouth*, 53 m.

—*Newton Abbot to Torquay*, 6 m; *Kingswear (for Dartmouth)*, 15 m.

—*Kingsbridge Road to Kingsbridge*, 10 m.

This line skirts in turn the estuary of the Exe, the open sea, and the estuary of the Teign, as far as Newton Abbot, beyond which it rises and falls again to the Dart, and for the greater part of the remaining distance skirts the southern side of Dartmoor. The scenery throughout is very interesting.

From *St. David's Station* at Exeter the line proceeds with the Exe on the left-hand, flanked by sandstone cliff, to *St. Thomas' Station*, which accommodates the residents in the southern part of Exeter. The Cathedral is not seen at first, but the modern spire of *St. Michael's* is a prominent object on the top of the cliff.

A little short of **Exminster** (4 m. *from Exeter*), the *Devon County Lunatic Asylum* is a noticeable object on the right of the line, and from Exminster itself we look across the widening estuary to *Topsham* (p. 33). The rising ground which culminates in Great Haldon, wooded almost to the summit, opens out on our right, and in another 2 miles we pass on the same side the tower, church, deer-park, and mansion of *Powderham*. Another mile brings us to the station at **Starcross** (Hotel: *Courtenay Arms*; Inn: *Railway, both close to the station*). This is a pleasantly situated little place when the tide is in, but it lacks the charm of the open sea. From it the tourist may ferry across to Exmouth, 1½ m. distant.

Powderham Castle, the seat of the Earl of Devon, is best visited from Starcross. (*Admission, at the Entrance on the Kenton road, 1¼ m. from Starcross Station, daily, when the family is not in residence, from 11 to 5 o'clock. Cards to be written for to "the Steward, Powderham Castle, near Exeter", 2 or 3 days in advance.*) It contains some good pictures. The exterior has little remarkable: the oldest part, of which two towers and the chapel remain, dates five centuries back; the rest is modern. The park is only separated from the estuary of the Exe by the railway, alongside which a road runs from Starcross Station. The greater part of it is level, but behind the Castle the ground rises gradually, and throughout it is finely wooded, principally with oak.

Beyond Starcross the line continues along the Exe estuary, on the far-side of which a full view of Exmouth presents itself. Just before the open sea is reached, a sandy promontory, or spit,

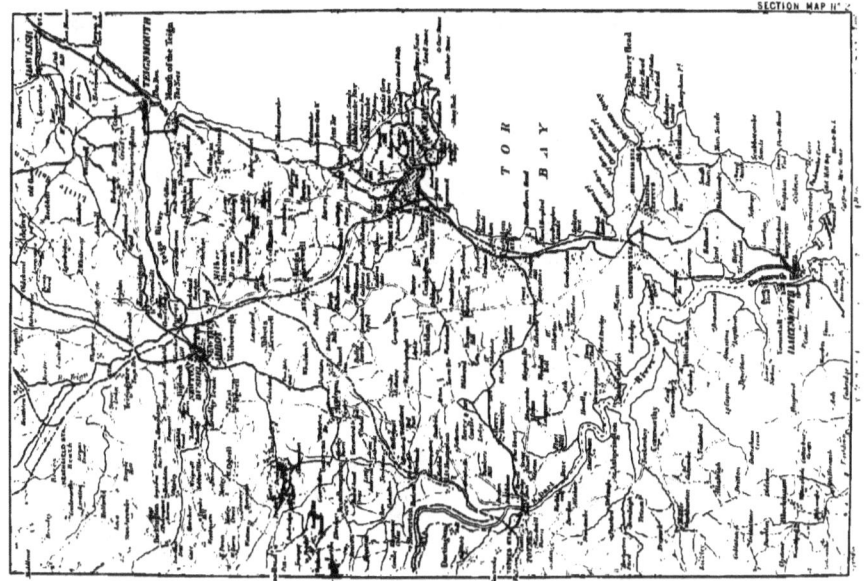

SECTION MAP No. 2

called the *Warren*, projects for nearly two miles, reaching apparently to Exmouth itself, but in reality admitting a passage (*ferry*, 3d.) of about a third of a mile in breadth between it and the opposite shore.

Hence with red cliffs on the right and on the left the open sea, separated from us only by a wall and a narrow promenade, we reach in 1½ miles Dawlish. The rocks in front, deeply hollowed, and in some cases insulated by the action of the waves, present fantastic shapes. *Rail continued p.* 40.

Dawlish.

Hotels :—*London* (H.Q.), in the town; *Royal*, *Albert*, opp. the station; *Coffee Tavern* (beds) near Station in Fore St.

Post :—*Del. London*, *7 a.m., North*, 10.30 *a.m.*; *desp., North*, 3.55 *p.m., London*, 11.50 *a.m.* and *9.20 *p.m.* [*Sundays also.*]

A pleasant feature of Dawlish, and one in which it resembles Bournemouth, is the open green space which lies between its two terraces and permanently secures its houses against overcrowding. This space forms a pleasant lawn, and is intersected by a clear streamlet crossed by bridges. The town recedes from the sea at right angles, and it is somewhat unfortunate that engineering necessities have obliged the railway to form a screen, though the evil has been mitigated by giving the obstruction the character of a viaduct, between it and the beach. Of Dawlish itself there is nothing much to be said except that the climate is warm and genial, the bathing very fair, and the opportunities for promenading, though somewhat limited in extent, very agreeable in character. On the cliff just south of the town is *Lee Mount*, sheltered by trees and provided with seats. It commands a fine view across the bay to Exmouth and the long line of cliff beyond. The walk to it may be continued past a roadside-inn, till, in 1¼ miles, a little by-road to the left leads under the railway to the sea-wall and promenade which continues for another mile and a half to Teignmouth.

Other **walks from Dawlish** are (1) along the sea-wall northwards to *Langstone Point*, 1½ *m.*, and thence across the *Warren* (*p.* 34) to the mouth of the Exe for Exmouth. The first part of the Warren is firm ground but the Exmouth end is loose sand. (2) To *Great Haldon* by the lanes which go north-westwards with the Dawlish Water on the left hand. There are various ways of making this expedition. Perhaps the best plan is to turn to the right nearly two miles on the way, and after ascending to a point where several lanes converge, to take one that bends sharply to the left, and make for an *obelisk*, which rises from the midst of the wood, and was constructed for a sea-mark. There is no way to its top, and no view from its base, but beyond it you may enter the open moor through a gate and follow the ridge of great Haldon as far as you please. The roads along and across this ridge are described *pp.* 36, 37.

Dawlish (over Holcombe Down) to Teignmouth, 3¼ *m.*, or to top of **Little Haldon**. Leave the church on the right hand and ascend by the shady lane which leads up to *Holcombe Down*. When in a little less than two miles you reach the ridge, you will come to a gate over which a lovely view across the Teign estuary to Dartmoor presents itself. Thence you may descend directly to Teignmouth, or turn to the right and proceed either to the summit ridge of *Little Haldon* (1½ *m.*) or to *Kingsteignton* and *Newton Abbot*—the latter about 8 miles from Dawlish.

The Parson and Clerk Rocks, nearly 1½ miles south of Dawlish, are the most prominent features of the sea-worn coast for some miles in either direction. The parson has not quite separated himself from the mainland, but the clerk, a stack of new red sandstone, is detached.

Rail cont. from p. 39. There are several short tunnels between Dawlish and Teignmouth. About half-way we have the *Parson and Clerk* (*see above*) on the left, and the recommencement of the sea-wall and promenade which extend to Teignmouth itself. *Rail continued*, *p.* 42.

Teignmouth.

Hotels: *Royal*, on the Den; *London* (H.Q.; good commercial); *Queen's*; *Railway*; *Temperance*, next the Station; *Globe Coffee Tavern* (beds).
Post: *Del., London. &c.,* *7 a.m.; *North*, 10.10 a.m.; *desp., North*, 3.40 p.m.; *London,* *9 p.m.   [*Sundays also.]

Teignmouth is most picturesquely situated at the foot of the southern spur of Little Haldon and in such a position as to command both a splendid expanse of open sea and a long reach of the river estuary. This advantage it owes in a great measure to a sandy spot, called the *Den*, which is now formed into a lawn and promenade with a handsome pier projecting from it. The estuary of the river, about four miles in length, has somewhat the appearance of an inland lake, and the beauty of the picture is greatly enhanced by the wooded little height, called the *Ness*, on the far side of the water. The long wooden bridge (built in 1825, and one of the longest in England) which spans the estuary about half-a-mile up it, is also a pleasing feature. The view up the Teign extends to those two notable outliers of Dartmoor, the Heytor Rocks. Teignmouth has two very ugly churches.

In the centre of the crescent on the Den are the *Public Rooms—*ball room, billiard room, &c., of Greek architecture, heavy and incongruous.

Teignmouth was twice burnt by the French—once in the fourteenth century, when it was only a village, and again in 1690, by Admiral Tourville, who destroyed upwards of a hundred houses, including the village of Shaldon, on the south side of the estuary.

Walks from Teignmouth.

(1.) To the **Parson and Clerk Rocks**, 1½ *miles north, by the sea-wall already mentioned.*

(2.) To the top of **Little Haldon**, *abt.* 3 *m.*, a delightful climb with views increasing in extent and beauty all the way. By diverging to the right in about 1½ miles, a pleasant descent into *Dawlish*, 2 *m.* further, may be made.

(3.) **To St. Mary Church and Torquay**, 8 *m.* By ferrying across the water from the end of the Den instead of going round by the bridge, a mile is saved, and the high road joined after a smart climb of a few hundred yards from the opposite side. This road continues parallel with the cliff, and from ¼ to ½ mile from it all the way to St. Mary Church, affording in a few miles a charming view down a little lateral valley to the villages of Stoke and Combe in Teignhead. At **Marychurch** (Hotel: *Brealey's Family*), it is best to turn to the left and proceed along the top of the cliff of Babbicombe Bay, and past Anstey's Cove, so as to enter Torquay from its east end.

Rail continued from p. 40. After quitting Teignmouth, a near prospect of great luxuriance, including some fine holm-oaks, is displayed on the right-hand side, and the northern shore of the Teign estuary is skirted till it ends in an expanse of marshy ground, at the extremity of which Newton Abbot is seen. As the train turns southwards towards the station, there is a good view up the Teign valley, on the right, the Heytor Rocks on Dartmoor being, as from almost all this region, the most conspicuous objects; to the west of them are the Saddle and Rippon Tor. *Rail to Plymouth cont.* p. 43; *Chudleigh and Ashton*, p. 84; *Moreton Hampstead*, p. 87; *Torquay*, p. 43.

Newton Abbot.

━━━━━◆━━━━━

Ref. Kms. **Hotels**: *Globe*, ¾ m. from Station, *Commercial* (H.Q.), ⅞ m.; omnibuses. *Queen's* (H.Q. ladies'), 150 yds. from Stn. *Bradley* (Q.) Market Place. *Lawson Coffee Tavern* (beds).

Post: *del.* 7 a.m.; (North) 10.25 a.m. *desp.* (North) 3.15, (London, &c.) 8.30 p.m.

Newton Abbot and *Newton Bushel* have of late years, owing to the rich and varied character of their situation and their abundant railway facilities, grown greatly in favour as places of residence, the population having increased 1,500 in the decade previous to the census of 1881. Parochially they have no existence, being both included in the parish of *Wolborough*. The *Church*, half-a-mile from the centre of the town and 150 feet above it, is not remarkable; but the churchyard is very prettily situated on a steep slope, and the views from the new road and walks all about it are charming, Heytor Rocks on Dartmoor being a conspicuous feature. As a tourist resort Newton is at a disadvantage. It is not on the sea, and it is too far from the moor, nevertheless the luxuriantly beautiful character of the hills on the slopes and at the foot of which it stands, renders the town a most agreeable resting place.

NEWTON ABBOT.

Newton contains two special objects of historic interest : the *stone* from which the first proclamation of William III. as King of England was made, and *Ford House*, a Tudor mansion, which was visited by Charles I. in 1625, then became the property of the Parliamentary General Waller, and lastly in 1688 received the Prince of Orange in the flush of his first proclamation. The *Stone* is in the centre of the town, and is now, with questionable taste, surmounted by a modern street lamp. Behind it, standing alone, is the tower which forms the sole remnant of the church of St. Leonard. *Ford House* is a little to the left of the Torquay Road, ⅜ m. from the centre of the town, and just across the railway.

The pleasantest stroll from Newton is by the north side of the Bradley Brook, which flows through the place, past *Bradley House*, in part a fifteenth century mansion, half-a-mile from the town. Beyond it the walk may be continued for half-a-mile, or a mile, and then the hill on either side climbed. Northwards, you will join the Newton and Ashburton road ; southwards, the return may be made through the village of *East Ogwell* and along the *Ogwell* ridge to the Totnes and Newton road. The country at the back of Newton is a region of little wood-crowned hills, steep and green, and commanding thoroughly Devonian landscapes in every direction.

Newton Abbot to Ipplepen, 3½ m ; **Tor Bryan,** 4½ m ; **Denbury,** 6 m ; **Newton Abbot,** 9 m.

The mileage is exclusive of the ascent of Denbury Down. That will add about a mile. The interest of the round is chiefly confined to the 2½ m. between Ipplepen and Denbury.

Follow the Totnes road for nearly 3 m. and turn to the right to **Ipplepen** (Inn : *Wellington*), whose 15th century church-tower is a conspicuous object. Large quantities of marble are quarried in this parish. After traversing the length of the village and passing the church at its western end, the view down a tributary valley of the Dart and away southward, for we are on high ground, is fine. The road soon drops to the stream across which, singularly prettily placed, is **Tor Bryan,** which gets its prefix from the rock-crowned tors around, and has a roadside *inn* with the uncommon sign *Church House*. The church is worth a visit on account of its screen and old glass. At the top of the village turn to the right and ascend to a cross-road on the slope of **Denbury Down.** If driving, the carriage should be sent on to *Denbury* (Inn : *Union*) by the right-hand road (¾ m.) and the Down climbed for the sake of the view. On the top of the hill is a large earthwork. From the camp a track zigzags down the north side of the hill to the road and the village of Denbury, whence a straight course due east for nearly 2 m. brings us into the Newton Abbot road by which we set out.

Newton Abbot to Torquay, 6 m ; and **Kingswear (Dartmouth),** 14 m. From Newton to Torquay the line follows the course of a valley, the hills on either side, though of no great height, shutting out all distant view. The route on to Kingswear, which is very charming, is described in the Torquay Section (*p.* 53).

Rail continued from p. 42. From Newton to Totnes the distance is 9 miles, and the railway passing from the Teign to the Dart at their lowest levels crosses a col more than 200 feet high. The summit is reached about half-way at *Deignton Tunnel*, on both sides of which the gradient is severe, that on the Totnes side being 1 in 40. The view is limited by low hills on both sides for almost the entire distance. Before entering the tunnel the line winds through a well wooded dell and a quarry of richly-tinted limestone. A few yards short of Totnes the Dart, here a dark and tranquil stream, is crossed, and a peep up the valley towards Ashburton obtained. On the left front are seen the Castle and Church of **Totnes,** *p.* 60 ; *Totnes to Ashburton, p.* 74.

From Totnes the line again makes a considerable rise to a level

of between 300 and 400 feet, which it maintains with a few minor
depressions, as far as Cornwood station (8 miles short of Plymouth),
a little beyond which the steep descent to the Plym commences.
Throughout this distance it skirts the southern slopes of Dartmoor,
presenting on the right hand beautiful peeps into the recesses of
the moor from several lofty viaducts which it crosses, and on the
left a wide prospect over the elevated region of the Southern
Hams, the "Garden of Devon."

The first station is **Brent** (7 m. *from Totnes* ; *Royal Oak*, close
to the station), situated on the Dartmoor Avon. The *church* has
a Norman tower.

Brent Hill (1,000 *ft.*, 1 *m.* from station) an outpost of Dartmoor, is an
excellent view-point. Cross the line by the bridge at the west end of the
station and in 300 yards take the second of two adjacent footpaths. After two
fields this enters another lane close to a farm, but at once starts up again. The
view includes Buckfastleigh and Ashburton, much of Dartmoor, and, far away,
Exmoor. Southward, the South Hams to the sea. A descent may be made into
a rough lane that leads into the Buckfastleigh road. About 3 miles on the
Ashburton road is the village of *Dean Prior*, where Herrick the poet was vicar
and in the church of which he was buried in 1674. Dean Prior, formerly a
Tudor mansion, now a farmhouse, was in Herrick's time the residence of Sir
Edw. Giles for whose tomb in the church he wrote the epitaph "No trust to
metals, &c."

The line turns southwards and in 2 miles reaches **Kingsbridge Road Station**, the nearest to Kingsbridge town. There
is a fair-sized inn, a few yards from the station, and coaches run
to Kingsbridge about three times a day ; *fare*, 2s.

Kingsbridge Road to Loddiswell, 7 m.; **Kingsbridge**, 10 m.
This route is mostly over the upper level of the South Hams, and presents for
the first two-thirds of the way few features of interest. On the left, in about 2
miles, we pass *Fowellscombe*, an old Tudor mansion. As we recede from Dartmoor, its southern heights from Brent Hill westward become prominent in the
rear, while many miles in front a long and flat ridge, abrupt at both ends, shows
us the position of Bolt Head and Bolt Tail. The village of **Loddiswell** lies
at the beginning of a steep slope to the Avon valley. It is picturesque
and untidy - not to say dirty. Not the least characteristic part of the
village is its inn. Beyond it, continuing the descent, we cross the green
strath of the Avon, and at once commence a corresponding ascent, from
the top of which another drop by the side of a richly-wooded glen, called *Combe
Royal*, introduces us, after another slight rise, to the main street of **Kingsbridge**, *p.* 66.

From Kingsbridge Road the line continues to work round Dartmoor, and on approaching Ivybridge presents a charming view,
left, down the Erme valley, especially as we cross the **Ivybridge**
Viaduct and draw up at the *Station, see p.* 118. From the viaduct
the view up the narrow glen *on the right*, through which the Erme,
almost hidden by foliage, escapes from the wilds of Dartmoor, is
as delightful as it is momentary. *On the left* the only disfiguring
feature is the tall chimney of the paper mills. Down the valley
we see the tower of the mansion of Fleet, and to the left of it the
spire of Modbury church, while far away in the same direction
that of Churchstow rises to the right of Kingsbridge (unseen) and
above the long level promontory which is terminated in either
direction by Bolt Head and Bolt Tail.

Two miles beyond Ivybridge we get a wider and scarcely less beautiful view towards Dartmoor from the *Blatchford Viaduct*. The foreground is richly wooded and threaded by the Yealm, which two miles higher up flows through a romantic scene called the *Hawns and Dendles*. Beyond the viaduct is **Cornwood Station** (see p. 129), and a few yards further we cross the *Slade Viaduct*, the last upon our route, and little if at all inferior to any in the charm of the landscape seen from it. By a long and severe gradient affording a good view of the receding heights of Dartmoor on the right, the line then descends to **Plympton**, (p. 129). There is a true Devonian richness in the scenery hereabouts.

A little further the Launceston branch converges on the right. On the same side after crossing the Plym, we gain our first sight of the fortifications of Plymouth—a green smooth hill crowned with earthworks. On the left the Plym widens into the *Laira Estuary*, across which the rich woods of *Saltram* descend to the water's edge—a picture when the tide is up. *Laira Bridge* is seen some way ahead, but instead of making for it we enter a shallow valley, and passing *Mutley* and *North Road*, neither of which are convenient for the town, arrive at **Plymouth** (*Mill Bay*) p. 133.

Torquay.

Stations: *Torquay* and *Torre*, 1 m. apart and both about 1 m. from centre of the town. Hotel omnibuses at *Torquay*.

Hotels: *Imperial* on E. side of the bay close to the sea 1½ m. from Sta., cab 2s.; *Victoria* and *Albert* in Belgrave Road, ½ m. from Sta.; *Torbay*, W. of the Harbour, 1 m. from Sta. Commercial and family hotels: *Royal*, in the Strand, *Queen's* (H.Q.) a little further on. *Western*, at the Sta.; *Union*; *Gibbon's.—Jordan's* and *Pavilion*, both temperance; *Coffee Tavern* (beds) in Lower Union St.

Private Hotels: *Belgrave*, Belgrave Road; *Cumper's*; *Osborne House*.

Cabs: (luggage to or from Station, 2d. each article carried outside) one-horse for 1 to 3 pers., 6d. per half-mile; for more than 3 pers., 1s. first ½ m., each additional ½ m. 6d. By *time* for 1 to 3 pers., 2s. first hour, 1s. each ½ hr. addit.; for more than 3 pers., 3s. and 1s. 3d. each ½ hr. addit. After 7 p.m. in winter or 9 p.m. in summer minimum fare 1s. 6d. and (more than 3) 2s.

Rowing Boats: with man, 1s. 6d. first hour, after that 1s. per hr.; without man, 1s. per hr.

Theatre in Abbey Road.

Post Office, in Babbicombe Road: principal mails *del.* (London, etc.) 7 a.m.; (North) 11 a.m.; *desp.* (North) 2.50 p.m.; (London) 8 p.m. Sunday *del.* 7 a.m.; *desp.* 8 p.m.

Torquay (*Pop*. abt. 25,000) contends in honourable rivalry with Scarborough for the right to be considered the Queen of English watering-places. It is not for us to attempt to settle so delicate a question between competitors both so fair, and yet of such different types of beauty. Of the Devon resort here are a few of the merits:— a mild and equal climate, soft but not damp in winter, warm but not sultry in summer; a situation sheltered on the north and north-east, but open to the sea and its breezes on the south; abundant and excellent accommodation for visitors; a copious supply of pure water brought from Dartmoor; model drainage. The characteristics of Torquay that at once strike the traveller are newness and greenness. The town is wholly the creation of the last 60 or 70, and very largely of the last 30 years. Three hills that rise rather abruptly from the margin of a small bay (an offset at the north-west corner of Torbay) have their feet and the intervening valleys occupied by terraces, while on their sides, up to their summits, rise handsome villas, set in ornamental and well-timbered grounds. Behind these there is a higher range also dotted with similar houses. As seen from the bay (the best view), or from near the railway station (the next best view), the effect of the white limestone houses, rising one above another amid a wealth of foliage is delightful. Torquay is essentially an aristocratic place, and though it cannot, considering the high quality of its entertainment, be considered unduly expensive, yet it does lay itself out more for those who have well-stocked purses than for persons who can only afford an economical resting place. It has two distinct "seasons." The winter and spring fill it with invalids and convalescents, to whom genial temperature and bright and pleasant surroundings are of more benefit than "doctor's stuff." The summer and autumn bring large numbers of visitors, who find in its charming bay and in the neighbourhood, inland and coastwise, an endless variety of delightful rambles and excursions. Shady avenues and magnificent "drives" are not the least attractive features of the place. Of public buildings there are not many that call for notice. The mother church is *St. Saviour's, Tor*, which is of small interest architecturally, having been restored in 1849, and since enlarged. There are monuments to the members of the Cary family, including a fair brass, dated 1581, and in the *Ridgeway Chapel* an effigy of John Ridgeway, grandfather of Thomas Ridgeway, first Earl of Londonderry. The rest of the churches are modern. *St. John's*, Early English, by the late Mr. Street, is exceedingly beautiful, and has a not very common feature—a marble *lavacrum*, for baptismal immersion.

Between the station and the town is **Tor Abbey** (R. S. Cary, Esq.), built about 1555, by the above mentioned John Ridgeway. It occupies part of the site of the Norbertine Abbey, founded by William Lord Brewer in 1196. Of the ruins of the abbey the most important remains are the entrance to the *Chapter House* (a fine round arch in good preservation); the 14th century *gateway*; the *Refectory* (used as a R. C. Chapel from 1777 to 1854, when the Church of the Assumption was opened); the 13th century *grange* (now stables), called the *Spanish Barn* from the fact that the prisoners taken in the *Capitana*, an Armada ship, were temporarily confined in it; and a square massive tower. When the mansion was undergoing restoration in 1876 two crypts were discovered, one under the refectory, and the other close by. The latter from its rather elaborate columns and the good details of the mouldings throughout was evidently an important part of the monastery, but for what purpose it was employed is uncertain. *The ruins are not shown to the public.* About half-a-mile north of the abbey, and close to Tor Station, is **St. Michael's Chapel**, on Chapel Hill, which is reached by a gate leading into a plantation. The ruins are Early English, but of no great interest. The original purpose of the chapel, and whether it belonged to the abbey or not, are alike unknown. It has a plain stone roof, and is built of limestone, varied with new red sandstone dressings. From its conspicuous position it is a well-known sea mark, and it is said that "up to within the last half century, when any foreign vessels arrived in Torquay, the crews of which were Roman Catholic,

they invariably paid a visit to St. Michael's Chapel."—*J. T. White.*
The view from the hill is ample reward for the short stroll.

The only other architectural antiquity in the immediate vicinity of the town is *Ilsham Grange*; see below.

The Harbour consists of an outer and inner basin, and the Pier (toll, 1*d.*) which shelters the latter is a favourite promenade, especially when many yachts are in port.

Close by are the **Baths** and **Saloons** and the *Ladies' Bathing Cove*, and at the end of Beacon Terrace the *Torquay and South Devon Club*. Passing the Club, and turning shortly to the right, we reach the *Imperial Hotel*, and beyond it a public pleasure ground commanding a fine view of Torbay. "Land's End" is the name given to the termination of the walk in this direction, and "London Bridge" is a natural arch of limestone in the promontory just beyond. The *Gentlemen's Bathing-place* is below this promenade. A pleasant walk is to proceed past the Club and ascend the hill, taking the first turn to the left, and then the next on the right. This leads to the open limestone plateau known as **Daddy Hole Plain**, so called from the largest of several chasms. The particular Hole was formed about a hundred years ago by a natural subsidence, and is in no wise remarkable. The Coast-guard station is on the Plain, whence there is a good sea view eastward to Hope's Nose.

From the Plain we can descend to *Meadfoot*, a sandy bay separated from Torquay by Park Hill, girt with newly-built terraces. The *Shag Rock* is off its western, and the *Thatcher Rock* off its eastern end. The *Sea Road* is carried along the top of the Torquay sewage tunnel to the eastern end of the bay, whence a good road runs up Ilsham (or Ilesam) Combe, and so to Anstey's Cove and Babbicombe. **Manor Gardens** (public) occupy the hillside above. The pedestrian wishing to extend his walk to Ilsham should leave a large villa, *Kilmorie*, on his left, and take a path through a gate across a field, and so into the road to Hope's Farm and **Ilsham Grange**. The latter belonged to Tor Abbey, and much of the old building remains. The farm was under the charge of a resident monk, and the three-storied 15th century building in which he lived and had a small chapel is standing. The ground floor was used for offices, the first floor, reached by an external staircase, contained the chapel, and above that was his cell. The dimensions of the chapel, which stands nearly N. and S., are about 12 ft. 6 in. by 9 ft. 6 in. and 8 ft. 6 in. high. The floor of the room above has perished. The *altar* was at the end next the farmyard, and traces of a *credence* remain on its east side. On the left of the window over the altar, is a slit which enabled the monk to command a view of his workmen below, and in the ground floor is a similar opening, apparently for the same purpose. The bell-cot is still in position on the ridge of the roof.

The return to Torquay can be made by the road that joins the Babbicombe Road at Wellswood, by there turning to the left. The Lincombe Drive is a fine drive on the left, a short distance from this turn.

Kent's Cavern is rather over a mile from the Strand by the Babbicombe Road. At Wellswood turn to the right. After passing a fountain, a direction notice makes the way clear. *The charge for one, two, or three persons is 1s. 6d. Larger parties 6d. each. Time taken, about half-an-hour. Open from 10 a.m. to 5 p.m.* The cavern consists of two parallel caves connected in one place with one another. The double entrance is on the eastern face of a low limestone cliff, and the length of the accessible portion of the cavern is about a furlong. From the roof depend stalactites, and the floor was, until broken up for exploration, covered with stalagmites. The size of the cavity varies from less than a yard to more than 20 yards in breadth, but in height nowhere reaches 20 feet. As far as beauty or anything to see is concerned, those who know the magnificent Cheddar caves will find Kent's Cavern of comparatively little interest. It is on account of the bones, &c., found in its floor that it has obtained a world-wide renown. The first bones were discovered by Mr. Northmore in 1824, and between 1825 and 1841 the Rev. J. McEnery, chaplain at the Abbey, disinterred a large number, as well as many flint instruments. In 1846 the Torquay Natural History Society took up the matter, and was enabled to confirm Mr. McEnery's work, but strangely enough the scientific world received its report with sceptical indifference. However, in 1858 another cave was discovered at Brixham, which was systematically examined by Mr. Pengelly, and yielded similar results to those of Kent's Cavern. "The antiquity of man" thenceforward became a question of popular interest, and a careful investigation was determined on under the supervision of a committee of the British Association. The names of Lyell, Lubbock, Phillips, Boyd Dawkins, and Pengelley upon that committee guarantee the accuracy of the facts reported.

First or uppermost we found huge blocks of limestone covering in every direction the entire chamber. Beneath and between these blocks was *black mould*, largely vegetable, from 3 inches to more than a foot in depth. Below that was *granular stalagmite* from an inch to more than 5 feet in thickness, and averaging 16 to 20 inches. In one part of the cavern beneath this stalagmite, and covering an area of 100 square feet was a *black band* consisting mainly of charcoal. Below that a light-red loam, mixed with angular pieces of limestone which we named *cave-earth*. In another part of this cavern we found beneath this cave-earth a layer of *crystalline stalagmite*, and under it another deposit called *breccia* i.e. a cave-earth of higher antiquity. The following table gives a rough list of the objects found in the several layers.

In the *Black mould*: Whetstones; plates of slate; pieces of smelted copper; bone combs like shoe-horns with teeth at the broad end, some ornamented; spindle whorls; flint flakes; amber beads; charred wood; bones and teeth of man, pig, dog, badger, brown bear, short-fronted ox, red deer, sheep, goat, hare, rabbit, water-rat, seal, birds, and fish; shells of snails, limpets, whelks, cockles, oysters, mussels, pectens, solens, and cuttle fish and hazel nuts. *No extinct animals.* These "finds" may be referred to Romano-British and pre-Roman times.

In the *granular Stalagmite:* Shells of cockles and cuttle fish; impressions of ferns; charcoal; bones and teeth of bear, elephant, hyæna, horse, fox, and man, with flakes and cores of flint.
In the *Black band*: 366 flint tools; flakes and cores; a bone awl; a bone harpoon; a bone needle with eye; burnt bones; remains of ox, deer; horse, badger, bear, fox, rhinoceros, hyæna.
In the *Cave* earth: Whetstones; hammer stones; flint stones and plates; a bone pin; two bone harpoons; charcoal; burnt bones; coprolites of hyæna; remains of cave lion and another *felis*, wild cat, cave hyæna, wolf, fox (various), glutton; badger, cave bear, grizzly bear, brown bear, mammoth, rhinoceros, horse, urus, bison, "Irish elk," red deer, rein-deer, hare, lagomys, voles (various), *Arvicola gulielmi*, beaver and *Machairodus latidens*.
In the *Crystaline Stalagmite*: Bones of bear only.
In the *Breccia* (or older cave earth): Immense number of teeth and bones of bear and three undoubted flint implements.

Abridged from a lecture by Mr. Pengelly.

Of the "antiquity of man" as indicated by the above layers it may suffice to point out that the black mould carries us back 2,000 years. The granular stalagmite alone must have taken a prodigious time to form if we may judge of its rate of accumulation by the film over the name of "Robert Hedges of Ireland, February 20, 1688." In 200 years that film has become about $\frac{1}{20}$th of an inch in thickness. In the Cheddar caves, discovered in 1828, a stalactite and stalagmite were found separated by a drop of water only, and the years that have since elapsed have not, to the naked eye at least, diminished the interval.

The *Torquay Natural History Society's* **Museum** contains a fine collection of the objects found in the cavern. (*Admission to Museum*: *Non-members*, 1s., or *member's order*; to *Reading Room*, 1s., and *member's order*.) Lectures are given weekly from November to May.

Walks and Excursions from Torquay.

Distances reckoned from the Strand.

1. Anstey's Cove, Babbicombe and St. Mary Church.

Anstey's Cove is a pretty but rather over-praised little bay about half-a-mile beyond Kent's Cavern. It may be reached direct by the Babbicombe road, but for the pedestrian the walk by Ilsham Combe or further east by a path over the hill commanding Hope's Nose and so to Ilsham, is better. The Cove owes its picturesqueness to the limestone, which forms its northern side, and to the ruin-like crags of the same rock, beautifully overgrown, in its midst. Of its other attractions the local poet shall be allowed to tell:—

"Picnics supplied with hot water and tea
At a nice little house down by the sea.
Fresh crabs and lobsters every day;
Salmon-peal sometimes, red mullet and grey.

The neatest of pleasure-boats let out on hire,
Fishing-tackle as good as you could desire.
Bathing-machines for ladies are kept,
With towels and gowns all quite correct.
Thomas is the man who supplies everything,
And also teaches young gentlemen to swim."

The same notice done into Latin elegiacs may be read over the door of this "universal provider." The Italian villa, **Bishopstowe**, built by Bishop Philpotts (*d.* 1869), is close to the road at the head of the Cove. **Babbicombe** (*Royal Hotel*; *Cary Arms* on the beach) is about 2 *m.* from Torquay Strand. The road crosses Babbicombe Down, of which a portion only has been preserved from the builder, who of late years has transformed a retired hamlet into a considerable and fashionable town. The view from the Down up the coast is very beautiful though not so fine as that from the hill west of Lyme Regis. The cliffs near by, much cut up by little coves and varied in colour, and either abrupt or draped on their slopes with rich wood, are the beginning of a sweep of coast that extends into Dorsetshire. Teignmouth, Dawlish, Exmouth, Beer Head (chalk-cliffs), Golden Cap (flat-topped hill, near Charmouth), and the gleaming quarries of the Isle of Portland, are all in sight on a clear day. Babbicombe itself has been spoilt, but of its perfect beach of fine quartz, and the beautiful Early English church of *All Saints*, by Butterfield, it may well be proud. The latter is exceedingly rich with Devonshire marbles and glowing with colour. At *Petit Tor*, on the north side of the bay, are marble quarries. Either to or from Babbicombe the pedestrian should walk over *Warberry Hill* (450 feet). Supposing him to return that way he must take a steep lane a little lower down the village than the "Rose Hill Hospital for Children."

St. Mary Church, about half-a-mile north-west of Babbicombe, is now a suburb of Torquay. The church has been entirely rebuilt and is handsome, especially the chancel. It contains a curious "Saxon" font, with a chain of seven ovals around the bowl, representing very unecclesiastical scenes. Notice a raven, vested as for the funeral of cock-robin, preying on a man. The mounting of the font is modern. Of far higher merit architecturally than the Parish Church is the *Roman Catholic Church*, by Hanson, of which a noticeable feature is the very graceful spire. *Blackler's Marble Works*, on the west side of the town and about half-a-mile north towards Watcombe, and the *Watcombe Terra-Cotta Works*, where the clay obtained from Watcombe is fashioned into articles both useful and ornamental, should both be seen, the latter especially.

2. **To Cockington**, 2 *m*; **Marldon**, 4 *m*; **Compton Castle**, 5 *m*.

Follow the Torbay road (the one going to the station), past Livermead House, and then turn to the right. The road ascends a pretty valley, passing a lodge of Cockington Court. The *church*, small and picturesque with ivy, is within the grounds of the Court. Returning to the cross-roads by the village smithy, we turn westward, and in a pleasant mile-and-a-half, strike the Newton and Dartmouth road at *Five Lanes*. The lane on the right across the main-road must be taken, and then a turn, left, brings us to *Marldon village* and *church*. The latter, restored, was built by the Gilberts of Compton about 1348. It contains memorials of that family, one of whom, Sir Humphrey, was the coloniser of Newfoundland. From the church a lane runs north to Compton village, at the end of which is **Compton Castle** (now a farm). Here was a stronghold as early as the reign of William I., and from about 1170 to 1310 it belonged to the De la Pole family, from which it passed to the Gilberts, of Greenway (*p.* 59), who erected the castle about 1420, of which the existing buildings are but a part. There is a good gateway, and near it a tower, originally one of four. The chapel, too, is fairly preserved. Mr. Parker says that, in the absence of a moat to protect the wall against being undermined, the numerous machicoulis were needed.

3. **To Berry Pomeroy Castle**, 8 *m*; **Totnes**, 11 *m*.

The above distances are by road. By rail to Totnes is 14 *m*. (changing at Newton Abbot). The pedestrian can shorten the walk by taking the train to Paignton, 2 *m*. (*For Paignton, see p.* 53.) Thence the Totnes road is to be taken. At *Collaton*, 1½-*m*. (good modern church; Inn) the road forks, and we take the right-hand branch.

About half-a-mile along the left-hand road, on the right, is *Blagdon House*, once the seat of the Kirkham family.

The road rises sharply to *Blagdon*, past which at cross-roads (caused by the running in of two by-roads), we take the by-road straight on, and turning to the left in ¼ *m*. arrive at the Lodge (where the key is kept), and enter the wood, through which the road winds down to **Berry Pomeroy Castle** (¾*m*., adm., 6*d*.). The Castle is situated near the head of a romantic and thickly-wooded glen, down which a tiny brook flows to join the Dart at Little Hempston, about 2 *m*. above Totnes.

History: Ralph de la Pomeraie was one of William the Conqueror's knights, and received, among many other manors, that of Berry. Here he is said to have built a castle, but the oldest part of the existing ruins—the south front with the towered Gateway and Lady Margaret's Tower at its east end—must be assigned to the beginning of the 13th century. The Castle remained in the possession of the Pomeroy family till the middle of the 16th century, when Sir Thomas Pomeroy (who had been a ringleader in the Rising of the West, in 1549), having been deprived of much of his property as a punishment for his rebellion, sold it to Lord Seymour of Sudely. It never belonged to the Lord Protector Somerset, to whom the Elizabethan mansion has sometimes, and therefore wrongly, been attributed. This mansion, built within the surrounding walls of the older work, was never finished, but is described by Prince (author of the "Worthies of Devon"), who saw it in its glory, as "a magnificent structure." The last occupant was Sir Edward Seymour, the head of the "Western Alliance," and M.P.

for Exeter in the reign of James II. Early in the 18th century, a fire, caused by lightning, so greatly injured the building that it was abandoned to decay. It is rather for its exceeding picturesqueness than for any important architectural features that it commends itself to the notice of the tourist. Ivy, trees, and moss drape and festoon the walls with a richness of green such as only a soft climate like that of South Devon produces. The visitor should by all means cross the glen and ascend the hill so as to look down upon the scene.

The village of **Berry Pomeroy** (*no Inn*) is about half-a-mile south-west from the Lodge, and has a *church* dating in part from the 12th and 13th centuries, but mainly Perpendicular. It contains two Pomeroy tombs, a remarkable one to Lord Edw. Seymour (d. 1593), son of the Lord Protector, and a good pulpit and screen.

The route onward to Totnes, 1½ *m.*, calls for no description. It passes through the village of *Bridge Town*, and then crosses the Dart.

Torquay to Paignton, 2 *m*; **Churston**, 5 *m*; **Brixham**, 7 *m*; **Dartmouth**, 9¼ *m. by rail.*

Those bound for Brixham branch off at Churston, as far as which place road and rail keep close company, the latter for the greater part of the distance being between the road and the sea. Brixham Quay by road is 8 *m.* from Torquay.

Torbay (about 4 *m.*, by 3½ *m.*) is in shape something like a roundbacked capital E, of which the upper member is the peninsula ending in Hope's Nose, and the lower that terminated by Berry Head. The central projection, broken off short, represents the square promontory of Roundham Head, just south of Paignton. The two enclosing headlands are of limestone with cliffs. On either side of the central promontory are fine sands, and the shore is low. As we skirt the bay, or better still, as we sail across it, the beauty and the sheltered position of Torquay are seen at a glance. The bay is an important haven for ocean-bound ships that encounter rough weather from the westward, and its waters are often covered with weather-bound vessels. It has, too, a prominent place in the annals of English history. Here, on the first of August, 1588, the first vessel captured of the Invincible Armada was brought into the bay by Drake, and left in charge of the Brixham fishermen. This was the *Capitana* already mentioned (p. 47) in connection with Tor Abbey. A hundred years later, on November 5th, William of Orange landed in the bay and slept in a hut at what is now Brixham Quay.

Paignton [Hotels: *Esplanade* (H.Q.), facing sea; *Gerston*, at station; *Commercial* (Q.), Dartmouth Road; *Town Bank House* (coffee-tavern, beds). Post del. 7.0, 10.40; desp. 2.50, 8.10; Sun. 7.30. Pop. 4,610] is distant from Torquay 2 *m.* by rail, and the same distance from the harbour by sea. A steam-launch plies hourly in summer. By road from the Strand it is 3 *m.* The town is nearly in the centre of Torbay, and has of late grown into a considerable watering-place. Its principal attraction is the fine sandy shore, perfect for bathing. There is also a pier, and the view thence of the bay is of great beauty. The *Church* (restored) has several features of interest. In the tower is a good Norman doorway, and the stone screen of the *Kirkham Chapel* is fine though much mutilated. The carved and painted wooden pulpit with a crucifix in the central panel is good. In the churchyard is part of an old cross, while an ivy-clad tower close at hand is all that remains of the old Episcopal Palace.

Immediately south of the town is the blunt promontory of *Roundham Head*, and beyond that *Goodrington Sands*, and then the picturesque little *Saltern Cove*. The rail and the road keep close to the sea past the latter, until then at the south-west angle of the bay strike across, but no longer in company, the peninsula between Torbay and the Dart estuary. *Churston Ferrers*, about $\frac{1}{2}$ mile from **Churston Station**, has nothing of interest to arrest the tourist. It is seen on the right of the line, soon after branching off towards Brixham (Quay). *For the line on to Dartmouth see p. 55.*

Brixham [Inns: *Bolton* (H.Q.); *Globe*, near the Quay; *Blue Ribbon, Coffee Tav.* (beds) in Fore St. Pop. 7,000] consists of two adjoining towns: Brixham, inland about $\frac{3}{4}$ m., and Brixham Quay, sometimes called respectively Upper and Lower Brixham. The station is 200 ft. above the quay, to which a steep descent is made by tortuous lanes. The old part of the town is very unsavoury. Referring to the landing of William of Orange, Macaulay says: " The whole aspect of the place has been altered. Where we now see a port, crowded with shipping, and a market-place, swarming with buyers and sellers, the waves then broke on a desolate beach; but a fragment of the rock on which the deliverer stepped from his boat has been carefully preserved, and is set up as an object of public veneration in the centre of that busy wharf." This memento has been removed to the pier, at the end of which is also a memorial of a visit by the Duke of Clarence in 1823. Brixham trawlers are known far and wide, and on Saturdays, especially, the harbour and inlet are crowded with them. Neither at Upper nor Lower Town is there any building of any architectural merit, and the Quay, except for the fish trade, has little interest. The breakwater is still unfinished.

Berry Head ($1\frac{1}{2}$ m.) to the eastward, should be visited. The way to it is by King-st. (out of Fore-st.) and the shore. Near the "old barracks" is *Ash Hole*, a cave in which Roman remains have been found. The promontory is limestone and contains several caverns, but the celebrated Brixham Cave already mentioned (*p.* 49) as having led to a thorough investigation of Kent's Cavern, is close to Upper Town, on Windmill Hill, and is known as **Philp's Cavern** from the lessee who "personally conducts" visitors. *Berry Head* (bury—a camp), was fortified by the Romans, but their works were destroyed when the five forts, now in ruins, were erected during the French war. The Head commands a fine view of the bay and of the coast eastward as far as Portland Bill, including Dawlish and Exmouth (Teignmouth is hidden), while the Hey Tor Rocks on Dartmoor are, as usual, conspicuous. Southward, close at hand, is Oxley Head, and beyond it Sharpham Point. *For coast-walk westward see p. 55.*

We now suppose the traveller to be continuing his railway journey, and to have returned to Churston Junction. Thence the line in about 1½ m. reaches the Dart, across which, as the trains descend the left bank to Kingswear, we get charming views up the estuary as far as Dittisham. The landlocked river has the appearance of a lake, and on the opposite shore, climbing the steep hill-side from the water's edge, rises Dartmouth. The town under a summer sky has an almost foreign look, and may remind the traveller of those which bask on the shores of the Italian lakes. At the **Kingswear** *Station* there is an Hotel—the *Royal Dart*, and the walk thence to the mouth of the river is one of the most beautiful in Devon.

The road from **Torquay to Dartmouth**, 10 m., turns to the right between Churston Station and Churston Ferrers, and gradually ascends to the watershed between Torbay and the Dart estuary. About a mile from the Station it again turns to the right and passes, left, *Lupton* (Lord Churston). Avoiding by-road, when the main-road forks take the left-hand branch. This soon begins to descend the valley to Kingswear. For *Dartmouth, see p.* 57.

Brixham to Kingswear by the Coast, 11 m. 5 hrs.

The distance above given is along the cliffs. The time stated is none too long if the many indentations of the coast-line are all to be explored. By not going out to the extremity of Sharpham Point, and by crossing from Scabbacombe Sands over Down End to the combe, with a streamlet on its south side, time and distance may be reduced about 1 hr. and 2 m. respectively. There is no public accommodation on the way, though by favour a crust of bread and cheese may be obtained at the Man Sands Coastguard station. Those who make either Brixham or Brixham Quay their temporary headquarters should make the coast from Berry Head to Mudstone Sands the object of a short excursion, and then they can avoid the somewhat difficult bit from Mudstone to Man Sands by proceeding by road from Brixham to the latter point.

The walk along the top of the cliff from Berry Head to Mudstone Sands presents little difficulty, and affords a fine though limited view of the limestone rocks that here form the rugged shore-line. *Oxley Head* is the first point, and then comes the needle-like projection of *Durl Head*, with a *Mew Stone* and the *Cod Rocks*, ¼ m. and ½ m. respectively out to sea. *Mudstone Sands* occupy the head of the bay of that name inside the far-projecting Sharpham Point, off which lies the Mag Rock. Sharpham Point is not worth attempting to reach, and the route onward as far as *Man Sands* is trackless, and necessitates a good deal of rough scrambling, but is quite possible to be followed. Whether it is worth his while the pedestrian must decide for himself. If from Mudstone Sands he turns inland toward Upton, he can follow a by-road over South Down, and at a cross-road turn to the left and descend to *Man Sands* with a brook and Coast-guard station. Thence the coast can be followed to *Scabbacombe Sands*, after crossing which a gate on the far side should be passed through, and a hedge followed over *Down End* and so down to the coast again. Thence onward the cliffs can be followed nearly to Kiln Cove, which is nearly opposite St. Petrock's Church at the mouth of the River Dart. The distance from the combe beyond Down End to Kiln Cove is from 3 to $4\frac{1}{2}$ m. according to closeness with which the sinuosities of the shore-line are explored. Taking it leisurely the traveller will be amply rewarded for his pains. *Ivy Cove, Padcombe Cove, Old Mill Bay*, which are successively passed on the way southward, are all delightful, but involve a good deal of up-and-down work that a summer's sun may tempt the traveller to abbreviate by crossing the several combes as high up as possible. From *Froward Cove* the coast turns westward, and we get a fine view across the mouth of the Dart and of the whole of Start Bay, terminated by the light-house crowned cliffs of Start Point. After passing Froward Point we reach the open inlet called *Newfoundland Harbour*, and fatigue may be saved by keeping well up and passing the combe at its head. Thence onward we have to quit the coast for a while, as the sea slopes above Kiln Cove form a warren which is closed to the public. The day-mark on the higher ground is a recent erection. On the far side of the combe ending in Kiln Cove, is a road which skirts the estuary to Kingswear, and affords charming views. Kingswear Castle (private) is below and opposite Dartmouth Castle.

Dartmouth.

Hotels: *Castle*, opposite the landing-stage; *King's Arms*, *Commercial* (H.Q.), near at hand; *Fairfax*, Coffee Tavern.
Also at *Kingswear* Station opposite the town, the *Royal Dart Hotel*.
Post: *del., London, &c., abt. 7 a.m.; North, 11.15 a.m.; desp. North, 2.10 p.m.; London, &c., 7.45 p.m.; Sun. 6 p.m.*

As we travel westward, Dartmouth (*Pop.* 5,600) is the first of those characteristically placed sea-ports which, owing to their position at the foot of hills shelving steeply to the sea, are but little influenced by the state of the tide. The mouth of the Dart is, proportionately to its width, flanked by higher and steeper hills than any other British river, and these hills descending at one sweep, green and luxuriant, to the water's edge, impart an aspect of beauty and completeness to the whole scene, which is, happily, not marred by any discordant features in the town itself. For better or for worse, the stranger contemplating a stay in Dartmouth, sees almost before he has boarded the steam-ferry at Kingswear the kind of habitation in store for him. In one peculiarity, the place resembles Barmouth, viz., that the lower stories of one house often look into the upper stories of another. In the principal part of the town, however, a lateral valley strikes inward and affords room for one of the principal streets.

Of old Dartmouth but little remains. The chief, if not the oldest relic, is the **Butterwalk**, on the right-hand side of the seaward end of the street we have just named. The lowest story of this includes a piazza, similar to those which extend the length of whole streets in Chester, and the grotesque carving of the period (17th century) abounds on the lintels and corbels. A very striking and successful attempt to reproduce the old style has been made in the street running parallel with the estuary, where a block of buildings, consisting of shops in the basement floor, is a noteworthy example of florid domestic Tudor architecture.

At the modest outlay of one penny the tourist may regale himself at Dartmouth with one of the curiosities of the South Hams—white ale, an unfailing recipe for a homely ache.

History.—The historic records of Devon are peculiarly interesting because they treat of many important personages who have been associated with the progress of the nation, and are not mere dry-as-dust annals. Dartmouth occupies a prominent place in them. It furnished 31 ships for the intended siege of Calais in Edward the Third's reign, a number inferior only to those supplied by

Fowey and Yarmouth. At *Greenway*, on the shores of the Dart, was born Sir Humphrey Gilbert, who appropriated Newfoundland in the name of the "Virgin Queen." In the same reign the godfather of Davis Strait, a native of *Sandridge*, on the banks of the same river, made Dartmouth his starting point on two expeditions. On the *Anchor Stone*—a rock in the channel of the river, a little above Dartmouth, Sir Walter Ralegh, presumably at low water, enjoyed his pipe. In the Parliamentary war the town surrendered to Prince Maurice after a month's siege. It was also the birth-place of Newcomen, who invented the stationary steam-engine, and by the aid of steam drained the Cornish mines.

The only remarkable **Church** in the town is **St. Saviour's**, which was consecrated by Bishop Brantingham of Exeter, in the fourteenth century. It stands to the south of the Butterwalk. The oaken screen, the stone pulpit, elaborately carved, and the Jacobean *west* gallery, an unusually fine example, are one and all worthy of notice, as is the brass slab in honour of the patriotic John Hawley, who reposes between his two wives. On the south door is some quaint iron scroll-work. As a whole the building sorely needs restoration. The **Church of St. Petrock** and the scanty remains of the old **Castle** are at the harbour mouth, a mile south of the town, and reached by the street and road which run parallel with the estuary. Neither would call for notice but for the situation, which is most picturesque. On the way to them may be noticed a church whose tower on close examination is found to have been built on the economical principle of having one side only—the front one.

St. Petrock's has three aisles of equal length, and the south side of its tower is ivy-clad. On the north side of the narrow estuary are one or two villa-mansions and *Mount Ridley*, a fort of importance in the Parliamentary War.

Dartmouth to Totnes, by *steamer*, 10 m.

Steamer once or twice a day according to tide. Fares, 1s. 6d., 1s. 3d. *Return,* 2s. 6d., 2s. *Also a small steam-launch once or twice a day.*

The Dart estuary between Totnes and Dartmouth is one of the finest navigable river-pieces in the kingdom, only surpassed, perhaps, by that of the Wye, though it must be acknowledged that the Fal and the Tamar are dangerous competitors. This part of the river has been paid the somewhat doubtful compliment of being called the "English Rhine," and there is no doubt that travellers who have not been led to expect too much by extravagant laudations will thoroughly enjoy exploring its beauties.

Starting from the landing-stage at Dartmouth we pass close to the *Britannia Training Ship*, and for two miles up that reach of the river which we have possibly already overlooked from the Torquay and Dartmouth railway. From this reach a considerable creek branches out on the left, and on its south side we call at **Dittisham** (2 *inns*), a village occupying the neck of a promontory, and famous for plums and cockles. On the opposite side, from a steep bank, as finely wooded as any on the route, rises *Greenway House*, the birth-place of Sir Humphrey Gilbert (*p.* 58), and near this, too, in mid-stream, and visible at low water only, is the *Anchor Stone*, a favourite smoking-haunt, says tradition, of Sir Walter Ralegh.

The wide part of the stream opposite the Dittisham promontory is *Galmpton Bay*, and beyond it we·obtain, on the right, a view of *Sandridge*, the birth-place of Davis, the navigator, but now a modern Italian mansion. Then, on the right, just beyond a little creek, a momentary and beautiful glimpse is obtained of *Stoke Gabriel* church and vicarage, the former displaying a red-belted tower. Opposite to it is *Bow Creek*, a narrow and picturesque inlet. Then, after calling off *Duncannon* we sweep round to the left and enter the serpentine windings of **Sharpham**. Here from the water's edge upwards, the banks are richly wooded with lichen-clad oak and other timber. In a silvan dingle on the left is a Swiss-looking little boat-house, and on the same side the mansion of *Sharpham*, white and square, crests the hill-side. Sharpham is noted for its rookery and heronry.

Beyond Sharpham the river forms several channels with intervening islets, and then enters a long straight reach, forming a vista finely terminated by the tower of Totnes church, and a ridge of Dartmoor. On the right hand is the *Totnes Rifle Range*. The landing stage is a few hundred yards short of Totnes Bridge, close to which are the *Seymour* and *Seven Stars Hotels*. It is nearly a mile to the station.

Totnes.

Hotels: *Seymour, Seven Stars*, close to the bridge, at the lower end of Fore Street, half-a-mile from the station. *Castle* (Q.), top of Fore Street. *Coffee Tavern* (beds), High Street.

Post: *Del.*, London, 7 a.m.; *North*, 10.30 a.m.; *desp.*, *North*, 3 p.m.; London, 8.25 p.m.

On the ground both of picturesqueness and antiquity **Totnes** (*Pop.* 4,100) has claims on the tourist's attention. Setting aside the apocryphal part of its history, attested, nevertheless, by the circumstance that the very stone on which Brutus of Troy landed is still to be seen, the town boasts a charter dated 1205, and the old piazza form of street-building to a greater extent than any other town in the kingdom, except Chester. It has also two archway gates—one on the steep ascent from the station to the castle, the other in the main street, just below the church.

The visitor having only a limited time at his disposal is recommended, if he has arrived by train, to ascend at once to the Castle by the steep by-road which begins a little below the station and passes under the *North Gate*—the way is obvious; if by boat, to pass from the bridge up the main thoroughfare—Fore Street—under the archway of the *East Gate*, and to visit the church, which is on the right hand a little higher up, on his way to the castle. In the square, a few yards on the town side of the bridge, a monument to William John Wills, who was "the first of mankind to cross the Australian Continent," and who "perished in returning," may be noticed, and in the pavement, on the N. side, just above Station Road, is the *Brutus Stone*, above mentioned.

Totnes Church (*key at Sexton's house, north side of church*) is a handsome structure with a fine Perpendicular *Tower* surmounted by crocketed pinnacles, and displaying several elaborately carved niches. It is built of red sandstone and is much weathered. The *South Porch* is also a noticeable feature, as are the south façade and the buttresses. The *Interior* of the building has lately undergone considerable renovation. The stone *Rood-screen*, a very fine one, has been restored; an oak *Reredos*, relieved by gilt, has been introduced, and a new pulpit made out of the tasteless altar-piece which formerly disfigured the church.

On leaving the church the visitor may take a peep into the **Guildhall**, the quaint simplicity of which is striking. The oaken stalls, old and correspondingly uncomfortable, are still retained for the Corporation. The building is part of the *Priory of St. Mary*, founded by Judhael de Totnes.

Proceeding up the street we turn to the right at the *Castle Hotel*, and reach in a few yards the entrance to the Castle.

Totnes Castle. (*Free. Ring the bell at the Entrance.*) This ancient keep, the only part of the original building remaining, and similar in many points to that at Launceston, stands on a lofty cone-shaped mound at the upper end of the town. Its reputed founder was a Norman baron, Judhael de Totnes, who came over with the Conqueror. It consists of two circular stories, of which the upper one is so much less in circumference than the lower as to admit of a walk round it. Like the church it is built of red sandstone, and is covered with ivy. The floor is a pleasant greensward. There is a small chamber in the wall on the west side. The upper story has ramparts to which one may ascend and walk round.

The *view* from the battlement over the town and down a long reach of the Dart is perfect of its kind, the point of observation being almost equal in height to the pinnacles of the church. In the opposite direction the cemetery is seen close to the railway, and a ridge of Dartmoor in the distance. Heytor Rocks and the Saddle are visible. On this side of the castle there is a pleasant walk through the trees and by the moat.

A pleasant stroll at Totnes is along the *Public Walk*, below the bridge, and past the landing stage of the steamers.

Nearly two miles from Totnes is **Dartington** Hall, which, as well as the church of the same name, has many points of interest. It is reached by crossing the railway and taking to a field-path almost ¾ m. from the town—a delightful walk. The Hall comprises part of the old mansion of the Hollands, Dukes of Exeter. The *Great Hall*, now unroofed, is 70 feet long by 40 feet wide, and contains a huge fire-place. The *porch* has a groined roof, and the *kitchen*, with some of the outbuildings surrounding a quadrangular court, still remains. The inhabited part, on the west side, was rebuilt in the reign of Elizabeth, when the house fell into the hands of its present occupants—the Champernownes. Beside it is a beautiful terraced garden.

The *Church*, which is close to the Hall, has a Perpendicular body and a Decorated tower. It contains a Tudor pulpit, the remains of a richly carved screen, and a monument to Sir Arthur Champernowne, 1578, his wife, and seven children.

The visitor may continue his walk to *Staverton Station*, one mile further and in a beautiful part of the Dart valley, which is now greatly resorted to by fishermen. Notice the beautiful bridge.

Totnes to Dartmouth, by the river, 10 m.

Steamer once or twice a day, according to tide. Also a small steam-launch about as often.

Fares: 1s. 6d., 1s. 3d. *Circular tickets issued from Torquay, vid Newton Abbot (in either direction),* 5s. 9d., 3s. 9d.; *also at proportionate fares from Plymouth and Exeter.*

Route more fully described the reverse way on p. 58.

The landing stage at Totnes is a few hundred yards south of the bridge, and nearly a mile from the station. Close to the bridge are the *Seymour* and the *Seven Stars* Hotels.

From Totnes the river pursues a straight course for nearly a mile, affording a fine retrospect of Totnes Church, with Dartmoor in the background. On the left is the Totnes *Rifle Range*. Then, after dividing into several channels separated by islets, it enters the horse-shoe windings of **Sharpham**, passing between banks luxuriant with foliage to the water's edge, and affording, after the second break, a view of *Sharpham* itself on the right hand. At the mouth of a dingle on the same side is a picturesque little boat-house. Then, on the left, after calling off the hamlet of *Duncannon*, a brief but beautiful glimpse of *Stoke Gabriel Church* is obtained. Opposite to it is the picturesque inlet called *Bow Creek*, and beyond it, on the left, *Sandridge House*, the birth-place of Davis, the navigator. Then, on the right, come the promontory and church of *Dittisham*, opposite to which, on a beautifully wooded slope, is *Greenway House*, the birthplace of Sir Humphrey Gilbert (*p.* 58). At Dittisham, where are two *inns*, a call is made, and then passing the *Anchor Stone* (*p.* 59), visible only when the tide is low, we notice the railway from Torquay descending the hill-side on the left, and after passing the *Britannia Training Ship*, reach the pier at **Dartmouth**.

For Dartmouth, see p. 57; *to Ashburton, p.* 74.

Dartmouth to Kingsbridge by Slapton Sands.

Dartmouth to Stoke Fleming, 2½ m; *Sands Hotel,* 6½ m; *Torcross Hotel,* 8 m; *Kingsbridge,* 15 m.

Torcross to Salcombe (by the Start and Prawle Point), abt. 15 m.

Coach daily about 9.30 a.m; *fare,* 3s., *also about* 4.30 p.m. *on arrival of* 9 a.m. *from London. Fare,* 3s.

Besides the tourist hotels at Slapton Sands and Torcross there are inns at the several villages on the route.

From the centre of Dartmouth the road passes southwards towards the harbour-mouth, turning inland up-hill at the little creek about half-way to St. Petrock's. Pedestrians who have not already visited the harbour-mouth should, undoubtedly, make the circuit by it. From St. Petrock's (*p.* 58) a path ascends the cliff, forking almost at once. Take the higher (right-hand) branch.

DARTMOUTH TO KINGSBRIDGE.

Then a considerable farm is passed, 200 yards beyond which a lane strikes to the right into the coach-road. In front appears the tower of Stoke Fleming Church, to which our route is continued some little way inland, and there we rejoin the coach-route. The *détour* adds about half-a-mile to the distance.

Stoke Fleming (Inn: *London*) occupies a commanding position, its church-tower being useful as a sea-mark for Dartmouth Harbour. The church itself contains two good brasses, one bearing date 1361. From about the entrance to the vicarage there is a fine view across Slapton Sands to the Start Light-house. Our road then drops to the sea at *Blackpool* (one of the loveliest spots imaginable for a watering-place), a picturesque little inlet, whence it rises again to the hamlet of *Street*. Another descent leads to the long, straight beach, called **Slapton Sands**—a remarkable bank of shingle, 2 miles long, with the sea on one side, and a fresh water lake on the other, each almost within a stone's throw of the road, and only a few feet below. The fresh water is contributed by two or three small streams, whose united force has not been sufficient to prevent the sea from raising the barrier thus interposed. It abounds in fish—pike, perch and rudd,—and in winter time is a favourite haunt of wild fowl. About half-a-mile from its commencement is the *Sands Hotel*, and at its southern extremity the *Torcross Hotel*, Q. (Post: *Del.* 8.25; *Desp.* 4.55; *Sun.* 9.20 *a.m.*; post town, Kingsbridge), both favourite resorts during the summer on account of the bathing and the facilities for sport which they afford. The proprietor of the *Torcross Hotel* has made and stocked an additional "lea" (or lake) of about 35 acres, between the old quarry and Beesands. Torcross is the nearest head-quarters for the Start. *Coach route continued p.* 65.

Torcross to Start Point (4 *m.*), **Prawle Point,** (9 *m.*) and **Salcombe** (15 *m.*). Country inns at Prawle; pub-ho. at Beesands and Hallsands. This is a rough, up-and-down walk, but should not be omitted by any one who wishes to acquaint himself thoroughly with the south-coast of Devon. The only place on the way affording sleeping accommodation is the little Prawle Hotel. The distance by *road* is 9 miles.

The cliffs recommence at the Torcross Hotel, whence a rough stair leads to their summit. In less than a mile comes a steep descent to the beach again, at an old slate quarry, below which is the new "lea" already mentioned. Hence you proceed along the shore to the little hamlet of *Beesands*. After another ascent of the cliffs, you may either pass above or descend to the hamlet of **Hallsands**, where the *London Inn* offers passing refreshment, if nothing more. Hence to the Point is about 1½ miles, alongside the cliffs again. Patches of cultivation vary the green slopes that descend to the verge.

The **Start Lighthouse** stands about 100 feet above the level of the sea and at the extremity of the Point. The light revolves every minute and is visible 20 *m*. The promontory consists of a rocky ridge sloping on both sides to the sea, and broken into an endless variety of shapes on the more exposed side, by the repeated assaults of sou'westers. The northern side, owing to its comparative freedom from violent storms, is much smoother. The name is probably derived from the Anglo-Saxon *Steort*, a "tail," and a glance at the map seems indirectly to confirm this derivation, when we note the corresponding and very similarly formed western extremity of this most southerly promontory of Devon, and find it called Bolt "Tail."

It is worth while to proceed from the Start itself to the west point, which is in reality a part of it, but for reasons unknown is called *Pear Tree Point*. From it the rugged inequalities of the Start are seen to advantage. A feature of the coast hereabouts is the crystal vein of quartz which runs in stripes down the cliff.

Hence as we proceed the cliff itself almost vanishes, and cultivation extends nearly to the water's edge, notwithstanding the fact that the shore is exposed to the full force of the prevalent winds. The strata, which here dip sharply seaward, act as a natural breakwater, and so defend this cultivated belt from the attack of the waves which but for this would inevitably demolish it.

The next break in the shore is at *Lannacomb Mill*, which is turned by a brooklet about 2 miles in length. Beyond it the cliffs again recede, forming, as it were, a double terrace along the lower of which you proceed till you reach a little recess in the rocks, affording just enough accommodation for a few fishing boats. Beyond it **Prawle Point** stands boldly out to sea. This headland, though exceeded in height by several others near at hand, is one of the most remarkable on the south coast. It is composed of gneiss rock, so broken up as to present the most irregular outline of any for miles round, and pierced at its extremity by an archway large enough for boats to be rowed through in calm weather. The rock is diversified with herbage and the thrift or sea-pink that flourishes so abundantly on our south-western shores. The view is good but limited. Westward on the far side of the Salcombe estuary, the superior height of Bolt Head bounds it, and eastwards it does not extend beyond the Start.

From Prawle Point you may either turn inland and join a lane leading from the hamlet of *East Prawle* to *Portlemouth*, or you may continue up and down along the shelving shore, dotted with gorse and here and there displaying ivy-clad cliffs, to the latter village. All along this shore, almost as far as Plymouth, the coast-path is more or less intermittently marked by white stones, placed by the coastguard. At *Rickham*, about a mile short of the Salcombe estuary, is the *Coastguard Station*, and here, in any

TORCROSS TO KINGSBRIDGE.

case, it is best to turn inland to *Portlemouth*,* about a mile distant. The village is placed on the crest of a hill commanding a fine view westwards. From it an abrupt descent leads to the ferry on the opposite side of which stands **Salcombe** (*p.* 69).

Coach route continued.—From Torcross Hotel the road bends round Slapton Lea, and, after skirting its opposite side for a short distance, turns inland and passes a little to the left of the handsome church of *Stokenham*, Perpendicular in style, and ivy-clad. Beyond it is the village (*inns*). Thence the route is continued to *Frogmore* (*inns*), where a branch of the Salcombe estuary is passed at its termination, and so on through one or two more villages, placed in the midst of pleasant rural landscape, to *Charlton*, a little beyond which the main part of the estuary—at high tide a ramifying lake, at low tide a wilderness of sand—necessitates a turn to the right. A short distance further the tide-way is crossed by a bridge, beyond which the road makes another sweep round to the left and right in turn, and then runs alongside the water to *Kingsbridge*, p. 66.

---

* In the church, an ancient dilapidated structure, are an old font and a richly carved screen.

Kingsbridge.

Hotels: *King's Arms* (H.Q.); *Albion*; *Coffee Tavern* (beds) in Fore St. Several inns nearer the water.

Post: *Del., London, &c.*, abt. 7 a.m.; *North*, 6.30 p.m.; desp. *North*, 11.30 a.m. *London, &c.*, 6.30 p.m.

Coaches: (from the *King's Arms*) to Kingsbridge Road, Dartmouth and Plymouth, see yellow sheet.

Steamers: to Salcombe and back as often daily as tide permits; to Plymouth, see yellow sheet.

Kingsbridge (*pop.* abt. 2800) owes its importance mainly to its distance from a railway station. The nearest is Kingsbridge Road, 10 miles away, to which there is a coach about 3 times a day. This remoteness makes the place a local centre for a wide surrounding area, which would, if railway communication existed, do its marketing at Plymouth. The town, which consists in the main of one long street descending to the water, is situated in a luxuriant hollow at the head of the Salcombe estuary, and presents a pleasant well-to-do appearance. The geniality of its climate is attested by the fact that oranges ripen in the neighbouring glade of Combe Royal, and further proofs of it may be seen in the garden of the King's Arms Hotel. Kingsbridge *Church*, early 15th cent., is cruciform with a central tower and spire. Besides one or two monuments of some interest it retains portions of a good screen. There is an interesting *Museum* in the Town Hall.

Kingsbridge was the birthplace of Dr. Wolcot (1738—1819) known as "Peter Pindar." In the part of the town called *Dodbrooke*, white ale, a beverage which boasts a high antiquity, is said to have been first brewed.

Kingsbridge to Kingsbridge Road. *Coach about 4 times a day. Fare: 2s.*

This route commands a good view of the southern range of Dartmoor for a great part of the way. It is given the reverse way p. 44.

Kingsbridge to Torcross Hotel, 7 m.; **Slapton Sands Hotel**, 8½ m.; and **Dartmouth**, 15 m. *Coach daily abt. 8.45, a.m. and 3.30 p.m. Fare, 3s.* This route is given the reverse way p. 62.

There is nothing of special interest after the Salcombe estuary is left behind, in about 2 miles, till Slapton Lea is reached, a little short of *Torcross Hotel*. Hence the road goes the whole length of the low and narrow bank of shingle, which has the sea on the right hand and the fresh-water *Lea* on the left. Beyond this it rises and falls (affording a fine view, looking back, to the Start), through the hamlet of *Street* and the village of *Stoke Fleming*, a mile or so beyond which begins a sharp descent to **Dartmouth**. Besides the hotels at Torcross and Slapton there are several village inns on the route.

Kingsbridge to Aveton Gifford, 4 *m*; **Modbury**, 8 *m*; **Yealmpton**, 13½ *m*; and **Plymouth**, 20½ *m*; *For Coach see yellow sheet.*

This is a pleasant enough drive, but the inland scenery of the South Hams, through which it passes, is in no way remarkable. Those who come for scenery will cling as far as possible to the coast, and should proceed by steamer from Kingsbridge to Salcombe, and thence visit Bolt Head and Bolt Tail.

The *road* ascends from Kingsbridge to *Churchstow*, which contains one of the most conspicuous church-towers in South Devon. Thence it drops to *Aveton Gifford* (*inns*), where the Church has good, late 14th century, screens (restored) in the two east bays on each side of the chancel. Between this and the old-world little town of **Modbury** (Inns: *Davis'*, *White Hart*) an up-and-down course is pursued. Modbury lies at the foot of steep hills, which its streets ascend on either side. The *Church*, with an octagonal spire, stands high up. It contains some monuments of the great Devonian family of the Champernownes, who occupied Modbury Court from the beginning of the 14th to that of the 18th century. Of the house, which was held for the king during the Civil War, there are only the scantiest remains at the west end of the town.

The nearest station to Modbury is Ivybridge, reached in 5 miles through Ermington, and in about 4 by a short and intricate cut, chiefly footpath. The town has no claim on the tourist's attention, except as a convenient resting place at one end or the other of his exploration of the coast scenery between the Salcombe estuary and the mouth of the Yealm, and even for this purpose it is only to be recommended because between it and the sea there is practically no inn accommodation. The scenery on these coast-routes is described in the routes which take Salcombe and Ivybridge as their starting point at one end, and Plymouth at the other.

Two miles beyond Modbury the road crosses the Erme a few yards short of one* of the drives to *Fleet House*, a modern mansion

---

* This drive—a private one—extends for 3½ miles along the western bank of the Erme, through a richly-wooded glen, over which it commands a succession of lovely views. It comes out at Mothecombe, within half-a-mile of the same river. This is by far the most interesting route to the coast hereabouts, if permission can be obtained to use it.

with a tower, for a long time the residence of the Bulteel family, but now occupied by J. Mildmay, Esq.

Beyond this point there is nothing of note, unless it be another entrance to *Fleet House*, until in 3 miles we cross the Yealm a little short of Yealmpton village. Hence the Yealm flows through a silvan dingle well seen from the road, to its estuary, which commences almost at once and continues for several miles between steep and richly-wooded banks, ending in a scene of great beauty at Yealm Mouth (*p.* 131). **Yealmpton** (*Inn*) has a handsome church rebuilt by Butterfield. It contains a brass to Sir John Crocker (*d.* 1508). On the north side is an inscribed stone of granite over 6 feet high, and bearing the name GOREVS, or TOREVS.

Beyond Yealmpton the silvan grounds of *Kitley* extend from the side of the road to the bank of the expanding river. From **Brixton** (1¼ *m. further; inns*), there is a cross-road to Plympton Station (3½ *m.*), commanding a rich and beautiful view in the direction of Dartmoor, as it breasts the ridge which looks down upon the flourishing villages of Plympton Earle and Plympton St. Mary. From the ridge a short cut may be made down a lane which leaves Plympton Earle on the right hand.

Between Brixton and Plymouth (5½ *m.*) the most noteworthy objects are the *limestone quarries* as we approach Laira Bridge (*double toll*) and the entrance to *Saltram*, a few yards short of the same structure. Close at hand is the *Morley Arms Inn*. The view up the Plym estuary from the bridge is good, but the entrance to Plymouth uninteresting. The coach stops at the Royal Hotel. *For Plymouth, see p.* 133.

Kingsbridge to Salcombe, Bolt Head, and Bolt Tail.

Boat to Salcombe, 4 *m.,* 2 *or* 3 *times a day according to tide. Fares, First,* 6d.; *Return,* 9d.; *Second,* 4d.; *Return,* 6d.

Salcombe to Bolt Head, 2 *m*; *Bolt Tail,* 7 *m*; *Hope* (*Inn*), 8½ *m*; *Kingsbridge,* 14 *m.*

We have chosen to return to Kingsbridge because the walk along the coast from Hope to Erme Mouth (10 *to* 12 *m.*) is tedious, and there is nothing more than the roughest inn accommodation on the way. Almost all the intervening coast may be seen from the high ground about Bolt Tail. Salcombe itself may also be regained in about 5 miles by an inland road from Hope, passing through Marlborough, or the walk may be comfortably ended at Aveton Gifford, to which a succession of lanes leads from Hope through South Milton, and a little to the left of Churchstow, beyond which the Kingsbridge and Plymouth road is joined.

Under a bright sun and with the tide well up, the sail from Kingsbridge to Salcombe is very pleasant. The steamer-stage is about half-a-mile south of Kingsbridge, and is overlooked by an inn. The estuary, ramifying in all directions, is flanked by low and verdant hills sprinkled here and there with wood. Its arms make the nearest road-route circuitous, the distance being 6 miles. Approaching Salcombe the tide-way narrows, and the hill on the left crowned by *Portlemouth Church* descends steeply to the water's edge.

Salcombe (Hotels : *Marine, Victoria, King's Arms. Post del.* 8,30 *a.m.* ; *desp.* 4.25 *p.m. Pop.* 2,000) is about as far from a railway station as any place in England, the nearest being Kingsbridge Road, 16 miles by highway. Consequently its almost unique attractiveness for those whose chief comfort depends on warmth or who think more of a few exotics growing out of doors than of the most beautiful and luxuriant native growth, has so far remained practically undiscovered. The estuary on which the little town stands, though not the mouth of any particular river, resembles in shape the trunk of a tree with a number of branches extending on both sides. In its more inland parts, it is, except for the hour or two of high tide, a wilderness of yellow sand, but at Salcombe itself there is deep water at all states of the tide, the only difficulty in utilising which, as a harbour, arises from the reefs and rocks which block its entrance. The water is beautifully clear and the hills which on the Salcombe side are pleasantly wooded, have a greater height and abruptness on the opposite, or Portlemouth, side.

The little town itself consists of a long street of true Devonian narrowness, running alongside and a little above the shore, and ascending at its northern end to a more open road, around which are several pleasant villas. Aloes, oranges, and lemons growing unsheltered in the gardens, and myrtles in the hedgerows attest the sheltered character of the situation and the general warmth of the climate. The Church is modern.

To the pedestrian Salcombe's chief interest lies in its being the handiest starting or finishing point for the coast-excursion to Prawle Point and the Start eastwards, and to Bolt Head and Tail westwards. These four capes stand out almost in a line from 4 to 7 miles southward of any other part of Devon,—due probably to the fact that the slate and gneiss of which they are composed offered a more stubborn resistance to the attacks of the ocean than the softer strata which form the coast on either side. Together they form by far the most rugged part of the south coast until the granite cliffs of western Cornwall are reached.

Salcombe to Prawle Point, 6 *m.*; **Start Point,** 11 *m.*; **Torcross Hotel,** 15 *m. Route the reverse way, p.* 63.
Small inns at Prawle ; Public-houses at Hallsands and Beesands.

Cross the ferry and ascend to *Portlemouth* (*p.* 65). Thence follow a lane southwards to *Rickham*. From the Coast-guard station there is an up-and-down path along the shelving shore to Prawle Point (*p.* 64), between which and the Start the cliffs recede so as to form terraces. A little beyond the Point you come upon a primitive little roadstead with some half-dozen fishing boats, and

1½ miles further, is *Lannacombe Mill*, where a streamlet about 2 miles long joins the sea. Then, climbing again, we proceed by *Pear Tree Point* for the sake of the view which it affords of the wilder side of the Start. Thence round a little bay to the *Lighthouse* (*p.* 64), and in another 1½ miles you reach *Hallsands*, where is a small public-house. Torcross is 3 miles further, the path being by the cliff and the shore alternately.

Salcombe to Bolt Head &c. (*route continued from p.* 69). Quitting Salcombe by the narrow street which runs southward we pass in a mile the scanty remains of the old *Castle*—the shell of a round tower or two rising between the road and the sea. So resolute and admirable was the four months' resistance offered here by Sir Edmund Fortescue to the Parliamentary forces in 1645 that, when at last he capitulated, he was allowed to march out with the honours of war. A short distance further the road descends to the *North Sands*, a little below which may be seen the fossil remains of a hazel wood. The wooded height and the house between which we next pass are called the *Molt*, and belong to Lord Courtenay. Then, after descending again to the *South Sands*, the regular road ceases, and we climb to the *flagstaff* on the Head by a zig-zag cart-track. Between the flagstaff and **Bolt Head** itself is another shallow depression, which we may cross or not, as we please. The view from the flagstaff is a fine one. Prawle Point is seen to advantage across the Salcombe estuary, in which are several reefs and rocks, including a *Mew Stone*. Those who proceed to the head itself will get a nearer view of the rocks, amongst which is a cavern called *Bull's Hole*, locally reputed to extend a distance of 2 miles to Saw Mill Cove, which we shall pass presently. Below the head, too, is a small area of beach, called *Stair Hole*, reached by a narrow cart-track.

From the signal post or the head we proceed westwards, crossing in the former case the depression already mentioned, near its head, and slightly climbing again to the *Clewer Signal-post*, beyond which comes a sharp drop to *Saw Mill Cove*, the only break in the cliff between the Head and Tail. Opposite to it, a rock, called the *Ham Stone*, stands out to sea, and close to the outlet of the small stream which threads the hollow is the fabled western entrance to Bull's Hole. Hereabouts, the track is marked by a succession of white stones, which direct the coastguardsmen on dark nights. The level-topped height to which we now climb is called *Bolbury Down*. All the way the view down the rugged, splintered cliff, seawards, is very fine. The path, however, leaves the edge of it some little way on the left. Several landslips are noticeable from the edge. In one of them, called the *Rotten Pits*, the rocks have fallen tumultuously, but have been arrested in their fall, and suggest a still impending destruction. Further on the disturbance shows itself in a number of crevices treacherously overgrown with grass and gorse, and of unknown depth. This is evidently the result of the cracking, as the other is of the actual downfall of the cliff. The crevices are called *Vincent's Pits*.

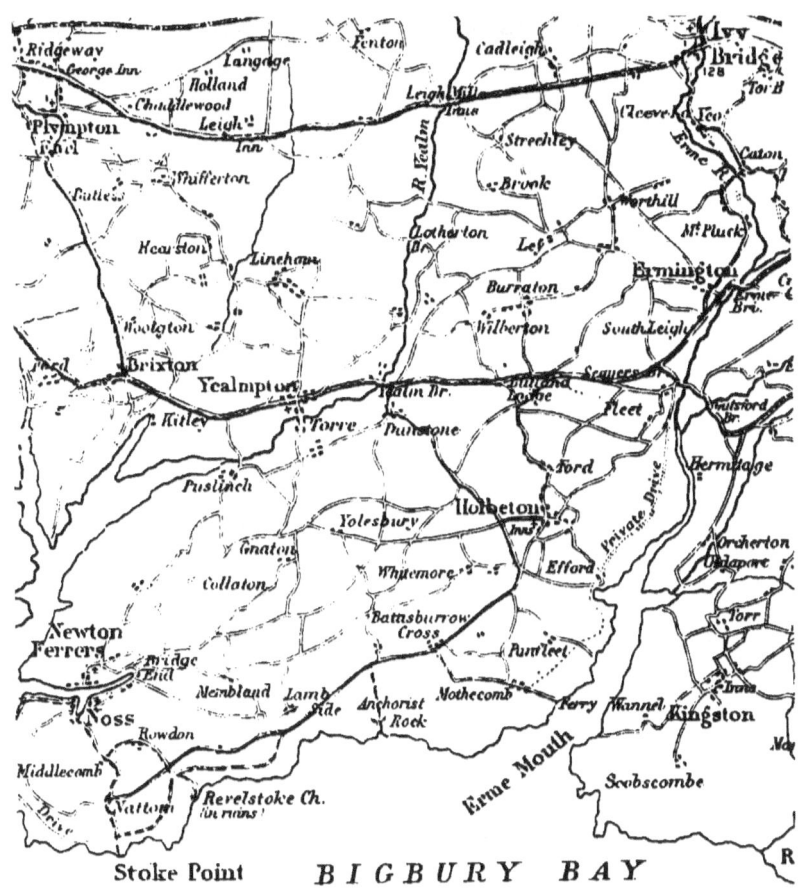

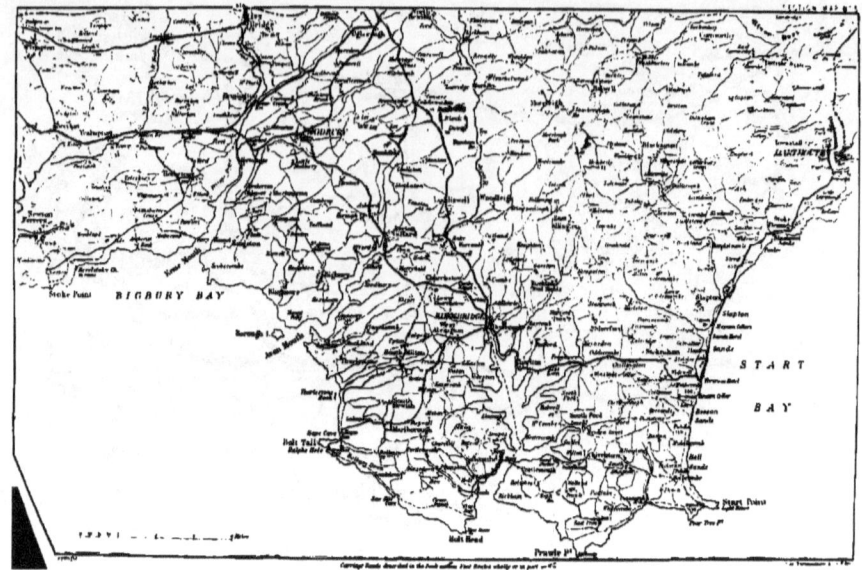

As we proceed beyond the highest point, or rather part—for the down is very level—of our walk, Bigbury Bay comes into view in front, to the right of the Tail. On its shore, just below us in the hamlet of Hope, and further away are seen the arched *Thurlestone Rock*—an islet of red conglomerate—and *Borough* or *Burr Island* opposite the mouth of the Avon. A cultivated combe on the right descends straight in the direction of Hope, but there is no path down it and it is best to continue round **Bolt Tail**, though the route is circuitous. A little short of the Tail itself is a chasm called *Ralph's Hole*, from its having been the resort of a smuggler of that name, and close to the point is *Ramillies Cove*, where the Ramillies frigate was wrecked in 1760, with the loss of the greater part of a crew numbering 700.

The view now extends beyond Yealm Mouth to the Mew Stone, opposite the near side of Plymouth Sound, and to Rame Head on its far side. In clear weather Dodman Point, in Cornwall, may also be seen. A sharp descent to the right now brings us to the sea-level and, half-a-mile further, to **Hope**, a wee place in itself, but a muckle one for crabs. The *Yacht* inn offers welcome refreshment and, if need be, a bed. The general appearance of the hamlet and cove is very primitive and picturesque.

At Hope the interest, even of the coast, ceases for awhile. Those who are resolutely bent on following it may plod their way onward to *Thurlstone* and *Bantham*, then ferry across the Avon, and pass through one or two inland villages to *Kingston*, whence they may descend to the Erme and cross to Mothecombe. This walk, however, we do not recommend, nor have we taken it ourselves. Its general character is well seen either from Bolt Tail on the one side or from Stoke Point, near to which we shall resume our description (*p.* 120) on the other.

From Hope back to *Salcombe* direct the road goes inland, and passes *Marlborough* with its conspicuous church spire: for *Aveton Gifford* or *Kingsbridge* it is best to follow the shore-line for about a mile, and then take a lane which runs inland to *South Milton*, whence the Kingsbridge road goes north-east and the Aveton Gifford road north.

DARTMOOR SECTION.

Dartmoor.

Regarded as a mountain district, Dartmoor is one of the dullest and dreariest uplands of any extent in Great Britain; but as the chief irrigator of Devonshire, the fountain head of the half score or so of perennial streams which give to the county the greater part of its beauty and fertility, it claims our deepest admiration and gratitude. In describing Dartmoor it is customary to generalise freely on its "sternness," "sublimity," and "poetic delight." If long lines of bare hill, scarcely undulating as much as a league-long roller of the Atlantic, fitly illustrate sternness, then Dartmoor is stern; if peat-bog, partly covered with cotton-grass vegetation be sublime, then Dartmoor is sublime; and, lastly, if floundering about for several successive hours in an alternation of ruts, morasses, and scrub heather represent "poetic delight," we obtain that feeling to perfection on Dartmoor. Otherwise it is what we have described it to be—in itself the quintessence of unlovely dreariness; but surrounded, fringed, and even pierced by scenes of beauty which owe their existence in a great measure to the principal cause of that unloveliness, the capacity for gathering and retaining moisture. The granite tors which rise at intervals from some of the ridges, or crown the more peaked summits, are striking objects—some picturesque, others grotesque—but their want of coalescence, if we may use the term, with the body of the hills on which they stand, prevents their contributing, as the craggy crests of our northern mountains do, to form an impressive whole. They are *on* the moor but not *of* it, excrescences rather than component parts.

The whole of central Dartmoor consists of a number of these ridges—the two principal extending from east to west, and a series of minor ones diverging at right angles from these two, and trending north and south respectively. A few of the outlying tors, especially on the west side, are peaked, and Cawsand Beacon, the frontier hill to the north-west, has a hog-back outline, like that of the Wrekin, which in the pervading absence of any outline at all, has won for it a local reputation for beauty.

In venturing on these remarks, we are anxious not to discourage tourists from putting them to the test of experience. Those who have learnt to appreciate the health of body and exhilaration of spirit which are the natural products of the pure bracing air of a continuous upland region, need be no Mark Tapleys to enjoy a trudge over even the dreariest of the long Dartmoor ridges, and all will delight in the one or two oases which the moor itself possesses, and the really glorious views obtained during the walks which we shall describe over what we may call the frontier heights of the moor.

And now a word or two as to the bright side of the picture.

Whatever we may think of the moor, there can be no question about the Dart, and we may take that river as representative of a multitude of other streams which equally belong to the same region—some of them little inferior to the main river in size or beauty. The Teign, the Taw, the Okement, the Tavy, the Plym, the Yealm, the Erme, and the Avon are all fed by the rains which descend on Dartmoor. It is to the valleys formed by these rivers, and to the fertility caused by them that Devonshire owes by far the greater part of its beauty;—in fact the Exe, the Torridge, the Tamar, and the East Lyn are the only other rivers of any importance in the county. As soon as ever these streamlets escape from the morasses which form their fountain-heads, the interest of the scenery commences. Bright and transparent as only a granite bed can make them, they run sparkling down the deepening valleys, receiving almost continuously fresh tributaries, and, as they sink lower and lower, causing the feet of the inhospitable hills on either side to grow green with meadows and luxuriant with trees. Then issuing from the moor, they wind onwards between banks whose fresh verdure is spangled with wild-flowers, and overshadowed by water-wooing trees. Hills of lesser height, but far more graceful lines, clothed here and there with wood from head to foot, rise sometimes from the water's edge, at others from the skirts of intervening meadows. Here and there timber of nobler growth, and towers rising above the abundant foliage betoken the residence of a well-to-do lord of the soil, and lastly, after a short but merry life, they flow with slackened stream into their estuaries, whose lofty cliffs are still green and wooded on the inland slopes, though many of them present to the sea bold scarps of bare weather-beaten rock.

This is no attempt at fancy writing. It is a simple and faithful description of the course of nearly all the Dartmoor streams mentioned in the foregoing paragraph.

Antiquarian. A complete survey of all the antiquities of Dartmoor would require far more space than is at our disposal. The traces of the "old men" may be briefly summarised as consisting of stone avenues, hut circles, maenhirs, or longstones, and clam (or stone slab) bridges. Of these, the last-named are by virtue of their situation across the bright granite-bedded streams the most picturesque objects, as they are the best preserved. There are two districts especially strewed with old-world remains.

viz., the North Teign valley about and above Castor, and Mis Tor moor between Princetown and Merrivale Bridge. Of these the first-named group is described under Chagford Section; the second, on the route from Tavistock to Princetown. Of cromlechs, Devonshire only possesses one erect, and that has fallen and been re-erected. It is called the Spinster's Rock, and is described in the Chagford Section. Most of the remains are near streams and are on the fringes rather than in the heart of the Moor. In many cases stream-tin works appear to have been the attraction, and the refuse heaps still occur by the side of the streams. In this connection the ancient Stannary (or Tin) parliament held on Crockern Tor calls for mention, and north of it the gnarled Wistman's Wood, popularly reputed to be a remnant of Dartmoor *Forest*. The finest clapper-bridges are Post Bridge and Belleyer Bridge, on the same stream between Postbridge and Dartmeet. Of many smaller bridges, a noticeable single-slab is that across the Wallabrook near its junction with the North Teign, to the northwest of Castor. There are no ancient buildings of the mediæval period on the moor.

The antiquities and legends of the moor are admirably treated in *Dartmoor* by J. Ll. W. Page (Seeley & Co., 1889; 7s. 6d.).

(1) Dartmoor from Ashburton.

Totnes to Buckfastleigh, 7 *m*; **Ashburton**, 9½ *m*. This is as pretty a little railway journey as can be imagined, though there are no places on the way at which the tourist, unless he be an angler, will probably wish to halt. For the first 7 miles the line follows the windings of the Dart, which alternates between pool and rapid, and is flanked by a narrow belt of meadow and pasture, hemmed in on both sides by soft woodland slopes. At *Staverton*, the first station, 3 *m*., we have an example of an attraction which the Dart possesses probably to a greater degree than any other English river, viz., picturesque bridges. Grey with years and graceful in proportions, they are almost without exception festooned with ivy, fern, and other greenery.

Buckfastleigh (Inn: *King's Arms*) lies a little to the left of the line, and is disfigured by an unsightly chimney. It is a small town employed in the manufacture of serge. The *Church*, crowned by a spire, stands on the top of a hill, whose sides are scarred by black marble quarries. It is reached from the town by an unconscionable number of steps.

What little remains of the old **Abbey of Buckfastleigh** is a mile north of the town, on the east side of the Dart. It dates from the reign of Henry II., and was accounted the richest Cistercian house in Devon. All but an ivy-mantled *tower*—called the *Abbot's*—has given place to a modern mansion. The so-called *Abbot's Way*—a track across some of the wildest parts of Dartmoor, towards Plymouth, and still traceable in places—had its beginning here.

During the remaining 2½ miles of the route to Ashburton the line is separated from the Dart by a low range of hills.

Ashburton.

Inns: *London*, West Street; *Golden Lion*, (H.Q.) North Street, each about ¼ m. from the Station. *Clarke's Coffee Tavern* (beds). 'Buses meet the trains.

Post: del., 7 *a.m.*, and 4.30 *p.m.* (*London, &c.*); 11 *a.m.* (*North*). - Desp. 2.30 *p.m.* (*North*); 6.45 *p.m.* (*London, &c.*).

Pop.: *Under* 3,000.

Ashburton is one of the old Stannary towns of Devon and boasts an antiquity of which there is very little trace in its present appearance. It is built cross-wise, its streets being named after the four cardinal points, though in reality their direction is that of the half points. The inn accommodation is comfortable but quite unpretending.

In 1646 Ashburton was occupied by Fairfax, who took up his quarters at the "Mermaid" Inn, now a shop in North Street, otherwise the history of the town has been uneventful.

The Church is a handsome cruciform building of different styles, Decorated and Perpendicular, and has a good wagon roof. It has been well restored. The church-yard, entered from the south side of West-Street, is prettily planted.

The situation of Ashburton, in the bosom of green and richly wooded hills, is attractive, but the chief interest of the place to the traveller is its favourable position for the following excursions. There is, perhaps, not a prettier drive in Devon than the "Buckland Drives"; no pleasanter walk over the outskirts of Dartmoor than that which includes Buckland Beacon, Rippon Tor, and Heytor Rocks; no more varied or less fatiguing route into its inner recesses than that to Widdecombe-in-the-Moor, and no more convenient way of crossing the moor by carriage than the road to Two Bridges and Tavistock or Princetown.

Excursions from Ashburton.

(1) The Buckland Drives. Ashburton to Holne Chase, &c., 10 m. *Open to the public on Tuesdays, Thursdays and Saturdays. Carriage and pair*, 15s.

This is the favourite excursion from Ashburton, and a very beautiful one, whether by carriage or on foot. As a great part of it is through wood and on low ground, it is one in which even the pedestrian may with advantage for the nonce consent to drive. If he walks he should combine a great part of it with a moorland climb over Buckland Beacon, Rippon Tor and Heytor Rocks, descending from the last named either to Bovey Tracey or to Ashburton again, or he may take the Drives on his way to Widdecombe-in-the-Moor.

The Route. Quitting Ashburton by North Street we cross the little bridge on the left at the far end of the town and follow the Tavistock road half-a-mile beyond it. Here the road forks, and we take the right-hand branch, continuing along it till in a third of a mile it bends to the right. At this point our route passes through a gate straight on, and in another 200 yards or so diverges to the right. From this part of it there is a pretty view southwards down the Dart valley to Brent Hill. Then, passing through another gate, we ascend along the side of a hill, from the wooded slope of which rises a tor, *Auswell Rock*, also called *Hazel Tor* and *Lion Rock*. Below the road, on the left hand, the river winds round the deep horse-shoe ravine which encircles **Holne Chase**. Overhanging the stream about the crown of the bend is the rock called the *Lover's Leap*. This is one of the most charming parts of the drive, which a little further on re-enters the Buckland public road just opposite a wall running up to Buckland Beacon (*p.* 77). Another mile brings us to *Buckland Church*, a building of mixed architecture, romantically placed in a grove of lofty trees. The new church across the valley is *Leusdon*. Two hundred yards beyond Buckland Church the private drive is re-entered on the left hand and a descent made to the *Webburn*, a small but beautiful tributary of the Dart. Alongside of this the road winds back again to the latter river, which it reaches about half-a-mile higher up the stream than the **Lover's Leap**—a name given to the most striking bit of rock scenery in this part of the valley. The rock rises almost perpendicularly from the water's edge. The view from it, though limited in extent, is very beautiful.

From the Leap the drive is continued down and alongside the river to **Holne Bridge**,—perhaps the most characteristic of all the romantic bridges which span the Dart. Here the Tavistock road, by which we started upon our outward journey, is re-entered, nearly 2 miles from Ashburton. The remainder of the route calls for no special notice.

(2) **Ashburton to Buckland Beacon, Rippon Tor, Heytor Rocks, and back (or to Bovey).**

Ashburton to Buckland Beacon, 3 m ; *Rippon Tor*, 5 m ; *Heytor Rocks*, 6¼ m; *Rock Inn*, 7 m ; *Ashburton*, 13 m. *(Rock Inn to Bovey Tracey*, 3 m.)

This is as easy and pleasant an excursion as any that can be taken by those who wish to make acquaintance with Dartmoor scenery without surrendering themselves entirely to its monotonous bleakness. All the hills mentioned are border heights, and while they command extensive views over the moor itself, they never lose sight of the luxuriant loveliness which surrounds it. Carriages may be taken the whole way, the road passing within half-a-mile of all the view-points. The *Rock Inn* is breezily situated on high ground, and affords sleeping accommodation. Pedestrians may easily make their way from Heytor Rocks to the small inn at Lustleigh, which is about 4 miles distant, or they may diverge by any of the roads marked on the map.

The Route.—Cross the bridge at the north end of the town, and take the right-hand branch about half-a-mile further. Guide-posts abound. The route to be followed is that to Buckland. If it be desired to include a portion of the Buckland Drives in the excursion, *see p.* 76. Otherwise, continue up the shady hill for nearly a mile beyond the point at which one of the Drives begins. At this distance the carriage-route turns to the right, out of the Buckland route, and pedestrians may either follow it till they are opposite the Rifle Butts on Buckland Beacon, or they may proceed along the Buckland road till they come to a wall which begins opposite one of the entrances to the Drives, and is continued upwards almost to the summit of **Buckland Beacon.** The latter is the more artistic route to this justly recommended view-point, as the general view is not presented until the top is gained. Looking southwards, we have the wooded slopes of Holne Chase, the Dart forming almost a circle round it, and Holne village, the birthplace of Charles Kingsley, rising from the hill-side beyond. Further off and extending in a semicircle, first westwards and then northwards, are the slightly undulating ridges which constitute the most elevated part of Dartmoor. Princetown, sombre and grey as the moor itself, may be detected by its church-tower in the far west, a little to the right of Tor Royal or Look-out Tor as it is locally called. Northwards of the town the billowy range extends to Cut Hill, the central point of the moor, rising but slightly above its fellows, but recognisable by the evenness of its wave-line on either side. Near at hand in this direction are the old church of Buckland, and the new one of Leusdon, to the left of which one may trace for some distance the course of the Ashburton and Tavistock road. Widdecombe lies hidden in the valley, beyond which rises the long level ridge of Hamildon Down. Rippon Tor is close at hand a little east of north, and to the right of it Great and Little

Haldon appear, forming the background to a valley of singular richness which stretches southwards to the Teign estuary and the sea. The estuary, as seen from here, has the appearance of a lake. To the right of it the spire of Marychurch overlooking Torquay rises from a level ridge, and further westwards are seen the ends of Bolt Head and Bolt Tail. The spire of Buckfastleigh church rises due south.

From Buckland Beacon to *Rippon Tor* the route is obvious. It follows the course of two walls a great part of the way, and crosses the carriage-route. On nearing the top we may note, some way to the left of the wall, a huge Logan Stone, which "may be moved by stamping steadily on the extreme end."

The view from **Rippon Tor** (1564 *ft.*) is more interesting northwards than from Buckland Beacon. It includes the ridge of which the fantastic Hounds Tor and Bowerman's Nose, opposite Manaton church, are the main features, to the right of which is Lustleigh Cleave. Cawsand brings the loftier ridges of Dartmoor to an end in the same direction. Southwards the green hills in the neighbourhood of Newton Abbot become more noticeable. North of the cairn is a rude cross cut on a rock *in situ*.

Descending abruptly from Rippon Tor, we again cross the road, and passing the *Saddle* reach, after traversing a level and rather swampy tract, the twin heights of **Heytor** (1491 *ft.*). These are two of the most remarkable tors on Dartmoor and means have been supplied for climbing them, so abrupt are their sides. Rising from the verge of the moor they command a prospect of great variety, fantastic rock and wild vegetation prevailing towards the north, and rich cultivation to the south.

The *Rock Inn*, visible from the tors, is a long half-mile West, and lies a little to the right of the carriage-road to Bovey Tracey, the descent to which little town, as well as the return to Ashburton, requires no description beyond that afforded by the map. The Heytor railway, which has long occupied a prominent position on the maps of the district, has ceased to be used, and the quarries are only occasionally worked.

Ashburton to Widdecombe-in-the-Moor, Chagford, &c.

Distances: To *Widdecombe*, 6½ *m.*; *Grimspound*, 10 *m.*; *Chagford*, 15 *m.*

— *Widdecombe to Postbridge (New Inn)*, 6 *m.*

— ,, ,, *Heytor Rocks*, 3 *m.*; *Bovey Tracey*, 7 *m.*

— *Grimspound to Postbridge*, 4 *m.*

— ,, ,, *Moreton Hampstead*, 6 *m.*

— *Postbridge* ,, *Two Bridges*, 3¾ *m.*; (*Princetown*, 5¼ *m.*) *Tavistock* 12 *m.*

This excursion is very interesting as far as Widdecombe and Grimspound, beyond which it is characteristically dreary in the direction of Tavistock, until the descent commences about 2 miles beyond Two Bridges; and of average merit, in the direction of Chagford and Moreton Hampstead. The route eastward from Widdecombe by Heytor Rocks to Bovey Tracey is a very pleasant one. All the routes named are practicable for carriages, except that to reach Postbridge by Grimspound involves a *détour* of nearly 2 miles.

From Ashburton either the direct road to Buckland (*p.* 78) may be taken, or on Tuesdays, Thursdays, and Saturdays the "Drives" may be followed to the same village.

Buckland Church, an ancient building of varied architecture, stands on high ground, but embowered by trees, on the left hand, a mile beyond the point at which the drive rejoins the road and the wall up to Buckland Beacon commences. Beyond it we continue along high ground, looking down on the left into the densely wooded Webburn glen, beyond which on the brow of the hill is seen the new church of Leusdon. In a little while the pleasant but sombre-looking upland valley in which lies Widdecombe comes into view in front—one of the most agreeable scenes of inner Dartmoor. The depression, shaped like a basin, is fertile in its lower parts and flanked by the green slopes of Hamildon Down on the west, and a succession of tor-crowned heights on the east.

Presently we descend to and cross the stream, beyond which a sharp angle made by the road may be cut off by an obvious footpath, passing a farm-house just before re-entering the main road about ¾-mile short of Widdecombe.

Widdecombe-in-the-Moor. Here there is no accommodation beyond that afforded by a small country inn, and no object of special interest except the old *Almshouses*, dating from the fifteenth century, and the **Church**. The latter building is, considering its situation, a very fine one. It has been called the "Cathedral of Dartmoor," and its size tells plainly of its having been built to accommodate a much larger population than now exists. The tower is said to have been built by a successful company of tin-miners. The style is Perpendicular, and the tower with its pinnacles is one of the best specimens of that style in the West. One of the pinnacles was destroyed in a terrific thunderstorm which occurred October 21st, 1638, during the progress of divine service. It was rebuilt in 1813, and the initials of the mason who accomplished the task (E. W.), appear on the restored pinnacle. The noticeable features of the interior are the wagon roof, the oak in the aisles, the new pews, which occupy the east-end only, the west part being left open, the oak-screen, much defaced, the pointed east window, and lastly the poetical record of the disaster above mentioned, which may be seen on the wall beneath the tower. The graphic style of this poem—the date 1786 is that of the board not of the verses—by Richard Hill, the village schoolmaster, may be gathered from the following quotation :—

> "One man had money in purse, which melted was in part,
> A key likewise which hung thereto, and yet the purse no hurt,
> One man was struck dead, two wounded, so they died two hours after,
> No father could think on his son, or mother mind her daughter.
> The different affection of people then were such,
> That touching some particulars we have ommitted much."

We, too, are compelled by the limits of our space to "omit much" of this account of the visitation, by which four were killed and sixty-two injured. The clergyman's proposal to go on with the service was not accepted. There is a record of the storm, in a pamphlet published the same year.

From Widdecombe we may proceed to Chagford, Bovey Tracey, or any place on the road between Moreton Hampstead and Tavistock, as stated in the itinerary which heads our description. The direct road to Postbridge is dull and well-nigh featureless. The road to Bovey ascends eastwards out of the valley, leaving a roughish line of tors on the left, and joining the previously described route from Ashburton to Bovey Tracey (*p.* 78) only a little below the summit of Rippon Tor.

Most tourists will wish to proceed onward to Grimspound, the carriage-route to which passes round the south end of Hamildon Down. Pedestrians are advised to ascend the Down and proceed northwards by its level summit-ridge. A farm road, the second on the left after leaving Widdecombe, leads a considerable way up, and then you have only to keep along the top, passing several barrows and Hamildon Cross—1854 is said to be the date of the letters only.

Grimspound itself lies in a semicircular depression on the north-west side of Hamildon Down. The walk to it calls for some patience, but when once the Pound comes into sight it is unmistakable : a large oval enclosure (154 by 121 *yds.*) surrounded by a wall or rampart, which in its ruinous condition rises 3 to 4 ft. above the level, and containing many hut-circles. Many of the stones are very large and the place is supposed to have been a fortified village, but has since been a cattle-gathering pound.

To reach **Chagford** we continue by Hookner Tor northwards for about 1½ miles, and then enter the Moreton Hampstead and Tavistock road, dropping down upon Chagford in another two miles from the slope of Mill Down.

For **Postbridge**, **Princetown**, or **Tavistock** we cross the stream and take a rough track which, passing a cottage at the outset, leads to the *Vitifer Tin Mine*, immediately beyond and above which the Moreton Hampstead, and Tavistock high-road is entered, close to *Bennett's Cross*, bearing the letters W.B., *i.e.*,

Warren Bounds, it being one of the bounds of Headland Warren. The *Warren House Inn* is then reached and in a little more than 2 miles further, after crossing Merripit Hill, one of the highest parts of the road, the *New Inn (Temperance)*—a roadside house, with some sleeping accommodation, a little short of Postbridge. For the rest of the route to Tavistock or Princetown, *see p.* 83.

Ashburton to Princetown or Tavistock by high road.

Ashburton to Tavistock Inn (pub-ho.). 5; *Dartmeet Bridge*, 7½; *Two Bridges (Inn)*, 12; [*Princetown (Hotel)*, 13½; *Merrivale Bridge (pub-ho.)*, 16; *Tavistock*, 20 m.
Coach, 3 times a week, to Princetown going by Holne Village, and Forest Inn returning by Dartmeet Bridge. Lunch at Duchy Hotel, Princetown.

This is the only carriage-road across Dartmoor, except the one from Moreton Hampstead to Plymouth, which it crosses at Two Bridges, whence either the route to Horrabridge by Princetown or the direct route to Tavistock may be followed. The former is perhaps the more interesting of the two. Those who adopt it may, if so minded, take train at Princetown and reach Plymouth by the Dartmoor line, which joins the Tavistock branch of the Great Western at Yelverton junction (*p.* 103).

Quitting Ashburton by North Street, and crossing the little bridge on the left at the far end of the town, we reach in less than 2 miles *Holne Bridge*, one of the most charming scenes on the Dart. It is at one end of the horse-shoe bend which enriches Holne Chase and, besides being a very picturesque object in itself, has most delightful surroundings of meadow and woodland. Beyond it the road goes south for a short distance and then turns west again.

About a mile beyond Holne Bridge, a road taken by the coaches strikes away to the left to *Holne village* (1½ m. distant), the birth-place of Charles Kingsley. Now there is nothing remarkable about it except its lofty situation and a remarkable epitaph—nearly undecipherable—which runs as follows:—

" Here lies poor Ned
On his last mattras bed
During life he was honest and free
He knew well the chace
But now has run his race
And his name was Collins
D'ye see ? "

From Holne Village the road (*see map*) follows an up-and-down course to Forest Inn, beyond which it crosses Hexworthy Bridge and rejoins the main road.

Leaving Holne Chase on the right, we have to make another drop to reach the river again at **New Bridge**. Here the stream commences the bend which ends at Holne Bridge, and embraces the most beautiful scenery on the Dart. In the middle of October we have seen the whole landscape aglow with the resplendent tints of the dying foliage, and except, perhaps, the Windcliff, can call to mind no scene where they appear with more telling effect. Every shade of autumn foliage is represented, though, if we mistake not, there has been a great cutting down of trees within the last few years.

From New Bridge the road rapidly ascends, passing in a mile or so the new church of *Leusdon*, some way on the right, and the *Tavistock Inn*, and then, after continuing over high ground (1169 *ft.*) for some distance, drops to *Dartmeet Bridge*, a few yards below which the streams of the East and West Dart unite. On the right as we drop to the bridge is *Yar Tor*, " having the appearance of a hill fortified by the engineering of nature herself."

Beyond the bridge the road again rises (1057 *ft.*) and maintains a high level to Two Bridges, passing about half-way *Dennabridge Pound*, a gathering-place for cattle, but retaining inside in the wall the " judge's chair " a relic of the tin-streamers' meetings here. The " council table " is at Dennabridge farm.

At **Two Bridges**, a little short of which the main road over Dartmoor, from Moreton Hampstead, converges, there is a good inn, the *Saracen's Head*, the most central place of entertainment on Dartmoor.

Two Bridges to Okehampton, 17 *m.* 6-8 hrs. This is a fair day's walk though the distance is comparatively small. There is no inn or habitation until Belstone is reached 2½ miles short of Okehampton, and if Yes Tor be included in the route there is no inn at all. That at Belstone is a small public-house. The central point is Cut Hill, which though destitute of all beauty or peculiarity of shape, is always recognizable by its appearing slightly higher than the average of the surrounding ridges and by the corresponding character of the gradual slope on either side up to the cairn which crowns it.

From Two Bridges there is a choice between two ridges striking northwards. The better one to take is reached by following the Tavistock road for about a quarter-of-a-mile, and then entering a cart-track, which crosses the Cowsick stream, and leads up to a farmstead. [There is a clapper bridge higher up.] Hence we soon enter on the bare moor, and have only to keep the high ground over a succession of tors (see map; Row Tor, right, has a block on top) to reach the central point of our route—*Cut Hill*. On our right soon after starting, we look across the Dart to Crockern Tor (*p.* 122) and the famous Wistman's Wood —a patch of oak scrub on the far side of the stream. Westwards, as we rise, Great and Little Mis Tor, two of the finest on the moor, appear above an intervening ridge.

Cut Hill (1981 *ft.*) is about 6 miles from Two Bridges. A turfy cairn marks its highest part—to say " point " would mislead. The *view* from it is, "of the moor, moory "—in fact, there is little else, except that westwards we get a glimpse of the rich country beyond Tavistock, over the deep depression of Tavy Cleave, the whale-back of Kit Hill, with its lofty chimney shaft, serving as usual to fix the different objects of the landscape. High Willhays and Yes Tor, the crowning heights of the moor, dominate the scene a little west of north, and the swelling outline of Cawsand Beacon—another whale-back · is about the same distance east of north. The moor between these two heights is split up into parallel ridges separated by the Taw, the East Okement, and one of the latter's tributaries, as well as by a stream which passes under Yes Tor into the West Okement. Over any of these ridges we may continue our route, which passes for the first mile or two over the most fatiguing part of the moor—the nucleus of its streams. It is simply a vast peat-bog, passable enough in fairly dry weather, but at all times wearisome from the unevenness of the ground, which is broken up by a succession of ruts only a few feet apart.

In any case we shall pass a little to the left of the swampy hollow in which the main waters of the Dart are gathered. Half-a-mile or so further the Taw takes its rise, and follows such a course that if it were connected with the Dart the two would form a continuous straight line north and south. A little north-west of this debatable ground between the two rivers, lies **Cranmere Pool**, which, whatever it may once have been, is now merely a black peaty depression with a small cairn in the midst. (*See p.*).

⁎ From this point, by going almost due east, we may reach, in a walk of about three hours, Chagford. *This route and that to Lidford are given p.* 99.

For *Okehampton* we may proceed either to the West or to the East of Taw Head. If Yes Tor is to be included in the excursion, we must go decidedly to the West, and continue along the level ridge of Okement Hill, which trends north-westwards between the sources of the East and West Okement. Beyond it we cross the head of another tributary of the West Okement, and proceed over High Willhays (*p.* 107) to Yes Tor—for a description of which, and the route to Okehampton, *see Excursions No.* 2, *p.* 107. The simplest way is to proceed about a mile along the ridge in a north-westerly direction, and then to descend to the Meldon Viaduct, whence Okehampton is reached by road in 3 miles.

If Yes Tor be omitted there is still a choice of routes, the most direct being due north from Cranmere Pool along the ridge between the valleys of the Taw and the East Okement. Along the latter part of this route we pass a succession of tors which make the going very rough, but drier than the average. A third, and perhaps the easiest way of all, is to bend slightly to the N.E., from Taw Head and to keep that stream and an intervening tributary one on the left. By this route you will shortly enter a rough cart-track which passes to the left of Cawsand Beacon,—always recognizable by its shape—and crosses the river a little short of *Belstone*, whence by road it is 4 miles to Okehampton. A shorter route in distance, but scarcely in time, is by a foot path which drops to the E. Okement valley in its prettiest part, and passing under the railway, reaches Okehampton in about 2½ miles from Belstone. For particulars enquire at the public-house at Belstone.

Those who diverge at Two Bridges for Princetown and Horrabridge will find the route, as well as the pedestrian one across the Moor from Princetown to Ivybridge, given under Tavistock. For *Tavistock* our road ascends for nearly a mile, and then drops slightly to another little tributary of the Dart, after crossing which it climbs again to a still higher point (1490 *ft.*) where the road from Princetown joins it. From this point, North Hessary Tor is on the left, and Little and Great Mis Tor—two of the finest on the Moor—1 mile and 1½ miles respectively on the right. The latter are described in our excursions from Tavistock.

A steep descent of 1½ *m.*, during which there is a fine view in front, comprising a number of tors, of which Staple Tor is the chief, brings us to Merrivale Bridge. The Merrivale Antiquities (*p.* 116) are on the left of the road, ¼ *m.* short of the bridge, beyond which there is a small *public-house*. Vixen Tor, rising west of the stream and south of the road, is one of the most curiously-shaped on the Moor. Another rise to 1081 *ft.*, succeeded by a sharp fall (with a view which includes Brent Tor, Kit Hill, Tavistock and Saltash Bridge), a stretch of level ground, and yet another descent to Tavistock, brings our journey to an end.

For **Tavistock** *see p.* 111.

Dartmoor from Chagford.

Newton Abbot to Chagford.

1. **By rail to Ashton, thence by road to Dunsford Bridge, path to Clifford Bridge, and road to Chagford,** 24½ m.

2. **By rail to Moreton Hampstead; thence by coach,** 17 m.

Choice of routes to Chagford. Both of the above are more or less beautiful throughout, especially the first, which follows the Teign most of the way and may be recommended to pedestrians, while visitors with luggage, who choose Chagford as head-quarters, will do best, perhaps, to go through at once by Moreton Hampstead, and to make the places of interest passed near-at-hand objects of excursions from Chagford. It should be remembered, however, that several of these places are in themselves tourist resorts, and that they offer very fair accommodation. On the direct route such accommodation is to be had at Bovey Tracey, and Moreton Hampstead. There is also a small inn called *Cleave Hotel*, in Lustleigh village, within a short walk of the Cleave. Moreton Hampstead is a dull country town, but a convenient starting-point for those who wish to cross the moor by carriage, though this can be done by routes somewhat rougher, but more picturesque to begin with, from Bovey or Chagford.

Bovey Tracey (*p.* 78), very pleasantly placed and with good inns, is the nearest station to the Heytor Rocks and Bottor, both famous view-points.

On the longer route Chudleigh has a very fair inn and should be made a halting-place on account of its picturesque limestone gorge. About 1½ m. up the valley from Ashton, the present terminus of the railway, and at Dunsford (7 m. from Exeter, *see pp.* 37, 86) there is good old-fashioned accommodation.

(1.) **Newton Abbot to Chudleigh** (*rail*), 6¾ m; **Ashton**, 11 m; **Dunsford** (*road*), 15 m; **Clifford Bridge**, 18½ m. **Chagford**, 24½ m.

Heathfield (4 m. from Newton) is the junction for Ashton. From it the line at once makes a great sweep eastwards, and by a steep gradient drops to *Chudleigh*. Just before reaching that station a glimpse on the right-hand of the limestone cliff of Chudleigh Rock is obtained between the masses of foliage which surround it. **Chudleigh** (Inn: *Clifford Arms*; *Pop. abt.* 2,000; station ¾ *mile from the town and rock*) is a sleepy market-town 10 miles from Exeter on the Plymouth road. In 1807 some 200 houses were destroyed by a fire, and later on the opening of the South Devon Railway diverted the stream of traffic that till then passed through it. From these disasters the place has never recovered. Its claims on the tourist rest on its Rock and its position as a fairly convenient centre from which to explore a pleasant bit of country.

The **Church**, in no wise remarkable, retains its original tower, which was built about 1259, but has been since altered. The main body of the church is some 60 or 70 years later, and the south aisle and the chancel screen are both 16th century. The latter has panels with alternate figures of Apostles and Prophets. The only tomb that calls for mention is that of Sir Pierce Courtenay (*d.* 1605) and his wife. This is in the chancel. The church was restored in 1870.
Between the station and the town the road which turns off near a blacksmith's shop leads to **Chudleigh Rock**. After following this road for a short distance, pass through a swing gate to a path skirting an orchard in which are the scanty remains of the *Bishop's Palace*. When the path enters a bit of woodland the Rock is only a few yards onward. This is a fine and lofty limestone crag embowered in trees and richly draped with creepers. It rises abruptly from a narrow wooded gorge through which a tributary of the Teign flows to join that river near Chudleigh Station. The descent to the stream whereon is a pretty cascade, should be made, as the glen and rock are then best seen. An obvious footpath leads to the platform at the top of the crag, and this, too, should be visited for the sake of the lovely view. In the Rock are two caves. The entrance to one of them is from the woodland about half-way between the stream and the summit. This is the *Pixies' Hole*. It is about 130 feet in length, and at the end is a rock called the *Pope's Head* into which, in order to disarm the mischievous inhabitants of the cavern, it is (or was) the duty of the visitor to stick a pin. There is another cave, called *Chudleigh Cavern*, on the other side of the rock. It is approached by the sward and orchard behind the Rock on its north side, and is under lock and key (*admission 6d.*). By proceeding up the glen from the Rock, the *Riding Parks* and **Ugbrooke Park** (Lord Clifford) can be visited. From the top of *Black Rock*, which is passed on the way, a fine view of Chudleigh Rock is obtainable. The chief attraction of Ugbrooke is the beautiful park (*the public can use the drive on Mondays*). The Ug forms a pretty artificial lake on the west of the mansion, and the south-side of the valley especially, is rich with grand masses of foliage. Down to the middle of the 16th century Ugbrooke belonged to the see of Exeter, and was attached to the palace whose fragments we passed between Chudleigh and the Rock. The house is an 18th century castellated building, and in the adjoining chapel is a tablet to Sir Thomas, first Lord Clifford, whose initial formed that of the celebrated Cabal. In addition to a considerable collection of pictures, including several by Old Masters, there is a State bedroom which contains a bed with hangings of "curious" needlework, designed by Mary, wife of the 9th Duke of Norfolk. The Romano-British *Camp*, on the high ground of the park should be visited for the sake of the view it commands. On the north-side of the lake, on *Mount Pleasant*, is a tree planted by Cardinal Wiseman. Leaving the park on the south-east the walk may be extended to the village of **Ideford**, which is at the foot of Great Haldon and about 2½ *m.* from Chudleigh; and thence to Dawlish, 6 miles from Chudleigh.

From Chudleigh the line follows the bottom of the valley, which is sweetly wooded. The Teign is crossed and recrossed on the way to Trusham Station, about which the sides of the valley are arable.

Trusham village (Inn) is ¾ m. from the station behind the hill on the right.

Continuing our journey the valley soon becomes finely timbered, and the white block of *Cannonteign Lodge* stands amid dense woods on the left. When it is passed look out immediately on the same side for the old **Manor House** of **Cannonteign**. It is now a farm, and is a fine ivy-mantled, gabled pile, though its immediate precincts are somewhat marred by the refuse heaps of an abandoned mine. **Ashton** *Station* is the present terminus of the branch. *Ashton village*, or *Church Town*, as it would be called in Cornwall, is a mile or so over the hill, east of the line.

On leaving Ashton Station cross the bridge, hard by, over the Teign. If a visit is intended to *Cannonteign* go straight on, but if bound for the Upper Teign and Chagford, turn to the right. The road is pleasantly wooded, but has no feature calling for remark until at ¾ m. the church and village of *Christow* are a few hundred yards on the left. There is nothing to tempt us to leave the main route which in summer is fragrant with sweet woodruff and meadow-sweet. At 1½ m. from Ashton is a little Inn, *Teign House*, much frequented by Teign anglers. Thence onward the road is pleasant, but calls for no further comment, until it turns sharply to the right, and crosses the Teign, of which a pretty view is had up and down stream. Turning to the left, beyond the bridge, we still keep near the stream, and get soon another pleasant view of it and of Dunsford with its lofty church-tower. Then, at a junction of roads, turn to the left. In a few yards the road for **Dunsford** (Inn: *Royal Oak*) strikes off up the hill on our right.

We still, however, keep straight on, and can obtain casual refreshment at the *Half-Moon Inn*, on the near side of *New* (or *Steps*) *Bridge*, by which we again cross the Teign. We are now on the high-road from Exeter and Dunsford to Moreton Hampstead and Plymouth. For the upper Teign we turn, right, a little up the hill, along a cart-track through the copse wood. This in due time leads to a meadow, which should be skirted along its upper edge till we regain the cart-track beyond it. The cart-track, still through thick woodland, leads us to a deserted cottage, where a water-course runs down to the right, above another meadow, along which we pass, keeping well away from the water-course to avoid wet ground. A gate at the end of the meadow opens on to a path through the woodland, and presently the country becomes fairly open alongside the stream. The amount of wood to be traversed varies from year to year, according as the undergrowth is cut. Soon we obtain a characteristic bit of the Teign valley—steep hills, here and there broken by rock, and elsewhere clad with oak scrub. In 2½ miles the path leads out into the rough road at *West Place* farm, adjoining **Clifford Bridge**. This bridge is picturesque with ivy, and should be viewed from below by crossing it and turning a few steps down-stream. From this point it is only anglers who follow the stream, and they have a rough time of it. We mount the long steep road that sets engineering at defiance, and for the best part of a mile, regardless of the toils of man and beast, goes nearly straight up over *Wooston Down*. About a mile from the bridge the remains of an earthwork are on the right, on the bluff over the Teign. When a fork in the road is reached take that to the right across the open down (the left-hand road goes to Moreton Hampstead). Westward we get a fine view of the wooded gorge, down which the Teign flows, between the opposite heights of Cranbrook and Prestonberry Castles. No direction is needed hence onward, except to say avoid all branch roads and keep straight on. Close to **Cranbrook Castle** a direction post indicates the grass-track that in a couple of hundred yards leads to it. It is worth visiting as a fair sample of hill-forts, but chiefly for the fine view of the gorge. *Fingle Bridge* (*p.* 95) is just below it, but down a zigzaged and very steep road. Continuing our route we soon begin a very steep descent to *Whyddon Park*, and get a good view of Chagford. The high-road from Moreton is then joined, and accompanied by the telegraph wire we reach our destination. For **Chagford** *see p.* 92.

2. **Newton** to **Teigngrace**, 2 *m*; **Heathfield**, 4 *m*; **Bovey**, 6 *m*; **Lustleigh**, 8½ *m*; **Moreton Hampstead**, 12 *m*; **Chagford**, 17 *m*.

About 5 *trains a day to Moreton Hampstead*; 35—40 *min.* '*Bus* 3 *times a day to Chagford*; 1 *hour.*

The Moreton branch leaves the main line a short distance on the Exeter side of Newton, and for the first 3 miles follows the valley of the Teign, hereabouts wide and somewhat marshy. A view of the twin Heytor Rocks, due north, is obtained at once. A little to the left of them are the Saddle and Rippon Tor. The Perpendicular tower of Kingsteignton Church rises on the right as soon as we diverge from the main line, and 1¼ *m.* further the spire of *Teigngrace* is close to the line on the left. On the same side the granite portals of Stover Lodge, a seat of the Duke of Somerset, are seen. Beyond *Teigngrace* we leave the main valley of the Teign, which comes down from Chudleigh on the right, and enter that of its tributary, the Bovey. *Heathfield*, the junction for Chudleigh and Ashton, stands as the name implies, on a heath— still bright with gorse and well-sprinkled with fir trees. Close to this station, and a little short of the next, Bovey Tracy, are some large *Pottery Works*. Those at Bovey were established as far back as 1772, and enjoy a high reputation. Visitors are allowed to inspect them. *Rail continued p.* 88.

Bovey Tracey (Inns: *Dolphin* H.Q., between station and town; *Union*, in the town) is a pleasantly-situated little town on the slope of a verdant hill, which drops to the Bovey river. In itself it has nothing to specially detain the tourist. The *Church*, Perpendicular and restored, is dedicated to Thomas of Canterbury, and is traditionally said to have been founded by Sir William Tracey, one of Becket's murderers. It possesses a fine screen and rood-loft, and a stone pulpit ornamented with figures of saints. The new *Church of St. John* is a mile south of the town in a pretty grove of cedars and shrubs. The shaft and steps of an old *Cross* stand in the village, close to the Town Hall.

Here in 1646 Lord Wentworth, one of the cavalier generals, was surprised by Cromwell as the latter was marching through Bovey to the west.

The large building on the hill-side, east of the town, is the Devon House of Mercy. It was built in 1867.

Excursions from Bovey.

(1.) **Heytor Rocks**, 4 m.; (**Widdecombe**, 7 m.) and **Ashburton**, 10 m. *Route described the reverse way p. 77.* A delightful walk either to Heytor Rocks and back, or onwards over Rippon Tor and Buckland Beacon to Ashburton. The road crosses the railway at the station and ascends for the rest of the way. The old Heytor Railway, the course of which is crossed in about a mile, is no longer used, the granite quarries of Heytor having been all but abandoned. The rest of the way is mostly across the down. About half-a-mile short of the rocks, a gateway on the left opens on to a lane leading to the **Rock Inn**, a favourite little hostelry with excursionists, and offering some sleeping accommodation. *For* **Heytor** *see p. 78.*

The road onward passes between the *Saddle* on the right and *Rippon Tor* on the left, turning southwards round the latter about 2 miles beyond the Rock Inn. (The direct road from the turn leads over an intervening hill and reaches, in a short 2 miles, **Widdecombe-in-the-Moor.** *p. 79.*) Pedestrians will obtain the best views by merely crossing the road and ascending at once *Rippon Tor (p. 78)* whence, descending by the side of a wall, they may cross the road again at a slight depression, and reach the fine view-point, **Buckland Beacon** (*p. 77*), which is 1½ miles beyond Rippon Tor. The descent from Buckland Beacon is again by the side of the wall to the Ashburton and Buckland Road which is entered just opposite the gate of one portion of the Buckland Drives (*p. 76.*) Hence it is 2½ miles down-hill to *Ashburton, p. 75.*

Those who are returning to Bovey may get there in 8 miles by following the Chudleigh high-road for the first 6, and then taking a straight road on the left. Heathfield Station is on the main road, half-a-mile beyond the turning.

Bottor Rock. This is another fine view-point, though inferior to Heytor. It lies north of Bovey, and may be reached either by a lane striking from the village in that direction, or by taking one which starts to the left a few yards short of the church, and leads up to the little village of *Hennock*, before reaching which the shortest way is to turn again to the left up a narrow green lane. The whole round, going one way and returning the other, is from 4 to 5 miles The lanes about here are narrow and steep. The view from the Bottor Rock includes a great portion of the Teign valley with the Haldon Hills to the east of it, Heytor rocks, and many other eastern tors of Dartmoor to the west, with the long dull lines of the higher ridges of the moor in the background. Southwards are the green bowery little hills that cluster round Newton Abbot, and the level range extending from Teignmouth to Torquay and Dartmouth.

Rail continued from p. 87. After leaving Bovey the line crosses the stream and enters a narrow and very picturesque part of the valley, but the view is a good deal obstructed by the abundance of foliage. Then, as we near Lustleigh, the dull outline of the distant Dartmoor hills appears on the left, and on the same side we have a peep up the glen through which the Bovey hurries down from Lustleigh Cleave. *For continuation of rail see p. 91.*

Lustleigh (*Cleave Hotel*, a small inn) is placed in one of the most romantic parts of the valley, the surrounding hills being steep, rough, and variously wooded. The village is diminutive, and the church without interest, but the curious in such matters will find an ancient *inscribed stone* outside the door-cill of the main entrance. From the village many delightful excursions may be made in the direction of Dartmoor, which may be said to commence from the village itself. That which particularly belongs to Lustleigh is to the Cleave, Becky Fall and Manaton. It may be extended in many ways—to Heytor Rocks, to Widdecombe, or to Chagford.

To **Lustleigh Cleave.** All the roads about here are intricate. The carriage-road necessarily makes a considerable circuit. The best pedestrian route is by the road behind the inn and past the church; then turn to the right past the chapel, and follow the rough woody lane as it bends upward to the left and passes between a farm and its buildings, beyond and above which it strikes a cross-lane. Turn right and then left again up a rougher lane than ever. This brings you out on to the open ground, and a path winds onward between the granite boulders with which the hill is strewed to the top, the entire distance from Lustleigh village being only a little over a mile. The pile of boulders which crowns the crest of the hill on the left is locally called "Nutcrackers." The name is derived from a logan stone which, with the assistance of a fixed one close to, will perform the suggested operation. Hence you command the full length of the *Cleave*, a cup-shaped valley covered with a patchwork of wild vegetation and granite boulders. With a bright sun to show up the chattering little stream which threads it, and bring out its contrasting colours of grey rock, yellow furze, and the varied verdure—yew, ivy, and whortleberry —this valley, so near to and yet so far from the business of the world, is as refreshing a little picture as we shall meet with in all our wanderings, but it imperatively demands this bright condition of weather. Across the Cleave the tower of Manaton Church— almost the only artificial object near at hand—serves admirably to fix the proportions of the picture, and behind it, in a long line, some of the highest Dartmoor hills form the horizon. Southwards from Manaton runs a ridge of curiously shaped tors, commencing with Manaton Tor itself, just behind the village, and continued by Bowerman's Nose, Hound Tor, the Saddle, and the twin bosses of Heytor. Southwards and to the left of the last named, the strath of the Teign valley about Bovey Heathfield is seen, beyond which are Newton Abbot and the uplands between the estuaries of the Teign and the Dart. Eastward the prospect is bounded by the Haldon range.

DARTMOOR.

From this point the walk may be continued in various directions:—

(1) *Along the ridge northwards* for about a mile, passing an *Ordnance cairn*, and keeping at first a stone wall on the right-hand, till a compulsory descent is made towards a farmhouse called *Neighdon*. This part of the walk is good going over dry grass. At the head of the valley North Bovey church stands well, and beyond it is seen the whale-back of Cawsand Beacon. Behind, the Heytor Rocks and the Saddle form in combination miniature mountains which may call to mind one or more of the well-known outlines of Lakeland and elsewhere. Beyond Neighdon, a little burn and a field have to be crossed, and there a road is entered by which, in about 2½ miles, *Moreton Hampstead* may be reached either by descending direct to the valley and railway, or turning to the left and keeping awhile along the higher ground. This part of the route is dull.

(2) *South-westwards to Becky Fall (see below).*

(3) The pleasantest of all, *north-westwards*, first down to the river, which is crossed a little below some farm buildings called *Foxworthy*, by *Horseham Steps*, a natural bridge formed of granite blocks, whence it is a sharp but short climb to **Manaton**, as peaceful and secluded a village as even Dartmoor contains. Here is a small *inn*, the "Half-Moon." The church occupies a commanding position and has a good tower and well-preserved screen. In the churchyard is a venerable yew tree.

Of the many tors which surround this sweetly-placed village, and no part of Dartmoor boasts of a larger or more eccentric assemblage, *Manaton Tor*, a rocky crest sprinkled with holly, rowan and dwarf oak, should be climbed for the lovely view it commands, but the most remarkable is *Bowerman's Nose*, a long mile away, and on the far side of the little Hayne valley. Looked at from the north side this pile of rocks may certainly be likened to a human shape, and native credulity has seen in it a rock-idol. *Hound Tor* is the next to the south of the Nose, and the tourist would have no difficulty in continuing over it and working round the head of *Houndcombe* by Saddle Tor and Heytor Rocks to Bovey (*p.* 87). If he prefer the road there is a good one all the way, along the west side of the tors and down to Bovey as described on *p.* 78. The map is really the best guide in these variations, and we have tried to make it trustworthy. In returning direct by road from Manaton to Lustleigh, Becky Fall (*below*) should be visited.

Becky Fall (4½ *m.*). This pretty little scene is near the head of a densely wooded glen, whose waters are tributary to the stream that flows through Lustleigh Cleave. The *carriage-route* goes south from Lustleigh for 1½ miles and then ascends East Down, passing a hundred yards or so above the *Fall*, which is reached by a path. *Pedestrians* may turn to the right in about ⅙ mile along this road, and, after dropping to and crossing the Cleave, take a fairly

MORETON TO CHAGFORD. 91

direct course over the hill beyond, keeping the stream on the right. The Fall is a broken one, and except after heavy rain insignificant. Manaton is 1¼ miles further.

Rail continued from p. 89. From Lustleigh the line continues up the valley side-by-side with the road and a small tributary of the Bovey, until sweeping round to the right and then again left it reaches its terminus, *Moreton Hampstead*. The church, crowning a green knoll, is conspicuous on the right hand as we approach the station, which is a quarter of a mile from the town and below it.

Moreton Hampstead (Inns: *White Hart*, Q.; *White Horse*, both in the centre of town. *Post del., London, abt.* 7 *a.m.*; *North*, 6.45 *p.m.*; *desp., London*, 6.25 *p.m., North*, 1.50 *p.m. Pop. abt.* 2,000) is a town which at the best can only claim to be a convenient halting-place for tourists. In itself it has nothing to detain them, and pretty is the strongest epithet we can apply to the surrounding country. The best view-point is a meadow called the *Sentry*, in front of the church, whence a small reach of valley is seen and the moor about Heytor Rocks and Rippon Tor. The *church* itself, Perp., needs restoration. The tower has been rebuilt in poor fashion. There is some good tracery in the windows of the aisles. Near to the church and on the way to the Sentry field are an old *Arcade* bearing date 1637, and a *Cross*, all but the head of which has been ousted by a self-sown lime tree. This tree has had its top flattened and its branches trained into the shape of a bowl, the bottom of which once formed a fiddler's platform.

For the route across Dartmoor to **Tavistock, &c.**, *see p.* 101.

Moreton to Chagford, 5 *m.*; *'bus* 2 *or* 3 *times daily.* The road between these two places is on a par in interest with that of Moreton as a town. It follows the telegraph wire for most of the way. The country is pretty and undulating, but neither wild nor rich. From its highest part, soon after leaving Moreton, there is a wide prospect in front, including Cawsand Beacon. Then after a long and gentle descent it continues on the level to *Easton*, a group of farm buildings, nearly 3½ miles on the way. Here we turn left at right angles, climb a short rise, from the top of which the best view on the way is had, including the entrance to the Fingle defile, and after another fall and rise enter Chagford past the *Moor Park Hotel*.

*** Pedestrians may save half-a-mile at the expense of a few extra hills by diverging to the left about 1¾ miles on the way close to a white cottage, and following a tortuous lane through the hamlet of *Week*, whence Chagford is entered on the south side of the church. Those going to the *Moor Park Hotel*, however, save nothing by the cut.

Chagford.

Approaches : *vid* Newton Abbot, *p.* 87; *vid* Yeoford, *p.* 105.

Hotels : *Moor Park*, at the entrance of the town from Moreton Hampstead ; also, *Globe*, *Three Crowns*, near the Church ; *King's Arms*, in the main street. *Coffee Tavern* (beds).

Post : *Del. abt.* *7.35 *a.m.*, 7.30 *p.m.* ; *desp.* 1.15, *5.45 *p.m.*   [*Sundays].

Though by no means an ill-favoured town (*pop.* abt. 1,500) in itself, or in its pleasantly-wooded surroundings, there can be little doubt that Chagford owes its reputation as a place of popular resort jointly to its position in regard to scenery of which the actual ground on which it stands forms no part, and to its angling facilities. Within easy walking distance are some of the most interesting and wildest parts of Dartmoor, and the upper valley of the Teign. This river, flowing through defiles of singular loveliness, both above and below Chagford, forms, however, nothing more than a pleasing feature of a pretty undulating landscape for a mile or so of its course on either side of the town, which is placed on the brow of a hill about half-a-mile above it. The climate of Chagford is healthy and fairly bracing.

Chagford Church, restored, stands in a square, pleasantly-shaded churchyard in the higher part of the town. It is a well-to-do looking specimen of the Perpendicular style, but of no particular interest. Sidney Godolphin was killed, according to tradition, in the porch of the Three Crowns, which is still standing, during an attack made upon the Royalists here in the Parliamentary war.

The best living authority on the topography of Dartmoor is probably James Perrott, who has guided tourists—amongst them on several occasions Charles Kingsley—over its trackless wastes for about half a century. Though no longer a young man, he is still active and accessible to visitors at his little shop, in the centre of the town, where pedestrians may obtain good and unstinted advice, and carriage-folk may hire vehicles adapted to the rough roads of the moor. Carriages may, of course, be also engaged at the inns. We should not take this opportunity of thanking Mr. Perrott for the valuable and practical help which he has given ourselves, but for the fact that the acknowledgment is entirely unsolicited.

SKETCH PLAN OF
MERRIVALE ANTIQUITIES

SKETCH PLAN OF
GIDLEIGH ANTIQUITIES

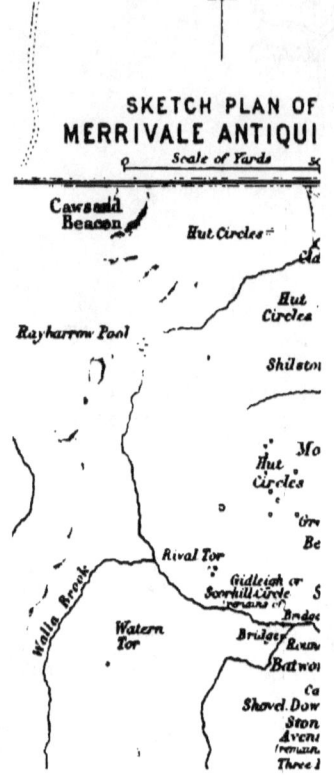

Excursions from Chagford.

₊ *Distances* in the moorland excursions are only approximate. and, as a criterion of the exertion entailed, are less instructive than the *times*, which are estimated for a good walker, a fair allowance being made for a leisurely observation of the various objects of interest met with on the way. The following is a list of these excursions and objects, all of which are afterwards described in the order given :—

1. Holy Street Mill.
2. Rushford Mill and Castle.
3. Gidleigh Castle.
4. Fingle Bridge, Drewsteignton and Spinsters' Rock.
5. Castor Rock, the Gidleigh group of antiquities, and Cranmere Pool.
6. Cawsand Beacon.
7. Grimspound and Widdecombe-in-the-Moor.

Lustleigh Cleave, Manaton, Bowerman's Nose, Hound Tor, Becky Fall, all of which may be made the object of longer excursions from Chagford, will be found described under Lustleigh (*p.* 89), whence they are more easily accessible.

1. **Holy Street Mill**, 1 *m.* Turn down the hill by the street opposite the west end of the church. When a dilapidated factory is reached, pass to the left of it. *Holy Street House*, whose unfulfilled promise of grandeur is a warning against not counting the cost, is close to the river, and the *Mill* is just beyond it, upstream. Without attempting to describe the exquisite beauty of the spot, we may say that the crumbling old mill, the swift, clear stream, and the richly-wooded glen, make up an ideal scene. The old bridge has disappeared, having been swept away some years since, but its absence does not prevent the perfection of the picture. As a practical bit of information we may say that the Ordnance map is wrong in placing a river-junction at Holy Street Mill. The stream coming down by Gidleigh enters the North Teign about half-a-mile higher up, at Leigh Bridge, which is close to the meeting of the two Teigns.

2. **Rushford Mill and Castle**, 1⅓ *m.*—The object of this walk is the pretty river-scene by the mill, and the view obtainable from the Castle. Follow the Moreton Hampstead road (the one that passes in front of the Moor Park Hotel) to the first fork, and there turn down to the left. The Teign is crossed at the foot of the hill.

A footpath across the fields on the left leads to a deserted factory, and the Castle, which is in full view above the trees, may be reached that way, but it is better to follow the road. This quickly brings us to *Rushford Mill*, where stepping-stones across the river make a still pool above—a pleasant feature in a scene of quiet beauty. Continuing along the road we turn up a lane on the left just beyond Rushford Barton, and through the wood reach the *Castle*, which is a modern shell erected with the object of improving the general picturesqueness of the views which embrace it. The view from it up-and-down the valley is deservedly much admired, and Chagford, backed by Natton and Mill Down, is seen at its best.

3. **Gidleigh Castle**, 2½ m. This walk involves much steep up-and-down hill work, and the pedestrian, taking things easily, will be an hour, more or less in reaching the Castle.

Turn down the hill by the street opposite the west-end of the Church (same as for Holy Street Mill). When a dilapidated factory is reached turn to the right, cross the bridge over the river, ascend the hill and turn to the left. Then avoid all turns until a stream is reached. Cross the bridge, ascend the opposite hill and take the first turn on the right to *Gidleigh Church*. This little fabric has been restored, and has a Perpendicular screen. The *Castle* is close by in a farmyard. The ruin consists of a 13th cent. tower, with a stone-vaulted basement. There are two staircases, one practicable to the first floor, on which grow two ash trees on either side of a fire-place. The other staircase enables us to reach the top of the walls. The ruins may form a bit for the sketcher. Their history is obscure.

4. **Fingle Bridge**, *by path*, 4 m; (*by road*, 5 m.); **Drewsteignton**, 5 m; **Spinsters' Rock** (*Cromlech*), 7 m; **Chagford**, 10 m.

(1) *Carriage-route*. This follows the Moreton Hampstead road as far as Easton, beyond which the route continues straight on by a narrow and almost precipitous lane along the south side of Whyddon Park, up to Cranbrook Castle and down by a tremendously steep zigzag to Fingle Bridge.

Cranbrook Castle (*about* 3½ m. *on the way*) occupies a large area of ground sloping towards the Teign from the crest of Whyddon Down. It lies a short distance left of the road, whence it is scarcely noticeable, and is approached by a green track starting from a guide-post directing to it. It is an old British camp and has a dry-stone rampart with a ditch on all sides except the lowest, which is towards the river. The view from it is extensive, especially northward, in which direction the river-gorge is so narrow and deep as to be imperceptible. Consequently Drewsteignton, which is a mile on the other side, appears within the range of an easy 20 minutes' walk. To the right of that village, and nearer at hand, is seen the rival camp of *Prestonberry* a green patch on the top of a hill sloping abruptly down to Fingle Bridge, which from this point is invisible. Beyond these the lower undulations of Mid-Devon extend far away to the skirts of Exmoor. Cawsand Beacon is a prominent object a little north of west, and to the left of it may be detected the crowning height of Yes Tor.

Returning to the road, we soon commence the abrupt zigzag descent to Fingle Bridge. Half-way down, a short reach of the Teign presents itself far below, bordered by a strip of level meadow and overhung by the screes and bare slope of Prestonberry. On both sides the road is densely wooded, principally with oak-scrub. At the bottom is *Fingle Bridge*.

(2) *By river-side footpath.* Leaving Chagford by the Moreton road, take the first turn to the left, and, after crossing the Teign and a tributary rill, enter a footpath on the right. This crosses the Moreton and Drewsteignton road, and shortly afterwards enters the *Fingle Glen* opposite Whyddon Park. The rest of the way, tracking the windings of the stream, which here becomes in places a rapid, is of the most charming description. The hills rise steeply from the banks, in some places covered, in others sprinkled with wood, and relieved here and there on the north side by bold faces of bare rock or sloping scree. A fine effect is produced by the way in which, as seen from various points, they overlap one another. The *Logan Stone* at the first bend is hardly movable. The scene altogether, for nearly 2 miles, is one of the best representatives of its kind—the V-ravine, if we may so call it —in Devon, and the stream is only surpassed by the rush of the East Lyn between Millslade and Lynmouth, while, if we search England through, the ravine is, perhaps, the finest of its kind, saving only the matchless Dovedale. Its weak point is rock.

Carriage and foot road meet at **Fingle Bridge**, a three-arched structure, narrow and buttressed, hoary with years and the growth of ferns and lichens, which the warmth and moisture of its situation have fostered. A little beyond it, on the right bank of the river, is a mill, beyond which there is only an angler's path.

Proceeding northwards from the bridge we ascend a narrow little defile between the Prestonberry Camp hill on the right and the woods of Piddledon Down on the left. After crossing the streamlet which flows down a grassy hollow between the latter and Drewsteignton, we may take a footpath up a field to the left and reach Drewsteignton in less than a mile. Those who wish to visit **Prestonberry Castle** must continue along the road till it joins another running east and west, and then wheel round to the right and attack the hill by its easiest slope. There is a path up it. Its description is substantially the same as that of Cranbrook Castle (*p.* 94), and most tourists will feel their greatest reward in the view it affords of Fingle Bridge and the Teign gorge.

Drewsteignton (Inns: *New, Old*) is a clean and comfortable-looking little village of one street, with a Perpendicular church, occupying a pleasant site on the north of it. The name is derived from that of an old lord of the soil, Drewe or Drogo. There is a direct path from it into the Fingle gorge, crossing a little intervening hollow.

The direct road back to Chagford turns to the left half-a-mile beyond the village, and is the same for the last mile as the one by which our pedestrian started for Fingle Bridge. Those, however, who wish to include the (Spinsters' Rock) **cromlech** in the excursion, must continue straight from Drewsteignton for 2 miles to Stone Cross, along a road which keeps to high ground throughout, and then, bending somewhat to the left, they will soon see that monument in a field on the left of the road, between it and a farm called *Shilston* (i.e., the shelf or hanging stone). As the only erect cromlech in Devon it attracts special notice. It fell down in 1862, and its re-erection cost £20, borne by Mrs. Bragg, the owner of the property. It consists of a slab 15ft. by 10ft. resting on three upright stones 6½ft. high. The name *Spinsters' Rock* is due to a tradition that its original erection was accomplished by three spinsters before breakfast.

Opposite to the Cromlech, in a deep hollow, is a small sheet of water called *Bradmere Pool*. Devonshire is not a lake district, or this pool would be ignored. It is only a water-filled quarry, or mine-work. The only lake on Dartmoor is Classenwell Pool, a tarn about 1¼ m. W. of Nun's Cross.

The return to *Chagford* is as straight as you can go along a lane which crosses the Teign a full half-mile short of the town, for which you bear to the left at an old factory.

5. To Castor Rock, the Gidleigh group of Antiquities, and Cranmere Pool and back to Chagford. *For Cranmere to Lidford, see p.* 99.

The whole of the antiquities about to be described can be visited in a round of from 4 to 5 *hrs.*, abt. 14 *m.*; by omitting the Grey Wethers the distance may be reduced to 11½ *m.*, see small print, *p.* 97. If Cranmere (nothing to see) be included, the distance will be 17 *m.* or 18 *m.*, and the time not less than 7½ *hrs.*

Of course the route may be taken the reverse way to that which we describe, but the one given is to be preferred, for the double reason that it leaves the best bit of scenery and the least fatiguing walk for the end of the round.

We leave Chagford by the south-west road that at once descends and, crossing a rill flowing to the Teign, ascends again to *Waye Barton*. Here we turn to the left, and, continuing the ascent, obtain a good view of Chagford by looking back. About ¾ *m.* from Waye the road forks, and by the right-hand branch we reach (3¼ *m.* from Chagford) *Metherall*, where the road bends to the right (bit of road connecting with Fernworthy omitted on old Ordnance). After climbing the hill, we diverge to the right into a meadow a little way down towards the Teign valley. The tors prominent across the stream are Frenchbeer, Middle Tor, and Castor. In line with Castor turn to the right and look out for **hut-circles**, of which there are several. Perhaps the best on the moor is across the next wall and near the stream. It may be recognised by a fair-sized thorn-bush inside. This hut-circle is enclosed by a wall of two courses of stones, together about 4½ feet high. The diameter is about 30 feet. One of the door-jambs still remains in position.

<small>The botanist, will, in June, find the comparatively rare fern moonwort, and the butterfly orchis abundant in the field in which is the hut-circle just described.
On the grass hill-side opposite, an isolated heap indicates a tumulus where there is a fine kistvaen with its cover complete. It was opened in 1879.</small>

We now return to the road and continue by it to *Fernworthy*, which is seen a short distance up the valley amid—for Dartmoor—a considerable group of trees. Before reaching the farm, the South Teign is crossed, 40 yards below an ancient *Clam Bridge*. *Fernworthy* is a flourishing homestead on the borders of cultivation. The house bears date 1690, but has been much altered since then. Passing in front of it, we reach the end of the road, and thence ascend by a rough lane, bordered by well-grown beeches, and striking over the moor due westward, soon reach the **Fernworthy circle**, 60 feet in diameter and of 27 stones, about 3 feet high. One stone is missing.

<small>It is from Fernworthy Circle that the round, of the antiquities, can be shortened as mentioned (*p.* 98.) To the S. of the Circle an Avenue of small stones extends for about 3 chains to a modern wall where it now ends. This Avenue appears to have been the continuation of one extending from Scorhill Circle to Fernworthy. To the N. of Fernworthy for 150 yds. the Avenue has disappeared; then for abt. 50 yds. it can be traced (see *p.* 93). Continuing in the same direction for about ¾ mile you will find a stone 5 ft. high, the only one now left of the "Three Boys" which are supposed to have been the supports of a Cromlech. Hence to the Longstone (*p.* 100) the destroyed avenue can be traced by the holes left. After visiting Scorhill Circle (*p.* 93) the return to Chagford is that given on *p.* 93. From Fernworthy to Scorhill this way is about 1¼ m. say ½ hr.</small>

Looking back, Blackingstone Rock (2 miles beyond Moreton Hampstead) is prominent eastward, and will be in sight for a great part of our round. As we near the top of *Long Ridge*, bearing a trifle N. of W. during the ascent, Watern Tor, north-west, appears to have three great towers of granite nearly close together, the two on the right hand separated by a chink. These, as we shall see, are a considerable distance apart on the ridge of the hill, but from our present view-point they are fore-shortened. It is useful to remember this, as this tor is a conspicuous landmark, but varies much in appearance.

From the top of Long Ridge we soon catch sight, due West, across the next combe, of a shepherd's cottage, known as "Teign Head" from its situation near the source of the North Teign (the source or sources are, however, some mile or more above this house). Our direct route (*but see small type p.* 98) for Cranmere lies through the yard of this cottage. To reach it make for a gateway in a wall, and then bear a trifle down stream, *i.e.*, to the right, to a *Clapper Bridge* of three spans. This bridge resembles that at Postbridge, but was built in the 18th century.

If instead of descending to the bridge we follow a wall running south, along the west flank of Long Ridge, we shall in a short mile come to the **Grey Wethers**—two sacred circles, now consisting of two semi-circles back to back at the eastern foot of Sittaford Tor. The circles, when complete, were each about 35 yards in diameter. The stones are about 4 feet high and roughly shaped. Of one circle there are 9 stones standing and 6 fallen; of the other 7 standing and 18 fallen remain. Wall-making is answerable for the removal of the rest. **Sittaford Tor** (1,764 ft.) should be ascended for the sake of its square logan stone which is not, however, very easily made to log.

From Teign Head [Shepherd's house] **to Cranmere**, 2¾ m., 1¼ hrs.

If bound for Cranmere it will be advisable to descend Sittaford and make for the Shepherd's house mentioned above, as the route given below is that which enables us to enter on the bog at a favourable point—a matter of some importance.

Pass through the yard and round to the back of the house, whence continue through a gateway, and ascend White Horse Hill, keeping nearly due West, but gradually bearing a little to the right-hand. When the top of the ridge, which is apt to be sodden, is attained there is a fine view looking back, in which Castor is very prominent. Keep along the ridge still nearly due West with a depression on the left, and mount a green stoneless ridge to a gateway in a wall. This wall runs nearly due North (right) and South (left). After passing through the gate the combe on the left is to be kept on that hand, and the boggy ground at its head rounded. Where we stand, looking right down this combe towards Sittaford Tor, the conical tor over a dip to the right is Belliver (2 m. S. *of Post Bridge on the Moreton Hampstead and Tavistock road*), and just West of South is seen Great Mis Tor. We turn our back on Sittaford and mount the hill to the remains of a peat cutter's stone hut, known as "*Mute Inn*." From the top of the ridge, it is necessary, if we are to find Cranmere, to note the chief points in the view. Due West is Hare Tor. To the left of it is Fur Tor crowned by church-like rocks; to the right of it the rocks of Great Links Tor form a rough castle and tower. Cut Hill, marked by an Ordnance cairn, is the rounded summit to the left of Fur Tor. It is only mentioned because of its central position in the moor, and has nothing to do with our guidance or our route. Great Links Tor gives the line we are to follow. It is necessary to mark its direction, because presently the dip of the ground will for a few minutes hide it from view. Yes Tor is prominent to the right of Great Links Tor. It appears as a huge ridge. The left-hand of this ridge, as seen by us, is High Willhays, the apex of Dartmoor. Between Great Links Tor and High Willhays, across the ridge at the head of the Dart valley on our left, is the deep combe of the West Okement. Now examine the ridge with a glass—if one is carried,—if not, carefully with the eye, and a long, narrow, dark depression will be observed. This is Cranmere, and to reach it we must cross the bog. There is no danger even in the wettest season, but at all times the going is bad, and sometimes particularly so. Keeping one's eye on Great Links Tor, we get as best we can across the gully-riven ground to the smooth green bog beyond. Henceforward it is only a question of plodding onward. **Cranmere Pool** has long been drained. It used to be considered dangerous to sheep, and so a cut was made, and its waters let out into the West Okement combe. It is a black peaty hollow with a bit of heather on the north side, whereon a dry resting-place can, in fine weather, be had. In the bed of the pool is a tiny cairn erected in 1854 by Perrott (the Dartmoor guide) of Chagford. Originally he placed a bottle within the cairn, and visitors to the place put their cards in it. For some years this receptacle was left undisturbed, but one day the cairn was found rifled, the cards gone, and only the broken bottle left. Since then 2 tins for a book and pencil and visitors' cards have been kept in the cairn, and it is to be hoped that no "'Arry" will again destroy the record, or fail to close the tins and insert them in their place, so as to make them safe from wet.

Cranmere Pool to Lidford, *abt* 9 *m.*, 3¼—4 *hrs.*

As far as the nature of the ground will allow, the traveller for the first two miles must keep a course due West, until, after going over Great Kneeset Tor, the long ridge of *Amicombe Hill* is attained. Then the most unmistakable route is to make for *Great Links Tor*, whence a track leads to the *Dartmoor Inn*, on the Okehampton and Tavistock road, 1 m. from Lidford village. There is, however, no difficulty in a more direct course. If this be determined on, the *Rattle Brook* combe must be crossed and Sharp Tor passed close on the left. Then comes another combe, also to be crossed direct, or this may be descended and the road so reached.

The **Return from Cranmere to Chagford** is for a mile or so nearly coincident with the final part of the approach to it given above. Due East is *Newlake*, with a fragment of rough wall. We make nearly straight for it. Avoid as much as possible the gully-broken bog and bear a little to the right of the direct line. In this way Taw Head is skirted. From it due North is *Hock Tor*; to the right of this and nearer is *Steeperton*, and more to the right and nearer still *Wild Tor*, with the huge back of Cawsand beyond. As we near the top of Newlake, bog gives place to hard ground. The view from the summit is a wide one. *South-west* is Fur Tor; then proceeding round to *West* are Hare Tor and Great Links Tor. *North-west* we have High Willhays, Yes Tor, West Mill Tor, East Mill Tor. *North*, Hock Tor, Steeperton, and Cawsand, *East by north* Watern Tor (now showing large rock-masses wide apart on the ridge). Wild Tor (fine rocks) is between us and Cawsand, now impressive by his mass. We make for Watern Tor, crossing the valley to a bit of path seen on its opposite side. The rocks of Watern Tor are curious on account of their laminated structure and the weathering of the edges. Strike down the valley towards the N.E. for a while and then bear eastward. Cross the little rising ground called *Littorally Tor* in the Ordnance Map. This brings us into the angle between the Walla Brook and the North Teign. Scorhill Circle and Longstone are seen just across the former.

The route back to Chagford is given below, where the round of the antiquities is continued on the supposition that Cranmere is not included in the excursion.

From Sittaford Tor we turn northward, and descend to the *Clapper Bridge*, which is seen crossing the stream just below the shepherd's cottage, noting on our way a waterfall on the, here rather diminutive, North Teign. Leaving the bridge, we follow down the stream to its junction with the Walla Brook. No direction is needed as the stream is sufficient guide. Its devious course when it trends eastward, just before we are opposite Watern Tor (4 rock masses), across the stream, need not be followed. It is better, then, to take a north-east course to the junction, where a modern bridge of two clamped granite blocks leads to the tongue between the streams. An old slab-bridge occupied the position of the new one till August, 1826, when it was swept away by a great flood.

Cross the Walla Brook by a *Clam Bridge*, a fine specimen of its kind (slab slightly arched 12 ft. by 3 ft., and about 1½ ft. thick), and take cart-track to the circle. **Scorhill Circle** is, perhaps, the best on the Moor. It is about 85 ft. in diameter, and consists of 25 stones standing and 4 or 5 fallen ones. The *Long Stone* is about 8 ft. high, and two of the prostrate stones are nearly as large.

Just below the junction of the streams is the *Tolmen Stone*, a
large block with a great hole through it, probably a pot-hole.
We now ascend by a wall towards Castor. This wall has been
partly built at the expense of the **stone avenue** that ran nearly
parallel with it. From the end of the wall the *Avenue* begins.
It is of small stones, and now varies in breadth owing to the
stones having been squeezed out of position by passing cart-
traffic. As we ascend the hill, another *avenue* comes in on the
left, and near the junction angle is a triple circle. Proceeding
over the brow, the main avenue ends with a *Longstone* 12 ft.
high (*p.* 97). We now return towards Castor, and after ascending
it (on the top is a large rock basin protected by a railing) descend
to the new road from Batworthy (N. Budd, Esq.). Adjoining
this, on the west slope of Castor, are many enclosures, large
and small, and on the left of the road (going towards Chagford)
is **Round Pound**, a walled enclosure in the shape of a
spherical triangle of about 70 feet diameter, with a 34 ft. hut-
circle within, and connected with the outer work by radiating
walls. Here we get a fine bit of the N. Teign glen. Turning along
the road, it is now all plain-sailing, chiefly down-hill, to Chagford,
and the route becomes very beautiful. The Teign gorge, near
Fingle Bridge, is a prominent feature in the scene. When an
iron gate is reached on the left, go through it, and after the next
iron gate turn to the left. An old farm-house on the right is soon
passed, and then for a moment, in a dip of the hills on the right,
are seen Heytor Rocks. Yeo and Southill farms are on that side
in a richly-wooded valley. Natton and Mill Down are over Chagford on the right, and we descend by a steep but pretty lane to *Leigh
Bridge*, at the junction of the North and South Teign. Here trees,
and moss, and stream compose a sweetly fresh and pretty scene.
Ascending the hill from the bridge, the *Puggie Stone* (with rock-
basin—ladder needed) is across a small field on the left. Soon
the narrow lane at a gate on the left gives a beautiful view of the
Teign coming down by Gidleigh Park. Going down the next steep,
note the *Cross* in the right-hand wall-bank. This used to stand in
Chagford, where the octagonal base, well ornamented, is now used
as a water-trough at Guscott's lodgings. We drop down to Holy
Street and so reach Chagford.

6. **Ascent of Cawsand Beacon**, 6 *m.*; 2½ *hrs.*

Cawsand is, from whatever point it is viewed, a tame-looking
round-backed hill, and only noticeable for its bulk. It is a
favourite ascent from Chagford, and the view from the summit,
on which there is a large cairn and sundry tumuli, is the best
obtainable on the northern side of the moor.

Leave Chagford as though going to Holy Street Mill, but at the
factory turn to the right and proceed to Gidleigh, (*p.* 94). The
map shews the route *viâ* Greenaway and Moortown. When

¾ m. beyond the latter a little brook is crossed, ascend the next hill and turn off left just before reaching *Shilstone Tor*. A course north-west will lead to the top, and no description is needful save to warn the tourist to avoid getting too much to the westward, *i.e.*, to the south side of the hill. *Raybarrow Pool*, of the Ordnance, is not a pool, but a "mire," or bog, and is the only really dangerous one on Dartmoor. It is quite impassable at all times, except in hard frost. Next, and little inferior, to it in extent and softness, is Fox Tor Mire, near Nun's Cross, but that is so obviously to be avoided by passers between Princetown and Ivybridge, that warning is scarcely needed.

The view from Cawsand (1,799ft.) is better than that from Yes Tor from the fact that the hill is on the edge of the moor. North and north-east is Exmoor, culminating in Dunkery Beacon, 35 *m*. distant. The wide, well-wooded expanse of Mid Devon is at our feet, while near at hand, West and South, are the finely ragged tors of Belstone, Hock, Steeperton, Wild Tor, and Watern; the last-named presenting its ridge of rocks end-on. South-east is the fine Castor rock. Of more distant points westward the most prominent are Yes Tor and Great Links Tor.

The return to Chagford cannot be much varied, as Raybarrow "Pool" forbids our descending the south flank. Those bound for Okehampton have an easy route by dropping gradually down (less that 2 *m*.) north-west to Belstone (*small inn*). The Taw can be crossed by some rocks just south of that village, whence the route to Okehampton (easily shortened and improved by taking a path which drops to the East Okement Valley), 4 *m*., calls for no description.

The nearest inn to Cawsand Beacon is the "*Taw River Hotel*" at Sticklepath, 6 miles from Chagford and 4 miles from Okehampton.

There is a tall Cross at **South Zeal**, 5 *m*. from Chagford on the road to Okehampton, and at **Sticklepath**, 6 *m*., a carved stone called *Ladywell*, 5½ feet high, close to an old fountain still used. A mile nearer Okehampton is another, 4½ feet high. There is no inscription on either, and their age and intention are alike unknown.

Chagford or Moreton Hampstead to Grimspound, Widdecombe, Ashburton, Princetown, Tavistock, and Plymouth.

Moreton Hampstead to Warren House Inn, 7 *m*.; *Post Bridge (Temp. Inn)*, 9 *m*.; *Two Bridges (Hotel)*, 12½ *m*.; (*Tavistock*, 20½ *m*.); *Princetown (Hotel)*, 14 *m*; *Plymouth (by rail)*,

— *Chagford to Post Bridge*, 8½ *m*.

Moreton Hampstead to Grimspound, 7 *m*.; *Widdecombe*, 9 *m*.; *Ashburton*, 15½ *m*.

— *Chagford to Grimspound*, 7½ *m*.

The road from Moreton Hampstead to Princetown, Tavistock, &c., is one of two main roads across Dartmoor, the other being that from Ashburton (*p.* 81). The two unite, or rather cross one another at Two Bridges, whence one road proceeds through Princetown to Plymouth, crossing the Plymouth and Tavistock railway at Yelverton Junction, and the other goes direct to Tavistock. Travellers from Chagford join this main road at Bector Cross, 3 miles from Moreton.

With regard to the respective merits of the routes from Ashburton and Moreton, it may be said that while the former presents in the neighbourhood of Holne Chase a scene of luxuriant beauty against which its rival has nothing to throw into the scale, the latter, crossing some of the highest ground of Dartmoor, conveys a decidedly more vigorous impression of the characteristic landscape of that elevated region. At the same time it cannot be denied that the pace of a carriage allows ample time for appreciating the attractions of both routes.

Those who are bound for Widdecombe, Ashburton, &c., quit the main route at Bector Cross, 3 miles from Moreton and a few yards beyond the point at which the Chagford road converges.

The Route. From Moreton this is over high ground of a fairly interesting character for the first few miles. From Chagford the road passes between Natton and Middleton Hills. In both cases extensive views are commanded.

To Widdecombe and Ashburton. The road to these places turns abruptly to the left at *Bector Cross*, and after a short drop rises again, and in 2½ *m.* at cross-roads turns to the right to Heytree Farm, ¼ *m.* further. Hence it is nearly a straight course of about 1½ *miles* to **Grimspound** (*p.* 80). From Grimspound onward the best way for pedestrians is southwards over the summit-ridge of *Hamildon Down*, from which in about 3 miles the descent to Widdecombe (*p.* 79) is obvious. Half-a-mile beyond Widdecombe a corner may be cut off by taking a short farm-road and then a footpath to the bridge over the East Webber stream whence the route through Buckland is fully described the reverse way on *p.* 79. Another way to Grimspound is by the new road striking southwards abt. 4½ *m.* from Moreton.

A mile beyond **Bector Cross** the road takes a wide sweep to the right (old road, traceable for some distance, attacks the hill at once), and a far-stretching view opens up northwards, to the right of the hog-backed Cawsand Beacon. It extends over Mid-Devon to Exmoor. Two miles beyond Bector Cross a new road, marked "Private," strikes off to Blackaton and Widdecombe.

Those who have climbed the hill by the old road must be careful in descending not to mistake this Private road for the main road.

Another rise and then a slight descent brings us to a cross marked W. B. and a way-side public-house, the *Warren House Inn*, beyond which we cross Merripit Hill. Looking back, we can trace in a hollow due east the rude circle of stones constituting Grimspound. Then a gradual descent brings us to **Postbridge** (*Temp. Inn*), with some sleeping accommodation. *Letters arr. & dep.* abt. 10 *a.m.* Post-town: *Princetown.*

Hereabouts, too, a few trees diversify the roadside. A few yards below the present bridge is the old *clapper-bridge*—the best specimen of its kind on the moor. It consists of four granite piers, on which rest slabs of the same stone 6 feet wide and 15 feet long, and, like all others of its kind on the moor, it is built without mortar.

Some of the wildest scenery of Dartmoor may be easily reached from Post Bridge, and an interesting walk may be taken by *Grey Wethers*, 3 miles to the north (*p.* 98) to *Chagford*.

Near Postbridge there are many of the characteristic antiquities of the moor —pounds, hut-circles, &c., but they are less interesting than the remains near Gidleigh and Merrivale Bridge.

Beyond Postbridge there is another slight ascent, and on the right of the road quite a luxuriance of evergreen wood around the shooting box of Mr. Bennett, of Plymouth. On the left *Belliver Tor* is a fine example of its kind, and after descending slightly to *New Bridge*, we have on our right front a line of tors, the best to look at being *Longaford Tor*, and, the most interesting to the antiquarian, *Crockern Tor*, the smallest and most southerly of the series. Here from 1305 to 1749 the Stannary (*i.e.* tin) Parliament of Devon met in the open air. It was composed of 24 stannators from each of the four stannary-towns: Ashburton, Chagford, Plymton and Tavistock, with Lord Warden of the Stanneries as president.

We are now approaching Two Bridges, and from the brow of the last hill, before reaching it, a glimpse of *Wistman's Wood*— an equally famous spot with Crockern Tor—may be obtained. It is an oak-scrub on the East of the Dart, and about a mile North of the road

At **Two Bridges** (*good inn—Saracen's Head*) the two Dartmoor roads cross one another, forming an angle so acute that travellers by the one or the other—from Moreton or from Ashburton—may proceed onward by either of the continuations, to Tavistock or to Princetown, without materially deviating from a direct course. For Tavistock we have already described the route on *p.* 83.

Rather more than half-way between Two Bridges and Princetown, we may note on the left-hand, as we cross a tributary of the W. Dart, another *clapper-bridge*, of the same character, but not so large as the one at Postbridge. For **Princetown,** *see p.* 116.

Princetown to Yelverton Junction, 10 *m.*, owing to the circuit necessitated by a descent of 900 feet, on an average gradient of 1 in 58; by *road* (see below) it is only 6 miles. The windings of the railway afford very fine views in nearly all directions, especially across the western skirts of Dartmoor into Cornwall. From the apex of the first loop (*see map*), the boldly shaped Vixen Tor (*p.* 116) is noticeable, also the Merrivale (*p.* 116) longstone; then, as the landscape widens out the most striking objects are the conical Brent Tor, Staple Tor—on which the chief rocks look like a pair of Cyclopean gate-posts—Kit Hill, in Cornwall, with its huge chimney-stack, Walkhampton Church and the Royal Albert Suspension Bridge over the Tamar at Saltash.

There are now small tourist hotels at *Dousland* and **Yelverton**. At the latter station we join the Plymouth and Tavistock branch, and continuing the descent, may notice on the left the churches of Meavy, Sheepstor and Shaugh Prior, the last named high up on the hill beyond Shaugh Bridge—a sweetly pretty spot marred by mining operations. Then come Bickleigh Station and the deep dingle of Bickleigh Woods; Plym Bridge, below on the right, Marsh Mills Station and the junction with the G.W. main line. For *Plymouth, see p.* 133.

The **road** between Princetown and Yelverton threads a number of tors (*see map*) and also commands from parts pretty much the same extensive view as the railway. Then, passing the hotels at *Dousland* (5 m.) and *Yelverton* (6 m.), it runs nearly the length of the breezy *Roborough Down* at an elevation of from 650 to 600 feet, and ends with an easy descent to Plymouth.

Dartmoor from Okehampton.

Exeter to Okehampton by L. & S. W. Railway, 26 m.

The London and South Western route from Exeter to Plymouth, is from 6 to 7 miles longer than the rival Great-Western route. The two together make the complete circuit of Dartmoor, the South-Western skirting its northern side just as the Great-Western does its southern. From Lidford, 36 m. from Exeter, the line belongs to the Great Western, the South Western having only running powers over it. The part extending from Lidford to the junction with the Great Western main line at Marsh Mills is the most beautiful on the route, and is described on *p.* 110. A new line (*p.* 110; L. & S. W. R.) is in course of construction from Lidford to Plymouth.

Route. Between *Queen Street* and *St. David's* Stations at Exeter, a distance of ½ mile, there is a descending gradient of 1 in 24. At St. David's, where all South-Western trains stop, the Great-Western line is joined. the two systems, oddly enough, issuing from the station in opposite directions to reach the same destination. Our present route, the South-Western to Plymouth, is for two miles identical with the Great-Western to London. Then it turns abruptly to the left, and threads the little valey of the Yeo. Just beyond the junction—on the right-hand side, but not seen—is *Pynes* (Earl of Iddesleigh). The first staion of importance is **Crediton**; Inns: *Angel, Ship* (H.Q.), *Bulles Arms, Coffee Tavern* (beds). The town lies out of sight on the right of the line. It was the original seat of the See of Devon (*p.* 29). For tourists it has no special attraction. Beyond it we come to **Yeoford Junction** (*inn close to station*), where the line divides the North Devon branch continuing straight on to Barnsaple, &c., and the Plymouth line bending sharply to the left.

Yeoford Junction to Chagford, 11 m. Omnibus daily in summer (Friday only in winter) in connection with the morning express from London (abt. 4 p.m. from Exeter). *Fare from Exeter abt.* 3s. The route passes through or near *South Tawton, Throwleigh, Whyddon Down* and *Sandy Park*. It is hardly to be recommended to the pedestrian, who, however, may improve upon it, by following an intricate succession of lanes to *Fingle Bridge*, and thence pursuing the north side of the Teign *to Chagford* (*see* p. 92)

From Yeoford for the first few miles the country has a barren and unattractive appearance. The next station is **Bow** ($5\frac{1}{2}$ m.), beyond which we come in sight of Cawsand Beacon, an outlier of Dartmoor, a long hog-backed ridge. Further away, and to the right of it are the more shapely Belstone Tors. After passing the next station, **North Tawton** (*inn*), the line crosses the Taw just as it issues from the wilds of Dartmoor.

This part of our route is on an almost continuous rise. Gradually the view northward expands till it reaches the southern flank of Exmoor. Crossing the picturesque valley of the *East Okement*, we proceed, still on an ascending gradient, to *Okehampton Station* (*Ref. Rm.* on up-side) which is situated high above the town on the slope of Dartmoor.

Okehampton.

Hotel : *White Hart* (H.Q.; *Fam. and Comm.*, 'bus) ; **Inns** : *Red Lion, Plume of Feathers*.

Post : *Del.* abt. 7 a.m., 3.30 p.m. ; *desp.* 2.40, 7.30 p.m.

This little market town (*pop*. abt. 2,000) lies in a pretty valley on the right of, and some way below the line, at the junction of the East and West Okement, and as seen from the station cannot be described as "ugly, dirty, and stupid" (*Kingsley*), though a nearer acquaintance may, to some extent, justify the dictum of the novelist. Around the town are many modern villas, much patronised by summer visitors who come here to enjoy the bracing air of Dartmoor, on whose northern skirts the town lies. The *Parish Church* is on a hill West of the town, and with the exception of the tower was rebuilt in 1842; a tombstone, said to be Saxon, is built into the wall outside, at the E. end, under the railings of the vestry steps. The *Chapel of Ease* in the main street has a good Perpendicular tower. **Okehampton Castle**, $\frac{3}{4}$ mile from the town, to the left of the Launceston road, on a bold knoll, round which winds the river Okement, is worth a visit. The pleasantest way is to go by the road which leaves the town by the post office.

When the castle appears on the left, take a footpath leading through the wood direct to it. The *Keep*, late Norman, crowns the knoll, and is mantled with ivy and embowered in a grove of oak and ash, that in summer shuts out the view of the stream which is heard below. On the lower ground towards the town are the remains of the *Hall* and *Chapel*, and in the latter a piscina, on the south side, is still perfect. With the exception of the keep the buildings are E. E. with a few pieces of Norman built in. The outbuildings were of considerable extent, as is indicated by the remains of walls on the lower ground near the stream. The return to Okehampton can be made direct in ½ m. by the river-side, by crossing a bridge, over which a path goes to the *Union Workhouse*, a comely building in a singularly pretty spot.

Excursions from Okehampton.

1. **To Belstone**, 3 *m. by path* (**Cawsand Beacon**, 6 *m.*), **Cut Hill**, *abt.* 10½ *m*; and **Two Bridges**, 17 *m.*

Route described the reverse way, on p. 82. This is the best pedestrian route over Dartmoor from north to south. It may also be commenced by taking the Yes Tor route next described.

To *Belstone* it is 4 miles by road, the Exeter road being followed for 2¼ miles, and then a by-way taken. A short cut may be made by ascending the valley of the East Okement, which goes under the railway about ¾ mile east of the station, and in another half mile or so ascending the steep hill on the left.

From *Belstone (public-house)* to the top of *Cawsand Beacon*, it is about 2 miles the river Taw being crossed a little above the village, and the summit gained by a long steady pull. *For the view, see p.* 101.

There is a choice of two ways from Belstone to Cut Hill. The nearest is due south over the long line of *Belstone Tor, Hock Tor*, and *Okement Hill*, passing in about 5 miles *Cranmere Pool*. Cut Hill is about 2 miles south from Cranmere. Its rounded summit, marked by a turf-heap and Ordnance cairn, appears a little higher than the surrounding parts of the Moor. The other route to it from Belstone is by crossing the Taw, as in making for Cawsand, and from the crossing following a cart-track which goes southwards under Cawsand and ceases some little way before the Belstone Tor route is joined on the boggy plateau between Taw Head and Dart Head. The two routes are separated by the desolate valley of the Taw.

For *Cut Hill, see p.* 82. From it the route, a trackless one, continues due south over a line of tors, which rise between the West Dart and the Cowsick stream. The map is the best guide to this route throughout.

2. **Ascent of Yes Tor from Okehampton.** (*a*) The easiest, but least picturesque way is to drive or walk by Dartmoor Gate to the foot of the final peak. The road branches off from the Station Road at the corner where stands a pillar letter-box.

A gate just below the station opens to a track that in a short distance joins the road mentioned above.

After crossing the bridge over the railway the *road* * route still ascends and passes the Artillery Camp, and so to *Dartmoor Gate*, whence a rough track leads nearly due S. to the Red Vein (Redavenn) stream. It is then a stiffish climb to the summit of Yes Tor (2,029 *ft.*), which is marked by a flag-staff that is used to signal "danger" when artillery practice is going on.

(*b*) Take *Castle Road* at foot of Station Road. This passes the pleasantly-placed *Union Workhouse*. A track leads on to the open fell-side of *Okehampton Park*. As we ascend, the castle on its wooded spur across the West Okement dominates the valley, and Okehampton appears to advantage behind us. The cart-track leads to *Meldon Viaduct*, about 3 *m.* from Okehampton. This frail-looking structure crosses the valley at a height of 160 feet above the stream. We pass under it and continue up the valley. About half-a-mile beyond the viaduct the Red Vein stream comes down a combe on the left-hand. Still ascend by the main stream under the crags of Shellstone Tor, right, until the rocks of *Black Tor* are above it on the left hand. Climb up to these (good view of the wild combe), and keep along the ridge for half-a-mile or so, bearing to the left. *High Willhays* (locally *Willis*) is the southern end of the mass of which **Yes Tor** is the northern. Its height, 2039 ft., makes it the apex of the moor. The view from Yes Tor is, of course, a wide one. North-east, on a clear day, it embraces Dunkery Beacon, and westward from it the outline of Exmoor with the softly beautiful expanse of the vale of the Taw between. Eastward, less than 4 miles off, is the huge lump of Cawsand, from which, carrying the eye round southward, the dreary waste of the bogs of central Dartmoor is embraced. South-west are prominent the castellated rocks of Great Links Tor, and far-away, in the same direction, the sharp outlines of Rowtor, Brown Willy, and Kilmar High Rock in the order named from right to left.

The *descent* to Okehampton is most easily made by descending N. to the Red Vein and so to Dartmoor Gate. This is given sufficiently under (*a*).

Yes Tor by Great Links Tor to Lidford.

This involves crossing the deep ravine of the West Okement. The map is guide enough, and in clear weather, noting the position of Great Links Tor, the way over Amicombe Hill is plain sailing. From about ¾ mile south of Great Links Tor a rough track descends to the road at *Dartmoor Inn*, 1 *m.* from Lidford village and 2½ *m.* from the station.

---

* The pedestrian should turn to the right to a cottage and take the foot-track up the hill beyond. This leads to the road and saves something in distance if not in time.

Okehampton to Tavistock.

Okehampton to Bridestowe, 6½ m.; Lidford, 10 m.; Mary Tavy, 13 m.; Tavistock, 16 m. The L. & S. W. R. new line from Lidford is given p. 110.

Beyond Okehampton the railway, continuing to rise, looks down upon the West Okement valley on the right. *Okehampton Castle*, on its wooded knoll, is well seen. The sparsely-wooded slope of the moor we are now traversing is called *Okehampton Park*. In three miles the river is crossed by the slender and lofty *Meldon Viaduct*, whence there is a hasty peep on the left into the narrow combe through which the W. Okement issues from the moor. A little further and close to the summit-level of the line between London and Plymouth the Holsworthy and Launceston (S.W.R.) branch strikes away on the right. After passing Sourton Church, close at hand on the same side, we leave Bridestowe (pronounced "Briddystow") village, 1½ miles away on the same side, and run to **Bridestowe Station**.

Bridestowe to Mary Tavy over Great Links Tor and Hare Tor, *abt. 9 m., 3½ to 4½ hrs. Route described the reverse way on p. 113.* Go left from the station and in half-a-mile, where the road joins the Okehampton and Tavistock main-road, turn up on to the moor between two houses, one of which is the *Fox and Hounds Inn*. The route to be followed, twice crosses a line of railway made for the conveyance of peat, and then, after dropping to a slight depression, rises steadily up the green hill-side to **Great Links Tor** (*p.* 115). Hence continue southwards along the wide ridge, boggy in places, which attains its highest point in **Hare Tor** (*p.* 114). From this point the descent commences. **Girt Tor** is crossed, and then a long slope leads down to cultivated ground again at the farm-buildings called **Lane End**. Hence to **Mary Tavy** (*p.* 114), where the train may be taken to **Tavistock**, either side of the river may be followed by roads (*see* map) described *p.* 114.

From Bridestowe the line continues along the slope of Dartmoor to Lidford. A depression in the moor about a mile short of the station reveals Sharp Tor and Hare Tor. Down this depression comes the Lid, forming a small cascade close to the line, on the other side of which are the village and castle. Between this and Lidford station which is a mile onward, a view is obtained of the upper part of the picturesque and richly-wooded ravine along which comes the G.W.R. from Launceston.

At **Lidford Station** (*Ref. Rms.*; Inns: *Manor Hotel*, Q., close to sta.; *Castle Inn*, in village, 1½ m. from sta.; *Dartmoor Inn*, 1 m., and *Lydford House*, Temperance, abt. ½ m. beyond village) we run on to the Launceston branch of the G.W.R. The history of Lidford goes back to Saxon times, when it was a borough of some importance and even had a mint but from the time of the Norman conquest it rapidly decayed. The parish includes the whole of Dartmoor Forest, the area being over 55,000 acres, but the population under 3,000. It is bordered by 23 other parishes.

The objects of interest here are the *Castle* and the *Cascade* and *Ravine* of the Lid. The **Castle** is conspicuous on a mound adjoining the churchyard. All that remains is the hollow shell of the *Keep*. The castle existed before the reign of Hen. III. Under Edw. III. it was made the Stannary prison and as such acquired an infamous reputation. Judge Jeffreys held a court here.

> I've ofttimes heard of Lydford law,
> How in the morn they hang and draw,
> And sit in judgment after.

The **Church**, Perpendicular, commands a wide view, and in the graveyard a curious tomb and epitaph to one " George Routleigh " should be noted.

The tourist who merely breaks his journey at Lidford should, if his time be short, omit church and castle, and visit the **Cascade** (*Fee* 2*d*) the shortest way to which is by a farm-road branching from the main road a few hundred yards from the station. The Fall, which in its upper part is a water-slide, has a total height of about 100 feet, and is picturesque both in itself and its surroundings. Some years ago an over-venturesome tourist missed his footing at the top of the slide and was precipitated into the pool below, whence he was rescued without serious injury, though stunned.

A longer but more satisfactory way to the Cascade is to continue on the main road to the village as far as the Lodge on the near side of Lidford Bridge. Here, on Mondays, the public are admitted to the path which threads the ravine above and below the bridge. The key is kept at the Lodge. *Fee optional.* Beneath the road-bridge a foot-bridge has been constructed, from which the defile—a mere rift in the rock—is seen to advantage. Turning up-stream, it is $\frac{1}{4}$ mile to *Kit's Steps*, where the Lid, when in flood, forms a series of fine cascades. Turning down-stream from the bridge, and passing in one place through a tunnel in the rock, we reach the foot of the Lidford Cascade (*see above*). This cascade is certainly the finest in the South of England, and, if seen in the gloaming, may fitly be termed the " Woman in White."

Lidford by Cranmere Pool to Chagford, *abt.* 18 m. 7-8 *hrs.* *fair walking.* This is a popular route across the moor from west to east or *vice versâ.* It is, however, one involving more fatigue than pleasure, and Cranmere Pool, whatever interest it may have, is extremely difficult to find, from the fact that it is a mere peat-hollow, only to be made out from a distance by those who know where to look and what for. We fancy it is missed oftener than found by the amateur explorers of its boggy environment.

Route. Follow the Okehampton Road to the *Dartmoor Inn* (2½ *m. from the station*). Then take a track which strikes nearly due East in the direction of *Great Links Tor*, which is seen a quarter of a mile or so to the left of an upright stone close to the path. Beyond this stone is a *hut*, which marks the end of the peat-railway from Bridestowe. Our course leaves this a little to the left also, and climbs the ridge of *Amicombe Hill*, which overlooks the valley of the West Okement, with Yes Tor across it, north-east. Avoid descending into this valley, and keep the ridge of Amicombe Hill until Newlake, its summit marked by a bit of wall,—is due East, 3 miles away. **Cranmere Pool** is a mile, as the crow flies, short of Newlake. Midway between the Amicombe ridge and the Pool is the tor called *Great Kneeset*—one of the most boggy hills on the moor though the bog, even in wet weather, is not dangerous. *For the rest of the route to Chagford see p.* 99.

Lidford to Yes Tor and Okehampton, 12 *m., abt.* 5 *hrs.* This is the same as the last described route as far as Amicombe Hill, in ascending which from the hut there mentioned, proceed north-east. *High Willhays* (pronounced "Willis"), the southern end of the Yes Tor mass, is across the Okement, and no direction is needed except to cross the stream as you may, and climb the hill. *For the descent to Okehampton see p.* 107.

Lidford to Tavistock by G. W. R. From Lidford Station the perfect cone of Brentor (*p.* 113) is seen on the right front. The line thence descends a narrow little valley, whose steep sides hide distant objects. Between Mary Tavy Station and Tavistock, on the right of the line, is *Kelly College*, a school for the sons of naval officers, the munificent foundation of Admiral Kelly, who left a very large sum for the purpose. The main valley of the Tavy is entered 2 miles short of **Tavistock**; *rail cont. p.* 126.

Lidford to Plymouth by L. & S. W. R. (not yet open, June, 1889; till it is, the trains use the G. W. R.). This line descends the valley under Black Down, left (parallel with the G. W. R.), to *Brentor*, 1½ *m.*

For the hill **Brentor** (1,100 ft.) cross the G.W.R. and follow road to (½ *m.*) the hamlet of North Brentor; turn to left and in about ¼ *m.* you will reach the high road at a point ¼ *m.* N.E. of the hill, *p.* 113.

After passing close to the G. W. R. Mary Tavy Sta., the line crosses to the W. side and follows that to **Tavistock** (6½ *m.*; station on the N. side of the town, ½ *m.* from G. W. Sta.; see *p.* 111). Beyond this it winds along the E. flank of Morwell Down and presently trends S.W. to *Beer Alston*, 12½ *m.* (where the station is a full ½ *m.* N.W. of the village). Then follows *Beer Ferris* (15 *m.*; ⅓ *m.* W. of the village). A mile onward the Tavy—⅓ *m.* broad—is crossed and then the Tamerton Foliot pill, ¼ *m.* broad. The E. bank of the Tamar is skirted to the Royal Albert Bridge (*p.* 141) and then the line runs inland to *St. Budeaux* (19 *m.*; 1 *m.* S. W. of the village but only ¾ *m.* from the Royal Albert Bridge by the shore road) another pill is then crossed with the road and G. W. R. viaduct, right. *Ford*, 21 *m.*, is convenient for Keyham (*p.* 138). The line then goes on to *Devonport* and (*North Road Station*) **Plymouth**, *p.* 133.

Tavistock.

Stations: *G.W.R.* east of the Tavy; *L. & S.W.R.* north of the town. They are ½ m. apart.

Hotels: *Bedford* ¼ m. from G.W.R.; *Queen's Head* (T.Q.) ½ m.; *Temperance*

Post: Open 7-8; Sun., 7-10. *Del. abt.* (*London, etc.*) 7 a.m., 7.15 p.m; (*North*), 12.40 p.m. *Desp.*: (*North*), 2.15 p.m.; (*London, etc.*), 8.30 a.m., 7 p.m. Tel. 8—8, Sun. 8-10.

Tavistock, in its more modern part, is a handsome town with several spacious thoroughfares. Its situation on the green well wooded banks of the Tavy, which rise more or less steeply on both sides, has facilitated the choice of conspicuous sites for its best buildings, and the appearance of the town as a whole is attractive.

Tavistock Abbey. The early history of the town is little more than that of the Benedictine Abbey, whose scanty remains, now almost lost to view amid the modern buildings which have been erected on its site and are to some extent adaptations of its different parts to modern uses, are by the river-side a short distance on the way from the G. W. R. station to the town. The *Bedford Hotel* occupies the site of the old chapter-house; a pinnacled porch is now a larder, and the refectory has been converted into a Unitarian chapel. In the churchyard, opposite the hotel, is a portion of the Early-English *Cloister Arcade*, popularly miscalled the *Tomb of Ordulf*, who completed the House, founded by his father, Earl Ordgar, in the middle of the 10th century. Of this building, however, no traces remain, as it was destroyed by the Danes in 997. *Betsy Grimbal's Tower* and other remains are in the Vicarage garden, and those interested in antiquities will there find: The *Nebarr Stone*, "Dobunnii Fabri fili Nabarr," with an Ogham inscription to the same effect on the edge; the *Sabine Stone*, "Sabini fili Maccodecheti," and the *Nepranus Stone*, "Neprani fili Condevi." Of these the first two were brought from Buckland Monachorum; the last was found doing duty as a "clam" or bridge, happily inscription downwards.

The **Parish Church**, opposite the Bedford Hotel, is a fine building, Perpendicular in style, with aisles extending to the full length of the nave and chancel and an additional south one of later date. The original building was dedicated by Bishop Stapledon, to whom a part of the choir of Exeter Cathedral is due, but none of it remains, except the Tower. The present fabric was restored in 1846. Among the several interesting *monuments* which it contains are an Elizabethan one to the eminent lawyer, Sir John Glanville, and those of the Bouchiers, Earls of Bath,

A *new church* occupying a conspicuous site on the Liskeard-road, west of the town, was built at the expense of the late Duke of Bedford. It is Romanesque in style.

The modern *Guildhall* was built to harmonize with the remains of the Abbey.

In a house at *Crowndale*, a mile from Tavistock and recently destroyed, Sir Francis Drake was born. His portrait, together with those of Pym and Lord William Russell, is to be seen in the New Hall, and his statue, by Boehm, at Fitzford, *p.* 124.

Dartmoor from Tavistock.

Tavistock is the chief head-quarters for the exploration of Dartmoor from its western side, though the completion of the railway to Princetown as a passenger line places several of the "lions" of the Moor which were formerly visited from Tavistock, within easier reach. *For that railway, see p.* 127.

We here give the excursions from Tavistock which include the chief objects of picturesque and historic interest within easy reach of the town, and also a short account of the routes across the Moor to Moreton Hampstead and Ashburton, already fully described the reverse way, *pp.* 80 and 101.

1. **To Brentor**, 4 *m.* and **Lidford** (*station*), 6½ *m*; (*village*) 7½ *m.* by road.

Remarks. The road to Lidford by Brentor goes considerably west of the railway route already described, Brentor being fully 2 miles N.W. of Mary Tavy Station in a bee-line. From either end it is quite unmistakable. Brentor is about 850 feet above Tavistock, and about 450 feet above Lidford. Its singular shape makes it a conspicuous object from all view-points for many miles round, especially from the north and west. It is about 1,100 feet above sea-level, but owing to the considerable elevation of the surrounding districts, its height, even on its eastern and steepest side, is not fully appreciated.

Route. Perhaps the best way (but see *p.* 110) of making the excursion is to take train to Lidford and walk back, and as the reverse route will be fully understood from our description of it this way, we shall suppose the tourist landed on *Lidford* (G.W.R.) platform. *For* **Lidford** *see p.* 108.

Hence the better part of a mile may be saved by following the railway a few yards towards Tavistock and then making for a footpath, which may be seen crossing a field a little above on the west side of the line. This leads through a farm and out into the main road about 1½ miles short of Brentor. At the cross-roads, a few yards on the Lidford side of the hill, is a roadside inn, the *Herrings Arms*. The way up the hill is on its northern side, the west side next the road being a considerable bluff of sheer rock.

Brentor is an almost perfect cone of volcanic rock. On the apex is a small weather-beaten *church*, dedicated to St. Michael, about 37½ ft. by 14¾ ft., with a low Early English western tower on the verge of the cliff. *The key is kept at the Stag's Head Inn.*

The view from the little churchyard is alone worth the walk, commanding, as it does, a great part of the western side of Dartmoor, and including an endless number of its tors, most prominent amongst which are Great and Little Links Tor, north-east; Hare Tor, and Fur Tor—the latter almost rectangular in shape—due east; and Great Mis Tor, with its ragged crest, south-east. The prospect, however, is one which can only be termed beautiful under a bright sky, as even the valley of Mary Tavy lacks that softness which is needed as a foil to set off the sterner features of the scene. To the south of Hare Tor is seen the combe of Tavy Cleave, and nearer, in the same direction, are many evidences of copper-mining. Eastward the view extends over the somewhat commonplace district watered by the river Lid and its tributary, the Lew water, to the far-off heights of Brown Willy and Rowtor. Launceston Castle is visible in this direction.

Returning to the main road we follow a course almost due south to Tavistock, the prospect on either hand losing its wildness during the descent to that town. From about half-way the view southward is delightful and truly Devonian.

Brentor to Mary Tavy Station, *nearly* 3 *m*. Follow the Tavistock-road, and take the second turn to the left. The by-road entered skirts for some distance a plantation, and then a guide-post "To Mary Tavy Station" gives the necessary direction. To **Brentor Station**, *see p*. 110.

(2) **Tavistock to Bridestowe** by **Mary Tavy, Hare Tor, &c.**

Mary Tavy (rail), 3 *m*; *Hare Tor* (foot), 8½ *m*; *Great Links Tor*, 11 *m*; *Bridestowe Station*, 13 *m*.

No pleasanter walk over the western side of Dartmoor can be taken than this. Allow three or four hours at least between Mary Tavy and Bridestowe (*pron*. Briddystow). Tourists with leisure may well make it a short day's ramble. The best variation is from Great Links Tor over High Willhays and Yes Tor to Okehampton, for which an additional two hours will be required. From Mary Tavy Station ascend the road on the east (*down*) side. Turn in at a gate on the right, a short distance up the hill, and cut off an angle by following a field-path. In the backward view Brentor rises in a true cone north-west, and in the opposite direction are great Mis Tor and Staple Tor, the latter crowned by rocks that may be compared to Titanic gate-posts. When after regaining the road the *Buller's Arms* public-house is reached, turn down to the left to **Mary Tavy** village. At the bottom of the hill a choice of routes is presented, (*a*) turn to the left and then shortly to the right, and so above the Tavy Valley on its western side, or (*b*), turn to the right, and, passing the church, descend to the bridge and cross the river. Then bear upward slightly to the left, and you will soon enter a road that keeps well above and parallel to the stream for about 1½ m., when it drops to *Hill Bridge*. Turning to the right at Hill Bridge and ascending the hill, the route (*a*) is joined in ¾ mile. Thence it is about half-a-mile to *Lane End*, where the open moor is reached; (*a*) is the shorter by a full mile, but (*b*) enables us to see *Mary Tavy Church* and *Cross*, both of which are good of their kind. The **cross**, which has an octagonal shaft, rises from a base of massive steps, the uppermost of which has the carving still fresh on its east side. A fine sycamore adorns the *graveyard*, against whose southern boundary will be found a row of antique gravestones, of which the earliest is "A. C. 90," that is 1690. Beyond the sycamore is a massive granite altar-tomb with a curious inscription "Heare: is: in: memorandum: of, &c., &c.," and against the south wall of the church (in the ditch) is a tablet to one Hawkins, a gentleman wrestler, whose family evidently resented his joining in the rough sport that proved fatal to him. Entering the porch note the good roof, a niche over the church door, and the stocks, a new set provided some 40 years ago "to frighten the troublesome boys." The **Church** is late Perpendicular, but contains older portions. It has been well restored. A good piscina is in the south aisle, and close to the door is a holy-water stoup. The rood-loft is gone, but the turret, containing the stairs leading to it, abuts on the north side.

Peter Tavy is seen across the stream on the opposite hillside. It can be visited by keeping on up the hill from the bridge, but this will further lengthen the route, (*b*) by over ½ mile.

We resume our description at *Lane End* mentioned above. One of the principal objects on our route, *Hare Tor*, has been visible for some time. It is the highest and most comely peak in a line of tors extending northwards. From Lane End the ascent, long and gradual, of **Great** (locally '**Girt**') **Tor** commences. On the right is **Tavy Cleave**, a narrow ravine through which the waters of the Tavy issue from the Moor; across it is Stannon Hill with a group of hut-circles. The rectangular *Fur Tor* is prominent in that direction, but is gradually overtopped by a lofty undulation of the Moor, on which an Ordnance cairn marks the position of Cut Hill.

From Girt Tor there is a fine prospect westward extending to the Cornish heights of Brown Willy and Rowtor. The whaleback Kit Hill with its crowning mine-stack is, as usual, the chief landmark. As we proceed to Hare Tor, the view improves. Lidford, at the commencement of the richly-wooded valley which is traversed by the railway to Launceston, is seen far down westwards, and beyond it Launceston Castle. **Hare Tor** has much more comeliness of shape than most of the Dartmoor heights, but it has no striking rock-outlines. From it our route, continuing northwards, crosses some boggy ground and leaves *Sharp Tor* and one or two other rocky excrescences some distance on the left—more so, in fact, than they are shown in the Ordnance Survey. The next prominent height which it crosses is Great Links Tor, a little short of which a rough track leading up from Lidford is crossed close to an upright stone, which seems to have served the purpose of a guide-post.

Great Links Tor is a huge boss of granite, and thoroughly Dartmoor in character. Below and eastward of it one is surprised to see a line of railway winding up almost to the highest part of the Moor. This was constructed by a Peat Company some years ago, but the capital was sunk and the scheme went into liquidation. At the terminus there is a solitary building for the accommodation of the workmen. [By diverging to this and crossing the long, level ridge called Amicombe Hill in a direction northeast (the map and compass are the best guides), the almost isolated mass, as seen from this point, of *High Willhays* is across the deep combe of the West Okement. *Yes Tor* is the northern end of this mass. *For the descent to Okehampton see p.* 107.]

A little to the left of Great Links Tor is **Little Links Tor**, a height of similar character, which may be taken on the route or not. A smooth descent follows to a small valley, beyond which, by climbing for a few hundred yards and crossing the railway, we may descend to the Okehampton and Tavistock road, which is entered by a little lane between two houses, one of which is the *Fox and Hounds Inn.* Bridestowe Station (*p*. 108) is half-a-mile further and 1¼ miles short of the village of the same name.

(3) **Tavistock to Princetown**, 8 *m*. By slight divergences to the north and south of this route the tourist may visit some of the most interesting tors and antiquities of Dartmoor. The first 6½ miles of it form the commencement of the carriage-roads across the moor to Moreton Hampstead and Ashburton already described the reverse way(*p.* 81), but of which we append to this description a summary.

The road crosses the Tavy and passes under the railway nearly half-a-mile north of the station.

Pedestrian Route to Merrivale Bridge, 4½m., preferable to high-road and equally short. Ascend direct from the station by a road which soon, bending to the left, becomes a wide path leading on to Whitchurch Down, a breezy greensward. Follow the telegraph-posts across it till you are several posts past an old *Cross* and a quarry. Then keep straight on to the east end of the Down (1¾ *m.*) where you will enter a lane which crosses a tiny brook and after passing two or three houses takes you to the open moor. Bear slightly to the left near a boundary wall and keeping the main path you will climb to another old *Cross*, whence it is ¾ *m.*—over a runnel into the main road near its highest point (1,075 ft.) between Tavistock and Merrivale, all but 4 *m.* from Tavistock.

The first mile is a stiff ascent, the next comparatively level; then, from cross-roads, the climbing begins again. A splendid retrospect reveals itself, including the conical Brent Tor, Kit Hill with its chimney stack, Saltash Bridge and Tavistock. We are now fairly among the tors. The first is *Cocks Tor* (1452 *ft.*) N. of the road, and beyond it the line of *Staple Tors.*

The most remarkable tor hereabouts is **Vixen Tor**, which rises a little below the level of the road ½ *m.* S. It has been likened to the Sphinx and can only be ascended by squeezing oneself up a narrow rift or rake in it. Its height is about 40 feet, and from either top or bottom there is a pretty peep into the wooded Walkham valley. On the top are 3 rock basins.

Staple Tor (1,482 ft.), with its gate-post-like rocks, commands a fine view. The loftiest of the rocks is said only to need the weight of a person on its summit to enable it to be slightly moved.

A slight descent now takes us to **Merrivale Bridge** (*Dartmoor Inn*), beyond which a long and steep ascent commences at once.

The **Merrivale Antiquities** (plan *p.* 93) all lie within half-a-mile of Merrivale Bridge. A footpath follows the course of the telegraph posts, and cuts off a circuit made by the road in ascending the hill. Follow the posts, which quit the road at a small quarry. The path at once enters the ground occupied by the *Stone Circles*, and beyond the third post passes through the *Pound*, a rude circle about 40 yards in diameter. In it, on the south side, two or three low stones support a circular flat stone, which is in reality merely a cider-press stone made to order some fifty years ago but not forwarded to its destination.

From the Pound go 150 yds. square to the right and you come to the *Avenues* near their east end. These consist of two parallel double rows of very low stones 35 yards apart, the lines which constitute each row being a yard apart. The north row is 196 yards long and the south 260. In the latter is a circle about 4 yards in diameter with a hollow in the centre, possibly a kistvaen. If from about 50 yards short of the W. end of the south row you go square to the left you will find in 130 yards a *Circle* of 10 low stones, 18 yds. in diameter, and 35 yards beyond them a *Longstone* 11 feet high. There is another *Longstone*, 6½ ft. high, 120 yds. from the east end of the south row.

Hereabouts is the point at which to strike out of the road for **Little** and **Great Mis Tor** (1761 *ft.*) a mile and a mile-and-a-half distant—the latter one of the most striking tors on the moor. The rocks are of great size and have a stratified appearance. On one of them is a rock-basin about 3 feet in diameter called *Mis Tor Pan*. From Great Mis Tor the view eastward is over the dreariest undulations of Dartmoor and westward into the smiling valleys which skirt them.

Our road now diverges to the right from the main Dartmoor road, and, skirting *North Hessary Tor*, passes the prison and enters **Princetown** (*Duchy Hotel*; *Post del.* 8.30 *a.m.*, *desp.* 5.25 *p.m.*), the highest place of any size in the kingdom, being 1,400 feet above sea-level. Fine air atones for a somewhat dreary situation. *For rail to* **Plymouth**, *see p.* 127; *Coach to* **Ashburton** *etc., p.* 81.

Of the prison—an uninviting subject to a holiday tourist—we shall only say here that it was built in 1809 for the accommodation of French prisoners of war, of whom at one time it held some thousands. Then, after years of uselessness, it became what it still is in 1850. The hotel is well spoken of.

Princetown to Ivybridge, over the Moor, 14 *m.*, 5 to 5½ *hrs.*
For reverse way see p. 121.

This is the best pedestrian route from the centre of the Moor to its southern edge. There are good inns at both ends. The highest part, lying between Nun's Cross and Erme Head, is trackless and hard to follow in consequence of the absence of all landmarks, and the boggy character of this part makes the journey anything but a pleasant one in bad weather.

The Route. Leave Princetown by a cart road, which forms a continuation of the main street leading from the church past the Duchy Hotel. This soon becomes a footpath skirting a wall and reaching, one mile from Princetown, a castle-like tor, called on the map **Tor Royal**, but locally known as *Look-out Tor*. Hence there is a fine view westwards over the Tavy and Tamar valleys to the Cornish Hills, while eastward the Moor stretches to its furthest limits in that direction, the prospect being down the Dart valley to Buckland Beacon and Rippon Tor.

Beyond Tor Royal the path, still hugging the wall, becomes very rough. Where the wall bends keep straight on, and you will soon cross a rough cart-track which descends a valley on the right, side-by-side with an artificial watercourse by which Devonport is supplied with pure water from Dartmoor. Half-a-mile further you come to a granite cross, called the **Nun's Cross**. This ancient relic is mentioned under the name of Siward's Cross in the "Dartmoor Perambulation" of 1240, and is supposed to have marked the boundary between the Forest and the Common belonging to Buckland Abbey. The supposition, that it was set up by the monks of Tavistock Abbey is supported by the fact that it lies in the track of the Abbot's Way, an old bridle path, which formed the direct route between the abbey and the Cistercian House at Buckfast—of which, we are told, there are still traces, though we have not ourselves come upon them. The Cross is 7½ feet high. It was thrown down in 1846 and broken but repaired and set up again in 1848. The inscription on one side is read (SI)WARD, that on the other is now said to be BOC LOND, but is really illegible.

A little beyond the Cross is a cottage (*milk*). Our route ascends the opposite hill, taking a direction rather east of south-east, so as to pass between the source of the Plym and the tributaries of the

Dart. Two large wheels and some adjacent cottages lying below on the left and across *Fox Tor Mire*—one of the worst bogs on Dartmoor—are called *White Works*.

When the summit of the ridge is reached, there is for some time no landmark at all, but the map will suffice. *Caters Beam*, a boggy watershed, has to be crossed. As Erme Head is approached, three heights appear to the southward crowned by small tors. The most westerly one, a long level ridge, is Staldon Down, and that on the left Three Barrows. Making straight for the latter you soon discern a depression in front. This is the upper Erme valley, along the left-hand side of which the route continues all the way to Ivybridge. **Erme Head** is to be known by a wilderness of stones, through which the diminutive stream makes its way. From it continue southwards, losing sight of the water for a while, until after crossing a small tributary you reach the spot marked *Redlake* (p. 121) on the map. A little beyond this and close to the river is *Erme Pound*, a large stone-wall enclosure (p. 121). Hence the track, marked on the map, is intermittently continued across another tributary, and then about half-a-mile above the stream until it passes between **Three Barrows** (p. 121) and *Sharp Tor*. Soon after passing the latter the tower of *Harford Church* may be detected rising above a small grove. The descent to this is easily made, and there a footpath leading past the rectory crosses a few fields and joins the carriage-road to **Ivybridge**, which is 2 miles beyond Harford. The *London Hotel* is at the entrance of the village, a little beyond the tall chimney of the paper mills.

Ivybridge.

Hotels: *London* (good and prettily situated, *King's Arms*, smaller but good.

Post: *Del., London, &c., about* 7.0; *North*, 11.30 *a.m.; desp., North*, 2.30; *London, &c.*, 7.45 *p.m.*

This village is charmingly situated in the richly wooded glen of the Erme, and of its kind there are few prettier spots in Devon. There are no "lions," and architecture is represented by an ivy-clad old church and a commonplace new one adjoining. A large paper-mill and an ornate nonconformist chapel are the only other buildings to be noted. It is for its river-glen and for the walks and drives,—southward in the South Hams district, and northward on the southern parts of Dartmoor,—that the village finds such favour with visitors, and the angler can get a good many small trout amid some of the sweetest bits of stream and woodland.

For **Cornwood, Hawns and Dendles**, etc., *see* p. 129; *for walk to* **Princetown** p. 121.

Ivybridge to Plymouth by the Coast.

Ivybridge to Ermington, 2½ m; *Holbeton*, 6 m; *Revelstoke*, 10 m; *Noss*, 12 m; *Yealm Ferry*, 12¾ m; *Wembury*, 14 m; *Turnchapel (Ferry)*, 19 m; *Plymouth (Barbican)*, 20 m.

A carriage may be taken as far as Noss. Village inns at Ermington, Holbeton and Noss. Route described the reverse way p. 130.

By far the most beautiful route for the first part of this round is by the private drive of the Fleet estate, which is entered half-a-mile beyond Ermington, and extends through the richly-wooded glen of the Erme to Mothecombe, whence a sharp ascent of a mile leads to the main route again, which is regained 1½ miles beyond Holbeton. The distance is very little increased by the *détour*, but whether the tourist may use the drive must be ascertained.

Another beautiful private drive has been constructed by way of Membland. It quits our main route about a mile short of Revelstoke, and winding round the slope of the cliff for a distance of 4½ miles descends to the Yealm Ferry. This *détour* adds 3 or 4 miles to the distance, but the commanding course followed by the drive as it passes above Stoke Point, and sweeps round Yealm Head, fully atones for the extra time and exertion. Whether this drive can be used must also be ascertained.

Several reasons combine to make Ivybridge the best starting point for this tour—the beauty of its situation, the convenience of its position on the railway, and its comfortable hotels.

From the Bridge itself, which is close to the *London*, the Plymouth road is followed past Tom's Hotel and the Post Office, beyond which the first or second turn to the left must be taken, and the Erme crossed just as it changes its character from a mountain stream to that of a quiet river. Half-a-mile further, where the road bends to the left, a lane, soon becoming a field-path, continues straight on, and rejoins the road in another half-mile at a farm called *Caton*. Hence, after recrossing the river, the road continues along its western side to **Ermington**. The spire of the church is as much twisted and out of the perpendicular as that of the famous one at Chesterfield, and one of the inns has adopted the well-known Land's End title of " First and Last." Half-a-mile beyond it, the *Fleet Drive* diverges on the left, and in another half-mile the high-road from Kingsbridge to Plymouth is joined. *Fleet House* is seen on the left, and at the Lodge of its western drive, a little over a mile along this high-road, we take a road diverging on that side, turning again to the left abruptly in a few hundred yards. The lane thus entered descends to the hamlet of *Ford* whence, by a smart rise and fall, it reaches **Holbeton** (principal inn, *George*). Here the cruciform Perpendicular church has been restored. The slim spire and tower are very graceful, and the village claims notice from its position in a pretty orchard-clad hollow. Rising again from Holbeton, the road continues over high ground which slopes on the left to the Erme estuary, whence, in 1½ miles, the road from Mothecombe and the Fleet Drive comes up. A little further, beyond some farm-buildings, on the same side, a pointed crag, called the *Anchorist Rock*, is noteworthy from its isolated position on a grassy slope. It is rather puzzling to get at, and not worth the loss of time.

In another mile or so, during which a wide view northwards to Dartmoor is obtained, is the new Membland drive, (*see small print p.* 119), left, and on the right the road to *Membland House*, the seat of Lord Revelstoke. Our road keeps to the high ground till, a mile further, it is crossed by the road from the old church of **Revelstoke**,—lying far below in a secluded grove close to the shore,—to Noss, which is really the chief part of the parish of Revelstoke, and contains the new church.

Most tourists will feel prompted to descend the little lane and examine more closely the strangely-placed old church, where the only sounds now heard are the wind in the sycamore-grove hard by, and the varying voices of the sea. The nave is in ruins, but the rest is roofed in, and is apparently late Decorated (but rude) in style. There are a south aisle, chancel, north transept and north-west towers, all more or less overgrown with ivy.

From the church it is worth the exertion to climb and continue along the cliff to *Stoke Point*, a rough headland rising from a bed of huge slabs of slate, and commanding a wider view eastwards than westwards. Striking inland from Stoke Point at right angles, and crossing a field or two, you will reach the farm-buildings of *Nattom* at the head of a narrow woody dell, down which a narrow lane leads to *Noss* (*see below*).

From Revelstoke by road, omitting Stoke Point, it is little over a mile to **Noss**, which, with the twin village of *Newton Ferrers*, occupies either side of a narrow creek opening on to the Yealm estuary. With the tide well up the appearance of the two nestling by the water-side between steep and pleasantly wooded banks is strikingly romantic, and the two churches, old and new, with their handsome towers contribute greatly to the effect. When the tide is out, however, and instead of water a bed of mud presents itself, the charm vanishes, especially under a hot sun, and one is scarcely surprised to read that the history of Noss contains stories of both plague and cholera. Even now the inhabitants cannot be congratulated on any extraordinary observance of sanitary principles.

The new *church*, built by Lord Revelstoke, stands high up on the slope of a monstrously steep hill which rises eastwards. The style is Perpendicular, and the material local stone, dressed with Dartmoor granite. Inside, the seats of carved oak, the altar triptych, the oak roof, and the carving of the side screens may be noted.

The **Ferry** over the Yealm is a little beyond the union of the Noss Creek with the main estuary. The chief feature of the latter is the deep clear water reflecting the green of the woods, which rise steeply from its edge. This is more noticeable as we climb the hill on the other side—at first by road, and then turning to the left by the side of a wall. As we proceed the view opens in front across the sea to the Mew Stone, Rame Head, with the Eddystone Light-house 10 miles out to sea beyond it, and the long level line of cliff, ending in Dodman Point, some 15 miles short of Falmouth.

This estuary of the Yealm, which we now lose sight of, is but little known, considering its proximity to Plymouth. Its features are not varied, but the narrow winding inlet with a tideway of green water, so tinted by the steep wooded slope above, and the one or two white cottages embowered in foliage on its very edge, give it a character unlike the other river-mouths along this coast.

Proceeding along the coast our track drops to the shore at the solitary time-worn little church of *Wembury*. Thence it proceeds along a little cliff running a few feet above the waves, which is continually crumbling, till it passes the *Mew Stone* and bends northward for Plymouth. From a lovely little green slope strewn with boulders and gorse the breakwater, Mount Edgcumbe, and the "three towns" come one-by-one into view, with the Cornish heights, localised as usual to the eye by the lofty tower on Kit Hill in the background. The purple tint of the rocky *débris* extending outwards to the *Shag Stone* may be noted, and then, still hugging the low coast-line except where an obvious short cut offers itself, we reach the little recess of *Bovisand Bay*. Hence we turn left and climb above *Staddon Point* and the *Bovisand Fort*, shortly afterwards entering a road which winds above the shore, and passing in front of the barracks and *Fort Stamford*, drops to the ferry at *Turnchapel*. Hence a steam-ferry crosses the Cat Water to the *Barbican* every half hour. From the Barbican it is nearly a mile to the G.W. station and quite that distance to the joint station at North Road.

Ivybridge to Princetown, (*pedestrian*) 14 m., 4½ to 5½ *hours*. *Described the reverse way, page* 117. This route, together with that from Princetown to Horrabridge Station, affords a sample of the several kinds of scenery that Dartmoor has to show. Leave Ivybridge by the road over the Ivy Bridge, to the right of the paper mill. In about 1½ m. soon after passing a new mansion, *Lukesland*, take a footpath in front, on the right of the road, over a stone stile at the entrance of a trifling bit of copse. This path leads past Tor Rock to *Harford Church*. *Crown Hill*, with its clump of trees, is now prominent westward. *Trentis Rock* is close at hand northwards, on the opposite side of the Erme, which comes down a comparatively straight and quite bare moorland valley. Take the footpath on the right past the north side of Harford graveyard. About 100 yards beyond a cottage, go through a gate on the right and keep a wall on the left hand. Where the wall ends, a faint track in the same general direction, well up above the stream, brings us to a tiny burn, just east of Trentis Rock. We cross this burn and scale the wall on the far side. *Sharp Tor* is the hill on the right front. Make for a gate in line with it, and then slant up the hill-side to the angle of walled enclosure, and thence climb to the top of the hill. Hence the view is a fairly wide one, but inferior to that from **Three Barrows** (1,522 *ft.*), which is the next summit, half-a-mile north, beyond a trifling depression. The tors immediately across the Erme Valley are Pen Beacon and Shell Tor (1,552 *ft.*), and southward over and beyond Harford is Pit Hill. Three Barrows is, as its name implies, marked by three heaps of stones, long since rifled of any buried relics they may once have entombed. The road marked on the map from this point to Erme Pound is an old cart-track that is only traceable in places. It runs to the right hand of a series of upright stones. Past a deserted wooden shanty, and gradually descending to the valley, it brings us to a low dry-wall enclosure, and then in another half mile **Erme Pound**, which is similar to but smaller than Grimspound (*p.* 80), and in a less ruinous condition. We now cross *Redlake* and another small valley, and then breast the hill, past a row of small stones—part of a line of stones which Mr. Page traced for 2 m. and more, from a circle on the W. of the Erme near Redlake—in a direction due north, to **Erme-head,** a mossy rock-strewed slope. When a large horizontal slab is passed, bear away gradually somewhat to the north-west, but avoid descending to Plym-head. From this point a detestable and long mile in a north-west direction, across a boggy watershed, called **Caters Beam,** brings us at length within view of the northern tors, whose broken outline is a welcome relief after the dull monotony that has been ahead thus far. Across the valley, due north, is *White Works,* and a couple of water-wheels mark the now deserted tin-streaming works. The depression is *Fox Tor Mire,*—with the exception of Rayborough on the southern flank of Cawsand Beacon, the only really impassable bog, after wet weather, on Dartmoor. Do not attempt to cross the valley direct, but still bear to the north-west, gradually descending towards the *Devonport Leat* and a cottage just beyond it. A glass of milk can be had before again climbing. **Nun's Cross** (*p.* 117) is just north of the cottage, and thence a rough track goes north to *Tor Royal* (or *Look-out Tor*), 1½ m. A wall on the right is followed during the latter part of this distance. From Tor Royal a good track on the east of the wall! ends to **Princetown** (*p.*116) whose churchtower is visible over the next ridge.

Tavistock or Princetown to Moreton Hampstead or Ashburton.

Tavistock to Two Bridges, 8 *m;* (*Postbridge,* 12 *m; Moreton Hampstead,* 21 *m.*); *Ashburton,* 20 *m.*

Princetown to Two Bridges, 2 *m;* (*Ashburton,* 14 *m*); *Postbridge,* 6 *m; Moreton Hampstead,* 15 *m.*

For Coach from Princetown to Ashburton see Yellow Sheet.

Routes described the reverse way; from Ashburton, p. 81, *from Moreton Hampstead, p.* 101.

The route from Tavistock to Two Bridges is identical with that to Princetown (*p.* 116) for the first 6½ miles, and the remaining mile-and-a-half, during which the road drops slightly to the upland hollow wherein lies the inn at Two Bridges, presents no object of special interest. At Two Bridges the road from Princetown, equally featureless, converges.

(1.) **To Moreton Hampstead.** Two of the wonders of the Moor are most easily reached by quitting the road at the first bend, about ¼ mile from Two Bridges. From the north side of the road rises **Crockern Tor,** by no means remarkable in itself, but historically famous as the meeting place of the Stannary (*stannum* = *tin*) Parliaments from 1305 to 1749. These parliaments were attended by delegates from the 4 Stannary towns, whose office it was to settle questions affecting the tin-mining industry of Devon. Half-a-mile north-west of this tor and on the east side of the West Dart, which we have just crossed at Two Bridges, is **Wistman's Wood,** popularly supposed to be a remnant of the old Dartmoor Forest, though it must be recollected that here, as elsewhere, the word forest probably meant nothing more than a large tract of waste and unenclosed ground. The wood consists of a weird group of stunted oaks, hoary with age, covered with moss and polypody, and embedded or growing on a hill-side thickly strewed with granite boulders. The name " Wistman " has been supposed to mean " wise men," *i.e.* the Druids, but " Wisht " is common in Devonshire for anything uncanny. The great block of granite on the top of Row Tor, at the head of the valley, is striking.

Between Two Bridges and Postbridge *Belliver Tor* is the only marked feature on the right, and on the left the barrenness of the Moor is relieved by the fir plantations included in the " new take" of Mr. Bennett, of Plymouth. For **Postbridge** (*Temperance Hotel*, a little beyond the Bridge) *see p.* 102.

Grey Wethers are 3 miles along the ridge due north and the other antiquities described on *pp.* 97, 98, may be taken on the way to Chagford.

Beyond Postbridge *Merripit Hill*, the highest point on the route, is ascended. During the corresponding descent Grimspound (*p.* 80) may be descried in a hollow due east, and north of the long level ridge of Hamildon Down. Pedestrians will most easily reach it by taking a track to the right at the Vitifer Mine, 2½ miles beyond Postbridge, but the carriage-road does not branch off for 2 miles further. The rest of the road is mostly on the descent, and commands extensive views to the north and east. At *Bector*, 3 miles short of Moreton Hampstead, the road to Chagford strikes away to the left.

For **Moreton Hampstead** *see p.* 91.

(2.) **Two Bridges to Ashburton**, 12 *m*. It is unnecessary to repeat our description of the points of interest along this route given on *pp.* 81, 82. *Dennabridge Pound* is passed in 3 miles; *Dartmeet Bridge*, with *Yar Tor* close at hand, in 5¼ ; the *Tavistock Inn* (a road-side house) 2¼ *m*. further. From the last-named a descent is made to *Holne Chase* (p. 76) which forms an irregular triangle with the Dart for its sides and the road for its base, and then after passing through ordinary country for 2 miles we enter **Ashburton** (*p.* 75).

Tavistock to Ivybridge by Cadover Bridge. 18 *m*.

Four miles of walking may be saved by taking the train to Horrabridge, and joining the main route at Walkhampton.

The first part of this walk or drive commands fine views from *Whitchurch Down*, extending over Tavistock in one direction and some of the most striking tors in the other. Then the road drops to the beautiful *Walkham valley* (*p.* 116) which it crosses to *Huckworthy Bridge*, ascending again at once to **Walkhampton** (*Inn*). Here the route from Horrabridge Station (*inn*), coming up above the south bank of the Walkham, joins the main road. Walkhampton *Church*, with its fine and pinnacled Perpendicular tower, is one of the most conspicuous objects for miles round.

Less than a mile beyond Walkhampton we cross the Princetown road and railway. There is an inn at the crossing. Then comes a descent, near the foot of which we have **Meavy** (*inn*), ¼ m. on the right, and **Sheepstor** 2 miles away on the left. This tor has a far more defined shape than the great majority of the Dartmoor hills. It is a fabled haunt of the Dartmoor Pixies, who found a congenial home in one of its cavities. The primitive little village of Sheepstor, containing about 100 inhabitants, lies beneath and on the western side of the tor. It has a Perpendicular *church* of granite, restored in 1862, and a *Priest's house* of the 15th century. In the churchyard is buried Rajah Brooke, who died at Burrator, in the parish, in 1868.

On the south side of *Meavy Bridge*, which our route crosses about half-a-mile from the village, and at the point where a by-road turns up the stream to Sheepstor, stands the **Merchant's Cross**, about 8 feet high, and with an incised cross on each face. It is the tallest ancient cross on the Moor. Beyond it, by attacking the hill-side at once, we may cut off an angle of the road, soon gaining open ground, by which, avoiding a turn to the left in about a mile, we descend slightly to **Cadover Bridge**. This crosses the Plym, and the road for some distance on either side of it is dreary. A **Cross**, long fallen, but replaced during the military manœuvres of 1873, stands about 18 inches above the ground in which its shaft is deeply embedded.

From the high ground beyond Cadover Bridge a fine view over Plymouth Sound opens to the south-west. In about 2 miles we pass a little to the left of the *Lee Moor Porcelain Clay Works*, and soon afterwards re-enter cultivation and descend through a wooded glade to **Cornwood** (*Inn, p.* 129). *Cornwood Station* is a long mile south of the inn, between the Slade and Blatchford Viaducts. For **Ivybridge** (*p.* 118), 3 miles, you keep straight on by a rather narrow lane, and crossing the Yealm and the South Devon railway, enter the village just below the station.

Tavistock to Gunnislake, 4 m. [Morwell Rocks]; Callington, 9½ m.; Liskeard, 18 m. 3 *hours by coach, which leaves the station abt.* 3.30 *p.m. on the arrival of the* 9 *a.m. train from London (Waterloo).*

The route is described more fully the reverse way, p. 111. For Tavistock, see p. 150.

The only good scenery on this journey is that of the Tamar valley, which is crossed at New Bridge, Gunnislake. A mile or so beyond Gunnislake, Calstock (*p.* 143) lies about 2 m. on the left of the main road, and is the only place on the road to Callington with good hotel accommodation.

The road turns to the right past the Tudor gateway of *Fitzford*, an ancient mansion of which it is the only relic remaining. The

TAVISTOCK TO LISKEARD.

view of the western tors of Dartmoor is good as we reach the higher ground, and the cone of Brentor, crowned with its storm-weathered church, is conspicuous on the right. When *Lumber Bridge* is reached the pedestrian may save ¾ m. by taking the old road (closed to vehicles) and going straight over the ridge to the Tamar at Gunnislake. The coach-road attains the same point by a series of zig-zags of easier gradient but sufficiently steep. From the top of this ridge a good westward view is obtained, including Kit Hill and, in order to the right of it, the Cheesewring, Shapitor and Kilmar Tor. The Upper Tamar valley and Gunnislake across it make rather a striking picture as, with the chimney shaft of Devon Great Consols mine away on the right, and immediately below us on that side a huge water-wheel, we drop rapidly by a wooded road to the Tamar at *New Bridge*—a bridge that the elevation of the western bank compels to be of arches of ascending magnitude.

From the junction of the old and new roads, just before we drop to Newbridge, a path goes off through the wood on the left to **Morwell Rocks**. These crags and pinnacles of limestone command a lovely view of the Tamar valley. They are themselves well seen after passing Gunnislake.

Gunnislake (Inns: *Cornish, Harvey's*), up the steep street of which the road runs, is quite without interest, and is a comparatively modern village. There are large granite quarries and brick works, and until recent years the rich copper mines of Devon Great Consols made it a busy place. Now those mines are far less productive and owe their chief profit to arsenic. As we wind sharply to the right around the eastern spurs of *Hingston Down*, a delightful view of Morwell Rocks, on the Devon side of the Tamar, is obtained, and Calstock church close to the stream on the near side is seen beyond. *For Calstock, an excellent centre for exploring much good scenery, see p. 143.*

Then, passing through the straggling street of St. Ann's Chapel (*Inns*), the road keeps high up along the southern slope of Hingston Down and commands the whole district extending to the English Channel. The lake-like reaches of the Tamar, Devonport, Mount Edgcumbe, Tregantle Fort, and, far out at sea, the Eddystone Light-house, are the main points. Just before reaching Kit Hill (1,097 *ft.*) we bear to the south-west and so enter **Callington** (*see p.* 151).

About ½ m. south from the cross-roads at the foot of Kit Hill, and a mile east from Callington is **Dupath Well**, with an ancient baptistery of granite. The stream flows through the building. A restored specimen of a similar baptistery is to be seen at St. Cleer, *p.* 149.

From Callington a sharp descent by the ornamental grounds of *Pencrebar* leads to the picturesque valley of the Lynher river at a second *New Bridge* where is a roadside *inn*. As we ascend the opposite side of the valley a nearer view of Cheesewring and Shapitor is obtained on the right, and then at 14 *m.* we reach **St. Ive** (*p.* 150) whence a descent, a mile long, with the lofty church-

tower of St. Cleer on the hill to the west and Carradon Hill on
the right across the valley, brings us to another stream. We are
now 3 *m.* from Liskeard but have yet another combe to cross before we arrive at our destination.
For **Liskeard**, *see p.* 148.

Tavistock to Plymouth by G.W.R.

Tavistock to Horrabridge, 4 *m ; Yelverton Junc.,* 5½ *m. Bickleigh,*
8½ *m ; Marsh Mills,* 12½ *m ; Plymouth (North Road),* 16 *m ;
(—Devonport,* 17 *m.) ; Plymouth (Mill Bay),* 16½ *m.*

This route is at present (1889) served by a double set of trains. The Great
Western, which starts from Launceston and runs to Mill Bay, the terminus of
that company; and the South-Western, which runs to Devonport. The divergence of the two is at North Road. The independent line of the latter company
(see p.. 110) is approaching completion. For *G.W.R. from Lidford, see p.* 110.

This route is perhaps the most beautiful round Dartmoor. The
line, a single one, is carried high up above the valleys of the Tavy
and the Plym, and affords extensive views of the western tors of
Dartmoor, and of the valleys which pierce that wild upland region.
   Quitting Tavistock we have the Tavy valley on the right, and
on the left the commencement of the rise for Dartmoor. On this
side the pretty village of *Whitchurch* crowns a low hill. A tunnel
succeeds, beyond which, as we cross the Walkham by a lofty viaduct,
we look down upon the junction of that stream with the Tavy on
the right-hand—a scene of silvan luxuriance, not improved by
the proximity of the *Virtuous Lady Lead Mine*—and on the left
the western slopes of Dartmoor burst suddenly upon the view.
They are especially well seen from **Horrabridge Station** (Inn :
Roborough Arms) whence, looking up the lovely Walkham valley,
we see Staple Tor, with its two rocks resembling a huge pair of
gate-posts, Mis Tor and Vixen Tor. The church of Walkhampton
with its lofty pinnacled tower is most conspicuous on the hill-side.
Beyond it the course of the Princetown railway, a series of serpentine curves, may be easily traced, especially if a train happen to be
climbing it. This railway joins our route as soon as we emerge
from the next tunnel at Yelverton Junction. Then Sheeps Tor,
with the towers of Meavy and Sheepstor beneath it, presents to
the eye a really mountain outline. The Meavy stream is below
us on the same side, and on emerging from a third tunnel we look
down on its junction with the Plym, which comes foaming through
a deep rock-strewed ravine from Cadover Bridge. *Shaugh Bridge,*
close to which the waters meet, is a most romantic spot, but the
bridge itself is hidden amidst a tangled wood of native growth,
From the angle formed by the two rivers rises the **Dewerstone**,
a huge block of granite festooned with ivy and crowning a steep
green slope rich in the vegetation of rowan, oak, broom, and wild
flowers. The rock itself has suffered a good deal from quarrying
operations, which have probably driven away the weird procession
of hunters, horses, and "swish" hounds which were formerly

wont to break upon the solemn stillness of midnight on this romantic hill. The way to it may be easily made out from the platform of **Bickleigh** *Station* (no inn). The course of the Plym between Cadover Bridge, to which point it flows over a dreary waste of moorland, and **Shaugh Bridge** is wild and beautiful. On its southern side rises steeply and thickly strewed with granite boulders *Shaugh Hill*, near the top of which stands **Shaugh Prior** (*small inn*), easily recognised by the Perpendicular tower of its weather-beaten little church.

At Bickleigh Station the narrow V-shaped *Bickleigh Vale*, a favourite pleasure haunt of the Plymouth folk, begins (*see p.* 128). The whole length of the vale is well seen from the railway, which is carried high above it, first on its right, and then on its left-hand side. The steep slopes are densely covered with coppice.

A few yards beyond the next station, **Marsh Mills**, our route joins the Great-Western main line, and for the remaining 5 miles is the same as that at the foot of this page.

Plymouth to Princetown by the Dartmoor Railway.

Plymouth to Marsh Mills, 4 m; *Bickleigh*, 8 m; *Yelverton Junction*, 10¾ m; *Dousland*, 12¼ m; *Princetown*, 21 m.

The opening of the Dartmoor railway has brought a great deal of the most interesting part of the Moor within 1½ hours' reach of Plymouth, and placed visitors in a position to commence their researches almost at its summit-level. The station at Princetown is 1,500 feet above sea-level, and the distance by road to it from Plymouth is 15 miles. A glance at the map will show how the difficulties attendant on this severe ascent have been overcome in the construction of the railway. By a succession of wide and almost constant S curves, which increase the distance between the junction with the main branch and Princetown from 6 to 10½ miles, the line winds upward to its terminus. The average gradient during this portion of the journey is about 1 in 65. Seen from below, the trains, gliding easily along the hill-side, hundreds of feet above the spectator, present a puzzle as to how they got there, which can only be solved by carefully tracking the course of the line all the way up. Over the Alpine passes, of course, the curves, or rather zigzags, are in places much more astonishing, but there is, we think, no instance in Great Britain of a passenger line reaching so great a height in so short a distance. Princetown is the highest collection of houses of any importance in the kingdom. From a tourist point of view the additional 4 miles add greatly to the interest of the journey, inasmuch as at one time or other during it he is going in every direction of the compass, and the views thus obtained are as beautiful as they are varied.

The Route. Quitting Plymouth at either of its stations we soon reach the *Laira estuary*, across which the woods of *Saltram* rise from the water's edge. *Laira Bridge* is seen some distance down the tideway. A portion of the earthwork defences of Plymouth appear on the left as the line quits the Great-Western main route, and enters Marsh Mills Station.

From Marsh Mills Station, a favourite walk, open to the public Mon., Wed., and Sat., threads the **Bickleigh Vale**. From this end it is entered by the old Dartmoor Tramway, which follows the course of the stream upwards. Beyond the pleasure of tracing a narrow, pleasantly-wooded valley, considerably spoilt by a railway, there is nothing to specially recommend this walk. The entire distance from Marsh Mills Station to Bickleigh Station is 4½ miles.

Beyond Marsh Mills the line, ascending rapidly, commands a full view into the once sequestered **Vale of Bickleigh**, a V-shaped depression, almost hidden by foliage more abundant than varied. This part of the valley ends at *Bickleigh Station*, beyond which are the Dewerstone, and the meeting of the Plym and the Meavy—scenes of great beauty, spoilt by a mine-chimney, already described on *pages 126-7*. After passing through a tunnel, Dartmoor opens out on the right, its nearest and most prominent height being **Sheepstor**, which rises behind the churches of Meavy and Sheepstor villages. Still ascending, we reach, a little short of the next tunnel, the diverging point of the moor line— **Yelverton Junction.** *Rock Hotel; passengers for Princetown change carriages.*

For the first mile or more the Princetown line runs parallel with the main road and the Devonport and Plymouth Leat. Then passing **Dousland** (*Manor Hotel*, rebuilt; also Private Hotel), a favourite resort with Plymouth folk in search of bracing air and pretty scenery, it sweeps round to the right, and makes the circuit of *Yannaton Down*, passing above the villages of Meavy and Sheepstor on the right, and affording a capital view of Sheepstor itself. After this horse-shoe bend we pass under the main road at a point little more than half-a-mile from where we left it, and as we ascend, the rich valley on the left becomes more and more clearly mapped out beneath us, revealing a scene of varied and rich beauty, which has few, if any, rivals in Devonshire. The lofty pinnacled tower, close below, is that of Walkhampton Church, and beyond it, across the lovely Walkham Glen, a line of tors extends northwards. The most noteworthy of them are Vixen Tor, a little above the Walkham stream and somewhat lower than the rest, and the Staple Tors beyond Merrivale Bridge. To the left of the latter the curious church-topped cone of Brentor is seen, and to the left of that, still further away, Launceston Castle. The sky-line is formed by the Cornish heights, chief of which are Brown Willy and Rowtor, and, nearer at hand, the hump of Kit Hill is made the most unmistakable object in the view by its mine-stack. On the right hand a succession of tors rises on the sky-line, the names of which will be best seen on the map. The sharpest winding on the route is made round King Tor, and the Merrivale longstone (*p.* 116) is easily seen below on the left. *North Hessary Tor* is the highest point on the left, and after passing it we at once enter Princetown Station. For *Princetown, see p.* 116.

Plymouth to Ivybridge (11 *m.*), &c.

The excursion to Ivybridge is a favourite one, and may be made to include much that is pleasant to see. The route is the same as that described on page 45, as far as the junction of the Launceston Branch, a mile beyond which is **Plympton Station** (Inns: *The George, abt.* ½ *m. from station, &c.*) The twin villages of *Plympton. St Mary* and *Plympton Earl* are bright, prosperous looking places, with *churches* of more than ordinary interest. That of Plympton St. Mary, seen close to the station, was restored in 1860, and its appearance is enhanced by the sward and evergreens of its churchyard. The *Tower* is Perpendicular and handsome. The other details are partly of that style and partly Decorated. The chief *monuments* are those of the Strode family, one of whom was one of the "five members" whom Charles I. attempted to seize in the House of Parliament. They are of the 15th and 17th centuries. Behind the church are the scanty remains of the *Priory of St. Peter and St. Paul* founded by Bishop Warelwast, nephew of the Conqueror, who built the Norman part of Exeter Cathedral. They consist of the Early English *Refectory*, and the Norman *Cellar* beneath it, the doorway of the latter being noteworthy.

Till 1832 *Plympton Earl* returned two members to Parliament. There are some fragmentary remains of the keep of a Norman castle which served as head-quarters for Prince Maurice in 1648. The surrounding earthworks are probably of older date. The other noteworthy buildings are the *Guildhall* bearing date 1696, and the *Grammar School,* built 30 years earlier. The latter has a piazza and adjoins the church and castle. In it Sir Joshua Reynolds was educated, his father having been master of the school. The house in which the great painter was born has been destroyed.

Beyond Plympton the railway ascends steeply passing a tree-crested height called *Hemerdon Ball.*

Cornwood Station (8 *m.*) stands between the *Slade* and *Blachford Viaducts,* from both of which lovely views present themselves both ways.

Cornwood village (*fair Inn*) is a long mile north of the station. To reach it, after entering the road, take the second turn to the right passing the church.

Cornwood Church. A picturesque lich-gate is placed over the steps at the main entrance to the graveyard of this well cared for and interesting church. The tower, perhaps Early English, is the oldest part. The body of the building consists of a nave with aisles, the latter of nearly equal height with it, and having each a transeptal projection of one bay. The plinths, buttresses and piers of the N. aisle are much more elaborate than those of the S. aisle, as though funds had failed to carry out the design. The chancel originally included one bay of the nave and this part has now an elaborate wooden roof. The windows reproduce the original tracery. Around the *sacrarium* is a (modern) low arcade of Derbyshire alabaster with dwarf shafts of Devonshire marble and serpentine, and enriched with slabs of Roman marbles. The massive altar-rails are of alabaster and marble and the handsome altar is of wood. Notice the rude Early Decorated, sedilia which show the age of this part of the chancel. To Lord Blackford (Sir Fred. Rogers) is chiefly due the renovation of this once disfigured church.

Hawns and Dendles. Conveniently visited from Ivybridge, whence the circular drive by Harford Bridge and Cornwood is about 9 miles, plus 2 miles' walking. This is the name given to a lovely bit on the Yealm, in which the stream descends a charmingly wooded dingle. Carriages can be taken as far the farm called *Combe* (*see map*), whence, breasting a small hill by a lane we emerge into a field and at once take a path that diverges to the left. Then keeping well up we come in about 10 minutes to a little *Waters' Meet*, above which on the right is a pretty fall. Then crossing the smaller stream and, just afterwards the main stream by a bridge, we ascend steeply to the highest bridge, near which there are other pretty falls. It is best to return the same way.

Ivybridge (11 *m*.) *see p*. 118. The station is high up above the village.

Plymouth to Ivybridge by the Coast, *about* 20 *m., a good day's walk.*

Route given the reverse way p. 119.

In summer there are occasional excursion steamers to Yealm Mouth, and the short trip is exceedingly pleasant, but the views of Plymouth Sound obtained from the high ground on its eastern side are so much finer than any to be had from the water that travellers who are free to choose are recommended to prefer the coast-walk. By sea to Yealm Mouth and back on foot by the cliff is a most delightful excursion from Plymouth. We leave Plymouth by the *steam ferry* that starts from the Barbican and crosses the mouth of the Catwater to *Turnchapel*. The road thence ascends to *Fort Stamford* and passes in front of the barracks, affording a fine view of Plymouth from Laira Bridge on the east round to Mount Edgcumbe to the west. Still ascending we reach *Fort Staddon* and obtain a yet better view, especially of the Hamoaze with Drake's Island in the foreground. Near the top of the hill a footpath on the right, which we take, winds along the slope and leads down to *Staddon Point*, where are a small pier and a large Coast-guard station, past which the track descends to the shore and has *Borisand House* on the left hand. Whitened stones on the green sea-slope now for a while mark the Coast-guard path, and when they come to an end no further direction is needed than to say keep close to the cliff. If the tide is out the rich purple of the rocks along the shore is noticeable. The off-lying rock is the *Shagstone*, abreast of which it is worth while to ascend the slope so as to come suddenly upon the view eastward, the prominent feature in which is the *Mewstone*. Westward across the Sound over Mount Edgcumbe rises the tower of Maker Church, while in a seaward direction juts out Penlee Point, and beyond it Rame Head crowned by its little chapel. A cart-track now leads down to a burn, on the far side of which more whitened stones mark the route, that, as it skirts the low cliff bounding Yealm Bay, is for a while somewhat tame. *Wembury Church* is seen ahead. Just before ascending to it we pass a tumble-down mill. The church is a mile or more from the village, which is up the valley. It is mainly Early Perpendicular and has a somewhat woe-begone appearance. What it contains we do not know, as the key is far to seek, but the tracery of the east-windows is good. A stiffish climb brings us in sight of **Yealm Mouth**, a most picturesque inlet, guarded on its east-side by an abrupt wooded headland. The ferry to Noss is some little distance within the Mouth, and to strike the road leading down to it, it is necessary to ascend the sea-slope a little, so as to avoid trespassing on a fringe of cultivation. First *Noss Church* and then *Newton Ferrers Church* appear up-stream above the trees with which the winding banks are clothed. The view back down the coast from the top of the road leading to the ferry is exceedingly beautiful, almost framed, as it is, by the mouth of the river. The Mewstone is still a fine object, and to the left of it juts out the Dodman, and in the dim distance part of the Lizard peninsula.

The steamers from Plymouth usually end their voyage at the ferry but occasionally, when the spring-tides serve, they ascend the river nearly 3 *m.* further to Puslinch.

The new coast road from Noss round by Revelstoke Church, and so to the high road for Holbeton, is seen winding up the hill across the river. It is the private property of Lord Revelstoke, of Membland, and can therefore only be used by his permission.

After crossing the ferry the road to Noss follows the side of the river, across which is seen the village of **Newton Ferrers** (Inn: *Dolphin*). For **Noss** (Inn: *Swan*, a mere public-house), *see p.* 120. Proceeding up the valley, soon we take a pretty lane on the right-hand, and when this divides at *Middlecomb** farm take the right-hand lane. This by *Natton* farm leads out to the cliffs.

Stoke Point is formed of huge slabs of slate, and is the western limit of Bigbury Bay, which is bounded eastward by Bolt Tail. The view of the bay is softly beautiful. The cliffs vary much in height, and on either side of Erme Mouth are lofty. Avon Mouth is indicated by the off-lying Borough island. The little village of Hope is seen just inside the foreshortened promontory of Bolt Tail, and the bold cliff of Bolt Head bounds the view eastward. The church-tower on the sky-line midway between Borough Island and Bolt Head is Marlborough. Beyond

---

* From Middlecomb Farm the left-hand lane leads to Revelstoke Church (*p.* 132) abt. 1½ *m.*

the next small bay and headland we come in sight of *Revelstoke Church* nestling among trees close to the sea at the mouth of a small combe guarded eastward by a fine cliff.

Revelstoke Church is architecturally of little account. The south aisle, north transept, north-west tower, and chancel are still roofed in, but the nave is in ruins. As far as so rude a structure can be so described the style is late Decorated. The charm of the spot is the bright little green sward and the sheltering trees. If the traveller has ascertained at Noss that he may use Lord Revelstoke's new road, then he should follow it to the main road. Otherwise he must turn up the combe from the church. *For the route onward to Ivybridge, see pp.* **119-121**, *where it is described the reverse way.*

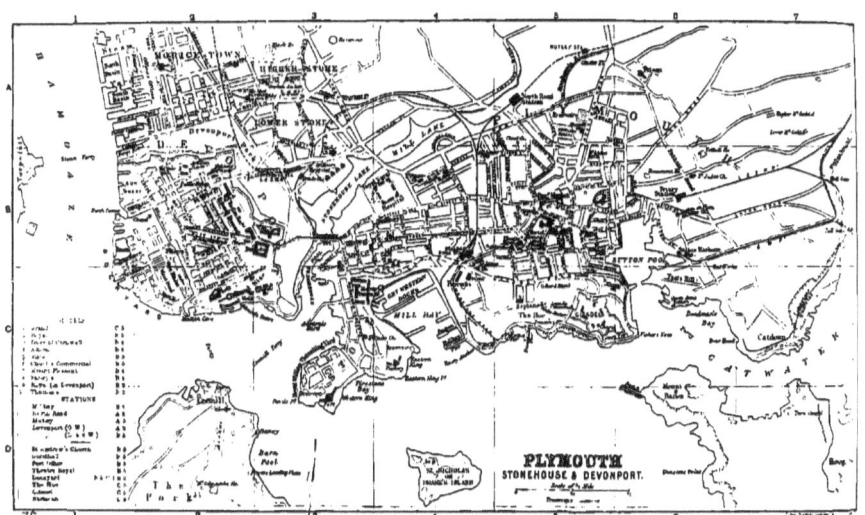

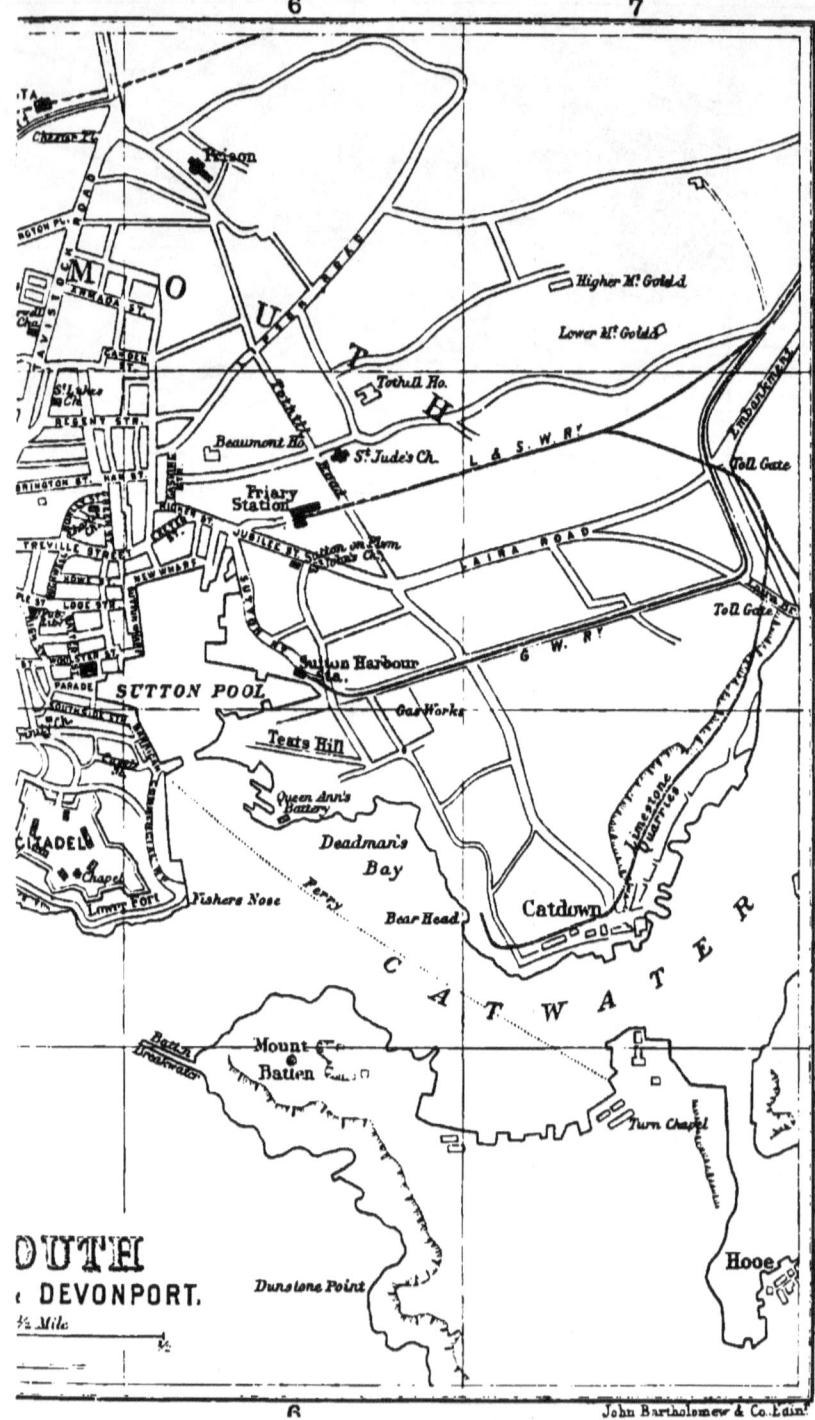

Plymouth—Stonehouse—Devonport.

Principal Hotels (in Plymouth): *Grand* on the Hoe; *Royal, Albion*, in Millbay Road; *Globe*, in George Street; *Farley's* (H.Q.) in Union Street; *Duke of Cornwall, Mount Pleasant*, opposite Millbay station, *Chubb's* in Old Town Street; *Sleeman's Coffee Tavern* (bds), Old Town St.; (in Devonport)—*Royal* (H.Q.), *Thomas'*, in Fore Street.

Railway Stations: *Millbay*, G.W.R., near the Docks and the Hoe; *North Road*, G.W.R., and L. & S. W. R. jointly, in the northern suburb, a full mile from the Hoe; *Devonport*, G.W.R., in Lower Stoke; *Devonport*. L. & S.W.R., near Military Hospital.

Ferries: *Barbican (Sutton Pool)* across Catwater to Turnchapel and Oreston; *Admiral's Hard (Stonehouse)* to *Cremill (Mount Edgcumbe)*; *Mutton Cove (Devonport)* to *Cremill*; *Ferry Road (Devonport)*, across Hamoaze to Torpoint.

Post: *Head Office* opposite Guildhall. Open 7-9, Sun. 7-10 a.m. Principal Deliveries, abt., 7 a.m. (*London*); 11.40 (*North*). Despatches, 1.45 p.m. (*North*; 12.10 p.m. Sundays); 7.30 p.m. (*London*).

Telegraph Office always open.

Tramcars *run from the east-end of Union Street, Plymouth, to Fore Street, Devonport.*

Population *of the three towns (exclusive of Army and Navy),* abt. 140,000.

With regard to the hotel accommodation of Plymouth we may remark that the *Grand* is finely situated on the Hoe; the *Duke of Cornwall, Albion* and *Mount Pleasant* are close to the G.W.R. terminus (the *Mount Pleasant* on a somewhat smaller scale than the others, reasonable); the *Royal* is a well-known family hotel, while the *Globe, Chubb's*, and *Farley's* are all good family and commercial houses.

Plymouth, Stonehouse, and Devonport form really one town. The two first are conterminous along Phœnix Street and Manor Street to Mill Bridge, and the last-named is only divided from them by Stonehouse Pool and Lake, the names given to the lower and upper parts respectively of the inlet crossed by Stonehouse Bridge.

Outline of the History of the Three Towns. A few years ago, in digging the foundation for Fort Stamford across the Catwater above Turnchapel, a British cemetery was discovered. From the articles found (see below under *Athenæum*) it has been inferred that there was a considerable settlement thereabouts during the Roman occupation of the island. The site of Plymouth itself does not seem to have been occupied at this early period, but at the time of the Domesday survey Sutton Prior and King's Sutton were two fishing villages near by Sutton Pool, the present Harbour. During the next 300 years the many-branched Sound

and its sailors came to hold an important place in our naval
annals, and in 1439 Plymouth was the name given to the town on
its incorporation. Thence onward the story of its rise is chiefly
remembered on account of the great captains, who, sailing from
its creeks, established the supremacy of England alike in naval
prowess and maritime adventure. Hawkins and Drake are house-
hold words in this connection, and Humphrey Gilbert, Thomas
Cavendish, and Howard of Effingham, all at one time or another
added lustre to its name. It was naturally made the rendezvous
when the Armada was expected, and it is said that the first news
of that ill-starred expedition was brought to Drake whilst playing
bowls on the Hoe. Hither returned Ralegh from that luckless
voyage that was followed by his execution, and hence it was that
the Mayflower sailed. In 1670, or thereabouts, the citadel on the
Hoe was built, and a few years later Plymouth Dock began that
career which obtained for it incorporation as Devonport, in
1824.

With the growing numbers and increasing size of England's
ships the wealth and importance of the three towns has grown
too, until as an arsenal they rank next after Portsmouth.

Walk through the Town.

From a tourist point of view, the town—as a town—has little of
interest, but the elevated esplanade, called the **Hoe**, has a wide
reputation on account of the view it commands. It is approached
from Mill Bay Station, by the street branching right of the Duke
of Cornwall Hotel. Taking our stand above the new pier, we
have on the left-front the high ground of Mount Batten with the
Catwater on its inner flank. Immediately across the Sound
stretches, some $2\frac{1}{2}$ m. distant, the low-line of the Breakwater,
terminated eastward by a day-mark, and westward by a lighthouse. Beyond it, 14 miles seaward, rises the lofty column of the
new Eddystone. St. Nicholas, or Drake Island, a strongly-for-
tified rock, is on our right front, and beyond it rise the richly-
wooded steeps of Mount Edgcumbe. On our right are the many
masts that indicate the neighbourhood of the Great-Western
Docks.

At the east end of the Hoe "*Smeaton's Tower,*" *i.e.* the old
Eddystone Lighthouse, has been rebuilt on the site of the
Trinity day-mark, that used by its skewness to be no ornament to
the promenade. Just eastward of this is the **Citadel**, built about
1670, principally to guarantee the loyal behaviour of the town.
As a fortification it is out of date and of small importance, but
the walk around its ramparts affords even a more varied view
than the Hoe, whence it is easily approached. The entrance is
on the north side, first through a gateway defended by guns and a
portcullis, and then, after crossing the ditch, by an ornamental

gateway, a good specimen of late 17th century work. The walk round, which the zigzag walls afford, is most tortuous. On leaving the citadel the passing visitor, desirous of seeing the chief features of the town, should descend *Castle Street* to the *Barbican*, which has a most fishy odour, and the Harbour (*Sutton Pool*), and then proceed by *Southside Street* and the *Parade* to *Notte Street* and *St. Andrew's Street*, in both of which are some interesting Elizabethan fronts. **St Andrew's** (or *Old Church*), at the junction of the street of that name with Bedford Street, is the only church in Plymouth calling for more than mention. It dates from the middle of the 15th century, and has a fine western tower. · Under the direction of the late Sir G. Scott, it was well restored in 1874-5. The most noticeable thing about the church is its size: 184 ft. long, 69 ft. wide, including aisles, 95 ft. including transepts. The aisles extend the whole length of the nave and chancel, and the comparative lowness of the building increases its apparent area. The stained-glass *windows* and chief fittings are modern. The *reredos, pulpit, bishop's chair,* and *font* should all be noticed, as should the good wagon *roof.* Of *monuments* the most important are the so-called Citadel Monument of Sir John Skelton (*d.* 1672) and his wife; a bust of Zachary Mudge, vicar (*d.* 1769), by Chantry; and that of Dr. Woolcombe (*d.* 1822), by Westmacott, an excellent work—"Medicine tending the Poor." In the south aisle is a marble tablet to the memory of Charles Matthews, the actor, who died in Lockyer Street, in 1835:—

"All England mourned when her comedian died,
A public loss that ne'er might be supplied."

South of St. Andrew's is a portion of the old Cistercian Abbey.

The new *Guildhall* and the *Municipal Buildings*, of which the lofty tower is a conspicuous object in views of Plymouth, occupy the sides of the square adjoining the church. Both externally and internally these are of great merit, and it is to be regretted that lack of breadth in the square and the inharmonious Post Office somewhat detract from their effect.

The new **Guildhall** (Norman and Hine, architects) was opened by the Prince of Wales in August, 1874. Externally notice the carved groups: (*left* of main entrance) Painting, Music, Sculpture, War, Peace, and Religion; (over the entrance) "Fame rewarding Industry and Virtue;" (*right* of the entrance) Architecture, Astronomy, Mechanics, Commerce, Plenty, and Law. The *Hall* is 146 ft. by 58 ft. exclusive of narrow lean-to aisles that seem scarcely in keeping with the dignified central area. At one end is an orchestra and a fine organ, at the other a large balcony. The richness of the interior is largely due to the good stained-glass of the windows, of which there are seven on each side. Their subjects, commencing at the east end of the hall, are:—

North Side.
1. "Masonic."
2. Napoleon at Plymouth, on board the "Bellerophon."
3. Final repulse of Royalists before Plymouth, Dec. 3rd, 1643.
4. Sailing of the "Mayflower" from the Barbican.
5. Proclamation of William of Orange.
6. Landing of Katherine of Aragon at Plymouth, 1501.
7. "The Priory" window. What is now Plymouth was formerly in part subject to the Prior of Plympton, and known as *Sutton Prior*.

South Side.
1. Black Prince embarking for Poictiers Campaign.
2. Descent of the Bretons on Plymouth 1403-4.
3. Drake inaugurating Plymouth Leat water-supply.
4. The Armada announced to the bowl-players.
5. Ralegh landing from Guiana, 1618.
6. William Cookworthy, the first maker of English Porcelain from "China-clay."
7. Commemorates the opening of the hall by the Prince of Wales in August, 1874. (a poor composition.)

The *statues* between the windows represent: Arthur, Alfred, Cnut, William I., Henry I., Richard I., Henry VI., Henry VIII., Edward VI., Elizabeth, O. Cromwell, Charles I., George III., William IV., and Queen Victoria.

Of the **Municipal Buildings**, opposite the Hall, the visitor should inspect the Council Chamber, a fine room with some Royal Portraits, and the Mayor's Parlour, containing a contemporary portrait of Drake, dated 1594, and many mementos of old Plymouth.

At the west end of the Municipal Buildings is the statue of Alfred Rooker, Mayor in 1874.

If from this point the visitor desires to visit **Charles (or New) Church**, he should cross Bedford Street and proceed by Old Town Street, Treville Street, and Norley Street. *New* Church points to the time (previous to 1640) when St. Andrew's was the only church in Plymouth. It was built between 1640 and 1657, the works having been stopped during the siege, and was dedicated to King Charles the Martyr soon after the Restoration. It is a good specimen of 17th century Gothic.

The **Athenæum** (at the corner of the street so-named, near the Royal Hotel and Theatre) is the home of the Plymouth Institution and the Devon and Cornwall Natural History Society. The museum contains the important "finds" discovered in the ancient cemetery at Stamford Hill, including a rare bronze mirror. There are also fossils from the Oreston quarries.

The **Plymouth Public** and **Cottonian Library** is on the north side of Cornwall Street (and must not be confounded with the Plymouth Free Library that occupies the old Guildhall in Whimple Street). The *Cotton Collections* are open to the public on Mondays; on other days application must be made to the Librarian. They take their name from their donor, the late W. Cotton, Esq., of Ivybridge, and consist of valuable books, MSS. prints, drawings, &c., and three portraits by Reynolds.

It only remains to say that the lofty spire seen from the train as we enter Millbay Station is that of the R.C. Cathedral in Cecil

Street, an Early English work by Hanson, built in 1856-8. Opposite to it is a convent of Teaching Nuns, whose schools adjoin.

Stonehouse takes its name from the solitary house that for a long period was the residence of the Stonehouse family, to whom the manor belonged. As already mentioned, it is practically part of Plymouth, and lies between it and the creek called Stonehouse Pool and Lake. Its sole object of interest to the visitor is the *Royal William Victualling Yard*, an immense establishment nobly housed, where everything connected with the commissariat of the Navy is exemplified on the largest scale. During working-hours the public are allowed to inspect the various processes, and the Bakery and Coopers' shops are of special interest.

The area of the Yard exceeds 13 acres, and was either reclaimed from the sea (about 6 acres) or levelled by removal of the rock.

The way to the Yard is by Durnford Street, past the Royal Marine Barracks. After passing St. Paul's Church turn to the right. The entrance to the Yard is by a fine archway, surmounted by a colossal statue of William IV. Just within the entrance are the Offices of the Police, who "personally conduct" visitors. Nothing more ample can be desired than the information that these cicerones, with perfect courtesy and much patience, supply, but the tour of inspection is, as for instance at Portsmouth Dockyard, necessarily perhaps, made so rapidly that most intelligent visitors, not accustomed to the Yankee pace of "doing" Europe, will long for the opportunity of leisurely investigation. To appreciate the handsome elevation of the principal block of buildings it requires to be seen from the Hamoaze, or, say, Admiral's Hard. The visitor should not fail to go round the southern extremity of the peninsula by *Western King Redoubt* to *Devil's Point*. There are seats by the way, and the walk commands delightful views of the Sound and the Hamoaze. In the opposite direction towards Eastern King Redoubt is the *Winter Villa* belonging to the Earl of Mount Edgcumbe, who is lord of the manor of Stonehouse. From the hill, above the redoubt just named, on which stands the official residence of the Queen's Harbour-Master, there is a wide view and a complete bird's eye one of the G. W. Docks at Millbay. The *Long Room*, once a well-known assembly-room, now a school for Marines' children, is passed in descending this hill towards the town.

Devonport can be readily reached from Plymouth in various ways. Tramcars run from Union Street by Stonehouse Bridge to Fore Street, close to the entrance to the Docks. A pleasant way is to take a boat (*Fare 2d.* or *3d.*) at Admiral's Hard, Stonehouse, to Queen's Steps under Mount Wise. In this way a full view will be obtained of the principal front of the Royal William Victualling Yard, and from the summit of *Mount Wise*, is a specially fine view of the Sound, the Hamoaze and their surroundings. The view seaward is utilised to signal Government vessels passing up or down channel. The public are not admitted to the Semaphore office, whence this is done. The large brass gun on the Parade was taken by Sir John Duckworth from the Turks, and is an unpleasant reminder of the rough handling experienced by the English fleet in repassing the Dardanelles under that commander. Notice the bronze statue of F. M. Lord Seaton.

From Mount Wise, or by the tram, we make our way to the principal entrance to the **Dockyard**. This is, of course, the sight of Devonport. The Police take visitors round at 10, 11 a.m., 2, 3, and 4 p.m., but the Rope Factory, employing nearly 150 young women, is not shown except by special order. Description is uncalled for, but it may be of interest to the visitor to know that the 70¼ acres of the present Yard are the lineal descendants of the little establishment begun by William III. Now some 3,000 hands are employed at a weekly wage of nearly as many pounds.

On the north side of the Dockyard, and entered from Queen Street, is the **Gun Wharf**. The chief sight in it is the *Armoury*, whose walls are covered with various weapons, disposed more or less ornamentally. No respectable applicant is refused admission.

Proceeding northward by *New Passage Hill* and *William Street*, we reach the entrance to **Keyham Steam Yard**, where, as its name implies, all that belongs to the repair of marine engines, and the construction of boilers, &c., is carried on. The steam-dock accommodation is the largest in the kingdom, and the principal shops and offices form a large quadrangle about 800 ft. long and 350 ft. broad, with a girder-roof of glass covering the whole area. At present the yard occupies about 72 acres, but the Government have bought the land as far as Weston Mill Lake, with a view of eventually enlarging the works to 120 acres. " *Thor*," the great steam-hammer of this yard, should be enquired for. It is capable of delivering a blow of a 100 tons or can be so adjusted as to crack but not crush an egg or nut.*

The **Breakwater** is about 2½ m. from the Hoe, and a boat there and back can be had for 2s. and upwards, according to the number of passengers. It is obviously an expedition only to be undertaken in calm weather, as the sea makes a clean breach over it at other times. Begun in 1812, this gigantic work took 30 years to complete and cost 1½ millions. It is formed of rough granite blocks, but the upper part is paved. Its ground plan is the segment of a hexagon of 1,000 yards radius, *i.e.*, the central portion, 1,000 yards long, has at either end arms bent back at an angle of 120 degrees. These arms are each 350 yds. long, and the western

---

* The **Old Block House**, ½ m. west of the Steam-yard and a little north of the Devonport stations, should be visited for the unique view from it.

one carries a lighthouse, and the eastern one a day-mark. Opposite and inside the centre of the breakwater is an iron-clad fort, heavily armed, and the channels at either end of the work are commanded by land forts.

Excursions from Plymouth.

1. **To Ivybridge** by the coast, *p.* 130; by rail, *p.* 129.
2. ,, **Falmouth** by coast, *p.* 161.
3. ,, **Princetown** ,, rail, *p.* 127.

4. **Saltram** (Earl of Morley), the woods of which are seen across the estuary of the Plym as we approach Mutley from the east by rail, can be reached from Plymouth by crossing Laira Bridge over the Catwater, or by taking the train to Marsh Mills Station. The Park is opened to the public on Mondays, and is a delightful place to ramble in, but the Saltram Gallery of pictures, formed under the direction of Sir Joshua Reynolds, and containing, in addition to its other treasures, 16 portraits by that master, can only be seen by order from the Earl of Morley. Of the Reynolds' a very striking one is *Cleopatra* (Kitty Fisher) dissolving the pearl, and, to name but one or two of the general collection, there are: *Bacchanals*, by Titian; *Marriage of St. Catherine*, by Corregio; *his Wives*, by Rubens, &c.

5. **Mount Edgcumbe**. *Open to the public on Wednesdays. On other days only by special order to be obtained at the Manor Office, Stonehouse. Ferry from Admiral's Hard (Devonport) to Cremill at the half-hours, returning at the hours.*

To the beauty of Plymouth Sound and the charm of the prospect from the various view-points in the Three Towns, Mount Edgcumbe, with its sweet alternations of swelling greensward and waving woods, is by far the greatest contributor. The house itself has but little to do with the effect. The eastern aspect of the slope which the grounds occupy protects the foliage from the blasting effects of the prevalent south-west winds, and the trees grow almost from the water's edge.

From whatever point in the Three Towns the Sound be crossed, *Cremill* is the landing place. Close to it there is a pleasant and comfortable inn, the *Mount Edgcumbe Arms*. The *Higher Lodge*, through which carriages enter the grounds, is a third of a mile up the road, but pedestrians can enter at Cremill itself. In either case the House, almost hidden by trees, is about ¼ mile away. It is a castellated mansion built in 1550 by Sir Richard Edgcumbe. The original round towers, however, were pulled down in 1762, and the present square ones substituted for them.

The **House**, not shown to the public, has a fine Hall, and contains many family pictures, amongst them works of Lely and

Sir Joshua Reynolds; also several of the sovereigns of the Stuart period.

The **Gardens** occupying the lower ground close to the entrance from Cremill, and to the left of the main avenue, are only to be seen by special order. They are divided, like those at Chatsworth, into Italian, French and English, and are similarly adorned with busts, fountains, &c. In the Italian is the *Orangery*, opening on to a delightful terrace. The French is characteristically prim, and the English has a beautiful lawn and many noble trees, including a very fine cedar.

The **Grounds** occupy the whole of the peninsula between the Sound and the Hamoaze, except the comparatively small area taken up by the Gardens, and the strip of shore between the public road to Cawsand and the Hamoaze itself. To walk fairly round them will occupy a long hour, but several hours may be most enjoyably spent in exploring them. Commencing with the eastern or lower side, we may make the circuit of the *Amphitheatre*, with its "insuperable height of loftiest shade, cedar, and fir and pine and branching palm" to *Milton's Temple*, wherein is a bust of the poet with the above quotation below. A little further we come to some modern ruins, then *Lady Emma's Cottage* and the *Red House*, close to Redding Point. Next we pass the *New Fort* at the foot of the tiny Picklecombe, and reach the *Huntsman's Cottage* in the valley of Hoe Lake, whence we bend back towards *Maker Church* (*p.* 145), and return to our starting point. Time after time, during our circuitous walk, we have had lovely views, but the most comprehensive to be obtained is from *White Seat*, which occupies a commanding position in the deer Park, near half-a-mile east of Maker Church and above the Amphitheatre. Close to the high road, a few hundred yards below Maker Church, is an ancient baptistery.

6. **St. Germans River, &c.** A pleasant excursion by boat from Plymouth is up the Lynher Creek or St. Germans River. In this way Trematon Castle, Antony House, St. Germans and Port Eliot can be visited.

Trematon Castle (2 *m. West from Saltash Station. The grounds are open to the public, who enter at the Higher Lodge, on Wednesdays*) is a moated 13th century ruin standing well up on a partly artificial mound overlooking the creek. It now belongs to the Duchy of Cornwall. The mansion (not shown) is modern, and was built, it is said, partly of materials obtained from the ruins.

Antony House, the seat of a branch of the Carew family, is on the opposite side of the creek. The direct route to it from Plymouth is by ferry to *Tor Point*. The fine woods are well seen as we proceed westward by rail from Saltash. The house, built in 1721, contains a considerable collection of *pictures* (not shown to the general public; they can only be viewed by permission which is occasionally granted). The two portraits, by Holbein, of Sir William Butts, physician to Henry VIII. and of Lady Butts, are celebrated works by that painter. In the park is a fine group of evergreen oaks planted in 1725.

The village of **Antony** lies more to the west on the high road from Torpoint to Looe. The church has a good tower and some interesting glass, and contains the tomb of Richard Carew, author of the " Survey of Cornwall." Ascending the creek after passing Antony, we enter a comparatively narrow channel softly hung with rich woods to the water's edge. After passing the mouths of two arms of the creek going off north and south respectively, we shortly afterwards come to two other branches, on the point between which is **St. Germans** (*Station on the Cornwall Railway, 9½ m. from Plymouth.* Inn: *Eliot Arms*). Here two items are of much interest,—the church and Port Eliot. The **Church** down to 1049 was the Cathedral of Cornwall. The West front is Norman and has a fine, deep-set West doorway. The towers are Norman below, that N.W. being Early English, and that S.W. Perpend. above. The Nave lost its North aisle about a hundred years ago, and the chancel fell in 1792. The South aisle is partly Early Decorated and partly Perpendicular. The 3-tier Perpendicular window at the east of the Nave, a fine niche on the South aisle, and a quaint and very early Miserere should all be noticed. There is a good monument to the Hon. G. Eliot, killed at Inkerman, Nov. 5, 1854. **Port Eliot** (Earl of St. Germans. *The Park may be visited any weekday by applying to the gardener*) is close to the church and occupies the site of a priory that soon after the dissolution became the property of the Eliot family, in whose possession it has since remained. There is a good collection of pictures including many by Reynolds, and a portrait of John Hampden, date 1628, and interesting as being the only one known, as well as one of his friend, Sir John Eliot.

7. **River Tamar to Weir Head.** This excursion should be made by all visitors to Plymouth who have a day at their disposal. During the season there are excursion steamers, and this is the quickest and least expensive means of locomotion, but the tourist with time at command will find his account if he charter a boat and make a long day of it. The first part of the voyage is up the *Hamoaze*, at the entrance of which *Tor Point* is on the left, and the quays and docks of Devonport on the right. Then, as the St. Germans river estuary opens on the left hand, we come in sight of the **Royal Albert Bridge** at Saltash. This, one of Brunel's greatest works, was opened in May, 1859. The total length is 2,240 feet, in 19 spans. The two spans which cross the river are each 455 feet and give a headway at high water for about 100 feet. Considering the engineering difficulties and the vastness of the work, the cost, nearly a quarter of a million, cannot be considered

excessive. The narrowness of the roadway above is not the least striking feature as we pass under it.

Saltash (Inn: *Green Dragon*), which is at the western end of the bridge, is a station on the Cornwall Railway, and from it the bridge can be visited on foot (enquire at the station). As seen from the river, the village is very picturesque and old-fashioned. Those who halt there should visit the *Chapel of St. Nicholas*, with a so-called Saxon tower, and proceed by the Callington road, about a mile westward, for a splendid view of the Tamar. The estuary now expands to some ¾-mile in width, and at high-water is a beautiful lake with many far-reaching arms. **Landulph Church** is seen a-head across the arm that runs up to Botes Fleming. In it is the tomb of Theodoro Paleologus (*d.* 1637), a descendant of the Eastern Emperors of that name. On our right-hand is *St. Budeaux Church*. The high ground north-west is Hingston Down, terminating westward in Kit Hill, and north-west we catch sight of Great Mis Tor, on Dartmoor. The second arm on the right-hand is the *Tavy* estuary, divided from the silvan Tamerton creek by the woods of *Warleigh* (house and grounds not shown). In about 3 miles onward, at the village of *Hall's Hole*, the river makes a huge loop at the head of which stands **Pentillie Castle** (Col. Coryton). The mansion is modern and of no particular interest, but the grounds are delightful. On *Mount Ararat* is a tower built by Sir James Tillie (*d.* 1712), who is buried beneath it. (*For an order to view the grounds apply to B. Snell Esq., Wayton, Hatt.*) The river now gradually narrows, becomes very pretty, and ceases to be an estuary at Cotehele Quay, — the usual landing-place for **Cotehele House** (Dowager Countess of Mount Edgcumbe), which is generally shown to visitors. To make sure, enquiry may be made of the agent, Manor Office, Emma Place, Stonehouse. The *Ashburton Hotel*, at Kelly Rocks, near Calstock, is an excellent resting-place from which to explore the neighbourhood. It is about 10 minutes' walk from the house. Cotehele House, so-named from the family to which it belonged down to the middle of the 14th century, and whence it passed by marriage to the Mount Edgcumbes, is a granite castellated mansion, quadrangular in plan, and chiefly of Early Tudor date. It is placed well above the Tamar and surrounded by fine woods of which chestnuts are the characteristic growth, and in itself and in its contents claims careful examination. The antiquarian should endeavour to pay his visit at a time when he will not be worried by a number of excursionists. The *Hall*, 44 ft. by 23 ft., has a good open roof, and is hung with armour, weapons, and hunting relics. The *chapel*, with an interesting East window, still retains its original screen and fittings. A volume might be written if we were to describe all the inns and outs of the mansion, and its wealth of old tapestries and furniture. Instead, we content ourselves with bidding the tourist pay the place a visit. The intelligent cicerone who shows the house makes no charge for his services, but well earns a "tip." On a rock overlooking the river is a small *chapel*, built by Sir Richard Edgcumbe, about 1486, as a thank-offering for his escape from the clutches of Richard III., who had good grounds enough to regard him as a supporter of Richmond. The story goes that Sir Richard, when pursued, flung his cap with a stone in it into the river, and so led his foes to think he was drowned. He retired to France till Henry VII. became king, when he returned and built the chapel.

After another bend of the stream the uninteresting village of **Calstock** (Hotels: *Tamar, Ashburton*, see *p.* 142), famous for strawberries and cherries, is on the left-hand bank. Here it is open to the traveller to land and proceed on foot 1¼ *m.* by *Harewood House* (Duchy of Cornwall offices) to the ferry at **Morwellham Quay** (small Inn: *Ship*). The river, closely fringed by woods, again makes a great bend and more than doubles the distance between these points. From Morwellham Quay the tourist may ascend to the summit of *Morwell Rocks*, but is advised to rejoin the steamer or his boat and ascend the river to Weir Head. These 2 miles are the finest part of the voyage. *Calstock Church* is seen high up on the Cornish Bank, and then on the Devon side we pass under the lofty ribs and crags (of limestone) known as **Morwell Rocks**. The scene here is striking and very beautiful and second only to that from the summit of the rocks themselves. At Weir Head is the basin where the steamer stops and turns. A pleasant way of reaching the summit of the rocks is through *Gunnislake* (*p.* 125) to *New Bridge*, ¾ *m.* after crossing which, and ascending the opposite steep a track strikes off to the right near the junction with old Tavistock road. This track leads through the woods out on to the rocks, the tops of which can be visited in succession. The view of the Tamar valley, immediately over which we stand at an elevation of some 300 feet, is delightful. From the rocks a descent can be made by the Inclined Plane to Morwellham Quay. Before descending, however, the antiquary may visit the farm-house of *Morwellham*, which stands on a knoll about half-a-mile from the river. It is an old Manor House, has a 15th century gate-house, and formerly belonged to Tavistock Abbey.

The pedestrian, bound for Tavistock, can proceed from the farm north-west to the Tavistock road, which he will join a long half-mile off Lumber Bridge. The distance is about 3½ miles.

8. **Eddystone Lighthouse.** This, the best known of British lighthouses, is distant 14 *m.* from the Hoe, whence the tower and light are visible in ordinary weather. A visit to it forms a favourite excursion from Plymouth. Its exact situation is lat. 50° 10′ 49″ N., long. 4° 15′ 53″ W., and the nearest point on the mainland is Rame Head, distant 9¼ *m.* The reef of gneiss rock,

on which the tower stands, being submerged at high water, was in the early days of Plymouth a source of peril to navigators making the Sound. The *first* lighthouse, erected by Mr. Winstanley, was of stone. It stood only 6 years, and was swept away by the Great Storm of Nov., 1703, when its builder, who was on a visit to it, perished with his handiwork. In 1706 Mr. Rudyerd, a London merchant, commenced the *second* lighthouse; it was of wood, was completed in three years, and lasted till Dec., 1755, when it was destroyed by fire, on which occasion one of the lightkeepers was killed by the melted lead from the lantern roof. On June 12, 1757, was laid the foundation of the *third*, or *Smeaton's Tower*, which has lately been re-erected on the Hoe. It was 2 years in building, and till 1882 remained uninjured by more than a century of storms. Its total height was 94 feet, and the column was of broad red and white bands, and modelled to the shape of an oak trunk. (The secret of its strength can only be understood by examining a detailed model such as that at the South Kensington Museum, made by a former light-keeper.) It was from no defect in the structure, but from the destructive action of the sea on the portion of the reef on which it stood, that the necessity for the *fourth*, the present, tower arose, and it was a happy thought that suggested the preservation of Smeaton's work as a day-mark on the Hoe. That work has supplied the model of most of the lighthouses since built in situations exposed to the sea, and the new one is in essentials only an enlargement of its predecessor. Sir J. N. Douglass, acting for the Trinity Board, was the engineer employed, and the site selected is only a short distance from that of the old one. From July, 1878, to the autumn of 1881 the new work was carried on, but little or no progress could be made during the winters. The top stone was laid by H.R.H. the Duke of Edinburgh June 1, 1881, and the light (a white double-flashing half-minute one, visible $17\frac{1}{2}$ miles) first exhibited in March, 1882. The lantern is 133 feet above high water, and 50 ft. higher than Smeaton's. With a view to breaking the impact of the waves on the tower the basement is a solid cylindrical mass of granite, forming a kind of platform 44 feet in diameter, and 22 feet high. From this rises the tower proper, $35\frac{1}{2}$ feet diameter at base, and $18\frac{1}{2}$ feet below the lantern. The cost of the whole work was £80,000.

A marvellous incident connected with the removal of Smeaton's tower is worth preserving. Mr. W. T. Douglass, a son of the chief engineer, was superintending the lowering of some portion of the upper part when the giving way of the gear hurled him from the top, and he escaped destruction on the exposed rock below only by the opportune inflow of a great wave. Happily he sustained no serious injury.

PLYMOUTH EXCURSIONS. 145

9. Rame Head *viâ Cremill*, 5 *m.*, returning by **Penlee Point and Cawsand to Cremill**, 11¼ *m.*

** *Distances from Cremill which is reached by ferry from Admirals' Hard.* This little pedestrian round is worth making. Rame Head can be approached within a short distance by those who drive, but there is no coast *road* from Rame Head to Penlée Point. The carriage, after setting down near Rame Head, should be ordered to Cawsand if the visitor only desires to walk that far from the Head, a distance of 3¼ *m.*

The landing place at Cremill is close to the Lower Lodge of Mt. Edgcumbe Park and the *Edgcumbe Arms Hotel* (good). Thence the road runs straight up-hill, past a day-mark obelisk on the right, and affords a good view of Mt. Edgcumbe House, and from time to time a pleasant backward prospect of the Hamoaze. At ½ *m.* we pass the Higher Lodge. The village below on the right is Empacombe, and far away winds the arm of the Harbour that runs up to Millbrook. By a well shaded but steep road we climb to the top of the neck on which stands, its tower conspicuous far and wide, **Maker Church**, Perpend. There are monuments to the Mt. Edgcumbe family, but little else. (*Key kept at the Vicarage.*) From the road, which now for a while is fairly level, we get a good view northward and just a peep of Plymouth Sound on the left-hand. At the fork, a short way beyond the church, the road on the left winds down to Cawsand. We take the right-hand one. At the next fork, 2 *m.* from Cremill, that to the right goes to Millbrook, and we take the left-hand. Then we drop sharply, and, avoiding roads right and left, climb again, getting a lovely view eastwards of the little bay on which Kingsand, half-hidden, stands. The Sound, too, is well seen with the pyramidal Mew Stone and the Breakwater. We now have sundry old and new fortifications on the hill close on our left, and then pass through a gate where the road becomes a mere farm-track. Rame Church is seen from the top of the hill, and then a steep drop brings us to the picturesque hamlet of *Forder*, 3¼ *m.*, where, crossing the brook, we turn to the right. The road we are now upon is that from Cawsand to Rame. Another ascent brings us to the few houses that constitute the latter village, where we bear round to the left past a tree in the middle of the road.

The road to the right, with telegraph posts, is a fine one, and skirts Whitesand Bay along the top of the cliff to Tregantle Fort. If this be taken then Plymouth can be reached from Tregantle *viâ* Antony (*p.* 141) and Tor Point (*Steam Ferry*).

Rame Church, 4 *m.*, Perpendicular with earlier portions, is weather-beaten and rather woe-begone. It has a thin square tower with narrow lights and a small spire. The south aisle is pretty with ivy, and from the ill-kept churchyard the sea is in sight. Taking the farm-road which has the church on the left-hand, we soon obtain a good view of the ragged cliffs that slope to the shore of Whitesand Bay. When the farm-road turns sharply left, keep straight on and pass through a gate. Tregantle

S. Devon. L

Fort is now in sight on the right, and the view on that side extends from headland to headland as far as the Lizard peninsula. Eddystone Lighthouse is on the left of **Rame Head**, which is now close at hand in front. The Head itself, a true *promontory*, is connected with the peninsula of which it forms the extremity by a narrow neck, some 4 yds. wide, sloping steeply on the east and having a cliff on its west side. A sharp little climb brings us to the ruined **St. Michael's Chapel** that crowns the hill. This chapel, abt. 20 ft. by 10 ft. inside measurement, with walls 3 feet thick of unhewn stone, has nothing about it by which its age can be determined. It is still roofed in, but all the wrought stone, except that of the eaves of the roof and two small pieces at the spring of the arch of the East-window, has been removed. The entrance is near the west end on the north side. In addition to the large East-window opening there is a window towards the east end of the south side. A niche on the north side of the East-window seems to be part of the original building. At some time or other a floor existed some 6 ft. 6 in. above the ground, as the walls still show the holes where the joists were inserted, and a window has been made high up at the west end to light this upper chamber. The view of the cliffs, as framed by the door, is good. The head commands a long coast-line. The rocky pyramid eastward is the Mew Stone off Yealm Mouth, and the headland seen to the right of it Stone Point, beyond which is Bolt Head. Looking westward, Looe is across the bay, and to the left of it, we make out St. George's Island, and then, one beyond the other, Dodman Point, Zoze Point, and the long low promontory of the Lizard.

The horse-path to Penlee Point is seen along the cliff-slope from the chapel. To reach it leave the signal house with its prone staff on the left and follow a wall. We see now the fine rocky cove that lies under the neck of Rame Head, and gaining the horse-track need no further guidance. **Penlee Point** is a mass of dark quartz-streaked rock at the foot of a green slope $1\frac{3}{4}$ m. from the chapel. Notice, looking back along the coast, the almost columnar appearance of the rock caused by the vertical tilting of the strata. Onward, on the hill-top, is a *Folly Tower*, a useful day mark, and a flag-staff, just below which is Lugger's **Grotto**. This is said to have been made by the Lieut., R.N., whose name it bears, as a remedy for the gout! It is a shallow cavity in the rock (in which seats have been hewn) with a common-place front carried on arches. In itself it is not worth a thought, but the view from it of the Sound is magnificent. The long line of wall seen on the opposite hill-side marks a Government shooting range.

From the grotto a road begins which runs through Penlee plantations to Cawsand and affords peeps of rocky coves and of the Sound. **Cawsand** is prettily placed at the head of a bay, but is only a poor fishing village. On the hill above it is a fort, besides which there is a Coast-guard station and one or two small public houses. Kingsand adjoins it, and has at any rate the advantage of a cleaner shore, with rather curious rocks. There is a small inn, *King's Arms*. It is a steep climb to get away from Kingsand. When the narrow road reaches the hill top, follow it to the right, past a fort, soon after which an obvious track goes off on the left and leads to the road past Maker Church and so to Cremill, 11¼ m.

If the road to Millbrook be taken from Cawsand, then by a short *détour* from the former place *Inceworth* can be visited, where there is an interesting, Decorated, chapel, now desecrated. Thence by way of St. John's, prettily situated at the head of a creek, and with a church, partly Norman, the road to Tor Point (ferry) can be reached. Cawsand to Tor Point, 6½ m.

Plymouth to Truro, *by rail* 54 m.

The starting point for this route is *Mill Bay Station*. All trains, except two early morning ones and the evening "Dutchman," stop at all stations and take about 2½ hours to reach Truro.

Soon after leaving *Devonport* Station the line crosses a creek, and we get a good view of the Hamoaze. About a mile onward is the **Royal Albert Bridge** (*p.* 141), which affords a magnificent prospect on either hand. On the right the Tamar and the Tavy, uniting their waters, widen to a lake, across which is seen Landulph Church (*p.* 142), while the western tors and slopes of Dartmoor supply the background. Beyond *Saltash*, after affording a fine back view of the Bridge, the line skirts the Lynher River, and, passing *Trematon Castle*, on the right, crosses several creeks, which, with the tide up, present delightful river scenes, whereof the woods of *Antony*, reaching to the water's edge, are the chief feature. **St. Germans** and Port Eliot are described on *p.* 141. From the Station little is seen of them, but there is a pleasant greenness about the line here. Then nothing calls for remark till we near **Menheniot** Station when the woods of *Coldrenick* are on the right, and we cross a deep and pretty valley by a lofty viaduct. Menheniot Station is 7 m. from *Looe* (*p.* 162). The village is a mile north of the line, and the spire, a comparatively rare feature in Cornish churches, is a conspicuous object. *Liskeard Station*, 4 m. further and 19 from Plymouth, is that at which pedestrians bound for Looe should alight, as the walk thence is to be preferred to that from Menheniot, and the distance down the valley along the canal-path is delightful and only a mile longer. *For continuation of rail see p.* 153.

Liskeard.

Railway Stations: *Liskeard*, G. W. R.; *Moorswater* (for Looe).
Hotels: *Webb's*, in the centre of the town, on the Parade; *Stag*, near the station; *London*, H.Q.; *Moon's Temperance*.
Post: *Del. London, &c.,* abt. *7 a.m.; North,* 1.30 *p.m.; desp., North,* 12.30*p.m.; London, &c.,* 6.35 *p.m.* *Sundays: desp.* 6.5 *p.m.*
Population: 4,479.

Liskeard is an ancient town and municipal borough, on high ground north of the line. In 1775 one of its representatives was Gibbon, the Roman historian. The town has little of interest to the tourist, but is a convenient centre for a few excursions. There is communication by coach with Tavistock on week days. The *church* is a large Late Perpendicular building and has been carefully restored. The west tower, of four stages, has curious gurgoyles below the battlements, and its west door is dated 1627. The most noticeable features are: the south porch with three (empty) niches over the doorway, the side ones supported on quaint corbels; and the pinnacles of the projecting bays of the south aisle. Of the *Castle* nothing remains, and its site is a shabby bit of turf with a few trees, not far from the church.

Excursions from Liskeard.

1. **To Looe,** 9 *m.* There is a choice of routes:—(*a*) *By rail* from Moorswater Station, a long mile west of and below the town. The line runs down a charming valley and is 6¾ *m.* in length, with an intermediate station at *Sandplace,* 2 *m.* short of Looe. (*b*) *By road.* This is a continuation of that from the town to the station, ¾ *m.* beyond which it reaches the valley, which it follows for half-a-mile and then crosses and ascends to *St. Keyne,* where the church is worth a passing glance. Thence it is 2 *m.* to *Duloe church* (restored), of which Dean Scott, of the "Lexicon," was formerly rector. The antiquary should enquire for the *stone circle,* which is near the church, a short distance left of the road. From Duloe the road descends to *Sandplace* and so to *West Looe.* (*c*) *By the canal-path.* This is the best route for pedestrians, who strike it by taking the road past the station, see (*b*). **St. Keyne's Well,** whose water is famous for securing the mastery to bride or bridegroom who first drinks it, is about 2 *m.* from the point where we reach the canal. To most people, however, the chief charm of

the walk is the pretty valley itself, which about Sandplace and thence to Looe is delightful. *For Looe, see p. 162.*

2. **To St. Cleer**, 2¾ *m*; **The Hurlers**, 6 *m*; **Cheesewring**, 7 *m*. This excursion will interest the antiquarian, and though the scenery on the way is hardly picturesque, there are many wide views that under a bright sky have a wild beauty of their own. The route we describe can only be taken by the pedestrian or by those who ride; but carriage-folk can approach within half-a-mile of the Cheesewring. The mineral line from Moorswater does not carry passengers, though permission to travel by it is occasionally granted. No objection is made to persons walking along it.

We leave Liskeard by Upper Lux Street, and at the top of the hill, at a junction of roads, turn to the left for St. Cleer, which is about 2¼ *m.* nearly due north. As we ascend St. Cleer Down the mineral line is crossed about a mile short of **St. Cleer**, which is on high ground and commands a wide view, in which Kilmar High Rock, or Tor, is conspicuous with its fine crest northward. The pinnacled church-tower at the head of the wide valley, eastward, is St. Ive (*p.* 150). St. Cleer is a village that owes its maintenance to the mines in the neighbourhood. Its name is the Cornish form of St. Clare, and has nothing to do with the word *clere*, applied to elevated sites, *e.g.* Highclere, &c., in Hants. The lofty and high-pinnacled church-tower is a prominent object for miles around, but the church need not detain the tourist. Its earliest part is Norman, in which style there are (renewed) square-headed windows, and a doorway on the north side. A little way beyond and below the church is **St. Cleer's Chapel and Well.** The old chapel 20 years ago was rebuilt, but the spring is as of yore, and the old cross is still standing. In a field, N.N.W., about a mile from the church, is **Doniert's Stone**, "Doniert rogavit pro animo." Doniert is said to have been a son of Caradoc, and to have been drowned in 872. An empty chamber was some years ago discovered beneath the cross.

Across the valley, about a mile east of the village, is **Trevethy** (or **Trethery's**) **Cromlech**. The upper slab, about 14 ft. by 9 ft., is pierced by a hole near its upper end. From the Cromlech the simplest way for the pedestrian is to get on to the railway, and to follow it, avoiding, however, the branch on the right, which runs east to Tuckenbury Mine. When he has proceeded along it about 1½ *m.*, the *stone circles*, called the **Hurlers**, are over the brow about ¼ *m.* on the left hand. Originally there were 3 circles, but the southern one, which was the smallest, has been nearly destroyed. The others, 115 ft. and 140 ft. in diameter, have only 6 and 10 stones still in position. The rest have either fallen or been removed. The **Cheesewring*** is only a mile to the

---

* The "Cheesewring Hotel," about 1 *m.* E., is an ordinary village inn.

north, close to a large granite quarry, which threatened to destroy it, but thanks to the Duchy authorities this vandalism has been prevented. It is a natural pile of granite slabs, of which the upper ones, resting on a comparatively small block, appear to be very insecurely poised. The view from the spot embraces both channels, but its most interesting features are the fine ragged *Kilmar High Rock* and the nearer *Sharp Point Tor*. *Brown Willy*, the highest of the Cornish hills, is seen north-west about 8 miles distant.

<small>The pedestrian bound for the north of the county should certainly go by way of Kilmar, and then he can strike a road just east of it at Beriow Bridge, from which *Five Lanes* (small inn) is about 5 miles distant up the valley. *Launceston* is north-east 7 miles, and the road—a succession of ups and downs—is pretty direct through South Petherwin; see our *N. Devon and N. Cornwall*.</small>

The traveller returning to Liskeard may vary his walk by going over *Caradon Hill* (1,200 ft.), and by Caradon Down to *St. Ive*, 6 m. this way from the Cheesewring. The coach from Tavistock passes through St. Ive (4 m. from Liskeard) about 5.15 p.m., but a seat cannot be reckoned on in the height of the tourist season. If permission to return by a mineral train can be secured, it should certainly be made use of, as the hills are steep and the scenery is too bleak to bear twice contemplating on foot.

3. **Liskeard to Callington**, 8½ m; **Gunnislake**, 14 m; **Tavistock**, 18 m. *Three hours by coach, which leaves Liskeard abt. 7.45 a.m., and connects at Tavistock with L. & S. W. R. train about 11 a.m. for North Devon, Exeter, and London (Waterloo).*

<small>The route is described the reverse way p. 124, &c.</small>

This journey is for the greater portion of the way too uninteresting and too toilsome to be recommended to the pedestrian. By coach it is pleasant enough in bright weather, and affords direct access from the West to Calstock (good inns) and the fine scenery of the Tamar about Morwell Rocks. *For the River Tamar see p. 141, and Calstock, &c., p. 143.*

We leave Liskeard by Upper Lux Street and at a junction of roads beyond Barn Terrace take the *second* turn on the right. The *first* turn is the old road, which is little if at all shorter, and more hilly. The two re-unite about 2½ m. onward. At 2 m. from the start we see a-head, across a deep valley, the prominent church-tower of St. Ive, the mile-long ascent to which begins at a small brook 3 m. from Liskeard. As we climb, the conspicuous flat-topped hill on the left is Caradon, and, looking back, the lofty and pinnacled tower of St. Cleer Church crowns the hill nearly due west. Mine-scarred hills bristling with chimney-shafts, and the little mineral line climbing round the southern slope of Caradon Hill, past South Caradon Mine to Tuckenbury Mine, are the only other features of a rather dreary picture. **St. Ive** (pronounced *Eve*) is a very small but neat village (no inn), with an interesting church mainly of the Decorated period. The south aisle and tower are Perpendicular, and the latter, as we approach from the west, appears to be crowded with pinnacles, which on closer inspection are seen to compose angular triplets of very graceful design. Soon after passing the village a fine view is obtained south-west to Devonport and the sea with Maker Church above Mount Edgcumbe. Kit Hill, the ever-visible summit of this district, is right-a-head, with the outline of Western Dartmoor on either side of it. At the sixth mile-stone we take the left-hand road (leaving the telegraph wire to pursue the old road) to *New Bridge**, where is a road-side inn close to the bridge over the Lynher river. The picturesque upper valley of this stream is well seen as we descend, and the Cheesewring (*p*. 149) and Sharp Point Tor (or Shapitor) rise conspicuous on its western side some 6 *m*. off. Another stiff climb, passing, on the left, the ornamental grounds of *Pencrebur*, brings us to **Callington**, where the coach stops for a few minutes at *Golding's Hotel*. Callington is a small and uninteresting town that lost its Parliamentary representatives in 1832. The only building of any note is the Perpendicular church, which is largely of granite, and contains a fine brass to Sir Nich. Assheton (*d*. 1465) and his wife, and the alabaster tomb of the first Lord Willoughby de Broke (*d*. 1503). The traveller by coach will not have time to inspect these memorials, but by getting down at the church he may examine the old *cross* in the churchyard, and then hurry to the hotel to resume his journey. For **Dupath Well**, which may be visited from Callington, see *page* 125.

Soon after leaving Callington a fine view opens eastward and southward, which widens and becomes very extensive as we ascend the slope of *Hingston Down*, and attain an elevation of between 600 and 700 feet. Kit Hill (1,097 feet) is immediately above on the left. The whole district south to the blue waters of the channel lies below us like a map. The Tamar and the Tavy appear as a land-locked lake. The Royal Albert Bridge across this united stream is well seen, and beyond we get Devonport, the Eddystone Lighthouse, Mount Edgcumbe, and (as a long line on the horizon) the profile of Tregantle Fort. Eastward the summits of Great Mis Tor and Sheepstor are prominent, and on the hill-side between them is Walkhampton Church. Far away to the south-east are the two tree-topped eminences so conspicuous from the higher ground above Ivybridge. The southern slopes below Hingston Down are celebrated for their cherry orchards and strawberry gardens, and the former in the early spring impart quite a snowlike appearance to the foreground.

At *St. Ann's Chapel*, a hamlet along the road near the eastern end of the Down, are two or three public-houses.

---

* Not to be confounded with New Bridge at Gunnislake which we shall reach further on.

The traveller bound for Calstock (*p.* 143) must now leave the coach and take a road on the right which in about 2 *m.* will bring him to his destination.

As the road sweeps round northward a good view is obtained across the river of **Morwell Rocks** and of the finely wooded Devon bank of the Tamar, and then, as we enter Gunnislake, **Weir Head** (the pool where the steamers from Plymouth end their journey) is below, and on the far side rises the Chimney Rock.

Gunnislake (*Inns*) is a large village devoted to the quarrying of granite and the manufacture of bricks. Another element in its prosperity was (rather than is) the group of mines hard by, known as *Devon Great Consols*. These mines are still worked for arsenic, but no longer produce the wealth of copper that rendered them famous. The Tamar is here crossed by another **New Bridge**, which has a curious appearance owing to the graduated height of its arches necessitated by the difference of level of the river banks. From the bridge the Ordnance map shows a nearly straight road over the next hill to *Lumber Bridge* and so to Tavistock. This is now only available for pedestrians, who by taking it save about ¾ *m.* in distance, but nothing in time, owing to its steepness. The new road zig-zags up and then down the intervening ridge. As we ascend, the tall chimney of Devon Great Consols is seen on the left, on which side immediately below the bridge is a huge water-wheel.

Where the new road crosses the old one, about ¼ *m.* from the river, a footpath goes off on the right through the woods, by which the top of **Morwell Rocks** may be reached, and a descent made to *Morwellham Quay*, whence the products of the mines are shipped. Thence the river can be crossed to **Calstock** (*p.* 143) by Harwood.

Gunnislake and the valley of the Tamar form a striking picture in the backward prospect, and the western tors of Dartmoor are well seen as we descend the hill into Tavistock, Brent Tor being conspicuous on the left hand. The gateway passed on the right as we enter the town is the only remnant of the old mansion of *Fitzford*. Here is Drake's statue by Boehm. For **Tavistock**, see *p.* 111.

4. **To St. Neot**; *by road*, 6 *m.*; *by rail to Doublebois Station*, 4 *m., and thence by road*, 3 *m.*

The road is pretty direct. Leave Liskeard by the Bodmin road, which descends to the valley running down to Looe near *Moorswater Station*. After crossing the mineral line and ascending the hill, at a junction of roads turn to the right, and then at the fork close by to the left. This road must be followed until, after crossing another valley down which one of the head-waters of the Fowey flows, a junction of roads below Bury Down is reached, when St. Neot is only ¾ *m.* onward down the hill. **St. Neot** (Inn: *Carloyan Arms*), as famous in the West country for its stained glass windows as is Fairford in Gloucestershire, has no attraction for the tourist beyond the *Church* (open from 10 a.m. until 4 p.m.) of which the tower, Decorated, is very fine. The windows alluded to above are 15 in number, and owing to long previous neglect had to be largely supplemented with modern glass when they were restored in 1829. They date from 1480, when the church was built, to about 1530. One, called *St. Neot's window*, depicts the marvellous life of that hermit, and another, *St. George's window*, the still stranger experiences of England's patron saint. The reliquary, that long preserved an arm of St. Neot, may be seen in the north aisle, and about a mile west of the village on *Conzion Down* is *Crow Pound*, where by his spell he detained some crows that he had been, as a boy, set to scare. It was this circumstance that led him to retire from the world. His *well* in a meadow near the church may still be seen. There lived two pet fish which by his merits were restored to life after having been respectively boiled and broiled for his dinner!—kinsfolk presumably of the two immortal fish which the poets tell us dwell in the sunless recesses of Bowscale Tarn in Cumberland.

Rail continued from p. 147. After leaving Liskeard Station, the line is carried by a lofty viaduct across the fine valley down which the mineral line from Moorswater runs to Looe. Passing *Doublebois* and then crossing some half-a-dozen viaducts on the way, we descend the left bank of the *Fowey river*, which here runs down a thickly-wooded valley that deserted mine buildings, hoary with age, now and again by no means disfigure. This is the finest part of the railway route between Plymouth and Penzance, and, in the time of autumnal tints, particularly beautiful.

Bodmin Road Station (*for Bodmin, Wadebridge and Padstow see our "North Devon and North Cornwall"*) is very prettily situated close to the Fowey and amidst abundant foliage, but the narrowness of the valley prevents any view beyond one of the pleasant greenery and, now and then, of the stream. Rather more than a mile onward **Lanhydrock** (Lord Robartes) is on the right. As there is no inn at Bodmin Road Station, this interesting seat will be most conveniently visited (*any week-day*) from Lostwithiel, the next station, from which it is about 3½ *m*. The chief feature of the grounds is a long avenue planted in 1648. The *House*, erected between 1636 and 1642 by the second Lord Robartes, afterwards Earl of Radnor, was burned in 1881 but has been rebuilt.

In the *Parish Church* behind the House are memorials of the Earls of Radnor.

Continuing our route, **Restormel Castle** (the keep, part of a tower, and a gatehouse are all that remain), built in the reign of Henry III., is seen on a hill above the line on the right. It is surrounded by a moat and very picturesque, and should certainly be visited by those who break their journey at Lostwithiel. *Rail cont. p.* 154.

Lostwithiel.

Hotels: *Royal Talbot* (H.Q.); *Bassett's Temperance*.

Post: *del. abt.* *7.15 *a.m.* (*London &c.*), 12.50 *p.m.* (*North*); *desp.* (*North*) 12 *noon*; (*London &c.*) *6.25 *p.m.* [*Sundays also.]

Population: *abt.* 1,000.

Here the trout-fisher will find one of the few good stations for his favourite sport in Cornwall. The situation, too, of the little town is delightful, and there are several objects of much interest to the general tourist. *Restormel Castle* has already been mentioned, p. 153, as well as *Lanhydrock*, both of which should be visited, and may be included in the same short excursion. In the town, the chief sight is the fine *Church of St. Bartholomew*, whose Early English tower is surmounted by an octagonal, Decorated belfry, each side of which carries a small gable, the effect being singularly graceful. In 1644, the Parliamentarians under Essex endeavoured to dislodge certain persons, who had taken refuge in the belfry, by exploding gunpowder, whereby the body of the church was much damaged, but the fine 14th century East-window happily escaped destruction. The curious font is worth notice.

The *Duchy House* retains some part of the early 14th century buildings, and the *Bridge* of 8 arches over the Fowey, which dates from the same period, is both interesting and picturesque.

Boconnoc (*house not shewn; permission to drive through the Park is given on leaving a card at the lodge*), the fine seat of Hon. G. Fortescue, is about 4 miles east of Lostwithiel. *The Park*, through which runs a small tributary of the Fowey, is well timbered and exceedingly beautiful. North-east of the house on a knoll is an obelisk and the remains of a small Royalist fortification. Charles I. had his head-quarters at Boconnoc, previous to the battle of Braddoc Down, 1644. The elder Pitt was born here in 1708, the house being then the property of Governor Pitt, his father.

Rail continued from p. 153. To Par Station nothing calls for remark. **Par**, the junction for Fowey and New Quay, distant respectively 4 and 21 *m.*, is of some importance on account of its mining and china-clay industries, to accommodate the products of which the late Mr. Treffry, of Place, constructed the harbour. Close to the station is the "Royal Hotel," which may be found useful by third-class passengers, who have to await the arrival of the " Dutchman" before proceeding by either of the branches, *see below*.

Between Par and St. Austell, the line for some distance is only a short distance from the coast, but the scenery by the way is mine-spoilt, and everywhere blanched with china-clay refuse. *Rail cont. p.* 158.

Par to Fowey, 4 *m*. The *Railway* route connecting these two places bends northward for a short distance, and, as far as *St. Blazey* (Pack Horse, Q.) is identical with the New Quay line. At St. Blazey we reverse engines, and passing under the main line, skirt for a few hundred yards Tywardreath Bay. Then the line enters a narrow green combe, passes through a tunnel into a similar combe at the other end, and finds its terminus on the banks of the Fowey estuary, and from ½ to ¼ *m.* short of the centre of the town, which is reached by the narrowest of streets. For Fowey see *p.* 165.

The *Road route* passes a small *inn* close to the bay and the rail, and then ascends, reaching in a couple of miles cross-roads, at the entrance to *Menabilly* (*p.* 166). A few hundred yards on the northward (Bodmin) branch is the ancient inscribed stone (*p.* 166). The Day-mark on Gribben Head is well seen from about here, and the road passing the entrance to Neptune Drive, drops into Fowey through a cutting in the rocks.

Par to Bridges Station, 4¼ *m*. (for the **Luxulion Valley**). No one who tarries in the neighbourhood of Fowey should omit this excursion.

The total walk need not exceed an easy **round of 3 miles**. There is a small inn close to Bridges Station (down-side of line), and another in Luxulion village, 5 min. distant. Simple refreshments may also be had at the Station Master's Cottage.

For a picnic party there are any number of pleasant spots wherein to set up a gipsy tripod—below the viaduct is a favourite one and at the smithy, on the way to and near the Colkerrow Quarry, a kettle might be boiled.

The walk we describe in large type includes the best points. Those who devote a day to the excursion will easily extend it, and include the points mentioned in the small print. Perhaps the best way for a **walk of about 4 miles** (not including the disused line to the Grinding Works) is to proceed, as in large print, to the Viaduct, then from the near end to turn down, right, into the valley, and there left, under the railway and Viaduct, and 2 *min.* beyond the latter to turn up to the right. This lands us on the tram-line, where we turn to the left and proceed as given in large type (where our road is said to *cross* the tram-line). In this way the return to Luxulion and Bridges would be by the small type route *via Mid Gready*.

Pedestrians who do not wish to return to Bridges Sta. can proceed to St. Blazey Station (for Fowey), or to Par Station on the main line without returning to Bridges Station. For this walk, see small print at the end of this excursion.

The Luxulion Valley is a deep silvan glen of much beauty (in spite of its noisy brook being thick and white with china-clay washings), and the great tors and stupendous "perched blocks" are very striking. The Treffry Viaduct, which spans the valley, is a noble work and fine view-point.

From the up-side of the station we ascend the road for a few yards, and then, from a stile, right, take the field-path, which in 5 *min*. leads to Luxulion village and church (restored).

About 70 yds. east of and beyond the church, on the left behind a pump, is an ancient **Baptistery** in good preservation. The *kolumbethra* is now dry, owing to the spring, which used to supply it having been drained by the railway-cutting. Down to about 1875 it was the village well. The bracket for the image still remains in the back wall of the well.

Here we bear round to the right, between the Post Office (left) and the School (right), and just beyond a bridge over the railway get over a stile. Hence an unmistakable path leads, in a few hundred yards, down the fields to the mineral line, used for bringing the granite from the quarries, along which we turn to the left. [N.B. This is not regarded as a trespass, and no risk is involved, because the trucks conveying the stone are drawn by horses.] A walk of 6 *min.* along the line (passing an old quarry, right, and a small reservoir, left) brings us to the **Treffry Viaduct**, 657 ft. long, 90 ft. high, from which we get a lovely view up and down the glen. At the far end of the viaduct is gear belonging to a quarry, but our route lies along the line that bends back to the left.

The line straight on from the Viaduct is now disused. It passes the ruins of a waterwheel, which worked the incline, and goes through a wood. In case the leat which brings water from the far side of the main valley is not in use, a waterfall is formed nearly 200 feet high, but this is seldom running except on Sundays, when there are no trains on the railway. Further on along this tramline are Grinding works, where the best China-stone for glazing pottery is prepared.

In 4 *min.* from the turn the line is crossed by a road, and 2 *min.* further another road crosses under the line. [The former of these we shall use presently.] Here, too, a disused branch line diverges, left, towards Luxulion. As we continue along our line, the scene on either hand is a fine combination of granite blocks, pools, and woodland, and the "perched" blocks will be noted. When the line begins to rise we may have to step aside to make way for trucks descending by gravitation. The botanist will note the sessile-fruited oak and the ordinary kind growing side by side, on the left, opposite a fine spring on the right. The former is the wood used in Westminster Hall which till recently was supposed to be chestnut. About 12 *min.* from leaving the viaduct there is a Smithy (*see p.* 155), on the left of the line, and behind it rises the largest of all the blocks, of which only a close view will reveal the true size. To reach it, turn to the left, by the spring and over the stepping-stones in the wall, whence a track will be found through the bushes. The group of blocks consists of three, and the largest, the **Giant Block**, under which there is a considerable space, we measured, roughly, and found to be quite 50 feet long.

We believe this is the largest block in Europe, larger than any of the famous boulders at the head of the Italian lakes. It may take rank with the largest known, the Agassiz blocks, in the Tijuca mountains near Rio Janeiro. The rock, which consists of large crystals of black tourmaline and pink felspar in a base of grey quartz, is called *Luxulianite*. It is only found in these blocks, and no dyke is known. The Wellington sarcophagus, in St. Paul's crypt, is of this stone.

If any visitor will be at the trouble of taking accurate measurements of the Giant Block, we shall be glad to hear the result.

Returning to the line we might diverge from it nearly opposite the Smithy to Colkerrow Hill, which commands a view towards New Quay and, in the other direction, of the channel near St. Austell. If, however, we keep along the line, 5 *min.* more brings us to the Colkerrow Quarry, and a climb to the head of it is rewarded by a fine view including the Viaduct.

A path, left from the quarry, leads to the ancient farm-house of *Mid Gready* (look inside the court-yard and at the well), and thence an old bridle-path brings us to a lovely slope leading down to the stream and then up to *Luxulion* village where the old Baptistery (*p.* 155) is on the right.

Our next object is to view the **Viaduct** from below, and we therefore retrace our steps along the line as far as the road which crosses it. There we turn down to the right, and in a minute or two join the road in the bottom of the valley and turn left. In 2 *min.* we are under one of the 10 arches of the viaduct. Continuing along the road, in 3 *min.* more we pass under the Railway, and then, if our return is to be to Bridges Station, we turn up and back, on the right, and, with a good view of the valley, rejoin our outward route at the little reservoir near the Luxulion end of the Viaduct.

Treffry Viaduct to St. Blazey Station, 50 *min.*, or **Par Station**, 1 *hr.* A pleasant walk. After going under the Railway keep to the road, that is, do not turn as for Bridges (see above) nor left at the house just beyond. A stiff ascent brings us in 10 *min.* or less to the top of the only hill we have to mount, and when a short distance down the other side a fork is reached, at an ivied cottage, we keep to the right. The road now descends through the beautiful demesne of *Prideaux* (Sir Colman Rasleigh), and at the foot of the hill (abt. ¼ *hr.* from the Viaduct) joins another road at some china-clay works, just short of which an obvious footpath, left, cuts off the corner. In any case we turn left when this other road is reached.

The route onward to the station is uninteresting. When we strike the street of St. Blazey, at right angles, turn to the right and keep on till the Church is on the right hand where the road, left (telegraph wire), is the way to the Stations. St. Blazey's is straight on. For Par Station, turn to the left where a high wooden bridge is seen on that hand and keep to the road, which shortly bears round to the right. When it forks, close to Par Station, take the left (upper) branch. The "Royal Hotel" is facing the steps leading to the platform; refresh.-room on up-side. *For* Fowey, *see p.* 165.

St. Austell.

Hotels: *White Hart*; *Globe*; *Queen's Head*, Q.; *Perry's Temperance*.

St. Austell (*pop.* 3612,) is in no sense a tourist resort, but is a convenient starting point for a walk by the coast to Falmouth, for details of which see *pp.* 166—70.

The church, the only object of interest in the town, was restored in 1870, and is one of the finest in the county. Especially noteworthy is the richly-ornamented Perpendicular tower, which has numerous niches and an elaborate, very graceful, upper story and parapet. The body of the church is of the same date as the tower, but the chancel is Early English, and the font Norman and curious. The traveller interested in mining should pay a visit to the colossal *Carclaze Mine*, 2 m. north-east by the Tregonissy road. This is a huge pit over a mile in circuit and nearly 150 ft. in depth. It is of unknown antiquity, and to within the last 30 years was worked for tin, but now yields large quantities of china-clay.

China Clay or Kaolin consists of disintegrated and metamorphosed felspar, and is obtained from highly decomposed granite. It is much used in the manufacture of paper and calico as well as for the finer sorts of pottery, from which circumstance it is often called Porcelain clay. **China stone** is somewhat similar, but contains quartz. It is a fair building stone, but is chiefly used in the manufacture of glaze for earthenware. Large quantities are raised in the neighbourhood of St. Austell.—*Harrison*.

The Bodmin road, which is spanned by a lofty viaduct, nearly a mile west of the station, passes at first through a very pretty and flowery little combe.

Rail continued from p. 155. Between St. Austell and Truro are two stations, *Burngullow* and *Grampound Road*. The latter is the nearest for *Probus*, 2½ m. A conveyance can be obtained at the inn close to the station, but the walk is a pleasant one, and passes *Trewithan Park*. Those interested in earthworks can visit one on *Barrow Down* within half-a-mile of the station, and another close to the north-east corner of Trewithan—a few yards along the road to St. Austell. **Probus** (Inn : *Hawkins' Arms*) is celebrated for its church-tower, which is of granite, and everywhere richly wrought. It is 108 ft. high (128 ft. including the pinnacles), and crowned by eight groups of five pinnacles. This fine example of Late Perpendicular was built in the reign of Queen Elizabeth. The rest of the church was re-built about 20 years ago. Two skulls, supposed to be those of St. Probus and St. Grace, found during the alterations built up into a wall, are now buried beneath the altar. In the Golden aisle, so called from a former mansion in this parish, is an early 16th century brass.

The road from Probus to Truro, 6 m., drops in a mile to a valley, which it descends for a mile and a half and then crosses **Tressillian Bridge**, close to the entrance gate house to *Tregothnan House*. This bridge witnessed the final collapse of the Royalist cause in Cornwall in 1646. After skirting the estuary for about a mile we ascend the hill past the well timbered grounds of *Pencalennick*, and then drop down to Truro, which we enter over Boscawen Bridge.

The *railway* as it reaches Truro is carried over two long valleys by long viaducts. A good view is obtained of the town on the left-hand. *Rail to Falmouth p.* 161 ; *Penzance, p.* 178.

Truro.

Railway Station, on high ground, ¼ m. W.

Hotels: *Red Lion, Royal* (H.Q.). *Good Refreshment House in St. Mary's Street on the south side of the Cathedral.*

Post: *Chief del.* (*London &c.*), 7.40 *a.m.*; (*North*), 2.10 *p.m.* *Desp.* (*North*). 12 *noon*; (*London &c.*), 5.20 *p.m.*

Population: 10,663.

A steep descent leads direct from the station to the centre of the town, which has wide streets with good shops and a well-to-do appearance. Since 1876 it has been the seat of the Cornish bishopric. The principal object of interest is the new **Cathedral** (consecrated Nov. 3, 1887; J. L. Pearson, R.A., architect; cost of site, £21,000, fabric, £74,000, fittings, £15,000). The best general view is from the bridge over the Fal, in New Bridge Street. In its incomplete state—central tower at present only carried clear of the ridge, and the nave, with western towers, yet to be built—the exterior gains in height and size by contrast with the houses which hem it in. A Late Perpendicular and richly-panelled aisle of St. Mary's Church has been incorporated on the S. side of the choir, but the rest of the building is Early English. To the W. of the aisle just named rises a Campanile, and the effect of this and the lofty clerestory is somewhat foreign. The stone is Mabe granite with Bath stone dressings.

From the Market Place, a narrow alley, called Cathedral Lane, leads to the S. transept entrance. The **Interior** is very beautiful and, thanks to the tender colours of the stonework, quite free from rawness. Standing beneath the Lantern of the **Great** (or Benson) **Transept** and looking eastward, the lofty choir, with groups of shafts rising to the simple vaulting, is very striking. Lower down, the triforium, rich with dogtooth and delicately-tinted shafts, leads onward to the Reredos, on which the Eastern Transept throws a flood of light.

Another beautiful view is between the many pillars towards **St. Mary's Aisle**. The latter is divided from the choir aisle by a narrow aisle and is on a lower level.

At the S.W. corner of the Great Transept is the graceful **Baptistery**, a memorial of Henry Martyn (1781-1812), the Indian missionary, who was a native of Truro. Against the wall of the N. arm of the transept is an interesting Jacobœan monument (removed from St. Mary's and refurbished) to John Roberts (1614) and his wife.

The *Stalls* of the Choir and the *Episcopal Throne* are of teak. In front of the bishop's desk are statuettes of Abp. Benson, Bp. Wilkinson, and Bp. Temple, and the first of these wears a *pallium!* The **Reredos**, 28 ft. high, is a mass of sculpture in Bath stone, and the idea of the whole is the One Sacrifice.

The Crypt—approached from the aisle adjoining St. Mary's Aisle—is used for vestries and temporary Chapter House.

In Pydar Street is the Royal Institution of Cornwall's **Museum** (*admission*, 6d.; *free Wednesdays after* 2 *p.m.*), which has a fine collection of Cornish birds, and some interesting local antiquities. All trace of Truro Castle, which stood at the top of Pydar Street, has disappeared. In Lemon Street is the monument of Richard Lander (*d.* 1839), the African traveller. Samuel Foote (1720-77), comedian, was born at the Red Lion.

Truro is admirably placed for many and varied excursions, and were we writing a handbook for residents it would be necessary to describe the expeditions thence:—to the North Coast about New Quay and Portreath; by rail to the great mining district about Redruth; eastward to Probus and the coast about Gerrans Bay. We have, however, the tourist public in view, and for them Truro is rather a city to be viewed in passing or to be visited from elsewhere, *e.g.*, from Falmouth. As regards the north coast we must refer to the companion volume of this series. For the other excursions above mentioned a reference to the Index to the present volume will show where the districts are described. In this place we need only mention that travellers who do not contemplate taking the river-route between Truro and Falmouth should, if time allow, walk or ride as far as Malpas (*pron.* Mopus), for a view of the fine river-scene thereabouts. **Tregothnan** (Viscount Falmouth) can be reached by crossing the mouth of Tresillian Creek at the Ferry (*Inn*). Tregothnan *house* is never shown to the public, but permission to view the *grounds* is sometimes to be had by applying to the Resident Agent, Tregothnan office, Truro. The return from Malpas can be varied by taking a lane that runs up the hill some half-mile beyond the Point. A somewhat longer route back may include *St. Clements*, (*small inn*) charmingly situated on the west of Tresillian Creek about a mile up it. In the Polwhele transept of the church is a memorial to the Rev. Richard Polwhele (*d.* 1838) the antiquarian, and author of the *History of Cornwall*. A curious feature of the church is the way light is admitted from the ridge of the roof. Between the church and the vicarage, near the gate leading to the latter, is an *ancient stone* some 10 ft. high inscribed *Isnioc Vital Fili Torrici* (Isniocus Vitalis, the son of Torricius). It has been rescued from doing duty as a gatepost. Its original site is unknown. By road, St. Clements is 2 *m.* from Truro, and the round by Malpas is about 5 *m.*

Truro to Perranwell (*for* **Carclew**), 4 *m*. Penryn, 8¼ *m*. Falmouth, 11¾ *m. by rail*.

The first part of this short journey passes through tunnels and heavy cuttings, which shut out all views. Perranwell is the station for **Carclew** (Col. Tremayne), to the gardens of which strangers can generally obtain admission by courteous application to the proprietor. The botanist will find growing wild the rare heath *Erica ciliaris* and be interested in the many fine foreign trees that have here been acclimatised. The village and church of **Perranwell** (or Perran-arworthal) which are passed on the way to Carclew are prettily situated at the head of Restronguet Creek. The name commemorates St. Piran, one of the twelve bishops sent by St. Patrick to evangelise the Cornish. His well is near the church. Resuming our railway journey nothing calls for notice till we approach Penryn when, from Treleever Viaduct, a good view down Penryn creek is obtained on the left hand, a view that is repeated after leaving that station.

Penryn (Hotel: *King's Arms*, II.Q.; *Vivian's Temperance*, Commercial Road) has nothing about it to attract the tourist, except that it is the starting place of 'buses to Helston and the Lizard. Its immediate surroundings, however, are pleasant and well timbered, and the view from the higher ground above the town down the lake-like creek towards Falmouth is pleasing. The parish *church* of St. Gluvias, overlooking the creek, has been restored, but is chiefly worth a visit on account of its situation. The town is a busy one and much occupied with granite and other works. The granite chiefly comes from the famous quarries of Mabe, 2 *m.* west, on the old Helston road. At Perranwharf is a large iron-foundry. Leaving Penryn, the line crosses a viaduct, and then, after a cutting, Budock Church with its low pinnacled tower is seen on the right. As we enter Falmouth, its well timbered suburb is on the left, and on the right we get a glimpse of the sea. The ticket-platform at Falmouth gives us our first good view of the Roadstead, and the Falmouth Hotel is on the right, close to **Falmouth Station**; *p.* 171.

Plymouth to Falmouth by the Coast.

Remarks. This is a pedestrian route, comparatively seldom taken by the tourist owing to its lying for the most part far from the rail. As a consequence the inn accommodation is scanty and chiefly adapted to local requirements. The points where sleeping accommodation can be had are Looe, Polperro, Fowey, Charlestown (the port of St. Austell), Mevagissey, Porthloe (2 small public houses) Porthscatho, and St. Mawes. The only points accessible by train are Looe (mineral line from Liskeard), Fowey,

Tywardreath Bay (from Par Station) and Charlestown (2 miles from St. Austell Station).

A good route for those who have already been to Rame Head from Plymouth is to proceed by rail to Looe. Thence walk *via* Polperro to Fowey, 11 *m*. After exploring the coast at Gribbin Head, or at any rate seeing the Grotto at Polridmouth, return to Fowey and take train to St. Austell, whence walk down the valley to Pentewan and on to Mevagissey. A lift may, perhaps, be obtained from St. Austell to Pentewan on the mineral line that runs close to the road all the way. At Mevagissey the *Ship* Inn, though small, is better than it looks. Thence along the coast there is no inn till we reach Porthloe, where the accommodation is very humble. At Porthscatho there is a fair inn, the *Plume of Feathers*, and at St. Mawes is a small commercial house, the *Fountain*. Should the tourist reach St. Mawes too late for the last ferry-steamer to Falmouth he can hire a boat. If, however, he proceeds by the coast-road from Porthscatho to St. Antony, he may there find it difficult after dusk to hail a boat for St. Mawes.

Plymouth to Rame Head, 5 *m*; **Looe**, 19 *m*. from Cremill.

For the coast as far as Rame Head, see *p*. 145. Returning from the Head, whence the whole sweep of Whitesand and Looe Bays, along the margin of which our onward route lies, is seen at a glance, we take the road along which the telegraph wire turns, just below Rame Church. This follows the cliff-top as far as *Tregantle Fort*, and is a Government road of modern construction and splendid going. In about 3 miles from Rame we join the road from Mount Edgcumbe and Cawsand. This still follows the top of the cliffs and we pass through the hamlet of *Crafthole*, beyond which our way continues along the cliff for several miles, passing *St. Germans Beacon* and then dropping to the shore a mile short of the little *inn* at *Downderry*. Hence the road strikes inland, but the pedestrian may continue along the shore for another mile to the farm-buildings of *Seaton*, and, crossing from the mouth of the stream of that name, ascend to the cliffs on the other side, and, after going slightly inland, continue along a cart-track which descends suddenly round the cliff into *East Looe*.

Looe (East and West; Inns: *Ship*; *Looe*, Q.; *Best's Temperance*; *for Menheniot 'bus see yellow sheet*) if it were more accessible, would probably be much visited. A quarter of a mile from the sea the estuary is crossed by an excellent bridge of many arches, whence the view of the two villages, lining either shore and mounting to some height the adjacent hills, is very pleasing. The streets of both villages are narrow, but both have fairly open promenading spaces between their densest part and the bridge, and the width of the river is almost in itself sufficient to prevent that straitened and choked-up appearance which, however picturesque, is a very doubtful recommendation from any other point of view. Altogether, the town and port have rather a foreign look, which is, perhaps, to some extent, the result of the vegetation, myrtles and hydrangeas, amongst other plants, flourishing in the open air, and the hill-sides being divided into small allotments of garden and orchard ground.

The little island about a mile south of Looe, reached past a Coastguard station and two houses, is *St. George's*, or *Looe Island*, which, in the spring of 1883, was associated with a melancholy yachting calamity whereby a family resident upon it lost their lives.

Very pleasant boating excursions may be made from Looe, subject to the state of the tide, which at new and full moon reaches its highest about 5.30. By far the most beautiful is that up the *Trelawne inlet*, which unites with the main Looe river half-a-mile above the town, and whose winding shores are fringed by steep and lofty hills, covered from head to foot with rich woods. On the right hand, as we ascend, are the lands of *Trenant*, and on the left are those of *Trelawne*, an old seat of the Trelawny family. Trelawne House is not shown to the general public, but permission to see the pictures and the chapel is occasionally given.

Looe to Moorswater, $6\frac{3}{4}$ *m. by rail*, **and Liskeard**, 8 *m.*—This little narrow-gauge line may be used by those who wish either to commence or to end their coast wanderings at Looe. The station is a few minutes' walk north of the bridge on the east side of the estuary. The line threads the valley of the Looe throughout, passing through pretty scenery, but only specially beautiful at the opening of the Trelawne inlet described above. At **Moorswater** it passes far beneath a handsome stone viaduct of the Cornwall line and from Moorswater Station to Liskeard (*p.* 148) is an uphill walk of about a mile.

Looe to Polperro, 4 *m*; **Fowey**, 11 *m*.

After ascending the steep and irregular street of West Looe, the carriage route onwards continues inland, but by far the best course for the pedestrian is by one which turns to the left, about a mile from the river-side, and passing some farms in a hollow between it and the sea, becomes little more than a cart-track across fields till it reaches the picturesquely placed **Talland Church** (restored, and with the tower detached from the body of the church), beyond which it drops to the sea-shore at Talland Bay. Hence the coast-path round the rocks to Polperro, about $1\frac{1}{2}$ miles in length, is very delightful.

Polperro (Inns: *Oliver's Tourist, Ship. Post del.* 8 *a.m., desp.* 4.50 *p.m.*).

Of all the narrow little ravines which offer to the landsman shelter from the sea-winds and to the mariner a few square yards of safe anchorage from the sea-waves of Cornwall, none is so narrow as that which contains this extraordinarily arranged group of human habitations. From whichever side you enter Polperro, you may almost jump down on to the tops of its houses before you see them, and so tightly have its habitations squeezed themselves together that it is only by actually wriggling your way through its so-called streets that you can get along at all. In on one side and out on the other is all the direction a guide-book can give to the tourist as to his progress through the village itself, and should it happen to be a hot day we fancy he will not be slow to attend to the latter part of this advice.

The valley into which Polperro has wedged itself is a perfect V, and its streamlet is a very narrow one, so that there is not even the breathing space afforded by a water-way of any breadth to relieve the pressure of closely-packed humanity. The most picturesque point of view is perhaps from the path by which we arrive from the eastward, just as we come plump upon the quaint little anchorage grounds which are walled off at the outlet of the stream.

A noticeable feature of Polperro is the richness of the vegetation in all such parts as are protected from the sea-winds.

The red grits and slates of the Lower Devonian formation are here well seen in the cliffs. Scales of such fishes as *Scaphaspis* and *Pteraspis* and spines of fishes (ichthyodurolites) occur, and suggest that the beds are of the same age as the Lynton beds of North Devon.- *Harrison.*

From **Polperro to Fowey**. The only *carriage road* (6 m. to Bodinnick Ferry) is, owing to the absence of finger posts, rather intricate to follow. At starting you can choose between the road which climbs the hill at once from the village, or proceed up the valley (abt. $\frac{1}{4}$ m.) to Crumple Horn, and there turn up to the left by the road on the S. side of the brook. These roads join about 1$\frac{1}{2}$ m. from Polperro. Both involve bad hills, the first is perhaps the better route. From the junction of the roads, the road runs N.W. for about $\frac{1}{2}$ m. (leaving Lansalloes village about $\frac{1}{2}$ m. to the left). It then in the course of the next $\frac{1}{2}$ m., zigzags left, right, left, right in quick succession, and then soon once more turns to the left and pursues, with a good deal of winding, a westerly direction. It passes Carneggan (3$\frac{3}{4}$ m.), Tredudwell (4$\frac{1}{2}$ m.), and about $\frac{1}{4}$ m. beyond the latter turns to the right down to Gregon (5 m.), where it crosses the stream and, ascending again, goes W., past Lamellion to Bodinnick Ferry (6 m.), the only place where vehicles can cross the water to Fowey.

There is no coast path west of Polperro. **Pedestrians**—the walk we describe is 6$\frac{1}{2}$ to 7 m. to Polruan—should proceed through the village of Lansalloes (2$\frac{3}{4}$ m.), the road to which diverges to the left, $\frac{1}{4}$ m. beyond the junction of the two above-named roads out of Polperro. The church of Lansalloes is a useful sea-mark. It is Perpendicular in style and seems to require restoration. A path, starting from the side of it and dropping into a little intermediate combe, leads to the Polperro and Polruan road. The rest of the route is over high ground, affording fair and wide views. The descent to Fowey Harbour through *Polruan*, is very steep. It is worth while, before commencing it, to turn aside to the top of the height on the left, for the sake of the view, which, like all views that include Fowey, is charming. Then, crossing the harbour by the ferry, we are landed at Fowey about a mile south of the station and almost underneath the Fowey Hotel.

FOWEY.

Fowey. (Hotels: *Fowey, Ship,* Q. *Post del. abt.* 7.20 *a.m.*, 1.30 *p.m.*; *desp.* 11.0 *a.m.*, 5.35 *p.m. Pop.*, 6,786. *Rail to Par, p.* 155.)

Fowey is, perhaps, the best example of a characteristic Cornish coast-town. The original part of it is wedged in so closely between the harbour and the rocks that, if in passing—say from the railway station—the visitor meet a vehicle of any description, he is almost bound to make a call at one of the houses in order to let it pass. Further southward, however, the gentler slope of the hills has afforded opportunity for building and arranging houses on more modern principles, and here a considerable hotel, the *Fowey*, has been erected as well as several villas—presumably for the accommodation of visitors.

Fowey at one time ranked amongst the first sea-ports in the kingdom—a position due, doubtless, to the depth and accommodation of its harbour, which in these respects may by compared with that of Dartmouth, to which it is similar. Fowey sent vessels to the Crusades, and for the projected blockade of Calais, in the reign of Edward III., it contributed 47 ships and nearly 800 men —numbers exceeded only by Yarmouth. Afterwards the "Fowey gallants," as they were called, so exasperated the French by depredations on the Normandy coast, that the latter attacked and set fire to the town. The defenders held Treffry—now Place—House, and in the end forced the enemy back to their ships. Fowey lost its importance through the piratical leanings of its people, and in the reign of Edward IV. had to hand over its ships to Dartmouth.

St. Catherine's Fort, originally built to defend the harbour, is now a ruin on the south side of the town, nearer to which, on each side of the water is a tower, said to have been built in the reign of Edward IV., and formerly connected by a chain boom.

Fowey Church, almost hidden from view except from the harbour side, is a remarkably handsome specimen, chiefly of 15th century architecture, the tower being the chief feature. The north aisle is about a century older and formed part of an earlier building.

Place House, the residence of the Treffry family, is a fine Tudor mansion, dating in part from the time of Henry VII. Its most striking features are two semi-octagonal bays of this date, richly panelled on the exterior of the upper storey, and bearing many armorial shields. A third bay of similar design is about a century later. The late Mr. Treffry (*d.* 1850) was the creator of the thriving port of Par, and to him is chiefly due the railway to, and the birth of, the young watering-place of New Quay on the north coast. Both port and town, in their present development, are the outcome of works that he planned and started.

The most conspicuous artificial object about Fowey is the *Rashleigh Mausoleum* on the top of the cliff overlooking St.

Catherine's Fort, and originally the site of the chapel of St. Catherine. It is reached by keeping as near as may be to the harbour-side, and passing Neptune House, beyond which a path leads up to it. It is shaped like a bell—four granite buttresses supporting a block of the same material, on which is a Maltese cross.

The walk along the shore can only be continued for a short distance beyond the Mausoleum.

In the promontory that divides the Fowey estuary from Tywardreath Bay, the extremity of which, Gribbin Head, is crowned by a party-coloured day-mark, is **Menabilly**, the chief seat of the Rashleighs. There is no particular object to be gained by going out to the extremity of the Head, though the view thence of the coast extends eastward to Rame Head, and westward to Black Head, just short of the Lizard, but every tourist should at least visit the **Grotto** at Pridmouth (or Polridmouth), which is reached through Hambland village. It is octagonal, and is entered through the jaws of a sea-monster. It is lined with an endless variety of minerals and fossils, and with stalactites on the roof. A granite table contains more than 30 kinds of that stone, all found within the county. Notice also two triangular links of chain, part it is supposed of an old harbour boom, which were found by some fishermen in 1776. About $1\frac{1}{4}$ m. from Fowey, on the St. Austell road, is *Four Turnings* and the entrance to Menabilly. By the side of the Bodmin road, less than a quarter of a mile from the junction is a *Longstone* (not to be confounded with that near Charlestown), about 8 feet high, inscribed: *Cirvsivs hic jacit, Crnowori filivs*, and having a Tau-shaped cross on the other side. *For the fine excursion to* **Luxulion**, *see p.* 155.

From Fowey it is well either to take a boat to Mevagissey or to proceed by rail to St. Austell (*p.* 157). In the former case the traveller will obtain a fine view of the bold rocks of Black Head and reduce the length of his next day's walk to some 20 m. even if he goes right through to St. Mawes.

St. Austell to Pentewan, $3\frac{1}{2}$ m.; **and Mevagissey**, $5\frac{1}{4}$ m. Facing the White Hart Hotel turn down the road on its left. This at once leads down to the valley of the little *Vinnick* brook, the water of which, thanks to the china-clay works above, is veritable whitewash. The road for a considerable distance has the mineral line alongside. At $1\frac{1}{4}$ m. is a shop with Post Office, at a fork beyond which take the right-hand road. The valley winds down between well wooded hills, and the line and the turgid brook are lost sight of in the thick growth of gorse that fills its bottom. **Pentewan**, $3\frac{1}{2}$ m., celebrated for its stone, guarded on the west by Pennare, a shapely but not remarkable promontory, has nothing beyond a small inn, the *Ship*, to detain the tourist. Hence to Mevagissey there is a choice of routes. [N.B. It is not possible to follow the coast below the cliffs even at low tide.] (i) A *cliff*-

path may be taken which leaves the shore behind a lime-kiln, and after reaching the top of the cliff soon drops again to a combe with a couple of cottages, between which and Mevagissey another hill has to be climbed and descended. This walk is not recommended as it runs too far from the edge of the cliff to afford any coast view. (ii) *By road*. This is a continuation of that from St. Austell. It at once ascends sharply. At the first fork take the left-hand branch.

<small>The right-hand road goes to St. Ewe. **Heligan**, the lovely demesne of J. Tremayne, Esq., is a short distance off this road on the left. The house is unworthy of the exquisite grounds. To visit the latter permission is necessary and without it, this route has no particular attractions. Mevagissey is reached in 3½ m. from Pentewan.</small>

When the hamlet of *Tregasick* is passed a very fine view up the coast is obtained, the chief points in which, in order eastward, are Black Head, Gribbin Head (day mark), Looe Island, and Rame Head with its little chapel. In the opposite direction rises the tower of Gorran Church. When cross-roads are reached, keep straight on and descend abruptly to **Mevagissey**. (Inns: *Ship, King's Arms*.) This is a large fishing village with a good harbour enclosed by two short piers. The houses rise tier above tier, and from their facing of light-grey slate have an appearance of newness. There is nothing in the place to attract the tourist, though if he be an archæologist he may visit the church (restored 1886), which has a curious Norman font. The *Ship* inn, though small, may be trusted for a well-cooked steak and a clean bed.

Mevagissey to Gorran Haven, 3 *m*; **Porthloe**, 11 *m*; **Porthscatho**, 17 *m*.

Ascending the principal street the road at once opens up a sweet coast view. Polstreath Cove, just east of the harbour, is very picturesque, and the rocks are fine. The view already described from the hill east of Mevagissey is repeated and improved, and off Rame Head rises the new Eddystone Lighthouse. Westward runs out the long and graceful Chapel Point. We then descend to *Porthmellin*, a little cluster of houses with a Lifeboat station, and small coves filled with the most pellucid sea-water. A few yards up the next hill take a path on the left. Another and still better coast view of seven successive bays is now obtained on our left. When the path, after crossing a field, reaches a gully turn down to the left and keep outside the cultivated ground and cross the base of Chapel Point* to the head of the next little bay. Climbing the green hill-side, Gwinges, a fine islet of rock, comes suddenly into view. From the top of the hill Gorran Haven appears across the bay. *Turbot Point*, which is now on our left, ends in a fine

---

<small>* The rocks from Chapel Point westward to Gerrans Bay are Silurian, and of about the same age as the Upper Bala beds. Fossils have been found at Carn Gorran.</small>

perpendicular cliff, draped with ivy, and frequented by ravens. Skirting the cliffs along the bay we come to *Great Carn*, where the Devonian formation for a short distance is interrupted by protruding masses of limestone, large blocks of which, interspersed in spring with blue bells and other wild flowers, are picturesque. When the Down becomes enclosed we cross two fields, and then a path leads down past a large Coastguard station to **Gorran Haven** (nearest *Inn* at Gorran church-town, 1¼ miles inland), a small fishing hamlet, devoted to crabs. There are a few lodgings in favour with artists. The 16th century chapel has been restored. From Gorran Haven the cliffs may be followed, or you may keep to the lane running straight up from the shore. As this quits the hamlet turn sharp to the left, breast the steep hill for 50 yds., when the lane will lead you through a gate to a farm. Keep straight on. *Baw Sand*, to which a track runs down, is then below, and without going much out of our way a dip may be had in the sea. **Dodman Point** is not yet in sight, being hidden by the uninteresting intervening corner of Penveor. When the cart-road turns to the right inland, if we intend going out to the Dodman we must skirt the cultivated ground along the cliff and make for a flagstaff. The ground is rough, but besides being able to trace the rampart, which in old days made the Point a cliff-castle, we get a wide view up and down the coast. Returning from the Point the best plan (in order to avoid the sharp dip to Hemmick Cove) is to take the road we left, and passing *Penare*, a farm-hamlet (whence the westward view is delightful, and more picturesque than that from the Dodman) to make straight for cross-roads near Gorran Church, whose pinnacled tower is seen a-head.

By taking the right-hand road at the cross-roads, **Gorran** church-town may be reached in about ⅛ m. There is a small inn close to the church.

We turn to the left, and at the next junction of roads keep on to the right. In ½ m. a footpath (public) is seen on the left running down a park-like field towards the little bay on which, with a good back-ground of timber, and a lake in front, stands the modern castellated mansion of **Caerhayes**. The plain, square tower of St. Michael Caerhayes is seen above the trees. The footpath, which we follow, rejoins the road close to the entrance to the grounds, and the tourist must be wilful indeed if he disregards the abundant notices not to trespass. You now climb the steep rock-hewn road on the opposite side of the bay. As the higher ground is attained, take the coast-road through a gate on the left. Soon there is a fine backward view of the abrupt crags of Lamb Sowdon and Greeb Point, and, in front, of the Gull Rock and Nare Point. When the little hamlet of *East Portholland* (*no inn*) is reached, and the head of the inlet crossed to *West Portholland*, it is better to quit the coast for awhile and take the road to Porthloe, 2 m. This goes up a long, steep hill. Where it forks take the left branch, and presently, avoiding a road running *back* on that side, take the next turn to the left. This ends at *Tregenna farm*, whence a footpath across fields develops into a pretty lane that soon rejoins the road, which descends sharply to **Porthloe**. (Inns: *New, Ship*.) The New Inn lets a sitting-room and bed-room, and, though small, is accustomed to cater for visitors. If the pedestrian has had enough of the coast, he can hire a vehicle to take him to Grampound Road Station (7s. *including driver's fee*). Porthloe is a little fishing village at the mouth of two narrow converging combes, and is well-known for its lobsters. The cove is rock-girt, and the Coastguard station, as at Gorran Haven, is about the only tidily kept domain. Just west of the village a very fine black chasm forms the second half of the bay and is well seen as we climb the steep hill-side to resume the cliff-walk. Notice the almost vertical lie of the strata on each side of the cove. Onward it is a pleasant walk, over turf for the most part, and there are no serious ups and downs for a while. *Nare Head* is a bold headland, but scarcely of sufficient individuality to tempt the possibly tired pedestrian out to its extremity. If he determines to cross the base of this promontory he should resume his coast-walk on the far-side of the dip that comes down from Carne, about ½ m. north from the Head. Here, on the sloping hill-side overlooking the bay, are **Giant Tregeagle's Quoits**, huge blocks of quartz.

Just beyond the hamlet of Carne, at the head of the next combe is **Carne Beacon**, a huge tumulus that, when opened in 1855, was found to contain a Kistvaen or stone burial-chest. Tradition says that Geraint, a king of Cornwall at the end of the 6th century, was here buried.

The cliffs now sink rapidly to *Pendowa Beach*, which we cross, and then take the road on its far-side, which shortly afterwards runs into that from Tregony (pronounced Tregŏny). When a fork is reached, by continuing along the left-hand branch, in ½ m. onward, we reach *Trewithan*, and 2 m. beyond that **Gerrans**. There is a public-house at each of these, and the church of the latter village is worth inspection. The tower and spire are Decorated. Notice also the curious tracery of the east window of the north-aisle. In the south porch is a *stoup*, and close by, in the grave-yard (which commands a fine view of Gerrans Bay with the Quoits conspicuous on the opposite cliffs) is a granite *cross*, about 6½ feet high.

Porthscatho (Inn: *Plume of Feathers*, fair) lies immediately below the church, and is reached by a sharp descent. It is a clean little village, glorying in much whitewash. Besides the inn there are a good number of small lodgings, which in the summer are much favoured by Truro folk. The village has no claims to be considered a watering-place, but is certainly a pleasant little spot. The bay on which it stands is almost perfectly rectangular, and is shut in north and south respectively by Pentelvadden Point and the Cabe.

Porthscatho (Gerrans) to St. Mawes and Falmouth.
From Gerrans there is a choice of routes to St. Mawes:

(i.) The direct one, 2½ m., is by *Polcuel Ferry*. Take the right-hand road from Gerrans Church, and then, ⅓ m. onward, a road going off on the right, which leads direct down to Polcuel Ferry. The afternoon steam-boat from Falmouth runs up to this point, but returns at once. If the traveller hits it off, he will in a few minutes find himself at St. Mawes, where a longer stay is made. Should he fail to catch the steamer, a ferry-boat (*toll*, 1d.) will take him across the water, and then a field-path runs over the hill to St. Mawes, which is less than a mile from the crossing. A delightful view of the winding sea-loch, as it would be called in Scotland, is obtained by the way, and at one point a dip in the eastern hill shows us, at the head of a minor inlet, a V-shaped bit of sea. At **St. Mawes** (Inn: *Fountain*, fair), there is nothing to see except the *Castle*, and that is of little interest. It was built in 1543 as one of the defences of Falmouth. Unlike the fast-held Pendennis it yielded at once to Fairfax in 1645. *Ferry, see below*.

(ii.) *By St. Anthony, about* 3½ m. Take the left-hand road from Gerrans. In little over a mile *Roseteage* is reached. This is only a farm, but is pleasant on account of its grove of ash, sycamore, and chestnut. Quit the road and take a field-path on the right. This quickly becomes a lane, a short distance along which a charming view of a winding and wooded creek is obtained on the right. Nothing calls for special notice for the next mile onward. Then we turn sharply down, to the right, towards *Place*, an in nowise remarkable mansion at the head of a small inlet nearly opposite St. Mawes. **St. Anthony Church** is at the back of the house, and is reached by a path, on the left, just before we arrive at the foot of the hill. It is well worth a visit as an example of Early English. Restoration has deprived it of all appearance of age, but the lines of the building are delightful. It is cruciform, and has a low central tower. On the south side of the nave is a good Norman doorway, with a lamb and a cross carved on the inner member.

If the tourist fail to find a boat at St. Anthony, he must shout for one, and if, too, he wave a signal of distress, he will have little time to wait before one will come over from St. Mawes. After nightfall, however, his chance would not be so good of securing assistance, and he had better sleep at Porthscatho than at St. Mawes, if he is too late to catch the last ferry-steamer, and does not want to charter a boat to Falmouth. The view of the little inlet in which Place is situated is very picturesque from the water.

From St. Mawes a steam-boat ferry plies to and from Market Strand (¾-m. from station), Falmouth, and takes about half-an-hour on the journey. The usual times from St. Mawes are 9¼, 11½ *a.m.*, 2¼, 5½ *p.m.*; but the last only in the summer months. *Fare*, single or return, 5½d.

Falmouth.

Hotels: *Falmouth*, close to the station and sea; *Green Bank*, overlooking the Harbour, nearly 1½ m. from the station; *Royal* (H.Q.), in Market Street, about a mile from the station. *Will's Temperance*, Arwenack Street.

Post: *Del. abt.* (London, &c.) 8.5 *a.m.*; (North) 2.45 *p.m.*; *desp. abt.* (North) 11 *a.m.*; (London, &c.) 4.30 *p.m.*; (Plymouth, &c.) 6.20 *p.m.*

Population: 4,373. (Parish 7,133.)

Steamers, see yellow sheet.

Falmouth, a port long well-known as the starting point of the Falmouth Packets, has of late years considerably declined in commercial importance, and is now chiefly used by vessels calling for orders. The last census showed a falling-off of about 20 per cent. in the population. But though its trade has diminished, its popularity with visitors seeking a picturesque resting place with a mild and equable climate, has of late years greatly increased. The town itself consists chiefly of a long, narrow and rather dingy street more than a mile in length, and running parallel with the west side of the Harbour. There are, however, some good shops, and a fair number of lodgings are to be found among the picturesquely placed villas &c. that dot the immediate neighourhood. The Hotel accommodation is good, and the situation of the *Falmouth Hotel*, on the neck of Pendennis Point and overlooking the Bay, is particularly pleasant. The bathing is safe, and plenty of machines are provided. Of public buildings the only one of any interest is Pendennis Castle, described below. The *Church*, which dates from 1663, is devoid of architectural merit. Of the old mansion of the Killigrew family, "*Arwenack*," on the left of the road from the station, there are some remains now in part converted into the estate office of the Earl of Kimberley, to whom this property has passed from the Killigrews. On the opposite side of the road is a granite obelisk erected near, but not on, its present site in 1738 as a memorial of the then recently extinct family.

It is on the charming scenery about its loch-like arm of the sea that Falmouth founds its chief claims on the tourist's attention, and even those who can only afford a few hours should visit Pendennis Castle and follow the castle-drive round the promontory on which the castle stands. The distance from the station and back again is about 1½ *m*. With more time at command, the excursion by steamer to Truro should be taken and a visit to St.

Mawes and St. Anthony across the inlet will also be found to open up scenes of much beauty. Those who make any prolonged stay at Falmouth will do well to provide themselves with Worth's *Guide to Falmouth* (Lake & Co., Truro; price, 1s.). **Constantine**, about 5 *m.* from Penryn, is one of the loveliest villages in Cornwall and has famous granite quarries.

Excursions from Falmouth.

1. **Pendennis Castle.** This Tudor fortification is still retained as one of the defences of the port, and is occupied by a detachment of the Royal Artillery. It was built in the reign of Henry VIII, and further strengthened by outworks under Elizabeth. The tower, of which the main work consists, remains much as it was at first, and numerous inscriptions preserve the memory of the King. It is of course now of far less importance and strength, and with its opposite neighbour St. Mawes Castle would, we imagine, soon be crippled by the power of modern artillery. It was to Pendennis, then held for the king by the gallant John Arundell of Trerice, that Queen Henrietta fled from Exeter in June, 1644. Thence she sailed to France, and in the following February, the Prince of Wales, afterwards Charles II., escaped from it to the Scilly Islands. Fairfax besieged it from March to August, 1645, when it had to yield to famine.

The *drive* round the promontory commands delightful views of the coast and of the Roads. Midway across the entrance to the latter is the Black Rock, marked by a beacon, and on the far side is St. Mawes and its Castle. From Pendennis Castle, about 200 ft. above the sea, the Harbour proper is fully commanded and on the creek at its head opposite Falmouth is the village of **Flushing**, said to enjoy the mildest climate in England. Numerous shipping is a pretty feature in the scene, which is softly beautiful with gently swelling hills, green and sprinkled with wood.

2. **To Truro**; *by water abt.* 10 *m.*, 1¼ *hrs. Fares, single or return,* 1s. *and* 9d. *Steamer (tidal) from Market Strand,* 1 *m. from the Station, during the Summer season.*

The first part of the voyage is down Falmouth *Harbour* and round *Trefusis Point*, memorable for the wreck of the *Queen* transport in 1814, when nearly 200 lives were lost. The point takes its name from an old mansion of the Trefusis family, that has long been a farm-house. We pursue our way up the mile-wide Carrick Road and passing Penarrow Point on the left, open up Mylor Creek, with the village of Mylor just within it, on the south bank. *Mylor Church*, close to the water, is Norman and has been recently restored. St. Just (in Roseland) Pool, where vessels lie in quarantine, is now on our right, and the village of *St. Just* is a short distance up the small creek beyond. Soon, on our left, we have the entrance of *Restronguet Creek* at the head of which is Carclew (p. 161), and then on the same side the lawns and woods of *Porthgwidden*, after which the Road abruptly narrows and we enter a winding river-channel. Then, ahead, the mansion of Trelissick comes into view on the left hand, and the scenery rapidly improves.

King Harry's Reach is the name given to the channel abreast of Trelissick, and the steep and richly-wooded banks on either hand are delightful. *King Harry's Passage* is the traditional name of the ferry which crosses the reach. An orchard-clad creek succeeds on the left, and then by *Tolverne Passage* we arrive off the mouth of the *Fal River* and enter *Malpas Road*. Lord Falmouth's splendid domain **Tregothnan** is now on the right, the mansion being high up above the river. Then the tower of St. Michael Penkevil is seen on that side, and on the opposite shore up a tiny creek the old church tower of *St. Kea*. In 1803 this church, far removed from the population of the parish, ceased to be used, and another—and an ugly one—was built about 2½ miles to the westward, but a small chapel has been retained, thanks to the late Rev. J. W. Murray. Another mile or so brings us to the end of the picturesque part of the voyage at the junction of the Tresillian Creek with the Truro River. Across the former of these is a ferry, and a small *inn* forms part of the little hamlet at the junction. The rest of the journey to Truro is uninteresting, and can only be made by steamer when the tide serves.

N.B.—Visitors staying at Falmouth are recommended to return from Truro by steamer, as the road route, 10½ m., presents no striking features, and the run by rail (*see p.* 161) is also of little interest.

3. To St. Mawes, St. Anthony, Porthscatho, &c.

Ferry from Market Strand at 10.30 a.m., 1, 3, 7 p.m. The 7 p.m. boat does not run in the winter half of the year. Return fare, 5¼d. Time to St. Mawes about ½ hr. The 3 p.m. boat goes on to Polcuel Ferry, but returns at once to St. Mawes. From St. Anthony to Portscatho is about 4 m. *For return boat see p.* 170.

The places named at the head of this Excursion are described under the coast route from Plymouth to Falmouth, and we here only give the necessary guidance for an easy day's ramble.

We suppose the tourist to leave Falmouth by the morning boat. In crossing it is quite possible, if he be a bad sailor, that he may find sufficient sea running to make him glad the transit to St. Mawes is but half-an-hour, as the Roadstead is unprotected from southerly winds. **St Mawes Castle**, a small edition of Pendennis, is well seen as we approach the eastern shore. From St Mawes a boatman will, for a few pence, row the tourist across to *Place*, an unimposing house at the head of a picturesque inlet. The pool that formerly lay in front of the house has been filled up, and the fish cellars known as Amsterdam, at the western entrance of the inlet, are no longer used. For *St. Anthony* lighthouse and *Zoze Point* the road from the landing-place passes in front of Place, and then turns up sharply to the left, but St. Anthony Church cannot be approached in this way. To reach that we go through the gate on the left of the house, and take a path that, in a short distance, goes off on the right. For *St. Anthony Church see p.* 170. Returning to the road, ascend the hill. We soon turn sharply to the left, and get now and again a view of the shore, which can be reached by a track that goes off on the right, and descends to *Porthbear Beach*. As, however, it is of no particular interest, and cannot be followed round the projecting headlands, we keep straight on. After having had a valley on our left for some time, when the road begins to descend, a good view up the Coast as far as the Dodman, past Nare Head and the Gull Rock, can be obtained by turning aside for a moment into the fields on the right. When the road descends to Porth avoid turns to the left, and ascend a rough lane, from near the top of which we get, on the left, a charming view of a winding creek. The lane then becomes a path, and skirts two fields to *Roseteage*, a farmhouse in a pleasant grove. Here the lane is resumed. Gerrans Church is seen a-head, and then we get a view of Gerrans Bay, with Giant Tregeagle's Quoits conspicuous on its far side. Carne Beacon (*p.* 169) is seen rising above the Quoits. For **Gerrans** see *p.* 169, *and for* **Porthscatho**, *p.* 169. From the latter place the tourist is recommended to return by *Polcuel Ferry*, for which route see *p.* 170. The walk we have described is about 7 *m.* If a longer one is desired, then St. Just may be included by proceeding north from Gerrans, ¾ *m.* to *Tregassa*, where we turn to the left, and then in about 1¼ *m.* onward to the left again. We then, in half-a-mile, reach the head of the main creek, running up from St. Mawes, from which St. Just is about 1¼ *m.* south-west. **St. Just, in Roseland** (*Rhosland*, the rough country), is so called to distinguish it from its namesake in Penwith, near the Land's End. The church is close to the water's edge, and the creek is pretty. There is a small inn, the *Ship*, in the village. A boat can, of course, be taken hence to Falmouth. By road to St. Mawes is about 2 *m.*, and the route thus extended about 10 *m.*

4. **To Helford Passage and back.**—A very pleasant walk of about 14 miles there and back, may be taken from Falmouth to Helford Passage—the out-journey being made by Budock Church and the village of Mawnan Smith, and the return by Mawnan Church and, for the last 3 miles, by the coast track. Either of these routes may also be recommended to pedestrians proceeding to the Lizard. There are small *inns* at Mawnan Smith and the Passage.

The footpath for Budock (2 *m.*) is a very good one. It leaves the Upper Penryn road—along which the telegraph goes—at its highest point, just above the Flushing Ferry, and crossing another road and the railway drops into a valley, beyond which it joins a farm-road leading directly to **Budock**. The tower of the church is a prominent object nearly all the way. There is nothing specially noteworthy about the building itself, unless it be the Norman arch of the porch and the pleasing appearance of the interior, which has been tastefully restored. Here is a brass to John Killigrew, the first Governor of Pendennis, who died in 1567. In the churchyard, near the porch, several old headstones, engraved with curious scrolls, may be seen. The services at Budock are attended by many Falmouth visitors during the season.

Passing out of the churchyard by the south gate we proceed by path and lane into the Falmouth and Mawnan road, which descends at once to a swampy little strath opening on to the sea at *Maenporth*. Here the coast-path, leading directly over the hill from Falmouth, joins our route. Above, on the right, rising from a mass of evergreens, is a picturesque gothic villa, appropriately called the *Crag*.

From Maenporth the road ascends again by a zigzag, which may be cut off by an obvious footpath. The top of this rise commands a wide view over land and sea, the higher part of Falmouth being, perhaps, the most interesting feature of it. In less than a mile a sign-post points to " Church," on the left, and " Mawnan Smith" on the right. The latter is our direction, unless we are going through to the Lizard and wish to see Mawnan Church and the beautiful peep from the churchyard on our way. The present excursion includes them in the return.

Half a mile beyond the turn is the village of **Mawnan Smith** (Inn: *Red Lion*). A pagoda-like erection noticeable on the way is locally called the *Tower of Folly*, but it serves the useful purpose of an Observatory. At the inn, our road turns abruptly to the left. A few yards may be saved by taking a footpath about 200 yards short of the inn. The stiles about here mostly consist of detached rectangular blocks of granite, let into the walls on either side, and so arranged as to form steps.

After continuing on the level for about a mile the road drops abruptly to the **Helford Passage**, where there is a small inn— *the Ferry-boat*—with sleeping accomodation for 3 or 4 visitors. The view up-and-down the Helford Estuary is very pretty when the tide is up. The flanking hills are low, but slope gracefully to the water's edge, and are in parts well wooded. Nearly opposite the inn are walls of the old Custom House, and up the creek, as far westward as the eye can range, the tower of Gweek Church rises from the trees.

Return from Helford Passage to Falmouth. An up-and-down footpath skirts the north side of the estuary eastwards for about 1½ *m.*, and is succeeded by a cart-track leading sharply up in half-a-mile to **Mawnan Church**, which is at the end of a

carriage-road from Falmouth. Though pleasantly overshadowed
by trees, the churchyard commands a lovely view, and the church
has lately been carefully restored. We now follow the Falmouth
road for about ¾ *m*., and at the finger-post, where we turned off to
Mawnan Smith village on our outward journey, turn to the right,
and retrace our steps to *Maenporth*. Thence we take the footpath over the hill, and in about 1½ *m*., passing the conspicuous
chimney of some chemical works, reach the shore again at
Swanpool, which is a little lake about a third-of-a-mile long
and some 200 yards broad, separated from the sea by a bar
of sand. Its name is derived from a swannery of the Killigrews
that has long ceased to be. To Falmouth we have a choice of
routes : (*a*) by cliff-path (1½ *m*.) which passes the bathing-place
called *Gyllyngvase*, and then joins the Castle drive ; or (*b*) by road
(1 *m*.) up the hill from the eastern side of the bar.

5. To Roscrow and Enys, *viâ Penryn*.

There is a choice of roads from Falmouth to Penryn. (i) That
by Basset Street and over Turnpike Hill is the *old* and shorter
one, and by it the distance is about 2 *m*. from the centre
of the town. Taking it, and turning off near the top of the hill at
a stile, the *Beacon*, which commands a fine view, can be visited.
(ii) The *new* road skirts the harbour-creek for a while and passes
the Ferry to Flushing, and then soon bends round and rejoins the
old road. This is an easier but slightly longer way, and misses
the fine view from the Beacon. By *rail*, Penryn is distant from
Falmouth *Station*, 3½ *m*., and the road distances above mentioned
are a mile longer from that part of the town. To reach **Roscrow view-point**, about 1½ *m*. from Penryn, follow the Helston
road, past Tremough, left (or better, ask permission to go through
the grounds and then turn to the right from the Upper Lodge),
to a junction of roads where turn to the right and then to the
left. A stile on the right is close to the spot, some 500 feet above
the sea, that commands the fine view which is the main object of
our excursion. This view extends north to St. Agnes' Beacon,
east over Roseland to the Dodman (seen through the dip already
mentioned as giving a glimpse of the sea eastward between Pen-
cuel Ferry and St. Mawes, *p*. 170), south to Pendennis, and north-
west to Carn Brea. South-west there is no prominent feature, but
on a clear day Row Tor and Brown Willy may be detected far
away to the north-east. Roscrow itself is near at hand below,
about half-a-mile to the north. We leave it on the left and proceed by road to Enys, to reach which we soon turn to the right,
as though bound direct back to Penryn, and then in another few
hundred yards to the left, and passing the railway, reach the
Truro road 2 *m*. north of Penryn. **Enys** adjoins this road on
the left, and to obtain another but very different view to that
described above, we ask permission to go a few yards along the
drive from the lodge. This view is a charmingly framed one. Its
central feature is Pendennis Castle.

6. **To Penjerrick**, *abt.* 3¼ *m.*

The nearest route to this pleasant seat, the gardens of which are open to visitors on presentation of their cards, is by Swan Pool through *Roscarrock*. It may also be taken on the way to Helford Passage (*see* Excursion 4) by proceeding 1½ *m.* by road, nearly due south from Budock Church. In this case, however, the onward route to Helford will be nearly straight, instead of by Maenporth, direct to Mawnan Smith, and the total distance will be about the same. The attractions at Penjerrick are the gardens and the lovely vistas that open between the flourishing and rare trees with which they abound.

7. **To the Lizard**, 18 *m.* direct.

This longer excursion can be made in various ways. *Omnibuses* run from Falmouth and Penryn to Helston (*p.* 181), and thence to Lizard Town. The *posting route* is *viâ* Gweek, at the head of the Helford estuary, and thence by *Trelowarren Park* (Sir V. F. Vyvyan, Bart.), through which permission to drive is freely given by the proprietor, and over *Goonhilly Downs*, and so into the Helston and Lizard road. Neither the route *viâ* Helston nor that *viâ* Gweek reveals any scenery worth mentioning, but Trelowarren Park is well timbered. By *pedestrians* the coast route should be taken, and if St. Keverne (*small inn*) and Cadgwith (*good hotel*) be made halting-places for the night, then much good cliff scenery may be inspected without serious fatigue. As far as Helford Passage the route is given on page 174. To save time the tourist will probably proceed that far *viâ* Budock or Swanpool to Maenporth, according as he starts from the upper or lower part of the town respectively.

After crossing the Helford Ferry, the road over the hill leads, in about a mile, direct to **Manaccan**, where the church, partly Early English, is worth looking at. Notice the Early Norman South door and the fig-tree growing out of the wall of the nave. The font, too, is interesting.

The pedestrian who intends to sleep at Cadgwith or Lizard Town had better proceed from Manaccan over *Roscreege Beacon* (380 ft., good view) to *St. Keverne*, nearly 4 *m.* by a rather devious and up-and-down course, for which the map is the best guide. If he determines to sleep at St. Keverne (*see below*), then from Manaccan **St. Anthony-in-Meneage** deserves a visit. It is on the little peninsula that separates the mouth of the Durra stream from the Hel estuary, and is distant about 1½ *m.* down the Durra valley. The situation is charming, and the little church, which is said to have been built as a thank-offering by some unknown travellers who escaped shipwreck and landed on the spot, is, possibly, in part, of the middle of the 13th century. A boat can be had to cross the Durra to *Gillan*, and then the coast-guard track, more or less distinct all the way, should be followed. *Nare*

Point, 1 *m.* from Gillan, is a fine headland ; and at *Porthalla*, a small fishing hamlet, about 1½ *m.* south of it, there is public-house accommodation. Thence, by the cliff, it is about 1½ *m.* onward to *Porthoustock*, a deep-set little cove with a coast-guard station, but no inn. Hence **St. Keverne** (Inn: *Three Tuns*, small ; '*bus to and from Helston twice a week*) is a mile or so uphill inland. The church, chiefly Perpendicular, is large, and its tower and spire are conspicuous far and wide. The village, without being remarkable in any wise, has a more picturesque garnishing of trees than is common in these parts. The extraordinary fertility of the soil, especially just south of the village, is famous in the neighbourhood, and the fields, with their wide path-wall divisions, owe their sunken condition to the removal of large quantities of the soil to less favoured regions.

From Porthoustock or St. Keverne the cliff-walk can be continued by the coast-guard track (rough and hard to hit) all the way to Coverack, 4 *m.*, and thence Cadgwith, 7 *m.* more, and is well worth taking. Off the shore, nearly due east of St. Keverne, are the *Manacle Rocks*, a dangerous reef on which in May, 1855, the *John* emigrant ship was wrecked, with the loss of nearly 200 lives. **Coverack** (small Inn and good lodgings), is a picturesque fishing village with a pretty little church restored 1885. Note the pulpit and font of serpentine. Not only to the geologist, for whom the coast hereabouts has much interest, but to the lover of quiet out-of-the-way nooks by the sea, Coverack will commend itself. The cliff scenery to the southward is very fine, and *Black Head*, about 1½ *m.*, is one of the finest bits of savage rock in the district. Supposing the pedestrian to follow the cliff-track, he ought to allow a good hour for the much indented two miles from Black Head to *Karakclews* (the grey rock), and then pushing onward past the sandy beach of *Kennack Cove*, he should turn inland, at *Caerleon Core*, to **Poltesco**, a hamlet famous for its serpentine quarries and in a fine rocky valley. Returning to the cliffs, Kildown Point and Ynys Head, with fine cliffs, are then passed, and Cadgwith (*p.* 188) is reached in another 1¼ *m.* From Poltesco by road through Ruan Minor (small restored church) it is only a mile to Cadgwith.

Truro to Penzance, *by rail* 25¾ *m.* ; 1 *to* 1½ *hrs.*

This route, for the first dozen miles, is through a mining district that of late years has suffered much from the low price of metals. As a consequence, abandoned mines abound, and add dreariness to a scene naturally devoid of anything approaching beautiful scenery. The line, too, as it strikes across to the neighbourhood of the north coast, is concerned more with the district treated of in our *N. Devon and N. Cornwall* volume, and accordingly we give but the briefest particulars of the journey. When **Redruth** (Inns: *Tabb's*, H.Q., *London* ; *Druid's Temperance*. *Pop.* 9,335),

9 m., is reached, mining is seen to be more prosperous; and then, on the left, **Carn Brea** (735 ft.) soon comes in view close to the line. It is crowned by an ancient castle at its eastern end, and on the summit is a monument to the late Lord de Dunstanville, of Tehidy.

Camborne (Inns: *Abraham's*, H.Q.; *Commercial*: Pop. 13,607) comes next, and is another mining town, close to which is the celebrated *Dolcoath mine* (tin and copper), which is worked to a depth of 2,250 feet, and can be visited. *Gwinear Road Station* is the junction for **Helston** (8 m.; *p.* 181). The towans about Phillack, whose church is surrounded by them, are on the right, on the way to **Hayle** (*White Hart*, H.Q.). This is the seat of considerable engine works, and the view from the line over its extensive quays and down the estuary is both interesting and picturesque. The church on the right hand is that of Phillack, and that on the left Lelant. Soon after leaving Hayle, St. Ives is well seen on the right, and over the hill appears the Knill monument. *St. Erth* is the junction for St. Ives, and thence the line crosses the isthmus, less than 4 miles in breadth, that connects the Land's End district with the eastern parts of the county. Ludgvan church is passed on the right, and then at *Marazion Road Station*, St. Michael's Mount is seen on the left (Marazion, *p*. 190, is more than a mile from the station). The railway now runs close to the shore, which is uninteresting, but Penzance appears to great advantage across the water, with Paul Church conspicuous to the left of it. On the right of the line the hill-sides form part of that rich market-garden-land so famous for the production of early vegetables. The church among the trees is that of Gulval. Stopping a moment to collect tickets, the train then enters **Penzance** station, a well-built structure of granite. *Omnibuses meet all trains. For Penzance, see p.* 192.

The Lizard.

Approaches: Rail to Helston, Penryn, or Falmouth, thence by omnibus to Lizard Town.

Under this name is included the whole of the peninsula south of the Helford estuary. The isthmus, measuring from Gweek, at the head of that tidal arm of the sea to Looe Pool, is a trifle over three miles in width. As seen either from the east or west the sky-line of the district is singularly unbroken, and a closer acquaintance reveals the fact that the peninsula is a tableland, with only comparatively minor undulations, and averaging from 200 to 300 feet above the level of the sea. Its greatest elevation is on *Goonhilly Downs* in the centre, where according to the Ordnance survey it reaches 368 feet. Geologically the peninsula consists of two formations, the division between them, to speak roughly, being a line drawn from *Polurrian Cove* on the west to *S. Keverne* on the east. North of this line the rocks are Devonian, south of it Trappean, of which last group Serpentine, so called from its resemblance to the skin of a serpent, is largely represented.

It is owing to this latter formation that the southern portion of the district is so generally barren, whilst its flora is distinguished by the abundant growth of the Cornish heath, *Erica Vagans*, a plant only to be found in England in this district and, according to Mr. Blight, on Conner Down, near Gwinear Road Station.

Most persons visiting the Lizard district proceed direct from Helston to Lizard Town, and from thence make such examination of the eastern and western sides of the peninsula as their time allows. This is certainly the best thing to do for those whose time is limited to a day or two, as within walking distance of Lizard Town are some of the most beautiful and interesting portions of the coast. Those with more leisure are recommended to make *Mullion* on the western side, and *Cadgwith* on the eastern side, as well as Lizard Town on the south their resting places. At each of these good accommodation is to be had, and in their immediate neighbourhoods are coast scenes that will richly reward the traveller who can allow himself sufficient time to examine them deliberately. There is little or nothing in the interior of the peninsula to interest the tourist, but its coast-line is as attractive as its inland portions are the reverse.

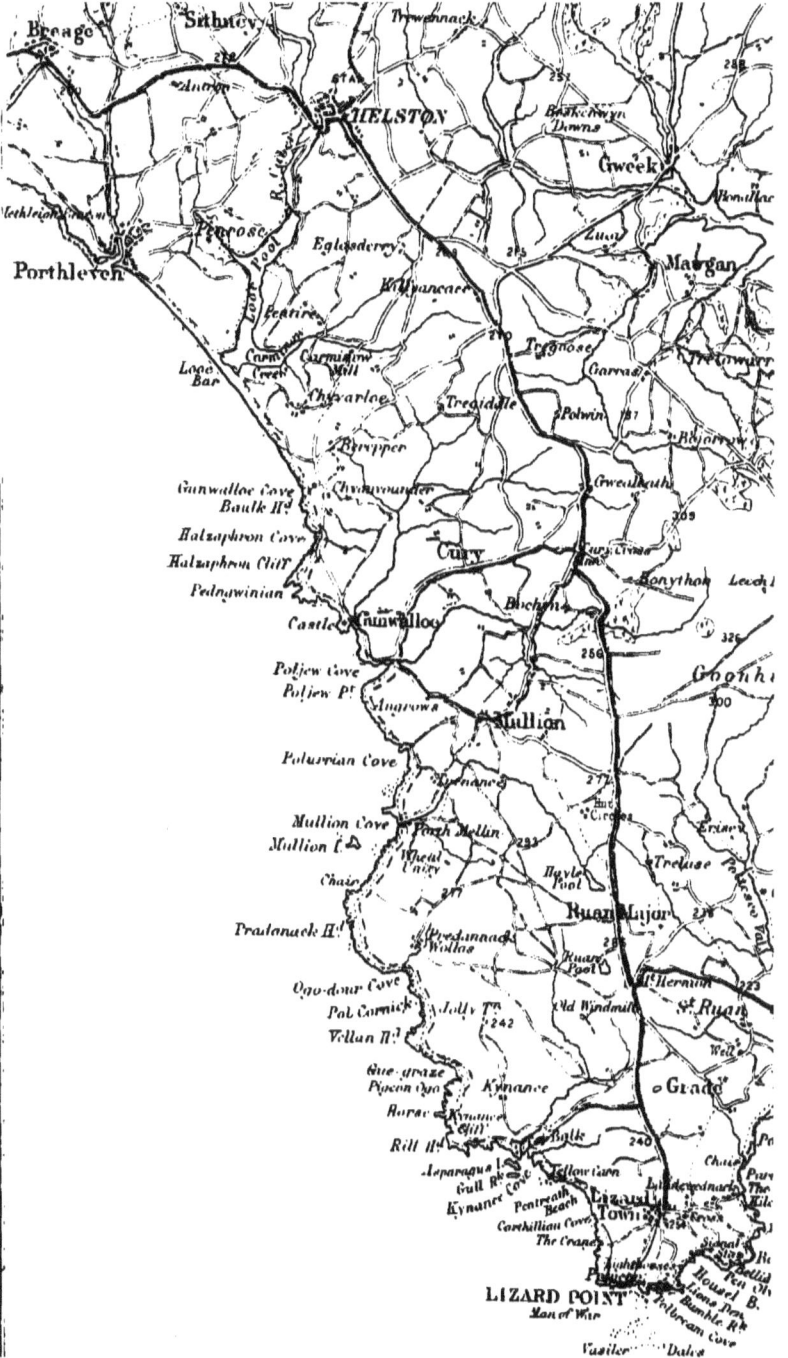

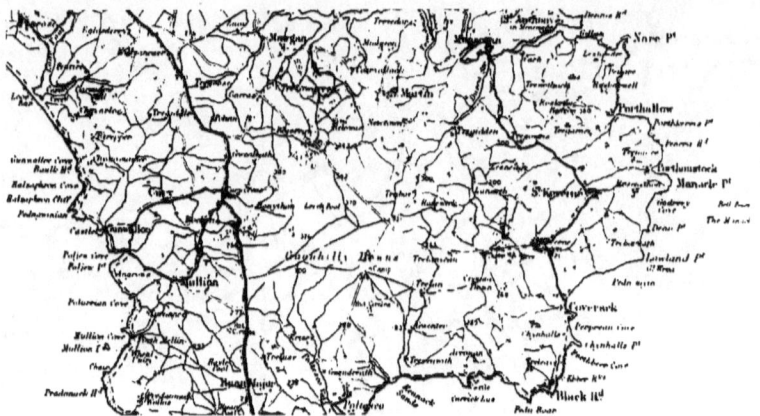

The road to Helston, whether from Falmouth, 12½ m., Penryn, 10 m., or Penzance, 13 m., is of little interest. On each route there is an omnibus service, the leisurely nature of which affords ample time to identify by means of the map the few objects seen on the way. On the road from Penzance, Godolphin Hill, 459 ft., and Tregonning Hill, 596 ft., are passed on the left hand; and at the village of Breag (*pron.* Brague) the church is noticeable, and the Looe stream is crossed as we enter Helston.

Helston (*Pop.* 3,432). Hotels: *Angel, Star* (Q.). 10 *min. from Station*; *Richard's Temperance*, Coinage Hall Street; *omnibuses to Falmouth, the Lizard, Penryn, and Penzance*.

This old-fashioned town, the terminus of a branch of the G.W.R., has little to interest the tourist. Turn to the right from the Station road and keep on straight down. At the bottom of the street is a memorial archway. The hotels face each other a little higher up.

Helston to Lizard Town, 10½ m.

This is the only route for which public conveyances are available. It requires but the briefest description, as it is singularly devoid of interest. Leaving Helston, the road at once begins to ascend to the watershed bounding the basin of the Helford river on the west. It keeps along this watershed for some 3½ miles, when it crosses a depression to *Cury Cross Lanes* (4¾ m.; Inn).

Here a road goes off on the right to *Cury* (1 m.) and *Gunwalloe* (2 m.; p. 182), and a little further on, one to *Mullion* (1¾ m.; p. 183).

Cury Church, restored, has a Norman south door with an enriched tympanum. The north aisle roof is of carved oak, and at the junction of the Bochym aisle and the chancel is a hagioscope. The rood-loft stairs remain, and in a bench-end near the door is a curious alms-box. A cross, 9 ft. high, is close to the entrance gate of the church.

Shortly afterwards as the road dips to the stream running to *Poljew*, on the left are the grounds of *Bonithon*, and on the right those of *Bochym*. At *Bochym*, a many-gabled and picturesque mansion amidst pleasant woods, are preserved some stone implements that in 1869 were found in a quarry hard by, and on the lower part of the estate, in a small plantation just outside the lodge gates, is a group of fine rocks, the topmost of which is called the Fire Rock. *Goonhilly Downs* are now on the left hand, and Cornish heath tells us that we have reached the magnesian soil that alone contents it.

We are now about half-way to Lizard Town, and the road thither is for the rest of the distance straight and in a direction due south. The tower-like object on the right of the road, just after passing *Ruan Major*, half-a-mile on the left, is the remnant of an *old windmill*. In the bare featureless district we are crossing, this almost becomes an object of interest, and apart from being a good landmark for those who, rambling, may have lost their way, it indicates to the traveller along the road we have come, that he is now only 2 miles from Lizard Town.

Lizard Town (Inns: *Hill's Lizard Hotel*, *Lugg's*, H.Q. *Post del. abt.* 10 *a.m.—Desp.* 2.30 *p.m., week days only. Telegraph Office*).

This, in spite of its designation, is a mere village, consisting of a few cottages, some fair lodgings, and the inns above named. It is situated about half-a-mile from the sea on the west and south, and half as much again on the east.

The *bathing place* is Housel Cove (*p.* 186), just east of the lighthouses.

Coast Walk round the Lizard Peninsula.

We now proceed to make the circuit of the peninsula, commencing at the north-west. The tourist, with either Mullion, Lizard Town or Cadgwith as his head-quarters will, with the aid of the index, readily turn to the description of such portions as he proposes to visit.

Helston by Penrose, Looe Bar, 3 *m*; **Gunwalloe,** 6 *m*; **to Mullion,** 7 *m*.

For nearly ¾-mile after quitting Helston we keep the Cober river on the right hand to the head of *Looe Pool*, a narrow lake about 1½ *m*. long, formed by the damming up of the river by Looe Bar, and formerly noted for a peculiar kind of trout. We then cross the stream and follow the west side of the pool, and through the Park of *Penrose* to Looe Bar, 3 *m*., a delightful walk. Looe Bar is formed of pebbles cast up by the sea. In times of flood it has to be cut through to relieve the pool, but this seldom happens more than once a year.

Carminowe Mill and all that remains of the Manor-house and Chapel of **Wynanton**, are on the bank of Carminowe Creek, on the east side of Looe Pool.

Crossing the bar, for the next mile the shore consists of small shingle and sand, and by following the wheel tracks quicksands will be avoided. Soon, after the cliffs approach the water-line, we reach *Gunwalloe Cove*, bounded on the south by *Halzaphron Cliffs*. Hence we get a pleasant view across Mount's Bay. Crossing the headland and skirting another small bay, 2½ miles from Looe Bar, we arrive at **Gunwalloe Church**, which occupies a dip, sheltered but slightly by the promontory called *Castle Mount*. The Church (restored) dates from the early part of the 15th century. The belfry-tower, formed of the solid rock of the hill-side on the N., S.

and W., is detached from the rest of the building. The bowl of a Norman font is under the west window, and has broad-arrows, symbolical of the Holy Trinity, round it. At the south-east corner of the chancel wall is a cross.

Proceeding onward we still follow the cliffs, till, in half-a-mile, we are overlooking the sandy inlet of *Poljew*. Passing round its head we quit for a time the coast, and mount the hill to *Mullion*.

Mullion (Inns: *Old, King's Arms*).

This church-town is 7 miles from Helston and 5 miles from Lizard Town by road. Its claims on the traveller are threefold: the church; the cove and the cave; and last, but not least, the excellent "Old Inn," happily still under the rule of Miss Mary Munday. Here, taking care to bespeak accommodation, the tourist will do well to tarry awhile. The *church*, Perpendicular, restored in 1870, is of considerable interest. Over the west window of the tower is sculptured a crucifix with St. Mary and St. John. Some portions of the old *rood screen* still remain, and the carved *bench ends* are considered by competent judges to be among the best, if not the very best, in the county.

Mullion by Mullion Cove and Kynance Cove (6 *m.*) **to Lizard Town**, 7½ *m.*

From Mullion the coast-walk can be resumed at the pretty sandy *Polurrian Cove*, which is about ¾ *m.* from the village, or at *Mullion Cove*, a trifle over a mile, south-west, where is a life-boat station. If possible choose a falling tide, towards low water, and if proceeding to Kynance, which also needs low water for its thorough exploration, there is no time to lose. *Mullion Cove* is very picturesque, and on the left a narrow natural archway leads to **Mullion cave**. This is a splendid recess, hollowed out by the waves, in the serpentine, and the view from within it is particularly beautiful. The entrance, like an irregular low pointed arch, exactly frames *Mullion Island*, which lies about a mile off the shore. In the mid-distance is an irregular islet, and the foreground is filled in by a smooth bit of sea, a patch of sand and a few rocks. To the left of Mullion Island we just catch sight of the Mullion Gull Rock. Returning to Mullion Cove by the way we came, a steep little climb lands us on the high ground, and we proceed southward towards *Pradanack Head*. If we are to reach Kynance before the tide flows we must make haste, for there is yet a good 3½ miles to traverse, by the cliffs.

The view from the high ground across the bay is delightful. We make out St. Michael's Mount and beyond it Penzance. *Mullion Island*, a cliff-girt little triangle rising to a point at its western apex, is now overlooked, and close under the headland is the *Gull Rock* above named standing up boldly.

Vellan Head is the next point passed, and then we skirt the margin of *Gue Graze*, which involves a descent to near the sea-level. Mounting again we have before us the curiously profiled *Horse*, which, as we proceed, we shall see is an "edge" far too sharp to tempt us aside to peril our necks by trying to ride it. On our way to it we can peer over a sheer, black precipice bounding a small semi-circular cove. Here, accessible only by boat, is a large cave called *Pigeon Hugo*.

The bold promontory next after the Horse is *Rill Head*, itself worthy of notice, but most in favour for the fine view obtained from it of Kynance Cove. **Kynance Cove**, however viewed, is certainly a remarkable spot. Perhaps it appears best from the Rill, when the tide is high. It then and thence presents itself as a cliff-bound bay, guarded on its further side by *Old Lizard Head*. From the midst of the bay rise numerous rocky islands of various shapes, all of fine outline, and most of them apparently so steep as to be unclimbable and certainly so on their western fronts. Viewed from *Tor Balk* on the other side of the cove, the scene is so different as hardly to be recognised as that of the same place, especially if now the tide has ebbed. We then have below us a sandy little cove, to which runs down a rocky irregular shore with a couple of cottages, and across the cove what from the west appeared as islands now seems to form a continuous headland. This is the view of the cove that on the whole most commends itself to us, and it is one which those approaching from Lizard Town and ascending the pile of rocks called the Tor Balk (corrupted into Tar Box) obtain. Nothing more varied and picturesque in outline than the "promontory" occurs on the Cornish coast. It appears nearly severed from the mainland, from which it at first stretches as a huge round-backed mass with turf on its summit, and cave-pierced cliffs on its eastern face. This is *Asparagus Island*. Thence seaward it suddenly rises in a ragged tor—the Kynance *Gull Rock*—beyond which, across a sharp dip, is the elevated and precipitous mass that forms its extremity. When the tide is out there are several caves that can be reached. Two, called the *Drawing Room* and the *Parlour*, are on the mainland opposite Asparagus Island.

That island itself has a cavern that pierces it, and a couple of blow-holes known as the "*letter box*" and "*post office*." It is easy to scramble on to *Asparagus Island* from the west, and not very difficult from the east. The *Gull Rock* is divided from it by a narrow channel, which the sea never quits.

We have hurried along to reach Kynance at low water. It is certainly not a cove to be hurriedly contemplated. Light refreshments may be had at the cottages, and comfortable lodgings too. The tourist will hardly fail to make some small purchases of serpentine or of the still more beautiful steatite as a tangible memorial of his visit. Those who care to be "personally accompanied" round the cove will in the season find a choice of guides.

Leaving Kynance, to resume our walk along the cliff, we first ascend to **Tor Balk** for the view of the cove described above, and then, crossing a tiny rill, climb for a little way. **Yellow Carn**, a sheer cliff of 200 ft. in height, is next on the right, and off it the isolated rock of *Enys Vean*. We then skirt the cliffs overlooking *Pentreath Beach*, after passing which a descent has to be made to another little stream at *Caerthillian* (*below*). We are now only half-a-mile from *Lizard Town*, and probably feel that we have earned refreshment. If so, our course is up the valley.

Coast route continued from Caerthillian by Lizard Lighthouses to Lizard Town, 2 to 2½ *m.*

The pedestrian anxious to push on and see as much as possible of the west of the peninsula before proceeding to Lizard Town, can from Caerthillian still keep to the cliffs. The serpentine is there quitted, and the patch of mica-slate that forms the south-west of the peninsula, entered upon. In a ¼-mile he will pass the little cove called *the Crane*, and ½-mile beyond that, arrive at *Old Lizard Head*. This is the name given to the westernmost of three adjacent points that form the south-west angle of the peninsula. The view back past Kynance to Rill Head is now particularly fine. On the way to the next cove we pass *Pistol Meadow*. Here were buried such of the bodies, some 200 in number, as were washed ashore from a terrible wreck that occurred in the early part of the last century. Anyone in the neighbourhood will tell the gloomy tale, but we have failed to get definite particulars as to date and name of vessel. Off the Old Lizard Head, a little to the east, will have been noticed two groups or rather broken ridges of rocks. On the easternmost of these a Government transport, with some 700 men on board, struck, every man of whom, with the exception of two, perished. The reef thenceforward has been known as *Man of War Rocks*, a name sufficiently like the old one, *Mên-an-raur* (great stones).

Polpeor Cove is now close by. This is one of the little fishing ports of the neighbourhood, and a lifeboat station. At low water a remarkable *cave* may be visited that runs through the western boundary of the cove. Just east of Polpeor we arrive at the southernmost point (lat. 49° 57' 32") locally known as *the Batha*. It does not appear to ordinary mortals to project further seaward than its immediate neighbours, but we do not venture to question the accuracy of the Ordnance surveyors. Above us now rise the twin towers of the **Lizard Lighthouses** (*visitors admitted except on Monday and after the lamps are lit*). These stand nearly 200 feet above the sea. They exhibit two fixed (electric) lights, and are provided with a Siren fog-horn against thick weather. Until the erection of the lighthouse on the Wolf Rock, off the Land's End, they were of even more importance than at present, as a ship coming up Channel by keeping the two lights in line thereby gives a wide berth of some 4 miles to that dangerous rock. The lighthouses *cannot* be visited after dusk, and to this rule the keepers are forbidden to make any exception.

Off the point just east of the lighthouses, to the edge of which the turf slopes rapidly, is the isolated rock called the *Bumble*, the base of which can be reached at low water. The bay to the east is Housel Cove, and the fine headland on its far side Penolver. Before striking inland to Lizard Town, the pedestrian should proceed a little way beyond the lighthouses to the **Lion's Den**. This is a pit similar to the Funnel near Tol-pedn-Penwith. It was formed suddenly during the night of February 19th, 1847, by the giving way of the roof of the innermost portion of *Daws Hugo*, a sea-cave that here runs under the cliff. At first its sides were sheer and its bottom level, and covered with the turf that had quietly sunk down some 40 feet. By degrees the sea washed out the soil, whilst the sides of the pit cracked and crumbled. It is now a square, rough-sided funnel communicating directly with the sea by the cave, and is interesting chiefly as showing the manner in which these cavities have been formed. We shall, near Cadgwith, see another example —the Frying Pan (*p.* 188)—of the same phenomenon. It is about half-a-mile by a rough road from the lighthouses to Lizard Town, *see page* 182.

Lizard Town to Housel, Belidden, Lizard Cove, and Landewednack, and back to Lizard Town, 2½ *m.*

The distances given in this and other cliff-and-cove excursions are only approximate, and are merely intended to furnish the visitor, unacquainted with the neighbourhood, with a rough estimate. **Housel Cove** is at the head of the bay of the same name. It is now approached from Lizard Town by a much better road than formerly, and is the recognised *bathing place*, and has a good sandy bottom, but is exposed in rough weather. Penolver is a fine object on its eastern side. From the head of the gully leading down to Housel we take the coast-path that runs eastward to **Penolver**. This rugged headland rises at its extremity in a pile of hoary lichen-covered rocks. On either hand the view is delightful—on the west the bay and cove of Housel, with the lighthouses and the Lizard Point and the Bumble on the far side. On the east we look down into the amphitheatre and narrow cove of **Belidden**, from which the Direct Spanish Cable is laid to Bilbao. On the opposite side of this bay projects *Beast* (or Bass) *Point*. Leaving Belidden, in a short distance we reach, near the edge of the cliff, an arrangement of rock slabs that is known as *the chair*, from which we get a noble view of the east side of Penolver. On *Beast Point* are the offices of the Direct Spanish Telegraph Company, and the Lizard signal station, with the name LLOYDS in enormous letters. Still keeping the coast-path we reach, after leaving Beast Point, *Hot Point*. Here is a *huer's hut*, such as is found on the headland at New Quay. It is used by the fishermen as a look-out, from which to observe the arrival of the pilchard shoals. The watchman from this point commands a magnificent prospect eastwards of the gently curving bay that extends to *Black Head*, its eastern limit, 4½ miles distant in a bee-line. The flagstaff on the cliffs on the left, 1½ miles off, marks the Cadgwith coastguard station. To the right of this the cliffs give place at Kennack Cove to a strip of sand. To the right of Black Head is seen Dodman Point beyond Falmouth, and in the extreme distance Rame Head on the west of the entrance to Plymouth Sound. The next cove—a small one, and though rocky not in any way remarkable, is *Kilcobben*, and then in a few hundred yards we descend sharply to **Lizard Cove** or, as it is marked on the Ordnance map, *Parn Voose*. This, like Polpeor already noticed (*p.* 185), is a little port, if such a term can rightly be applied to a cove where an occasional cargo of coals is landed and a few fishing boats are hauled up on the shore. From the cove we ascend by a steep road, ½-mile, to **Landewednack**—the Church Town of the parish. The church has several points of interest, the chief of which are the groined roof of the porch, the Norman doorway surrounding a smaller Perpendicular doorway, and the font, bearing the name of the rector, Richard Bolham, who carved it at the beginning of the 15th century. There is also a hagioscope. Landewednack is reputed to have been the church in which the last sermon in the Cornish language was preached, "not long before the year 1678." *Borlase*. It is the most southernly church in England. Returning to Lizard Town, ½ *m.*, an old and rude *cross* may be seen about half-way.

Lizard Town to Cadgwith. Weather permitting, and it needs a very calm sea, this expedition should be made by boat from Lizard Cove. Thence along the coast the row is not more than 1½ miles. The coast-guard path follows the top of the cliff, and is indicated in places by whitened stones. It calls for no particular description. The main object of interest on the route is the *Frying Pan*, near Cadgwith, and an account of this will be found *p.* 188. Supposing the tourist to have taken a boat at Lizard Cove, the first noteworthy object is the precipitous cliff, called the *Balk*. Half-a-mile beyond this he is off *Polbarrow Core*, where is a small cave (accessible only at low water) showing serpentine, hornblende, and diallage. Just beyond this, under *Carnbarrow*, is a natural archway, and then immediately we are opposite **Raven's Hugo**, so called from the birds that frequent a ledge on the face of the cliff above its mouth. This cave is of no particular interest, but its narrow entrance is draped with *Asplenium Marinum*, which here grows more luxuriantly than at any other spot we remember, except perhaps Mousehole.

Dolor Hugo is the next cave but one. It is always filled by the sea, and hence the necessity of a calm day if the tourist is to visit it. It is a grand cavern in the serpentine, and the colours of the rock at the entrance are singularly rich. The boat can enter but a short distance, and the recesses of the cave have in consequence never been explored. Less than a quarter of a mile beyond this is the **Frying Pan**. This originally was doubtless a cave, but the restless motion of the waves having eaten away the rock till a softer stratum was reached, the roof fell in, and, the *débris* having been gradually washed away, it assumed its present appearance. It is that of a huge funnel communicating with the sea by an archway. On its landward side it is nearly 200 feet deep. The boat enters by the archway, and a landing can be made on the little patch of shingle at the bottom of this singular cavity. The bushes growing from the cliff, high up, are tamarisk, and are said to be portions of a hedge that subsided. Returning to the boat we reach the pretty little village of Cadgwith after a short pull.

Cadgwith. (Inn: *Star Hotel. Post arr.* 11 *a.m., dep.* 1 *p.m., week days only; Post Town, Ruan Minor; nearest Telegraph Office, The Lizard; porterage,* 1s.) This is a charming little fishing village at the mouth of a picturesque valley, with a little brook. It is the best stopping place for those who wish to explore at leisure the coast by *Ynys Head*, just north of the village, *Caerleon Cove*, and *Poltesco* (p. 178), where the rocks are fine but not improved by the quarries. The pedestrian will find it a pleasant walk by the coast as far as *Coverack* (Inn), and thence by *St. Keverne* (small inns) across to the ferry on the *Helford River*, and so to *Falmouth*. The coast between Cadgwith and the Helford estuary is described the reverse way, *pp.* 177-8.

Helston to Penzance, *coast walk, abt.* 19½ m.

The first part of this route may be taken by Penrose and Looe Pool to Looe Bar, as given p. 182, by those who do not go that way to the Lizard. It will add, however, about 1½ m. to the distance named above. The sands can be followed westward from Looe Bar to Porthleven, but this 1½ m. is of no particular merit. From Helston most tourists will be disposed to get over the first 2½ m. of the alternative route, direct to Porthleven, by taking a Penzance 'bus that far. Then turning to the left, a road runs down a commonplace valley to the coast at **Porthleven** (Inn: *Commercial*), a port chiefly frequented by fishing boats. Considerable expenditure has, of late years, been made on the harbour, which its difficulty of access in rough weather hardly seems to justify. The place has nothing to show the visitor, except a handsome new Wesleyan chapel. The pedestrian bound westwards by the cliffs will probably be more interested in the inn, as he will find no house of refreshment on the way to Marazion.

Route. We take the road which ascends from Porthleven harbour to the western cliff, and soon get a good view of the sands eastward past Looe Bar to Gunwalloe and Halzaphron. Westward the view is bounded by the granite headland of Trewavas, with mine chimneys on its verge. For Trewavas Head it is necessary to keep the road for about 1½ *m.* further. It gradually ascends, and soon Sithney and Breage churches are conspicuous inland, and a church-like tower is seen on the face of Trewavas. At *Trewithack* take a farm-road on the left. This passes through *Trequean* farm to the head of a combe, where we turn to the right along a cart-track that soon becomes smaller as we near the edge of the cliff, along which we follow a wall. In front is a fine granite precipice, and looking back across the mouth of the combe we have skirted, the cliff is observed to have broad bands of granite. When a gate is reached, get over the wall on to the sea-slope above **Trewavas Head** and Mine, one of whose buildings is the church-like object previously noted. The mine is submarine, and used to yield copper but is now abandoned. Onward we follow for awhile the mine-road, and then take to the grass sea-slopes. Notice the finely-piled rocks at a point past the first mine. Next we reach the head of a cove, and pass above two more mines. Trewavas is well seen behind. Our track now for a little while has a wall on either hand, and then we follow a rough road past a cottage, and descend by a footpath that crosses two or three walls and then zigzags to *Pra Sands.* These are not good going, but the distance along them is inconsiderable. Near the west end of the sands take a lane inland, about half-a-mile, to **Pengersick Castle**, a Tudor ruin, of which a square tower with N.E. turret is all that remains. Within, some wainscoting may be seen. The key is kept at a cottage close by. Lying in the farm-yard solid stone barrels will be noticed, and on our return to the shore many hundreds of these will be found near a deserted mine. They are the cargo of a ship laden with Portland cement, that was wrecked here some years ago. We now ascend by a track to the cliff-top, and proceed to the savage **Hoe Point**, the rocks of which are pierced by three or more slits similar to that of Nanjizal. There is a fine chasm just east of the Point. We next cross a small combe, keeping the seaward side of a depression, and then reach *Prussia Cove,* that owes its name to the sign of a public-house long since closed. Here are a coast-guard station and a few cottages. Beyond the flagstaff we come to **Bessie's Cove**, which is very fine, especially as seen from its west side; and beyond it is a chasm into which the sea rolls with grand effect in rough weather. The sea slopes hereabouts are bright in the spring with abundant growth of wild squill and sea-pink. It is worth while proceeding out to **Cuddan Point**, which ends in a long ragged "edge." We now come in sight of St. Michael's Mount. The low and serrated Greeb rock is about half-way towards it, and close by on our right is the square form of Acton Castle, a modern erection of no interest.

Cuddan Point commands a view of the shore westward, which is comparatively uninteresting, and the pedestrian is recommended to turn inland by the lane past *Acton Castle* to the main road, which is reached in about a mile beyond it, at a point a little over 3 m. from Marazion Station. As we enter the town of **Marazion** we get one of the best views of St. Michael's Mount.

If the tourist so time his walk, he may proceed by the evening 'bus to Penzance from the point where the main-road is gained.

Marazion (or Market Jew).

Hotels: *Godolphin, Marazion.* A good hotel is needed.

This little town, 3 m. for Penzance and 1¼ m. from Marazion Station, has not much to arrest the tourist's attention except St. Michael's Mount, which is opposite to it, and is one of the chief "lions" of the district. The place appears, however, to attract a fair number of summer visitors, for whom there are several good lodging-houses. Both names by which it is known are said to mean "markets," and there is no doubt that it was in very early times a port of some trade.

St. Michael's Mount.

This is connected with the shore by a causeway ½ m. long, which is overflowed at high-water. *Boat-fare to the Mount, 6d.* The greenstone rock on the right of the causeway is called *Chapel Rock*, though of the chapel of St. Catherine, which is said once to have stood upon it, no traces are left. The Mount, as we near it, reveals at a glance all it has to show. Along its northern base is the village (Inn: *St. Aubyn Arms*, good), with the harbour on the west sheltering a few small craft. Above rises the steep granite tor of which the Mount consists, and on its top the castle with its square central tower. The height of the top of the tower above the shore at low water is 238 ft. At low water the circuit of the island can be made on foot, though the rough scramble is little remunerative. The ascent to the castle is by a steep rocky path, a little way up which we pass the *Giant's well*, that has nothing about it to interest us or to justify its name. Thence we ascend to a gateway, with the remains of a guard-house on the left and a sentry-box on the right. Still ascending, we reach a platform on which are guns bearing the arms of the St. Aubyn family, who have owned the Moun: for more than 200 years. On the left a flight of steps leads to the castle door. The two apartments that are of interest are the "chevy chase" **hall** and the **chapel**. The former of these was originally the refectory of the Priory, and gets its present name from the cornice, which represents the chase of a very varied quarry. The oak-roof is modern and heavy, but some of the furniture of the room is old and curious. The *chapel* is Perpendicular. In the south wall of the chancel a low doorway communicates with a small chamber, in which, when its entrance was discovered early in the present century, was found a skeleton alleged to be that of Sir John Arundell, killed in an attack on the Mount in 1471, when attempting to recover it from the Earl of Oxford, who, after the Royal victory at Barnet, had seized it by a ruse. These bones were buried outside the chapel on its northern side. A narrow staircase leads from the chapel to the top of the tower, whence a fine view of the bay and its shores is obtained. At the south-west angle is "*St. Michael's Chair*," so called, the ruin of a stone lantern from which a beacon-light used long ago to be exhibited for the benefit of the fishermen. The true "chair" is a rock on the west of the Mount. On the south side of the castle the proprietor (Lord St. Levan) has made considerable additions. We have only space for the briefest possible history of the Mount. Hither St. Keyne is said to have come from Ireland as early as 490 on a pilgrimage to a spot already hallowed by the appearance of the archangel Michael to some hermits. In 1047 Edward the Confessor granted it to *Mons S. Michaelis in periculo maris* off the Normandy coast, and a Priory of Benedictines was established here. It does not appear to have suffered as an alien priory in the 13th and 14th centuries, nor was it suppressed under the Act of 1414, though it was afterwards assigned *temp.* Henry V. to Sion nunnery. As already mentioned, in 1471 the Mount was seized by the Earl of Oxford, who here defended himself so gallantly that his offence was forgiven. Some few years later Lady Catherine Gordon, who had been married by James IV. of Scotland to Perkin Warbeck, "Richard IV.," took refuge here, and later on, when in 1549 the Cornish rose against the use of the reformed Prayer Book, the Mount passed more than once to and from the rebels and the royal forces. Like the rest of Cornwall, St. Michael's sided with Charles I., but was captured by the forces of the Parliament. The Mount eventually, soon after the Revolution, became the property of the St. Aubyn family, in whose possession it remains.

From Marazion to Penzance is a long 3 miles, quite devoid of interest, but the railway from Marazion Road Station is available for the last two of these.

Penzance.

Railway Station at E. end of town, about a mile from hotels on Esplanade, half-a-mile from *Western* or *Union*.
Omnibuses from station to Hotels, 6*d*.
Cabs   „   „   „   1*s*. (1 or 2 pers.), 1*s*. 6*d*. (3 or 5 pers.).
Hotels: *Queen's* (first-class: bed and attend. from 4*s*. 6*d*., dinner 5*s*.) and *Mount's Bay* (next door east), both on Esplanade.
Western (bed, breakfast and attendance, 6*s*.; H.Q.) in Alverton Street at corner of Clarence Street; *Union* (same prices) in Chapel Street.
Railway (close to station), and *Star*, in Market Jew Street. *Perrow's Temperance*, Chapel Street.
Steamer to Scilly Islands.—Cab from station or hotels to Pier, 1*s*.
Baths at west end of Esplanade.
Post Office (in Market Jew Street, 50 yds. E. of Market House): *Del* 8.30 a.m., 3.30 (North) and 7.15 p.m.; *Desp*. 6.15, 11.15 a.m. (North), 4.50 p.m. Sunday *Del*. 8.30 a.m., *Desp*. 4.30 p.m.
Telegraph Office always open.

Penzance, perhaps = "holy head", is an old town with a modern western extension. From the Station, Market Jew Street, nearly half-a-mile long, leads up direct to the **Market House**, a domed building with a classical façade, in front of which stands a *statue of Sir Humphrey Davy* (1778—1829), the eminent natural philosopher, who was a native of Penzance. Against the W. end of the Market House is a well preserved *old Cross*, and the junction of streets there serves as the Market Place. [By turning left here we should reach the Esplanade.] Keeping straight on we pass through the *Green Market*, a tiny square, and in 150 yds. more (beyond the Western Hotel) reach the **Public Buildings**, a handsome block containing the Guildhall, Municipal Offices, *Geological Museum* (good), *Public Library*, *Reading Room*, St. John's Hall (assembly room), Masonic Hall, etc. The *School of Art* and *Art Museum* are housed in a new building at the top of the new street, reached by turning left a trifle E. of the Public Buildings. This street leads down to the sea and Esplanade.

If from the station we skirt the Harbour, we see on our right the tower of St. Mary's, the parish church, and then, after crossing a swing-bridge, have to turn for a little distance away from the water because the sea-front is interrupted by business premises. Bearing left, as soon as we can, we reach the E. end of the **Esplanade**, about ½ mile long, a delightful promenade in full view of St

Michael's Mount. Westward the bay is bounded by Penlee Point, on the near side of which we see Newlyn and Paul Church on the hill. Eastward, beyond St. Michael's Mount, runs out Cuddan Point, and the view is unbounded in that direction by the long flat-topped Lizard peninsula.

Of the three **churches** in Penzance none are remarkable, but the bells of St. Mary's are sweet. The old part of the town, lying chiefly between Market Jew Street and the Harbour, is more or less quaint, and the street names now and again suggest inquiry into the history of the place; one reminding us that in days gone by Penzance was a tin-coinage town.

The new or western part of Penzance is bright and pleasant and offers a wide choice of lodgings; and of small lodging-houses there is also a long terrace on the eastern part of the Esplanade, not to mention other unpretending parts of the old town.

Climate. The annual rainfall is about 43 inches, and the winters are so mild that ordinary half-hardy plants, such as geraniums, remain out doors without danger from frost. In the summer the climate is distinctly relaxing but not particularly warm. The drawback of the place during a great part of the year is the frequent occurrence of what north of the Tweed would be termed "soft" weather. On the other hand there are pretty walks close by, and the cliff scenery westward to the Land's End is magnificent.

In 1595 a large part of the town was burned by the Spaniards. It became a tin-coinage town (tin blocks tested for quality by cutting off a *coin, i.e.* a corner) in 1663 and so continued till the practice was abolished in the reign of George IV. June 24 and 29 (St. John's and St. Peter's days) are local festivals.

Walks and Excursions from Penzance.

Distances reckoned from the middle of the Esplanade.

N.B. The distinctive scenery of this district is almost confined to the cliffs. For about 2 *m.* inland around the head of Mounts Bay the country is fairly timbered, the rocks being of slate. Outside that area, N. and W., granite prevails, and trees give place to a ragged and frequently furze-clad country of little beauty. The N. coast of the peninsula, W. of the Hayle estuary as far as Gurnard's Head, and again between Pendeen Watch and Cape Cornwall, is also fringed with slate rocks, but there are no trees there worth mentioning. That our pages may be of use to the antiquary, we point out the chief old-world relics, but it may prevent disappointment if we forewarn the ordinary tourist that none of them are objects of beauty.

Of **short walks** the best are: (i) To Gulval Church, 2 *m.*; (ii) To Madron Church, 2½ *m.*; (iii) To Mousehole, 3 *m.*; (iv) To Castle Horneck, 1¼ *m.* Of these, particulars will be found under the following longer excursions, except number (iv). To reach the field-path past *Castle Horneck* start by the road running W. from the Public Buildings (or from the top of Marrab's Road), and beyond the bridge over the stream at Alverton do not take the road, right, up stream, but a steep pitch just beyond that, on that side. A few yards up this, after a slight bend to the right, you bear round to the left, and then following the path, in half-a-mile or so, beyond Castle Horneck, the house seen on the right, you will join the St. Just road, and can turn *down* back to the town—a round of about 2½ miles.

To prolong this walk (3½ to 4 m. in all) keep *up* the road for ½ m. and then turn left. In about ½ m. further you will pass **Trereiffe** (*pron.* Treeve), left, and see the end of the house, clad with close-clipped yew. Just below it you join at right angles the Land's End road and (*a*) turning left can reach Alverton again, by a shaded road in a short mile. (*b*) By crossing the Land's End road you quickly reach a bridge over the stream flowing down the Newlyn valley, past some mills, to the bridge (1 m.) at Newlyn, whence it is about 1 m., by the coast-road, back to the Esplanade.

To Gulval Church, 2 *m.*; **Castle-an-Dinas**, 4¼ *m.*; and then back same way; or on foot to **Chysoyster**, 1 *m.*, and then by road back to Penzance, 4 *m.* more—total 9¼ miles.

From Gulval to Ludgvan Church, 2 m.

You can drive to Castle-an-Dinas gate, and if after setting down there the carriage be ordered to go to Chysoyster (2 m. by road *viâ* Badger's Cross), the intervening walk need not exceed 1¼ m. Chysoyster is only of antiquarian interest.

To **Gulval Church** there is a choice of routes, viz: *viâ* Bleu Bridge or by footpath from the Marazion road, *see below*.

We leave Penzance by the Marazion road, past the station, and on the near side of the Three Tuns Hotel, for the Bleu Bridge route to Gulval, turn to left and then immediately to the right. The road ascends (it leads direct to Zennor, see *p.* 205), and (¼ hr. from the hotel) we turn down from it, right, by the third road, the fourth opportunity counting a footpath, to **Bleu Bridge**, a pretty spot with an inscribed stone (6th cent.) at the bridge, "*Quenataus Icdinui Filius.*" Thence (by right-hand road) it is 10 min. walk up to Gulval Church.

Footpath to Gulval. This leaves the Marazion road on the E. side of the little bridge over a brook, just beyond Ponsondane, the private house whose small park the road skirts. When the footpath forks a few yards from the road keep to the right.

Gulval Church, partially restored, is not of much interest, but its graveyard, recently enlarged, is delightful. Outside the S. porch are the stump of an old cross and a stone, found a few years ago, perhaps a Roman milestone. The window tracery against the wall of the church belonged to the old E. window, which has been replaced by the larger and well filled Bolitho window.

By a pleasant lane it is about 2 m. east to Ludgvan Church (restored 1887), of which Dr. Borlase (1772), the antiquary, was rector for more than 50 years.

It is 1 mile due N. from Gulval Church to Badger's Cross, where we take the right-hand road and follow it for ½ m., and then diverge left up to **Castle-an-Dinas** (735 ft.) on which are the remains of a hill-fort, similar but inferior to Chûn (p. 206). The **view** includes: Merra Hill and Trevalgan Hill, with a bit of sea between them. East, Trink Hill and the N. coast as far as Trevose Head, with the round topped St. Agnes Beacon half-way. Still nearer and more to the right is Carn Brea with its monument. South, the whole of Mount's Bay. South-west the tower of Buryan Church breaks the sky-line.

Of *Roger's Tower*, modern, we do not know the history. About 200 yards below the top of Castle-an-Dinas is a *walled enclosure*, about 30 ft. by 20 ft., entered by step-stones in the wall. On the opposite wall are three tablets: No. 1 "J.H., 1812, aged 20," No. 2, "J.H., 1823, aged 63," No. 3, " E.S., 1812 (bis), aged 22 and 1." These commemorate a gentleman of Gulval (No. 2), his son, his daughter and her babe. Note the inscriptions, left-hand corner, "Custom is the idol of fools"; right-hand corner, "Virtue only consecrates the ground." The gentleman had quarrelled with the incumbent of Gulval and declined his offices and burial in the churchyard.

From the top of Castle-an-Dinas it is a short mile, about S.W., to **Chysoyster**, where a little above the farm are the remains of a considerable British village, consisting of hut circles or ovals. There is also, a short distance from these, an old stone arch, nearly hidden by gorse and brambles. It is called the *Giant's Cavern* but leads nowhere, as far as we could make out.

Our outward route is rejoined by road 1¼ m. S.E., at Badger's Cross, but the pedestrian may with no increase of distance cross the valley and hill to the W. of Chysoyster, and return to Penzance by the Zennor road *viâ* New Mill and Trevaylor (or Treyailer). To include Mulfra Quoit (p. 197) would increase the total round to a long 12 miles.

To Madron Church, 2½ m.; **Lanyon Quoit**, 4½ m.; **Nine Maidens**, 6 m.; **Mulfra Quoit**, 7 m.; **Penzance**, 12 m.

Beyond Madron Church there is little on this round to interest the traveller who is not an antiquarian. By an extra mile or thereabouts the antiquities: *Madron Well* (Baptistery), *Mên-an-tol* and *Mên Scryfys* can be included.

We start either by Causeway-head (the street N. from the Green Market) or from the Western Hotel up Clarence Street. The two streets converge at the Cattle Market, and still proceeding in the same general direction, by St. Clare Street, we ascend past the Recreation Ground (right), and then descend past the Cemetery with Madron Church conspicuous on the opposite hill. Just below the Cemetery Lodge (1 m. from the Esplanade) the road forks, and we proceed to the left through the hamlet of *Heamoor*.

Hea, a few hundred yards to the right from the Pub. Ho. at Heamoor, has a chapel, built on a rock where John Wesley preached; an inscription records the fact.

As we ascend towards Madron, the footpath runs inside the right-hand hedge, and looking back we get a peep of the sea and St. Michael's Mount. The mansion on the left of the road is Poltair.

Madron Church (2¼ m.; 350 ft. above sea-level) is the mother-church of Penzance. Externally it has nothing remarkable about it. On the N. side of the graveyard is a portentous mausoleum, and on the bank at the W. end is an ancient *Cross*. The interior, well restored in 1887, is very pleasing. Most of the woodwork (linen-panel bench ends in the body of the church, side screens of chancel and low chancel screen) is modern, but a few pieces of old carving are worked into the chancel screen, and in the S. aisle of the chancel are 14th century bench ends, found under the floor. The uprights in the chancel screen indicate work still to be done. The oldest part of the building is a Norman base of a pillar at the E. end of the S. aisle, and in this aisle is an Early English piscina, and another with sedile, also E. E., in the chancel. The rood-stair doorway is in the S. aisle, and on the opposite side of the church a corresponding recess.

<small>**To Madron Well** (Baptistery), nearly a mile, From N. porch of Madron Church go N., and when the village street forks to the left. Keep on past the Union Workhouse at the far end of which (550 yds. from church) take field path on the right, and where this, at once, forks, the right-hand branch. About 500 yards from the Union you will reach a bit of rough ground alongside a road and see two gates, on your right (there are three, but only two are at first seen). Go through the left-hand gate and follow cart track for 150 yds. Then take an intermittent foot-track, left, about parallel with the copse, to a granite stile (110 yds). Beyond this (140 yds.) are the ruins of the **Baptistery**. The walls are standing, and inside are the remains of stone seats as well as the altar slab (hole in it). The *Kolumbrtrha* is also intact, but dry, although the rimlet that supplied it is within a few yards. We were told by a native that another " well " did duty for divining, by pin-dropping, now that this, the real one, was in abeyance. Where it was we did not learn, but if such a substitute is a fact it may lead to confusion if local guidance is enlisted. Returning to the bit of rough ground we can go up the road to join the road for Lanyon—right at cross-roads.</small>

The road past the Union (see small type *above*) is the one we have to follow, and 2 miles bring us to **Lanyon Quoit** which was overthrown or fell, in 1815, and was re-erected in 1826, when the three uprights were cut down and the archæological interest of the monument destroyed. The cap-stone measures 18½ ft. by 13½ ft. at its N. end. It is now only 5½ ft. off the ground, but in Dr. Borlase's time a horseman could ride beneath it.

Lanyon Manor House, now a farm-house, a short distance beyond the Quoit, is still the abode of the decayed family of Lanyon, whose name comes from Lannion in Brittany.

<small>On the moors at a short distance to the right of Lanyon farm-house, in the direction of Carn Galva, is **Men-an-tol** (" the holed stone "). It consists of two upright stones, 3 and 4 ft. high, with, midway between them, a slab pierced by a hole nearly 2 ft. in diameter.
About 1½ m. N.E. on the W. side of *Gun-mèn-scryfys* (" down of the written stone ") is **Men Scryfys** inscribed *Rialobran Cunoval Fil* " (Rialobran the son of Cunoval) in letters not later than the 5th cent. Of the persons named nothing is known. The writer has not seen this.</small>

From Lanyon we take the road, N.E., to *Ding Dong Mine* (1 m.) said to have been worked before the Christian Era. On the hill, north of the mine, are the remains of a stone circle, **Nine Maidens**, but only 6 out of the original 22 stones are erect, one about 6 ft. high. Of the fallen stones, two measure 7½ and 6 feet. The S. side of the circle is interrupted by a low cairn, near the centre of which are the remains of a small cist.

It is about a mile E. to Carn Mulfra, on the N.E. side of which is **Mulfra Quoit**. The capstone has fallen, but three sides of the cist it covered, remain. We can return to Penzance (5 *m.*) from here, by the Zennor road, which descends to the Marazion road a little E. of Penzance Station.

Penzance (by *New Bridge*, 3½ *m.*) to St. Just, 7 *m.*

This is the dull road taken by the omnibuses (several times a day, 6*d.*). It is described *p.* 206 in the reverse direction.

Penzance (by *Sancreed*, 4 *m.*) to St. Just, 7¾ *m.*

We leave Penzance by Alverton St., and up the hill beyond Alverton take, at a fork, the left-hand road past Trereiffe (pron. Treeve), right. At cross-roads here, we keep straight on, and ascending the next rise note an old oak, left, which sends a limb over the road. At the top of the rise there is in the left bank an old Cross. Then we drop to *Buryas Bridge*, 2 *m.*, over a small brook. A few yards up the hill beyond, an avenue, on the right, leads to Nancothen, but we keep to the main road to *Drift* (2¾ *m.*), a hamlet at cross-roads, and there turn to the right for **Sancreed**, 4 *m.* The church (restored) has a good church-yard *Cross*, and is pleasantly surrounded with trees. Beyond the village our road passes between Sancreed Beacon, right, and Carn Bran, ½ *m.* to the left. On the latter are the remains of a hill-fort. A mile W. of it rises Pertinney or Bartiné Hill (689 *ft.*) and then, as we descend towards St. Just, there is a wide view in front. *For St. Just, see p.* 206.

St. Just to Sennen, 6 *m.*; Land's End, 7 *m. by road.*

This route is for the most part dreary and uninteresting. For the first 4½ miles, as far as the junction with the direct road from Penzance to the Land's End, it keeps a course a mile or more away from the shore. Unhappily, those who drive between the two places have no alternative route, and to add to its disadvantages the road by its windings on leaving St. Just makes two miles out of one.

St. Just by Whitesand Bay and Sennen Cove to Sennen, 5¼ *m.*, *or* **Land's End**, 5½ *m.*, *cliff walk.* The best plan for the pedestrian is to take the road south-west to *Boscregan*, 1½ *m.*

This is on the cliffs just south of *Pol Pry*—the "clay pool"—
where there are some caves in the cliff. From Boscregan there
is a Coast Guard path to Sennen Cove. Proceeding south and
crossing the stream from *Nanjulian*, the shore becomes lower and
less abrupt. A good raised beach may be seen here. In another
¾ m. we pass *Carn Creagle* with the Watch rock, and then at *Carn
Aire* arrive at the northern extremity of the beautiful **Whitesand
Bay**. At the southern extremity is the little fishing village of
Sennen Cove, and the three islets off it are, naming them from
right to left, *Little Bo, Bo Cowloe*, and *Cowloe*. The rock on which
the sea breaks between them and the Longship's Lighthouse is
Shark's Fin. The tourist should, if the tide allows, make his way
to Sennen Cove along the sands. Half-a-mile short of the cove a
tiny stream comes down at *Vellandreath*—" the mill in the sand "
—but the mill has long disappeared. Close to Sennen Cove is a
mass of protruded slate, the junction of which with the granite
will interest the geologist. From Sennen Cove we mount to *Pedn
mean du*, "Black Stone Head," and then the Land's End, the
westernmost extremity of Great Britain, comes into view. The
curious rock close to the shore is the *Irish Lady*, and the shape of
the top of it gives some justification to the name. A little way
onward we reach on the cliff-edge a "cliff castle," small but in
good preservation, called *Mean Castle*, and then if our destination
is Sennen (*Inn, below*), we strike inland ¾-mile. Should we, however, have determined on the Land's End Hotel as our resting-
place, we can still continue to follow the cliffs and shall get, as we
proceed, a good view of the stern cave-hollowed precipices on the
north of the actual **Land's End** (*p.* 199).

Penzance to the Land's End, *direct* 10½ m.

This is a dull walk and the breaks are to be preferred.

As far as *Drift*, see *p.* 197. There we keep on up the hill and at
the top see, a little to the left, 2 upright stones said to be monu-
mental. Descending again, at *Lower Hendra*, 3½ m., a few cottages,
we turn to the right. [The left hand road leads to St. Buryan and
the Logan Rock.] In ¼ m. another pillar-stone is seen on the
right. Beyond this, when after crossing the next dip we again
reach higher ground, the Stone Circle, **Boscawen-un**, is seen on
the left.

To reach it take the farm road left. This passes *Creuplol* (¼ m.) a rock with
cavities more or less like footsteps. Turning to the right at the farm-
cottages, *Boscawen-noon*, it is about 1 m. in all to the **Nine Maidens**, as this
"circle" is called. It consists of 19 stones and within, but not central, is a
Long-stone 8 ft. high. For another Nine Maidens see *p.* 197.

On the N. side of the main road are the remains of an *Ancient British
Village*, so says the new ordnance map. We have not visited them.

At (6 m.) *Crows-an-wra* ("the wayside cross") is an ancient
Cross. Avoiding diverging roads but after many windings we soon

begin to descend towards the coast and, at 9 m., reach **Sennen** (Inn: *First and Last House in England*), an inconsiderable village with a not particularly interesting church. A good many artists find farm-house lodgings here during the summer. It is a long mile from the village to the Land's End by road, but a footpath cuts off the angle.

The Land's End.

Here, on the headland next south of the "End," is the *Land's End Hotel* (closed Jan. to March). Those who can afford the time are recommended to sleep either here or at Sennen at least one night. The actual Land's End is a sharp slope of turf terminated by a cliff of columnar granite, between 50 and 60 feet in height, off the extremity of which a broken ridge runs out for some distance into the sea. The writer has visited the spot at all seasons and well-nigh at all hours. His memory especially retains a visit early one summer's morning, and another just before sunset on a bright January evening, on both which occasions the Scilly Isles rose sharp and clear. Early and late are certainly the most beautiful, because then not only does the light add to the beauty of the rock-colouring, but there are deep cool shadows. The early afternoon of a bright and hot summer's day is without doubt the least advantageous time, and Scilly is almost sure then to be lost in haze. If the tourist is fortunate enough to combine the witching hour with a bright sky and a good ground-sea, he will view the scene of old Bolerium at its best. The view northward is bounded by the fine headland of Cape Cornwall with the off-lying Brisons. Near by, in the same direction, is the **Irish Lady**, close under the cliffs of Gamper Bay. Westward immediately below is the Peal Rock, and across the restless waters of Kettle's Bottom is *Carn Bras*, on which stands the **Longships Lighthouse**, the lantern of which is 123 feet above high water mark. The keepers, four in number, only one of whom is on shore at a time, have frequently great difficulty in passing from the mainland owing to the prevalence of stormy seas. The Scilly Islands, when in sight, appear a little to the left of the Longships. The fine pinnacle of rock, near the cliffs on the left, is the **Armed Knight**. The dangerous *Wolf Rock*, about 6 m. south, has since 1872 been marked by a lighthouse. At low water a visit can be paid to the cavern that pierces the Land's End. It is about 50 yards through. If the tourist has not already come down the north coast from St. Just, he should avail himself of his visit to the Land's End to explore at least as far as **Whitesand Bay** in that direction, and there are interesting caverns between the Land's End and Sennen Cove.

Land's End to Trereen (for Logan Rock and Trereen Dinas), 4 m. by road.

This drive is of little interest, but except on foot along the cliffs, a magnificent walk described in the next section, the tourist has no other choice. From Trereen (or Treen), where there is a small *inn*, it is rather over half-a-mile to the **Logan**.

Land's End to the Logan, 6 to 7 *m*. **by the cliffs.**
This walk is justly considered to equal if not to exceed in grandeur and beauty of cliff scenery any other of equal length in these islands. It matters little in which direction it is taken, but the writer inclines to prefer that which he is about to describe, from west to east. The only point of importance is to choose a bright day and so to time the walk in either direction as to have the sun more or less behind one. Plenty of time should be taken, and if the latter part of a summer's afternoon and evening, say four or five hours, be allotted to the excursion, and a carriage be ordered to meet the pedestrian at *Trereen*, say half-an-hour after sunset, he will be able to thoroughly explore the ins and outs of this wonderful bit of coast without having to spare himself for the tramp back to Sennen or Penzance.

N.B.—Fern collectors will find abundant *Asplenium marinum* on the rocks along the cliff-top.

The first point on the cliff after leaving the Land's End is *Carn Creis*, and just off it lies the *Dallah* or Dollar rock. The **Armed Knight** is the fine pile a little beyond. As far as we have made out the resemblance, it is that of a giant mail-chested figure leaning against the pile, a projection of which does duty well enough for the bent knees of the knight. The other large rock close by is called *Guela*, which is said to mean the 'easily seen' rock. The point due east of these which we next reach is called *Carn Greeb* —the 'comb,' from a certain rough likeness of its crowning ridge of rocks to a cock's comb. Whether there is any connection between Greeb and Cribba (the headland west of Penberth cove) we do not know, but that is of similar character, and is said to mean the 'crested' head.

We now have immediately in front, and near the cliffs, **Enys dodnan**, 'the island with soil upon it.' Its summit is covered with turf, and its outer side pierced with a fine natural archway some 40 ft. in height. The rock may be reached at low tide by those equal to an awkward bit of crag-work. The chief reward to be obtained by this scramble is a really fine view of the Armed Knight through the arch of Enys dodnan.

We next reach the magnificent headland of **Pardenick**, " the assemblage of rocks." Here the columnar arrangement of the granite is very striking, and the colouring of the promontory, especially seen from the westward when the sun is low and the lichens are like gold, is exceedingly rich. Towards the outer end of the ridge and on the west of it will be noticed a rock apparently balanced on a mere point. The view of this headland from the east is not less impressive than that from the west. Passing *Carn Voel*—the piled cairn—and *Carn Evall* and below *Zawn Reeth*, "the red cavern," so named from the colour of the rock, we have before us the charming cove of Nanjizal or Mill Bay. The feature that at once arrests attention is a narrow vertical cavern through a headland called *Carn les Boel*. Here, if any sea be running, the effect of the cavern, now clear and now filled with foam, is particularly striking. **Nanjizal** itself—"the cove of the Vale" or "the vale of the bosom," as it has been variously interpreted, is of singular beauty, not its least attraction being the margin of pure white shell-sand to which a small brook bounds from rock to rock. Passing Carn les Boel we arrive at *Pendower Cove*, where, on the green slopes, is the *Boistow Logan Stone*. The long low point running out to sea to the south of it, with two or three islets at its extremity, is *Carn Barra*. Towards this we make our way, and then for the next mile have a grand walk, over turf, by the cliffs past Port Loe and *Guethenbras*, "the great cairn," to **Tol-pedn Penwith**—"the holed headland in Penwith." This headland vies with Pardenick in boldness. In calm weather it is, we think, less imposing, but when the huge rollers are dashing themselves in vain against the rugged sides, the sight is terribly grand. Its distinctive name is derived from "the Funnel," a deep chasm resembling the Lions Den at the Lizard, close to the edge of the cliff. These pits appear to have been formed by the roof of a sea-cave falling partially in, and the detritus then being in time carried away by the waters. The tourist will not find it difficult to get *down* to the mouth of the cave connected with the funnel, but the return *up* a nearly smooth slab, 7ft. high, is troublesome through lack of foot-hold. In any case whether the cave can be entered or not, a descent of the cliffs—inclined not sheer—should be made. Nowhere on our coasts are the cliffs on either hand more magnificent and especially at the *Chair Ladder*, where cubes on cubes of granite rise sheer as though built by the Titans. A little east of the cavern leading to the base of the funnel is another with a high narrow opening on the cliffs and running up to the turf. It is not safe to trust to the crumbling edges of this pit. The two beacons or sea-marks on the higher ground, when in line, give the direction of the *Runnel Stone*, a dangerous rock about a mile off this point.

Looking eastward from Tol-pedn Penwith, the conical headland with an islet off it, is *Polostoc*, "the cap," beyond which we reach *Porthgwarra*, said to be the descendant of a Breton fishing-village. The little cove is paved, and here two tunnels have been made through the granite cliff on the east. There is nothing to detain the tourist here, and the *disjecta membra* of fish and fishing gear give an untidy and at times an unsavoury air to the spot. Half a mile east of Porthgwarra we reach *Porth Chapel*, so named from a baptistery of St. Levan, the scanty ruins of which will be found near the cliffs before crossing the small brook that here runs down from *St. Levan* Church-town, ¼ mile up the valley. **St. Levan's Church** is small but interesting, and on the right hand as we approach the south porch with its sun dial, is a fine *cross*. There is another on the north side. In the porch is a holy-water stoup. The earliest portion of the church is the north transept, Early English. Some bench ends, the remains of the screen and the font, should be noticed, also the Lich-gate on the east side of the churchyard, through which goes the path to Porth Curnow (the Cornish Port) our next object of interest. It may also be reached from St. Levan by returning to the coast. The latter, somewhat longer, affords a fine view of Trereen Dinas. At **Porth Curnow**, where a valley opens to the shore, we have beautiful sands bounded on either hand by fine rocks. From this point the Falmouth and Gibraltar Cable is laid, the houses of the officials being in the valley. Under bright sunshine the lover of the sea will pause to note, how, as the long ground-swell rolls in majestically, the crest, as it breaks, shows cornelian and topaz tints of exquisite delicacy, and then runs over the sands in creamy foam. The number of rare shells to be picked up on the sands at Porth Curnow is considerable, and usually undamaged specimens are freely to be had beneath the little ridges of sand left by the ripples of the falling tide. After our walk thus far, a hasty dip, for which no better place could be devised, will refit us for a leisurely ramble towards **Trereen Dinas**, now ¾ mile to the east. If the tourist does not mind a steep descent he should certainly go down to *Trereen Cove*, which is just west of that promontory. This can be reached by a break-neck path, and from it as from nowhere else are seen the sheer cliffs and romantic towers and spires of the Dinas or Castle. The Logan rock is on the summit of the pile which rises abruptly on the right of a depression about the middle of the Castle. Returning to the top of the cliffs by the way we came we make straight for the isthmus, which connects the promontory with the mainland. The headland was once a cliff-castle, and its landward defences can be traced along a series of mounds. Passing through an entrance in another protecting bank that runs across the neck, we are opposite an opening between two huge piles of granite. Through this our path runs to the **Logan Rock**. To reach this rock a little climb up the rock to the right is required, but to anyone not troubled with over sensitive nerves there is neither difficulty nor danger, and we venture to add, no reward! The story of the upsetting of the rock in 1824 by Lieut. Goldsmith and its replacement by tackling borrowed from the Admiralty is too threadbare to be repeated. Those who are cragsmen can climb the highest point of the headland called Castle Peak, and there they will be rewarded by a really fine view of the coast in both directions and of the rugged castle itself. From the entrance to the castle it is a long half-mile to the "Logan" Inn at Trereen.

The path, a little difficult to hit at first, crosses at right angles to the wires, a wall just in a grassy corner, and having a slight depression on the right. For part of the way it is carried along the top of the wall. The inn lays itself out rather to supply the wants of the passer-by than those of the wayfarer, who would fain tarry for the night. It offers fair accommodation, however. From Trereen it is about 8½ miles *viâ* St. Buryan (*Inn*) to Penzance, and 3½ miles to Sennen and 4 miles to Land's End Hotel.

Penzance (by *St. Buryan*, 5½ *m*.) **to Trereen** (8½ *m*., for the Logan) **and the Land's End,** 12½ *m*.

As far as Lower Hendra, 3½ *m*., see *pp*. 197-8. There we ascend to the left and over the next brow, cross the valley by a kind of causeway. When over the next brow, a tall pillar-stone is seen on the right and then we descend to another small valley.

When, a few yards up the hill beyond, a by-road diverges, left, the archæologist may take it to St. Buryan and try and find the "Stone Cross" and "Stone Circle" shown in the new Ordnance map. We spent some time in vain, Jan., 1888.

St. Buryan (Inn : *Ship*) is a bleakly placed village (5½ *m*. from Penzance) only noticeable for its **Church**, of which the fine tower, 90 ft. high and over 400 feet above the sea, is seen far and wide. There is an old Cross close to the entrance to the churchyard, and another close to the S. Porch. Inside the church notice the beautifully carved beams and the panels at the back of a seat on either side of the chancel—these were parts of the roodscreen. Under the tower is a 13th cent. tomb with a French inscription : "Clarice, wife of Geoffrey de Boleit."

St. Buriena, one of the Irish ascetics (said to have been the daughter of a king), settled here in the 6th cent. Athelstan defeated the Cornish king Howel in 926--8, and in gratitude founded a collegiate church in honour of the saint, but of that nothing remains.

From St. Buryan to *Trereen* the route, 3 miles, calls for no description. The latter place is reached after a sharp descent to and climb out of the valley, down which a stream runs to *Penberth Cove*. At Trereen is the *Logan Inn*, and thence it is a long half mile to **Trereen Dinas**, or "Castle," and the **Logan Rock** (*for the Castle, &c., see p*. 202). The finest view of the promontory is from the west. **Penberth Cove**, ½ mile east, lying between *Cribba Head*—the crested head—on the west and *Pedn-sa-wanack* on the east, is worth including in a visit to the Logan. It is at the mouth of perhaps the pleasantest of the many pleasant little combes that nestle along the coast. Like Porthgwarra it is paved with large stones, and in a cottage or two live the few fishermen whose lobster-pots and other trade-gear lie about the cove.

From Trereen to the Land's End, 4 *m*., the road is dull. The cliff-walk is superb ; *see p*. 200.

Penzance to Newlyn, 1 *m*; **Mousehole,** 3 *m*; **Lamorna.**
5 *m by cliffs.*

This as far as Mousehole is a delightful drive or walk. From that village carriages going on to Lamorna have to take a very devious course inland of 3 miles, to attain a point that in a direct line is but little over 1½ miles. Pedestrians, west from Mousehole have a fine walk for most of the distance high up on the sea slopes.

We leave Penzance by the coast road from the W. end of the Esplanade and in 1 *m.* reach *Newlyn*, a quaint but ill-built fishing village. Over the bridge we turn to the left and soon make a turn inland and then a turn seaward down to the shore (on paper quite an undescribable labyrinth) and crossing a bit of sand ascend to the sea-front above the cliff. Hence to Mousehole the road overlooks Gwavas Lake, as this part of Mount's Bay is called. **Mousehole** is another fishing village. It is more artistic than cleanly, and will not, in spite of its old fashioned aspect, tempt the tourist to tarry. It occupies the mouth of two converging combes; at the head of one, half-a-mile north, is Paul. The derivation of 'Mousehole' is unknown, though it is quite certain that it has no connection with 'mouse hole' and the cavern close by so called. The village suffered from a descent of the Spaniards in 1595, who then also burnt Paul church and part of Penzance. The old manor-house, part of which is now the Keigwin Arms, should be noticed. The island opposite the southern end of the village is St. Clement's, and once had a chapel.

Paul Church has little claim on the tourist's attention except as the burial place of Dolly Pentreath, d. 1778. She is commonly said to have been the last person who spoke Cornish, but the truth of this is open to question. A granite memorial, recording her death, was in 1860 built into the church-yard wall. A field-path cuts off an angle of the road on the way back to Penzance.

For Lamorna we ascend the steep road which follows the cliff-top S. of Mousehole, but instead of taking the road which presently strikes up to the right we keep straight on and about 50 yards beyond the last of the cottages get over a stile on the right. This is the beginning of a footpath which soon joins another and runs more or less parallel with the coast along the sea slopes. It from time to time becomes a farm road as it passes successively through the farm hamlets of *Lower*, *Middle*, and *Upper Kemyell*, which being in sight of one another make the route unmistakable. From the last named the path gets narrow and steep as it drops to the hamlet of **Lamorna** (*Pub. Ho.*) at the head of Lamorna Cove. Here the granite quarries have greatly disfigured *Carn-du*, the eastern promontory.

A mile up the valley, pleasantly wooded, we join the lower road from Penzance to the Logan. Across it, seen from the road, is the manor house (now a farm-house) of **Trewoofe** (*pron.* Troof) with an old doorway. Turning left here it is ½ *m.* up to **Boleit** (*pron.* Belay—accent on 'lay'). Here Athelstan is said to have gained in 936 his final victory over the Cornish. Boleit means "the place of slaughter." Here also is a remarkable *fougou* (underground passage or cave) lined and roofed with slabs of granite. On the right of the road, just above the hamlet appear the two great pillar-stones, **the Pipers**. When the road runs into another at right angles take the footpath on its far side. This leads, in a few hundred yards, through the stone circle (of 19 stones and 76 feet diameter) known as the **Merry Maidens**—maidens and pipers turned to stone for dancing on Sunday!

This circle can be visited direct (abt. 1 *m.*) from Lamorna and the cliff walk next described joined at St. Loy. To do this take the road on the left a short distance inland from the Pub. Ho. at Lamorna. It is the one joined at right angles (see above) near the Pipers. From the Merry Maidens the path at once rejoins the road and ½ *m.* W., at cross-roads, is a *cross*. Here, or ¾ *m.* onward we can turn left for the cliffs.

Lamorna to Penberth, 4½ *m.* by the cliffs, and the Logan, 5½ *m.*

This extension of the walk in the last section will connect with that between the Land's End and the Logan and so complete the view of the south shore of the peninsula. The first point after quitting Lamorna is *Tater-du*. Thence round a bay and across a combe we reach *Boscawen Point*, having again entered on the granite which is here finely piled up. Treveen Dinas now stands boldly out to sea a couple of miles to the westward. From Boscawen we turn away a little from the cliffs to avoid the bad "going" along them, and then descend into a charming little wooded valley and by it rejoin the coast at **St. Loy's Cove**. From the top of the next headland, Merthen Point, we look right into *Penberth Cove*, but before reaching it have another combe or rather pair of combes to cross this side of Pedn-sa-wanack. (For Penberth and the Logan, *see pp.* 203, 202.)

To St. Ives, 9½ *m. by rail*, changing at St. Erth Jctn.

The route need not here be described, and for a full account of St. Ives (best Hotel: *Tregenna Castle*) see "N. Devon and N. Cornwall" guide. The object of this excursion is to obtain sight of the really beautiful bay, just within the western arm of which the town stands. The *town* will not long detain the tourist, but he may make it the starting point of a walk along the coast to St. Just, 14½ *m.*, and the Land's End, 20 *m.*, of which, as far as the former place, we append a brief description.

St. Ives to Zennor, 4¾ *m.*; **Trereen**, 6¾ *m.*; **Morvah**, 10¼ *m.* **St. Just**, 15 *m.* We leave St. Ives by a steep road that passes the Board Schools, and in 1¼ *m.* pass through the works of *St. Ives Consols*. The north side of Trevalgan Hill is then skirted, and then at 4¼ *m.* we sweep round the spur on which is **Zennor Cromlech**, said to be the largest monument of its kind in existence. The slab, 18 feet by 9 feet 6 inches, was formerly supported by 7 upright stones. One end of it now rests on the ground. The whole structure was in the early part of the last century buried up to the level of the slab. In ¾ *m.* onward we reach **Zennor** (*Inn*). The church is of no particular interest, but the font, late Decorated, is good, and there is a curious bench-end representing a mermaid. A Logan-stone, capable of being rocked, is just north of the church.

It is worth while from Zennor to make for the coast, and to follow it westward by Porthglaze and Rose-an-hale Coves to Gurnard's Head. If the road be adhered to, then for **Gurnard's Head** (Inn : *Gurnard's Head Hotel*) we turn to the right, at 1¼ m. from Zennor, to Trereen (*Inn*), whence to the extremity of the promontory it is about ¾ m.

The old name of the headland Trereen *Dinas* is still illustrated by the remains of walls across the isthmus, and the cliff-castle must, from its situation, which resembles that of its namesake at the Logan (*p.* 202), have been of great strength. Close to the cliffs on the isthmus are the remains of a little chapel with a granite altar slab.

[From Treleen the beehive hut of Bosporthennis can be reached in 1 m. Follow the Penzance road ¾ m, and then cross the hill on the right another ¼ m.]

A mile and a-half from Treleen, after passing the fine hill Carn Galva on the left, we reach the *Morvah and Zennor mines*. Here a *détour* may be made on the right, ½ mile, to *Bossigran*. This promontory, the head of which formed a cliff-castle, presents on both sides fine granite cliffs, and has also a Logan-stone. On its west-side is Porth Morna, the "monk's port." Returning to the road, at 9 miles, we proceed inland, for ½ mile, to the junction with the Penzance and Morvah road, and from the high ground of the *col*, between Chûn Hill (west) and Kerrow Hill, obtain a good view to the south-east.

[**Chûn Castle** and **Cromlech** (*below*) may be reached over Chûn Hill in 1 m., and thence it is about 2½ m. to St. Just.]

From the *col* the road doubles back to **Morvah**, 1¾m. Beyond Morvah a track, right, leads to some cottages and between two of them. Thence a good path leads in abt. 1¼ m. into the road to **Pendeen** (Inns : *North, Boscaswell*). *Pendeen Watch* is a fine headland, and to the east of it is Pendeen cove, a sandy bay with a coast-guard station. The rocks lying off the point are called the Wra or Three Stone Oar. Dr. Borlase, the antiquary, was born at Pendeen Farm in 1695. From Pendeen follow the road straight on past the Levant Mine, right. Then after crossing a valley you ascend past a large Wesleyan Chapel to **St. Just** (Inn : *Commercial*; 'bus to Penzance, 6d.), where the church (restored) is the only object of interest. Cape Cornwall and the Botallack Mine are within 2 m. For St. Just to the Land's End see *p.* 197.

St. Just by New Bridge, 3½ m., **to Penzance,** 7 m.
This, the route taken by the omnibusses, is devoid of interest. In 1½ miles after leaving St. Just, we have on the left the ragged topped Kenidjack Carn, and on the right *Pertinney* or *Batiné* (717 ft.), to the east of which is the nearly equal height *Carn Bran*, on which is an earthwork. At 2½ miles the road to Pendeen goes off left.

[For **Chûn Castle** and **Quoit** follow the Pendeen road, 1¼ miles, and then take a lane, on the right, for ½ mile. You are then almost under the castle, which is on the north. **Chûn Castle** is the best example of Cornish hill forts. It consists of an oval, 155 feet by 140 feet, round which runs a wall, with remains of chambers on its inner side. Outside this is a ditch 30 feet wide, and then another wall with a ditch beyond it. The entrance is on the west side, and the main ditch is in three places crossed by the walls connecting the two encircling ones. On the north of the enclosure is a well. The walls are of unhewn stone without mortar. About 250 yards west of the castle is the **Quoit**, which is formed of a slab, about 12 feet each way and 2 feet thick, resting on three supports about 7 feet in height.]

From *Newbridge* (3½ m.) a featureless 2 miles brings us to a roadside *Cross*, at the junction of a by-road. Hence a good view of Mount's Bay. About 100 yds. onward the road to Newlyn diverges on the right, but we keep straight on for ½ mile.

[Here, on the left, a pleasant lane begins which goes past **Castle Horneck** (house is seen on the left) and skirting the fields rejoins, in 1½ m., our road at Alverton, the hamlet immediately W. of Penzance.]

Continuing down the road we reach the hamlet of Alverton and pass through it to Penzance.

To Porthleven and Helston, by the coast, 19½ m.

This route is given the reverse way on p. 188. Tourists with time at command should certainly explore the cliffs between Cuddan Point and Porthleven. The Helston and Penzance 'bus can be used to a point 3 m. beyond Marazion (N.B.—Ask to be put down for Acton Castle) if the walk is to be taken eastward. If a return is to be made to Penzance then it is, perhaps, better to go by 'bus as far as the turn to Porthleven, 9½ m. from Penzance, and 1 m. beyond Breage. Between Cuddan Point and Marazion the shore is comparatively low and not worth following. The evening 'bus may be used, in either case, for the return to Penzance.

To Marazion and St. Michael's Mount, 3½ m.

These places are described on p. 190. About 2 miles from Marazion, on the left of the road to Camborne, is **St. Hilary's Church** where the fine Decorated tower is all that survived the fire of 1853. In the graveyard are an old cross and a Roman milestone found after the fire.

Scilly Isles.

Penzance to Scilly Isles.

Distance to St. Marys, 40 m. Time 4 hrs.
Steamer from Penzance Pier (abt. ¾ m. from station), twice a week in winter, thrice or oftener in summer, abt. 10 a.m. Letters arrive and depart by the steamer. Telegraph Office at St. Marys.

Inns: St. Marys, *Hugh House Hotel*, *Tregarthen's*; Tresco, *Canteen*; Bryer, *Mountain Maid* (no beds).

Agnes and St. Martins are the only other inhabited islands of the group.

On leaving the extension pier at Penzance, an excellent view is obtained of the shores of Mount's Bay and of Penzance, Newlyn, and Mousehole. Further on, Castle Trereen, capped by the Logan Rock, and bristling above and below with rocky peaks, makes its appearance, and soon after leaving it, we pass the bell-buoy which marks the **Rundle Stone**. The cliffs and islets around and about the Land's End now begin to appear, first Tol-pedn Pen-with, then in the distance Enys Dodnan, Land's End, and the Longships Lighthouse. As far as the Rundle stone the steamer keeps a course fairly close to the Cornish Coast, but when Tol-pedn Penwith is passed our way is more seaward, and clearing the Land's End we open up Cape Cornwall. About half-way from Penzance to Scilly we pass to the right of the **Wolf Lighthouse**. The Wolf rock, on which the lighthouse stands, was so called because of the roaring which wind and sea made when driven through a narrow aperture. This aperture was filled up with stones and pebbles by the fishermen, who imagined that the noise frightened away the fish!

Long before the cliffs of the mainland have faded from view, an experienced look-out will make out the Scilly Isles. These appear as low breaks upon the horizon, at first undefined, then showing themselves to be rocks and low banks. The rocks will shortly be found to be the eastern islands, Great Ganilly and Hanjague, and of the low lying-banks, that to the right, with a conical daymark upon it, is the eastern end of St. Martins, that to the left the island of St. Marys, with a telegraph tower upon its highest point. To Hugh Town, the chief collection of buildings in St. Marys and the destination of the steamer, there are two approaches by sea, and it depends upon the state of the tide which will be taken. By the direct approach we enter the Scilly Archipelago from the east, and pass through *Crow Sound* into *St. Marys Pool*, leaving St. Martins and Tresco on our right. Owing to the shallowness of the water at Crow Sound (Crow Bar, which extends from St. Marys towards St. Martins and Tresco, being at low tide little more than knee deep) this route, although the shorter, is not always available. The other approach to Hugh Town enters the archipelago on the south-east between the Gugh of Agnes and the south-western side of St. Marys, known as the Garrison, by way of *St. Marys Sound*, and so to St. Marys Road.

The Scilly Islands form an archipelago extending about 10 miles in length from N.E. to S.W. and with a maximum breadth from N.W. to S.E. of half that distance. By far the greater number are rocky islets, and the Scilly Rock, which lends its name to the group, is only one acre. The rock everywhere is granite, which weathers rapidly under the combined action of sea and air. Regarded merely as scenery the Islands do not rank high, but the seas are often grand. The climate is very equable in temperature, but fogs and storms are common. The soil, so far as there is enough to cultivate, is fairly fertile, and after having long sent us our early potatoes, it now produces, in early spring, immense quantities of narcissus, which are gathered in bud and sent off to Covent Garden. The early potato culture fell off when the increase of railway facilities made the yet earlier grounds of Southern Europe the source of our supplies.

Herodotus mentions, but not of his own knowledge, "the islands Cassiterides (*i.e.* tin islands) from which tin is brought to us," and Diodorus Siculus distinguishes between the islands and Cornwall as sources of supply. It is, however, more than doubtful if the former ever yielded any quantity of the metal, and the probable explanation is that Scilly was credited with the tin brought by sea, and Cornwall with that which arrived through Gaul.

The Arthurian legends place the Land of Lyoness between the islands and the mainland; *cf.* Tennyson's *The Passing of Arthur*, 57-62.

From the reign of Elizabeth till late in the last century the islands were held by the Godolphin family, now for many years they have been leased from the Crown by the family seated at Tresco Abbey (*p.* 214). During the Civil War the Royal cause was adhered to by the Scillonians, but the Parliamentary fleet, under Blake and Ayscue, took the islands in 1651.

St. Marys. (*Pop. abt.* 1500.)

The chief objects of interest in St. Marys, the largest and most important island of the archipelago, are:

(*a*) Peninnis Rocks. (*b*) Old Town with its bay and cemetery. (*c*) Giant's Castle, Porthellick Bay, and the Cromlechs on Clapper Down. (*d*) The view from the Telegraph Tower.

To a tolerably diligent pedestrian one day will suffice to inspect the lions of St. Marys. As a preliminary, however, it is advisable to walk around the *Garrison Hill*, which need not take up more than ½ to ¾ hr. We start from the Terrace, in front of *Hugh House Hotel*. Beneath us lies **Hugh Town**, with its empty streets and its gardens. On the ridge or table-land to the left stands the Telegraph Tower with its flagstaff beside it. Hugh Town is seen to occupy an isthmus, which connects the Garrison Hill with the main body of the island. The bay to the left, as you look towards St. Marys Church, is St. Marys Pool. This is divided into two coves by Cain Thomas, a bold stack of granite 80 feet high. The farther Cove is called Pormellin Cove, and the bay to the right hand is Porcrasa Bay, and, overlooking it to the north-east, is Buzza Hill, with a windmill. About a mile to the right, the rugged rocks of Peninnis ("end of the island") form the eastern horn of Porcrasa Bay. Having thus noted the view at starting, we proceed to make the circuit of the garrison, proceeding southwards. An excellent road runs round the hill, and, for the greater part of the way, follows the line of the fortification wall. For the first 300 yards or so it skirts the western side of *Porcrasa Bay*, on the opposite side of which, towards its south-eastern horn, the Tooth Rock and the Monk's Cowl, granite rocks, so called from their shape, stand out on Peninnis Down. At the point where the road is cut for a yard or two through the granite the island of Agnes first comes into view, and then, as we bend round to the right, we see the Gugh of Agnes, a peninsula separated from Agnes at high tide. Then we notice Agnes' Lighthouse, and in the distance beyond and over Agnes, the Bishop Lighthouse. As the road still bears steadily to the right, the island of Annet appears, and is easily recognised by the Haycock Rocks which stand out upon the horizon, and mark its north-western extremity. From the Haycocks, for a space, the open sea towards the west forms the horizon. Then the rugged islet of Minalto, with its satellite rocks, followed immediately by the southern hill of Samson, comes into view. At the point we have now reached, the Garrison Walk diverges from the fortification walls and begins to slope upwards. When the top of the ascent is reached, the northern hill of Samson makes its appearance, and apparently—but only apparently—continuous with it the island of Bryer. Bryer is separated from the adjacent island of Tresco by a pretty little strait with winding shores. Hangman Island, like a miniature St. Michael's Mount, rises from the water in its narrowest part. The white sand beaches of Tresco, behind them Tresco Abbey, the residence of the Lord Proprietor of the islands (T. A. Dorrien-Smith, Esq.), the island of Tëan, and the island of St. Martin complete the views to be had from the Garrison Walk. From the sights of this walk we must not omit the **Star Castle**, which we shall pass as we again approach our starting point. It is at present the residence of the Lord Proprietor's steward (Mr. Allen), but was originally a fort, built in the reign of Queen Elizabeth. Over the portal the date 1593 and the initials E. R. (Eliz. Regina) may be read. The higher part of the wall is pierced for the ponderous muskets which formed the lighter artillery of the day. From the date and initials placed over the lower gateway, by which the Garrison precinct is entered, we learn the date of the walls and platforms, G.R. (*i.e.*, George II.) 1742.

(*a*) **Peninnis** is approachable from Hugh Town in two ways. One, a make-shift path, skirts *Porcrasa Bay*, another, commanding better views of the sea and of the Western islands, ascends

Buzza Hill, passes the windmill and leads, by a lane which turns to the right, to a gate half-a-mile distant from the mill, and opens on *Peninnis Down*. Passing through the gate we make for a group of rocks a little to the right, and then below are seen the two points east and west of Peninnis, the latter, with its piled-up granite, being a very picturesque promontory. Midway between these points are the *Tooth Rock* and the *Monk's Cowl*, so called from their shape. These are part of a bold pile that, seaward, forms a precipice whose base is washed by the sea. The rocks here are everywhere fashioned by weathering into fantastic shapes, and their upper surfaces are occupied by rock-basins in various stages of formation or decay; some just forming, some fairly hollowed out, containing water and a few grains of granite, others disappearing, the outflow of water, at a particular point of the edge of the hollow, disintegrating the granite at that point and in time widening and deepening more and more, and turning the cup into a steep stone channel. A hundred yards or so onward is the **Pulpit Rock**, so named from its likeness to the sounding-board of a pulpit. This freak of nature is a slab of granite, kept in position by a block of the same material upon its northern end. The approach to the top of the sounding-board is easy, but to get beneath it involves a scramble. From the Pulpit Rock, northwards, a bay will be seen, alongside of which a tolerably-defined path takes us past *Carn Lea* to the old church at the head of the bay.

(*b*) This bay is called **Old Town Bay**, from the hamlet at its head, which was long ago the chief town of the island. The *Church*, part of which has been pulled down, formerly the only church on the island, now serves as a cemetery chapel. Inside, it has nothing of interest. The **Cemetery**, from its situation one of the most striking in the kingdom, has not been improved in appearance by the memorials which have been erected comparatively recently. The gratuitous ugliness of two obelisks, which have not even the justification of marking the resting-places of persons buried within the cemetery (one is to the memory of the late Lord Proprietor, who is buried at St. Buryan, on the mainland, and the other to a lady who was lost in the *Schiller*, in May, 1875), is remarkable. Many other monuments tell the sad tale of wrecks. The visitor will notice the Australian palms and the aloes which thrive here. There is nothing remarkable about Old Town, except, perhaps, the carn of rocks which stands in the middle of it, called *Castle Carn*, and on which is said to have stood the chief stronghold of the islands. No traces of this remain.

From near Castle Carn an opening in the houses to the south takes us by a path through the fields to the head of the eastern cove of Old Town Bay, called *Permynis Bay*, and from this point a rough path, hardly recognisable from time to time, goes along high-water line to the western slope of *Sallakey Down*.

(*c*) To reach **Giant's Castle** one can either walk round the coast, turning to the left from the head of *Permynis Bay*, or make a short cut up the hill across the Down. Giant's Castle may be easily recognised as the highest point of the Down overlooking the sea. It is one of those mysterious remnants of antiquity called "cliff-castles," and is the only one in the Scilly archipelago, though on the mainland of Cornwall and Wales they abound. Cliff-castles consist of some promontory or eminence abutting on the sea, and defended on the seaward side by inaccessible precipices. On the landward side they are defended by ditches and ramparts. Trereen Dinas (*p.* 202), on which is the famous Logan Rock, is one of the largest of such cliff-castles. By whom or for what purposes they were made is utterly unknown. Giant's Castle seems to have been defended by a series of terraces one above the other. Three at least may be made out, and these were formed partly by excavating the soil and partly by heaping up stones and boulders of granite wall-wise. The accommodation offered by it must always have been of the smallest. The granite shelves, on the summit, afford interesting examples of rock-basins past and present, and the sea-view thence is good. At our feet lies *Porthellick*, "the bay of willows," of which Giant's Castle forms the western horn. Opposite, across the bay, are the Clapper Rocks, and behind, to the north, Clapper Down. On a ledge a little below the Castle and to the west of it, rests a *Logan Stone*, which by continued pushing may be made to "log" very distinctly. From Giant's Castle to Porthellick the path lies along the western side of *Porthellick Bay*. Here the brig *Nerina*, of Dunkerque, came ashore keel upwards in the night 18-19 Nov., 1840. Four of her crew were in her and were saved, after an entombment of 70 hours. The upper part of the bay towards the north is left dry at high-water, and its eastern side is studded with granite boulders. At its northern end it is bordered by a strand of granite grains. Behind the strand is a slope of turf which stretches towards Holy Vale to the north, and is terminated by a large marsh-like pond of fresh water. The turf borders the granite strand the whole width of the cove, broken only by a strip of naked sand towards the east end, near where a little stream runs from the pond into the sea. Upon this little strip of sand hangs a tale, the only bit of romance that, as far as we know, clings to the islands. Let those who will, discredit it. This is how the tale was told us years ago :—

"When Admiral Shovel was sailing across the main on his way back to England, there was on board his ship a common seaman who kept for himself a reckoning of the vessel's course. This in itself was an unusual proceeding, very few sailors in those days possessing the necessary knowledge. The man declared that the ship's course would take her upon the rocks of Scilly, and this conclusion was brought to the knowledge of the officers. The unfortunate man was court-martialed on a charge of inciting to mutiny, and then and there convicted and sentenced to be hung at the yard-arm. Before execution he asked, and got leave, to read aloud a portion of Holy Scripture. The portion he chose was the 109th Psalm. It spoke of him who ' remembered not to show mercy, but persecuted the poor and needy man, that he might even slay the broken in heart.' It invoked upon him, among many other woes, fewness of days, fatherless children, and a posterity cut off. In a few hours the reckoning of the unhappy man was proved to be correct; the vessel struck upon the Gillstone Rock, and was lost. The body of the admiral, still alive (it is whispered that he was murdered for the sake of a ring he wore by the tenant of Sallakey farm), was carried by the sea to Porthellick, and for a while rested on the spot of ground marked by that strip of sand, and ever since that time the grass has refused to grow there!"

On Clapper Down, close to Porthellick, and bordering the bay to the east, some dozen barrows, called by the inhabitants *giants' graves*, are worthy of a visit. Their sides and ends are of small stones rudely built up, and the tops are covered by large granite slabs laid across. The earth seems to have been mounded around them, and this makes them conspicuous as we ascend from Porthellick to the Down. No remains of flint or other implements have been discovered, which might serve as a clue to the builders, or as to the state of Scilly civilisation that witnessed their erection. From Clapper Down, a walk across the island, north-west, along some of the excellent roads, which preserve the memory of the late Lord Proprietor far more worthily than the ugly erection in Old Town cemetery, brings us to the

(d) **Telegraph Tower.** This tower, stationed on Telegraph Hill, the highest point (158 *ft.*) in the island, is worth a visit on account of the extensive view of the islands which it commands. Its name is now misleading, as it has nothing to do with telegraphing, except as concerns the arrival of the Penzance steamer. It is a coast-guard station, and the coast-guard's man in charge readily permits visitors to ascend to the top of the tower, and is both willing and able to give the names of the numerous islands and islets in sight. To the north-east rises the eastern group of islands, Great Ganilly, Hanjague, and their satellites. To the north, St. Martins, stretching out low and long towards the west, then Tëan, St. Helens, and Mên-an-vawr, " great stones." The last named islets are seen from this point to great advantage. From these the eye passes to Tresco, Bryer, Samson, and the north-western rocks; and last of all in the far south-west, the Bishop Lighthouse, the Haycock Rocks, Annet, the Western Rocks, and Agnes, conspicuous by its lighthouse. There is nothing of sufficient interest along the north-east shore of St. Marys to require description. Should the tourist be at Scilly on St. John's Eve, he will witness a miniature carnival, such as is held at Penzance. Bonfires are lit in the square at Hugh Town and on St. Martins.

Remaining Islands.

The interest of the remaining islands of the Scilly group is mainly that attaching to the varied rock-forms which granite assumes when exposed to perpetual wind and rain, to lonely sequestered bays everywhere fretted by the sea into the land, and to the varying colour, under sunshine, of the water, according as it covers rock or sea-weed, or white sand. To these attractions the island of **Tresco** (*Pop. abt.* 400; *Canteen Inn*, 8*s.* a day) adds those of the Abbey Gardens and the Piper's Hole. The **Abbey Gardens**, together with the House, are the creation of the late Lord Proprietor, Augustus Smith, Esq. The gardens are opened to tourists, accompanied by one of the gardeners, at all times; fee according to the discretion of the visitor. They are remarkable in two ways. For the products proper to a garden,—flowers, shrubs, and dwarf-trees of the most various kinds,—and for an unrivalled collection of figure-heads and other memorials of wrecked ships, which either singly or in groups meet the eye at every turn. Of the vegetable products only a botanist or gardener could give an adequate account. To see the gardens to the best advantage they should be visited towards the end of June or the beginning of July. The mesembryanthemums, which will have been observed in great beauty and profusion on the walls and hedges of St. Marys, grow to still greater perfection, and in still greater variety here. There are said to be upwards of thirty species. Besides mesembryanthemums there are tree-ferns from Australia (somewhat draggled), rock plants from Madeira, a musk-shrub, a twig of which will retain its fragrance for weeks, and the largest but one, it is said, eucalyptus in Europe.

Piper's Hole (5*s.* for a party; apply at *Canteen Inn*), the other lion of Tresco, is somewhat disappointing. The local guide books lead one to suppose that it must be a vast underground cavern containing a considerable pool or lake, whereas it is, in reality, nothing but a somewhat narrow passage or shaft which runs underground for about 200 yards. About 100 yards from the entrance the passage dips and rises again, and the water which drips unceasingly from the top collects in the depression, and has to be traversed in a boat. The depth of the water varies according to the time of the year, and in winter in places is said almost to reach the roof. When the water, which extends for a length of some 20 yards, has been passed, the visitor is landed upon a beach of fine granite gravel which extends to the end of the Hole. The only noticeable thing about this point of the cavern is the disintegration of the granite, which here takes place from below and not from above as in the rock basins. The walls glisten with moisture and crumble to the touch for a depth of $\frac{1}{4}$ in. In returning, the visitor, whose eyes by this time will have become used to the gloom, will notice boulders in the roof, seemingly ready to fall down. Between the water and the entrance the floor of the cavern is strewed with similar masses that have fallen down in times past, and which, added to the darkness, make the entrance to this cave a rough walk.

Bryer (*Pop. abt.* 100. Inn: *Mountain Maid*; no beds), the island next to Tresco to the west, separated from it by a narrow strait fordable at low spring-tides, is worth visiting by those who can afford the time, on account of the views of rock and sea to be obtained in a walk round its shores, particularly to the west and north. To the south is **Samson**, the largest uninhabited island of the archipelago, separated at all times by deep water from Bryer, but at low spring tides approachable from Tresco along a narrow reef of rocks. Samson was converted by the late Lord Proprietor into a rabbit warren. One or two ruined cottages remain as vestiges of the few inhabitants some 50 years ago, and one or two barrows which were opened by the late Mr. Smith witness to a more remote occupation. To the west and south-west from Bryer an archipelago of rocks and islets, perpetually "laced with foam," opens upon the view, the most noticeable of which are Castle Bryer, so called from its shape, Gweal, Maiden Bower, and last, and among the least, the **Scilly Rock** (area 1 acre), from which the whole group takes its name. As seen from the north of Bryer this rock appears as a dark wall slightly elevated at two points towards its ends.

St. Helens. To the north-east of Tresco, separated from it by reefs and a deep sea-channel, rises St. Helens, or St. Elids, the latter the more ancient name. (*Boatman's charge from St. Marys*, 7s. 6d.) To reach it, a Lizard Point in Tresco, said to be exactly in the same latitude as the better-known Lizard Point, has to be passed. The boat lands one on a strand of fine white sand, on the south of the island, some few feet in width, between two rough boulder walls. Close to the landing-place is the *Pest House*, now long disused, and far on the way to ruin. On the top of the island, 135 ft. above the sea, are the relics of a *church*, said to be that of St. Helen, or Elid. Enough remains to show that there was once a building, but not enough to give any clue to its character, or even, indeed, to the lines of its foundation. Troutbeck, if we rightly remember, says that in his time the church was one of a double nave—the ruins at present to be seen suggest rather a single-aisled church, with a cell for the resident hermit at the west end. From the site of the church there is a magnificent view of the adjoining islands, particularly of those to the north. To the east is the low length of St. Martins. Still nearer, between us and it, and almost at our feet, the islet of Tëan, with its many bays—not unlike an immense cuttle-fish, petrified and grass-grown. To the north, rise—sheer out of the sea—the seemingly inaccessible heights of Round Island, the summit of which is a few feet higher than the spot on which we stand.

But the most remarkable object to be seen from this point is Mên-an-vawr, commonly called Man-of-War. In shape it is a pyramid, roughly-hewn and storm-scarred, divided into two segments by a narrow chasm, through which, from our position, the light streams and illumines the restless waters of the narrow strait beneath. On the north side of St. Helens those who are disposed for a scramble will find a *blow-hole*. Two caverns, one above the other, have been fretted into the granite. Through the floor of the higher and the roof of the lower cave, into which the sea enters, there is an aperture, and through this the air is either expelled or sucked into the lower cave, according as the advancing or receding waves fill it or leave it empty.

Agnes. (*Pop. abt.* 200.)

In Agnes, the southernmost of the inhabited islands, the most interesting objects are the lighthouse, the Punch-bowl, and the dried-up well of Sancta Warna. The **Punch-bowl** is a huge boulder of granite perched upon another boulder. It contains a rock-basin some 3 feet deep. A ladder is needed for inspecting it.

The **Well of Sancta Warna** is dried up, and is more interesting for its associations than for its surroundings. Here Sancta Warna is said to have landed after her voyage in a coracle across the Atlantic from Ireland; and here, in by-gone times, on Sancta Warna's day the natives of Agnes gathered together to pray for wrecks! The old fisherman, who years ago showed the well, expressed great doubts as to this latter fact: "They were very bad in old times," he said, "but not bad enough for that." Perhaps, as at Morwenstow, the petition was modified: "If wrecks there must be, let them be here." The coast of Agnes is low and uninteresting. Near the well is **Bead Bay**, so-called from the beads which strewed its shores after the wreck of a vessel bound for the coast of Africa. This wreck took place many years ago, but a bead can still, from time to time, be picked up on the sands. As one walks along the coast, carns or low-lying oblong heaps of stones, some of them nearly grass-grown, may be noticed. These, we were told, marked the resting-places of bodies thrown upon the shore by the sea, which were buried where they were found, until an Act of Parliament was passed directing the burial of such bodies in parish burial grounds. The *Gugh of Agnes* is a promontory, on the east of the island, that at high spring tides is turned into an islet.

To the west of Agnes, as far as the Bishop Lighthouse, are the Western Islands, the largest group of the Archipelago. They are full of interesting rock forms, infinite variety of sea-birds, and many seals. **Annet** is the chief accessible haunt of sea-birds.

St. Martins (*Pop. abt.* 180) is in itself devoid of special interest, but affords from the comparatively high ground (147 ft.), on which its day-mark stands, a good view of the archipelago.

N.B.—**Boatmen.** The men who pester tourists on their arrival at the new quay with cards, are quite capable of making a voyage to the nearer of the adjoining islands, such as Agnes, Tresco, or St. Martins. But among them there are some more qualified than others, and some are merely boatmen in the intervals of cobbling or gardening. For a longer voyage to the outlying islands, tourists are recommended to engage none but experienced men, and on no account to attempt boating by themselves. The seas of Scilly abound in lurking rocks, which only come out of their hiding when the boat is some two or three feet away from them. To the risk of reefs must be added that of capricious weather, which is often fatal to Scillonian navigators themselves. The best plan is to take counsel of mine host before embarking on a distant cruise.

Ferns. Scilly has a few ferns not easily procurable elsewhere *Asplenium lanceolatum* is found on St. Marys and Agnes *Lastrea æmula* and *L. spinulosa* in Hugh Town Marsh; *Ophioglossum lusitanicum* and *Botrychium lunaria* on St. Martins. *Asplenium marinum* is found on all the islands, and grows to great perfection at Peninnis, and *Osmunda regalis* flourishes on Hugh Town marsh.

INDEX.

N.B.—Where more than one page is referred to, that on which a locality is particularly described is placed first.

Telegraph Offices are indicated by * ; *Railway Stations* by †. The names in [*square*] brackets are required to complete the postal address.

Agnes, 216.
Anchor Stone, 59, 62.
Anchorist Rock, 119.
Annet, 216.
Anstey's Cove, 50.
Antiquities (Gidleigh), 96, 100.
— (Merrivale), 116.
— (Postbridge), 103.
Antony [Devonport], 141.
Armed Knight, 200.
*†**Ashburton**, 75.
— to Bovey, 77.
— ,, Chagford, 78, 86.
— ,, Princetown, 78.
— ,, Tavistock, 81.
— ,, Two Bridges, 81.
Ashe, 13.
*Ashton, 86, 37.
Asparagus Island, 184.
Answell Rock, 76.
Aveton Gifford [Kingsbridge], 67.
*†**Axminster**, 13.
Axmouth [Axminster], 17.

*****Babbicombe** [Torquay], 51.
Balk, the, 187.
*Bampton, 32.
Bartiné Hill, 197.
*†Bath, 9, 16.
Bead Bay, 216.
Beast Point, 186.
Becky Fall, 90.
Bector Cross, 102.
*Beer [Axminster], 19.
†— Alston, 110.
†— Ferris, 110.
— Head, 19.
Beesands [Knightsbridge], 63.
Belidden, 186.
Belliver Tor, 103, 98.
Belstone, 101, 106.
Belvedere Tower, 37.
Berry Head, 54.
— Pomeroy, 53.
———— Castle, 52.
Bessie's Cove, 189.
†Bickleigh [Tiverton], 32.
† ,, near Plymouth, 128.
— Vale, 128.
Bicton, 25.
Bindon Farm, 17.
Bishop Lighthouse, 216.
Black Head, 178.
— Hill, 34.
— Pool, 63.
Blagdon, 52.
Bleu Bridge, 194.

Bochym, 181.
Boconnoc, 154.
*†Bodmin Road, 153.
Boleit, 204.
Bolt Head, 70.
— Tail, 71.
Bonithon, 181.
Borough Island, 71.
Boscawen-un, 198.
Bosistow, Logan Stone, 201.
Bosporthennis, 206.
Bottalack Mine, 206.
Bottor Rock, 88.
*****Bovey Tracey** [Newton Abbot)
— to Ashburton, 88.   [87.
Bovisand, 121, 130.
*†Bow [N. Devon], 105.
Bowerman's Nose, 90.
Bradley House, 43.
Bradmere Pool, 96.
†Brampford Speke, 31.
Branscombe [Sidmouth], 19.
*†Brent [Ivybridge], 44.
— Hill, 44.
†Brentor, 112, 110.
*†Bridestowe, [N. Devon], 108.
— to Mary Tavy, 108.
*†**Bridport**, 3.
    to Charmouth and Lyme Regis, 3.
*†Bristol, 9.
*†Brixham [S. Devon], 54.
— to Kingswear, 55.
— Cave, 54.
Brixton [Plympton] 68.
*†Bruton, 3.
Bryer [Scilly Isles], 215.
*†Buckfastleigh, 74.
Buckland, 76, 79.
· · Beacon, 84, 77.
— **Drives**, 76.
*****Budleigh Salterton**, 35.
· to Sidmouth, 36.
Budock, 175.
Bull's Hole, 70.
*†Burngullow, 158.
Buryas Bridge, 197.

Cadbury Castle, 31.
Cadeleigh, 32.
Cadgwith [Helston], 188.
Cadhay, 25.
Cadover Bridge, 124.
Caerhayes, 168.
*Callington, 151, 125.
*****Calstock** [Tavistock], 143.
*†Camborne, 79.
Cannonteign, 86.

INDEX.

Cape Cornwall, 206.
Carndon Hill, 150.
Carclaze Mine, 158.
Carclew. 161.
Castle-an-Dinas, 195.
Castle Horneck, 194, 206.
Cawsand [Devonport], 146, 145.
— Beacon, 100.
*Chagford [Exeter], 92, 80.
— to Ashburton, 101.   [100.
— „ (over Cawsand) Okehampton,
— „ (by Cranmere) Lidford, 96, 99.
— „ Princetown, 101.
Chapel Point, 167.
Charlton, 65.
*Charmouth, 4.
Cheesewring, 49.
Chideock [Bridport], 4.
*†Chippenham, 2, 9.
Christow, 86.
*†Chudleigh [Newton Abbot], 85.
Chûn Castle, 206.
— Cromlech, 206.
Churchstow [Kingsbridge], 67.
*†Churston, 54.
Chysoyster, 195.
Clapper Down, 212.
Classenwell Pool, 96.
Clifford Bridge, 86.
Cockington, 51.
Collaton, 52.
*†Colyton [Axminster] 13.
Combe Royal, 44.
Compton Castle, 52.
Conig's Castle, 5.
†Cornwood [Ivybridge], 129, 45.
Cotehele, 142.
Coverack [Helston], 178.
Crafthole, 162.
Cranbrook Castle, 101, 87.
Cranmere Pool, 98, 106, 109.
Creagtol, 198.
*†Crediton, 104.
Cremill [Devonport], 139, 145, 133.
Crockern Tor, 122, 103.
Crow Pound, 153.
— Sound, 209.
Crown Hill, 121.
Cuddan Point, 189.
*†Cullompton, 11.
Cury, 181.
Cut Hill, 82, 106.

Dart, River, 57, 62, 74, 81.
Dartington Hall, 61.
Dartmeet, 82.
Dartmoor, 72.
— Antiquities, 73.
— Gate, 106.
— Inn, 107, 108, 109, 110.
*†Dartmouth, 57.
— to Kingsbridge, 62.
— „ Torcross, 62.
— „ Totnes, 58.
*†Dawlish, 39.
Dean Prior [Buckfastleigh], 44.

Dempswell Abbey, 11.
Denbury Down, 43.
Dennabridge Pound, 82.
*†Devonport, 133, 137.
— Leat, 122.
Dewerstone, 126.
Ding Dong Mine, 196.
Dittisham [Totnes], 58, 62.
Dodbrooke, 66.
Dodman Point, 168.
Dolor Hugo, 187.
Doniert's Stone. 149.
*†Doublebois, 153.
Dowlands landslip, 7.
Downderry, 162.
†Dousland, 128, 104.
Drake Monument, 112.
Drewsteignton, 95.
— Cromlech, 96.
Drift, 197.
Duloe, 148.
*†Dulverton, 32.
Duncannon, 59, 62.
Dunscombe, 20.
Dunsford [Exeter], 86.
Dupath Well, 125, 151.
East Budleigh [Budleigh Salter-   [ton], 25.
Eddystone Lighthouse, 143.
Erme Head, 118, 122.
— Pound, 118, 121.
*Ermington [Ivybridge], 119.
Enys, 176.
— Dodnan, 200.
Exe Valley, 31.
*†Exeter, 26.
— to Chagford, 37.
— „ Dawlish, 36.
— „ Dulverton, 32.
— „ Newton Abbot, 36.
— „ Teignmouth, 36.
*†Exminster [Exeter], 39.
*†Exmouth, 34.
— to Budleigh Salterton, 35.
Eype Down, 4.

Fal River, 172.
*†Falmouth, 171.
— to the Lizard, 177.
— „ Truro, 172.
Fernworthy Circle, 97.
Fingle Bridge, 95, 104.
Fitzford, 124, 152.
Fleet House, 67, 119.
†Ford, 110.
„ Abbey, 13.
„ House, 43.
Fox Tor Mire, 118, 122.
Fowellscombe, 44.
*†Fowey, 165.
Frogmore [Kingsbridge], 65.
*†Frome, 3.
Frying Pan, 188.
Funnel, the, 201.

Garrison Hill, 209.
Gerrans, 169.

Giant's Castle, 212.
Gidleigh, 94.
— Antiquities, 96.
Girt Tor, 114, 108.
Golden Cap, 4.
Gorran Haven [St. Austell], 168.
Grampound Road, 158.
Great Carn, 168.
— Links Tor, 115, 108, 110.
— Mis Tor, 116.
— Tor 114.
Greenway House, 58, 59, 62,
Greywethers, 98, 102.
Grimspound, 80, 102.
Gue Graze, 184.
Gugh of Agnes, 216.
Gulval [Penzance], 194.
*Gunnislake [Tavistock], 125, 152.
Gunwalloe, 182.
Gurnard's Head, 206.
Gwinges, 167.

Haldon Hills, 36.
Hallsands [Kingsbridge], 63, 70.
Halzaphron, 182.
Hamildon Down, 80.
Hare Tor, 114, 108.
Harford, 121, 118.
Hawns and Dendles, 130.
Hawksdown, 17.
Hayes Barton, 25.
*†Hayle, 179.
Hazel Tor, 76.
Hea, 195.
Heathfield, 84, 87.
Helford Passage, 175.
Heligan, 167.
*†Helston, 181.
— to the Lizard, 181, 182.
— „ Penzance, 188.
Hembury Fort, 14, 11.
Hemerdon Ball, 129.
*†Hemyock [Cullompton], 11.
Heytor, 78.
High Willhays, 107, 109, 82.
Hingston Down, 125.
Hoe Point, 189.
Holbeton [Ivybridge], 119.
Holcombe, 6.
Holne [Ashburton], 81.
— Bridge, 76, 81.
— Chase, 76.
Holy Street Mill, 93.
*†Honiton, 13, 23.
Hope, 71.
*†Horrabridge, 126.
Horseham Steps, 90.
Hound Tor, 90.
Housel Cove, 186.
Huckworthy Bridge, 123.
Hugh Town, 209.
Hurlers, the, 149.

Ideford [Newton Abbot], 85.
Ilsham Grange, 48.
Ippleden [Newton Abbot], 43.
Irish Lady, 198, 199.

*†Ivybridge, 118, 44.
— to Plymouth, 119.
— „ Princetown, 121.

Kelly College, 110.
Kent's Cavern, 49.
Killerton, 11.
King Harry's Passage, 173.
Kingsand [Devonport], 147.
*Kingsbridge, 66, 44.
— to Dartmouth, 66.
— „ Plymouth, 67.
— „ Salcombe, 68.
— „ Torcross, 66.
*†— Road, 44. [40, 87.
Kingsteignton [Newton Abbot],
*†Kingswear [Dartmouth], 55, 56.
Kit Hill, 151.
Kitley, 68.
Kit's Step's, 109.
Kynance Cove, 184.

Ladram Bay, 22, 36.
Ladywell, 101.
Laira, 45, 68.
Lambert's Castle, 5.
Lamorna, 204.
Landewednack, 187.
Land's End [Penzance], 199.
Landslip, 7.
Landulph, 142.
Lane End, 114.
Lanhydrock, 153.
Lannacombe Mill, 70.
Lansalloes, 164.
Lanyon Quoit, 196.
Leigh Bridge, 100.
Leusdon, 82.
*†Lidford, 108.
— Cascade, 109.
— to Chagford, 109.
— „ Okehampton, 110.
— „ Tavistock, 112.
Lion Rock, 76.
Lion's Den, 186.
*†Liskeard, 148.
— (by Cheesewring) to Launceston,
— to Looe, 148. [149.
— „ Tavistock, 150.
Little Links Tor, 115.
Littleham, 35.
Lizard, the, 180.
— Cove, 187.
— Lighthouses, 185.
*— Town [Cornwall], 182.
-- (by Cadgwith) to Falmouth, 187.
Loddiswell [Kingsbridge], 44.
Logan Rock, 202, 203.
Longships Lighthouse, 199.
*†Looe, 162, 148.
— Island, 163.
— Pool, 182.
— to Fowey, 163.
Lookout Tor, 117, 122.
Lostwithiel, 154.
Lover's Leap, 76.
Ludgvan [Penzance], 194.

Lugger's Grotto, 146.
Lumber Bridge, 125, 152.
*†**Lustleigh** [Newton Abbot], 89.
— to Moreton, 89, 90.
— **Cleave**, 89.
Luxulion, 155.
— to Par and St. Blazey, 157.
***Lyme Regis**, 5.
— to Seaton, 6.
*†Lympstone, 33.

Madron [Penzance], 196.
Maenporth, 175.
Maker, 145.
Malpas [Truro], 160, 173.
Manaccan [Helston], 177.
Manacle Rocks, 178.
Mamaton, 90.
— Tor, 90.
Man Sands, 55.
*†**Marazion**, 190.
Marlborough, 68.
Marldon [Torquay], 52.
†Marsh Mills, 127.
Marshwood, Vale of, 4.
Marwood House, 14.
*Mary Church [Torquay], 51.
*† — Tavy, 114.
Mawnan Smith [Falm'th], 175.
Mean Castle, 198.
Meavy [Horrabridge], 124, 126.
— Bridge, 124.
Meldon Viaduct, 107.
Membland, 120, 119, 131.
Menabilly, 166.
*†Menheniot [Liskeard], 147.
Men Scryfys, 196.
Merchant's Cross, 124.
Merripit Hill, 81.
Merrivale Antiquities, 116.
— Bridge, 116.
Merry Maidens, 205.
Metherall, hut circles, 96.
*Mevagissey [St. Austell], 167.
— to Porthscatho, 167.
Mewstone, 131, 121.
Mis Tor, Great, 116, 83.
— Little, 116.
— Pan, 116.
*Modbury [Ivybridge], 67.
Monk's Cowl, 210.
†Moorswater, 148, 163
Morcombelake [Bridport], 4.
*†Moreton Hampstead, 91.
— to Chagford, 91.
Morvah, 206.
Morwellham, 143.
— Quay, 143.
Morwell Rocks, 125, 143, 152.
Mothecombe, 67.
Mousehole [Penzance], 204.
Mount Edgcumbe, 139, 145.
— Ridley, 58.
Mulfra Quoit, 197.
Mullion [Helston], 183.
Mylor [Penryn], 172.

Nanjizal, 201.
Nare Head, 169.
Newbridge (Callington), 125, 151.
— (Gunnislake), 125, 152.
— (Penzance), 206.
Newlake, 99.
*Newlyn [Penzance], 204.
*†Newton Abbot, 42.
— Ferrers [Plympton], 120, 131.
Nine Maidens, 197, 198.
*†North Tawton, 105.
Noss, 130, 131.
Nun's Cross, 117, 122.

Obelisk, the, 40, 38.
*†**Okehampton**, 105.
— (over Yes Tor) to Lidford, 106, 107.
— to Two Bridges, 106.
Old Lizard Head, 185.
— Town Bay, 211.
Otterton [Budleigh Salterton], 25.
*†**Ottery St. Mary**, 23.
Oxley Head, 55.

*†**Paignton**, 53.
*†Par, 155, 157, 162, 165.
— to Fowey, 155.
Pardenick Head, 200.
Parson and Clerk Rocks, 40.
Paul, 204.
Peake Hill, 25.
Pear Tree Point, 64, 70.
Penberth [Penzance], 203.
Pencalennick, 158.
Pendeen [Penzance], 206.
Pendennis Castle, 172.
Pengersick Castle, 189.
Peninnis Rocks, 210.
Penjerrick, 177.
Penlee Point, 146.
Penolver, 186.
Penrose, 182.
*†Penryn, 161.
Pentewan [St. Austell], 166.
Pentillie Castle, 142.
*†**Penzance**, 192.
— to Helston (coast), 207.
— ,, Land's End, 198.
— ,, ,, (by Logan), 203.
— ,, Logan (coast), 204, 205.
— ,, St. Just, 197.
*†Perranwell, 161.
Perranwharf, 161.
Pertinney Hill, 197.
Peter Tavy, 114.
Pigeon Hugo, 184.
Pillesdon Pen, 4.
Pipers, the, 205.
— Hole, 214.
Place House, 165.
Plym River, 127.
*†**Plymouth**, 133.
— to Calstock, 141.
— ,, Falmouth, 161.
— ,, Ivybridge, 130.
— ,, Looe, 162.

INDEX. 223

*†Plympton, 45, 68.
Polbarrow, 187.
Polcuel Ferry, 170.
Polpeor, 185.
Polperro, 163.
Poltesco, 178.
Port Eliot, 141.
Porthalla, 178.
Porth Curnow, 202.
Porthellick, 212.
*Porthleven [Helston], 188.
Porthloe, 169.
Porthmellin, 167.
Portholland, 168.
Porthoustock, 178.
*Porthscatho [Grampound Road],
— to Falmouth, 170. [169.
Portlemouth, 65, 64.
Postbridge [Princetown], 102,
Powderham, 38. [123.
Pradanack Head, 183.
Prawle Point, 63.
Prestonberry, 95.
*†**Princetown** [Horrabridge], 116,
- - to Ivybridge, 117. [103.
— „ Yelverton, 104.
*Probus, 158.
Prussia Cove, 189.
Puggie Stone, 100.
Pulpit Rock, 211.
Pynes, 11, 31.

Ralph Hole, 71.
Rame, 145.
— Head, 146.
Ramillies Cove, 71.
Ravens Hugo, 187.
Raybarrow Pool, 101.
*†Reading, 2.
Redlake, 118, 121.
*†Redruth, 178.
Restormel Castle, 153.
Revelstoke, 132, 120.
Rickham, 64.
Rill Head, 184.
Rippon Tor, 78.
Rock Inn, 88.
Roscrow, 176.
Rotten Pits, 70.
Round Pound, 100.
Rowsedon, 7.
Rowtor, 82.
Royal Albert Bridge, 141, 147.
Rundlestone, 208.
Rushford, 93.

St. Ann's Chapel, 125, 151.
—Authony-in-Meneage, 177.
—— „ in-Roseland, 170.‡
*†— Austell, 157.
—— „ to Mevagissey, 166.
— Budeaux, 110.
— Buryan [Penzance], 203.
— Cleer [Liskeard], 149.
†— Erth [Hayle], 179.
*†— Germans, 141, 147.
— Helens, 215.

St. Hilary, 207.
— Ive [Liskeard], 150.
*†— **Ives**, 205.
—— „ to St. Just, 205.
— John-in-the Wilderness, 35.
*— Just-in-Penwith [Penzance], 206.
—— „ to Land's End, 197.
—— „ „ Penzance, 206.
— Just-in-Roseland [Grampound
Road], 174.
— Kea. 173.
— Keverne [Helston], 178.
— Keyne's Well, 148.
— Levan, 202.
— Loy's Cove, 205.
— Martins [Scilly Isles], 216.
*— **Mary Church** [Torquay], 51.
*— Marys [Scilly Isles], 209. [42.
*— Mawes [Grampound Road], 170,
173.
— **Michael's Mount** [Marazion], 190.
— Neot [Liskeard], 152.
— Petrock, 58.
*Salcombe [Kingsbridge], 69.
- - to Bolt Head, 70.
— „ Torcross, 69.
— Regis 19, 20.
*†Salisbury, 12.
*†Saltash, 142.
Saltram, 45, 68.
Samson, 215.
Sancreed, 197.
Sancta Warna's Well, 216.
Sandridge, 59, 62.
Saw Mill Cove, 70.
*Scilly Isles, 208.
— Rock, 215.
Scorhill Circle, 99.
*†Seaton [Axminster], 17.
- to Lyme Regis, 17.
- - „ Sidmouth, 18.
*†— Junction, 13.
Seatown, 4.
Sennen [Penzance], 199.
- - Cove, 198.
Sharpham, 59, 62.
Sharp Tor, 121.
Shaugh Bridge, 127.
— Prior, 127.
Sheepstor, 126, 128.
Shell Tor, 121.
*†Sherborne, 12.
Shute, 13.
Sidbury Castle, 22, 14.
*†Sidmouth, 21.
— to Budleigh, 25.
— „ Seaton, 25.
*†— Junction, 14.
†Silverton, 32.
Sittaford Tor, 98.
Slapton [Kingsbridge], 63, 67.
Sourton, 108.
Spinsters' Rock, 96.
Staddon Point, 121, 130.
Star Castle, 210.

INDEX.

*†Starcross, 38.
Start Point, 63.
Staverton [Totnes], 74.
Steps Bridge, 86.
Sticklepath, [Okehampton], 101.
Stoke Fleming [Dartmouth], 63.
— Gabriel [Totnes], 59, 62.
— Point, 120, 131.
Stokenham [Kingsbridge], 65.
*Stonehouse [Plymouth], 137.
Stover Lodge, 87.
Street [Devon], 63.
Swanpool, 176.
Symondsbury, 3.

Talland, 163.
Tamar River, 141.
Tamerton Foliot, 110.
*†Taunton, 10.
*†Tavistock, 111, 110.
— to Ashburton, 122.
— „ to Bridestowe, 113.
— „ Ivybridge, 123.
— „ Liskeard, 124.
— „ Moreton Hampstead, 122.
— „ Princetown, 115.
— Inn, 82.
Tavy Cleave, 114.
*†Thorverton, 31.
Teign Head, 97, 98.
— House Inn, 86.
— River, 86.
†Teigngrace, 87.
*†Teignmouth, 41.
— to Torquay, 41.
Telegraph Hill, 213.
Templecombe Junc., 12, 23.
Three Barrows Tor, 121, 118.
†Tipton [Ottery], 14.
*†Tiverton, 32, 11.
Tol-pedn-Penwith, 201.
Tooth Rock, 210.
*†Topsham [Exeter], 33.
Tor Abbey, 47.
— Balk, 185.
— Bay, 53.
Tor Bryan, 43.
— Royal, 117, 122.
*Torcross [Kingsbridge], 63.
— to Kingsbridge, 65.
— „ Salcombe, 63
*†Torquay, 46.
— to Totnes, 53.
*†Totnes, 60.
— to Dartmouth, 62.
Trefusis Point, 172.
Tregantle Fort, 162.
Tregeagle's Quoits, 169.
Tregothnan, 158, 173.
Trelawne, 163.

Treelever Viaduct, 161.
Trematon Castle, 140.
Trenant, 163.
Trentis Rock, 121.
Trereen Dinas (Logan), 202.
— — (Gurnard's Head), 206.
Trereife, 194, 197.
Tresco [Scilly Isles], 214.
Tresillian Bridge, 158.
Trevethy Cromlech, 149.
Trewavas Head, 189.
Trewithan, 158.
Trewoofe, 204.
*†**Truro**, 159.
†Trusham, 85.
Two Bridges, 82, 103, 123.
— to Ashburton, 123.
— „ Okehampton, 82.

Ugbrooke, 85.
Uplyme [Lyme], 6, 13.

Vellandreath, 198.
Vincent's Pits, 70.
Virtuous Lady Mine, 126.
Vitifer Tin Mine, 80.
Vixen Tor, 116, 83, 128.

Walkham Glen, 128.
Walkhampton [Horrabridge], 128.
Warberry Hill, 51.
Warren, the, 34, 33.
Watcombe, 51.
Webburn Glen, 79.
Weir Head, 143.
*†Wellington [Somerset], 11.
Wembury, 131, 121.
Weston Mouth, 20.|
*†—super Mare, 10.
Whitchurch, 126.
— Canonicorum [Bridport], 5.
Whitesand Bay, 145, 162, 198.
Whyddon Park, 87.
Widdecombe [Ashburton], 79.
Wistman's Wood, 122, 82.
Wolf Rock Lighthouse, 208.
†Woodbury, 33.
Wynanton, 182.

Yar Tor, 82.
Yealm Mouth, 131, 121.
*Yealmpton [Plympton], 68.
Yellow Carn, 185.
Yelverton Junction, 104, 126.
*†Yeoford Junction, 104.
— to Chagford, 105.
*†Yeovil, 3.
— Junction, 12.
Yes Tor, 107.

Zennor, 205.

London: J. S. LEVIN, Steam Printing Works, 75, Leadenhall Street, E.C.

Thorough Guide

Advertiser.

N.B.—Communications respecting Advertisements should be addressed to "M. J. B. BADDELEY, Bowness-on-Windermere."

Only appropriate Advertisements are inserted.

ALPHABETICAL INDEX
to
RAILWAYS, STEAMERS, HOTELS, HYDROPATHICS. &c.

Alphabetical order is strictly observed in this list.

Railways.	Page
Caledonian	9
Cambrian	8
Glasgow and South Western	7
Great Western	5
Midland	6
Midland Great Western (Ireland)	10

Steamers.	
Caithness, Orkney, and Shetland	11
Loch Lomond and Loch Long	13
Mac Brayne's (Glasgow and Highlands)	12

England.

ALPHABETICAL INDEX.

Coaches.
	Page
Lynton, Lynmouth, and Barnstaple	22

Hotels, Hydropathics.
Derbyshire (Peak District)	13–16
Devon and Cornwall	16–23
English Lake District	24–38
Ireland	38–42
Scotland	44–64
Wales	42–43

Miscellaneous.
Boyd, Bookseller and Stationer, Oban	57
Buxton Lodgings	15
Dictionary of the Clyde	10
Fountain Baths, Matlock, F. Howe	21
Ganson, Shetland	46
Holland, House Agent, Lodgings, Bowness-on-Windermere	38
Houldin, Mrs., Bookseller and Stationer, Ambleside	24
Portinscale Lodgings (Tower)	30
Shetland Goods, Laurenson & Co., North End, Lerwick	46

Hydropathics.
Place.	Name.	Shortest Telegraphic Address.	
Rothesay	Glenburn	Glenburn, Rothesay	61
Windermere	Windermere	Hydro', Windermere	34

Hotels in England and Wales.
Place.	Name of Hotel.	Shortest Telegraphic Address.	
Ambleside	Queen's, S'tation Waterhead	Queen's, Ambleside	24
Ashbourne	Green Man	Green Man, Ashbourne	14
Bangor (Upper)	George	George Hotel, Bangor	43
Bettws-y-Coed	Royal Oak	Oak, Bettws-y-Coed	42
Bideford	New Inn Hotel	Ascott, Hotel, Bideford	16
,,	Royal	Royal Hotel, Bideford	17
,,	Tanton's	Tanton's, Bideford	16
Bowness	(See Windermere)		
Buxton	Crescent	Crescent Hotel, Buxton	15
,,	George	George Hotel, Buxton	15
Coniston	Crown	Crown Hotel, Coniston	24
,,	Waterhead	Waterhead, Coniston	25
Dartmoor	(See Princetown)		
Dovedale	Peveril of the Peak	Nearest at Ashbourne, 4 m.	13
Eskdale	Woolpack	Nearest at Holmrook, 10 m.	25
Exeter	New London	Pople, Exeter	18

Place.	Name of Hotel.	Shortest Telegraphic Address.	Page
Grasmere	Prince of Wales	Brown, Hotel, Grasmere	26
,,	Rothay	Rothay Hotel, Grasmere	27
Great Langdale	New D'geon Ghyll	Nearest at Elterwater, 2½ m	26
Ivy Bridge	London	London, Ivybridge	22
Keswick	Blencathra	Jeffery, Keswick	29
,,	Keswick	Wilson, Hotel, Keswick	28
,,	Queen's	Queen's, Keswick	29
,,	Royal Oak	Royal Oak, Keswick	30
(**Borrowdale**)	Borrowdale	Askew's Bus, Keswick	30
(**Portinscale**)	Derwentwater	Harker, Portinscale	31
Llandudno Jnc.	Junction	Junction Hotel, Conway	43
Lynmouth	Lyndale	Bevan, Hotel, Lynmouth	19
Lynton	Royal Castle	Baker, Hotel, Lynton	21
,,	Valley of Rocks	Hotel, Lynton	20
Matlock Bath	New Bath	Tyack, Hotel, Matlock-Bath	16
Menai Bridge	Victoria	V'toria Hotel, Menai-bdge.	43
Penzance	Queen's	Queen's, Penzance	19
Plymouth	Grand	Grand, Plymouth	22
Porlock	Porlock Weir	Nearest at Minehead, 6 m.	18
Princetown	Duchy	Duchy, Princetown	23
Ullswater	Howtown	Nearest at Pooley Br., 4 m.	33
,,	Ullswater	Bowness, Patterdale	32
Wastwater	Wastwater	Nearest at Holmrook, 12 m.	36
Windermere	Crown	Crown Hotel, W'mere	36
,,	Lake Side	Walker, Hotel, Newby Bridge	37
,,	Low Wood	Lowwood Hotel, Ambleside	33
,,	Old England (Bowness)	Old England, Windermere	35
,,	Rigg's	Rigg, Hotel, Windermere	34
,,	Royal (Bowness)	Royal Hotel, Windermere	35
(**Troutbeck**)	Mortal Man	Nearest at W'mere, 4 m.	37

Hotels in Ireland.

Place.	Name of Hotel.	Shortest Telegraphic Address.	Page
Ardara	Nesbitt Arms	McNelis, Hotel, Ardara	38
Connemara	Renvyle House	Blake, Letterfrack	39
Dublin	Gresham	Gresham Hotel, Dublin	39
Giant's Causeway	Causeway	Causeway Hotel, Bushmills	40
	Royal	Kane, Causeway, Bushmills	39
Kil'aloe	Royal	Royal Hotel, Killaloe	42
Killarney	Graham's	Graham's Hotel, Killarney	41
Killybegs	Royal Bay View	McLoone, Hotel, Killybegs	41

Hotels in Scotland.

Place.	Name of Hotel.	Shortest Telegraphic Address.	Page
Aberfoyle	Baille Nicol Jarvie	Blair, Aberfoyle	44
Blair Athole	Athole Arms	Hotel, Blairathole	44
Braemar	Invercauld Arms	Invercauld Arms, Braemar	45
Dalmally	Dalmally	Hotel, Dalmally	54
Dunkeld	Royal	Fisher, Hotel, Dunkeld	46
Edinburgh	Clarendon	Clarendon Hotel	49
,,	Cockburn	Cockburn Hotel	48
,,	London	London Hotel	49
,,	Regent	Regent Hotel Edinburgh	47
,,	Roxburghe	Roxburghe Hotel	49
,,	Waterloo	The Waterloo	48
,,	Windsor	Windsor Hotel	47
Glasgow	Cockburn	Cockburn Hotel, Glasgow	50
Glenaffric	Glenaffric Hotel	Nearest at Beauly, 17 m.	50
Glenelg	Glenelg	Glenelg Hotel, Lochalsh	51
Inverness	Royal	Royal Hotel, Inverness	52
,,	Victoria	Victoria Hotel, Inverness	53
,,	Waverley	Waverley Hotel, Inverness	51
Lerwick	Grand	Grand Hotel, Lerwick	63
Loch Awe	Loch Awe	Fraser, Lochawe	54
,,	Portsonachan	Cameron, Portsonachan	55
,,	Taycreggan	Taycreggan, Portsonachan	56
Loch Lomond	Tarbet	Tarbet Hotel, Lochlomond	56
Oban	Great Western	Western, Oban	58
,,	King's Arms	King's Arms, Oban	59
,,	Royal	Royal Hotel, Oban	58
(Kilmelford)	Cuilfail	Cuilfail Hotel, Kilmartin	60
Pitlochry	Moulin	Moulin Hotel, Pitlochry	56
Portree	Royal	Royal Hotel, Portree	62
St. Fillans	Drummond Arms	Divie, St. Fillans	59
Shetland	(see Lerwick)		
Skye (Isle of)	Broadford	Hotel, Broadford	62
,, ,,	Kyle Akin	Hotel, Kyleakin	62
,, ,,	Sligachan	Nearest at Portree, 9 m.	62
Strathpeffer	Spa	Wallace, Strathpeffer	64

GREAT WESTERN RAILWAY.
TOURIST TICKETS,
FIRST, SECOND & THIRD CLASS.

Available for two Months, and renewable with exceptions, up to Dec. 31st, are issued in LONDON, during the Summer Months of each year at the following Stations and Offices:

STATIONS.

GREAT WESTERN RAILWAY.	GREAT WESTERN & METROPOLITAN RAILWAY.	METROPOLITAN RAILWAY.	DISTRICT RAILWAY.
Paddington		Aldgate	Mansion House
Westbourne Park		Aldgate	Blackfriars
Uxbridge Road	Notting Hill	Bishopsgate	Charing Cross
Kensington	Latimer Road	Moorgate St.	Westminster Bdg.
(Addison Road)	Shepherd's Bush	Farringdon St.	Victoria
Victoria	Hammersmith	King's Cross	South Kensington
(L. C. & D. Sta.)			Earl's Court

RECEIVING OFFICES.

5, Arthur St. | 43 & 44, Crutched Frs. | 193, Oxford St. | 26, Regent Street
4, Cheapside | 67, Gresham St. | 407, " | 269, Strand
29, Charing Cross | Holborn Circus | 23, New Oxford St. | 82, Qn. Victoria St.

And at the Offices of Mr. Jakins, Red Cap, Camden Town; Mr. Kingston, 11, Southampton Street, Fitzroy Square; Mr. Myers, 1a, Pentonville Road, and 343, Gray's Inn Road; also of Messrs. Cook & Son, Tourist and Excursion Agents, Ludgate Circus;

AND AT ALL PRINCIPAL STATIONS.

To the following well-known Watering and other places of attraction.

WEST OF ENGLAND DISTRICT,
Barnstaple, Bodmin, Clevedon, Dartmouth, Dawlish, Exeter, Falmouth, Fowey, Helston, Ilfracombe, Lynton, Minehead, New Quay, Paignton, Penzance, Plymouth, Scilly Isles, St. Ives, Teignmouth, Torquay, Weston-Super-Mare, Bridport, Dorchester, Weymouth, Channel Islands, &c.

NORTH AND SOUTH WALES DISTRICTS.
Aberystwith, Bala, Bangor, Barmouth, Bettws-y-Coed, Blaenau Festiniog, Carnarvon, Corwen, Dolgelley, Llandudno, Llangollen, Penmaenmawr, Rhyl, Chepstow, Tintern, Cardigan, Swansea, Tenby, New Milford, &c.

ENGLISH LAKE AND DERBYSHIRE DISTRICTS.
Windermere, Furness Abbey, Ambleside, Buxton, Matlock. Leamington, Malvern, Ross, Monmouth, Abergavenny, and to to Isle of Man, Waterford, Cork, Lakes of Killarney, Dublin.

Tourist and Ordinary Tickets are issued from and to the WEST of ENGLAND and the NORTH of ENGLAND and Scotland, in connection with the Express Service of Trains *viâ* the Severn Tunnel; also from and to South Wales by the same Service *viâ* Hereford.

Tourists by the GREAT WESTERN LINE—THE BROAD GAUGE ROUTE TO THE WEST OF ENGLAND—pass through the most picturesque scenery in Devonshire and Cornwall, extending from Exeter to Plymouth, Falmouth, St. Ives, Penzance and the Land's End; while the Broad Gauge Carriages running in the Fast Express trains to and from the West of England, for which they have been specially built, are THE FINEST RAILWAY CARRIAGES IN ORDINARY USE IN THE KINGDOM.

For particulars of the various Circular Tours, Fares, and other information, see the Company's Tourist Programmes, which can be obtained at the Stations and Booking Offices during the Tourist Season.

Paddington Station, April, 1890.   H. LAMBERT, *General Manager.*

MIDLAND RAILWAY.

The Picturesque Route between
LONDON & MANCHESTER, & LIVERPOOL,
Through Matlock and the Peak of Derbyshire.
EXPRESS TRAINS FROM and TO ST. PANCRAS STATION.

THE TOURIST ROUTE to SCOTLAND.
Viâ SETTLE and CARLISLE.

EXPRESS TRAINS from ST. PANCRAS, also from LIVERPOOL and MANCHESTER to EDINBURGH and GLASGOW, with connections to all parts of Scotland. Ordinary RETURN TICKETS between London and Stations in Scotland are available for one month.

Tourist Tickets.—From May 1st to Oct. 31st Tourist Tickets are issued from LONDON, and all principal Stations on the Midland System, to Glasgow, Edinburgh, Greenock, Ardrossan, Oban, Inverness, Aberdeen, and other places of Tourist Resort in Scotland; to Malvern, Matlock, Buxton, Ilkley, Harrogate, Scarboro', Morecambe, Blackpool, Southport, Isle of Man, the English Lake District, and all the principal places of Tourist Resort on the Yorkshire and Lancashire Coasts; and to Belfast, Portrush, Londonderry, Connemara, and the North of Ireland.

Full particulars of the Fares, and arrangements respecting the issue of Tourist Tickets, are given in the *Programmes* inserted in the Company's Time Tables, or can be obtained at any of the Stations on the Midland Railway, on application, during the season.

All Tourist Tickets issued to places in Scotland by Midland Route, at any time during the season, are available for the Return Journey, on any day, and by any train, up to and including the 31st of December.

Carriages.—The through Trains of the Midland Railway Company are formed of Carriages of the most improved description, fitted with an efficient continuous automatic brake, and all the most approved modern appliances.

Drawing Room Saloon Cars & Sleeping Saloon Cars.
Drawing Room Saloon Cars are run in the principal Express Trains of the Midland Company between St. Pancras and Nottingham, Sheffield, Leeds, Bradford, Manchester, Liverpool, Carlisle, and Glasgow; and *Sleeping Saloon Cars* between St. Pancras and Manchester, Liverpool, Carlisle, Edinboro', and Glasgow (also Perth during the summer months).

Passengers holding First Class Tickets are allowed to ride in the Drawing Room Saloon Cars attached to the Day Express Trains, *without extra payment*.

A charge of 5s. per berth in the Sleeping Saloon Cars is made in addition to the First Class Fare.

Dining Saloon Cars are attached to the 5.0 p.m. Train from London (St. Pancras) to Manchester, (passengers for Liverpool change into the other portion of the train at Manchester) and to the 5.20 p.m. Train from Manchester to London (St. Pancras), into which Passengers from Liverpool, etc., can change at Manchester; and to the 5.40 p.m. St. Pancras to Nottingham, Sheffield, Leeds, and Bradford, and to the 6.15 p.m. from Sheffield to St. Pancras. No extra charge, beyond the sum payable for the dinner will be made.

Third Class Tickets are issued by all Trains over the Midland system.

Saloon, Family, and Invalid Carriages, fitted with Lavatories and every convenience, can be engaged for the use of parties, by giving a few days' notice at the Station or to the Superintendent of the Line, Derby.

Pic-Nic, Pleasure, and School Parties are conveyed at Reduced Fares, particulars of which can be obtained at the Stations on the line.

Excursion Trains at very low fares will be run at intervals during the summer season to and from London, Liverpool, Manchester, Yorkshire, Birmingham, Nottingham, Derby, Lancaster, and Carlisle, and all the principal parts of the Midland system, particulars of which will be announced fourteen days prior to the running of the Trains.

Derby, 1890.   **JOHN NOBLE, General Manager.**

Glasgow & South-Western Railway.

Direct Route between Scotland and England.

Through Trains are run between

GLASGOW (St. Enoch) & LONDON (St. Pancras)

Via the GLASGOW & SOUTH WESTERN and MIDLAND RAILWAYS,

Giving a Direct and Expeditious Service between GLASGOW, GREENOCK, PAISLEY, AYR, ARDROSSAN, KILMARNOCK, DUMFRIES, &c., and LIVERPOOL, MANCHESTER, BRADFORD, LEEDS, SHEFFIELD, BRISTOL, BATH, BIRMINGHAM, LONDON, &c.

Drawing-Room and Sleeping Saloon Carriages

Are run by the Morning and Evening Express Trains between GLASGOW and LONDON.

LAVATORY CARRIAGES (First and Third Class) are run by the principal Day Express Trains between Glasgow, Liverpool, Manchester, Bristol, London, &c.

IRELAND via GREENOCK and via ARDROSSAN.

A NIGHTLY SERVICE is given by Messrs. G. & J. Burns' Royal Mail Steamers vid Greenock and vid Ardrossan, in connection with which Tourist Tickets are issued to KILLARNEY, CORK, CONNEMARA, GIANT'S CAUSEWAY, &c. For particulars of sailings, see Time Tables and Newspaper Advertisements.

FIRTH OF CLYDE & WEST HIGHLANDS,

Vid Greenock.

EXPRESS and FAST TRAINS are run at convenient hours between

GLASGOW & GREENOCK

(St. Enoch Station)   (Lyndoch and Princes Pier Stations)

In direct connection with the "Columba," "Iona," "Lord of the Isles," "Eagle," "Sultana," "Windsor Castle," and other steamers, sailing to and from KIRN, DUNOON, INNELLAN, ROTHESAY, KYLES OF BUTE, ARDRISHAIG, OBAN, INVERARAY, KILCREGGAN, KILMUN, LOCHGOILHEAD, GARELOCHHEAD, &c.

Through Carriages are run by certain trains between GREENOCK (Princes Pier) and EDINBURGH (Waverley), and by the Evening Express Trains in each direction between GREENOCK (Princes Pier) and LONDON (St. Pancras).

Return Tickets issued to Coast Towns are available for Return

AT ANY TIME.

Passengers are landed at Princes Pier Station, from whence there is a Covered Way to the Pier where the Steamers call; and Passengers' Luggage is conveyed *free of charge* between the Station and the Steamers.

ARRAN and the AYRSHIRE COAST.

From ARDROSSAN the splendid Saloon Steamer "Scotia" sails daily to and from the ISLAND OF ARRAN in connection with the Express Train Service.

An Express and Fast Train Service is given between GLASGOW (St. Enoch), PAISLEY, and TROON, PRESTWICK, AYR, ARDROSSAN, FAIRLIE, LARGS, &c.

For Particulars as to Trains and Steamers, see the Company's Time Tables.

JOHN MORTON, *Secretary and General Manager.*

CAMBRIAN RAILWAYS.
Tours in Wales.

BATHING, BOATING, FISHING (Sea, River & Lake), COACHING, MOUNTAINEERING.

1st, 2nd, and 3rd Class Tourist Tickets,

Available for Two Calendar Months, renewable up to 31st December, are issued from 1st May to 31st October at all the principal Stations in England and Scotland, and at Dublin, and other principal Stations in Ireland to

Aberystwith, Aberdovey, Towyn, Dolgelley, Barmouth, Criccieth, Borth, Harlech, Portmadoc, Pwllheli, Rhayader, Builth Wells, and Brecon.

The Scenery traversed by and adjacent to the Cambrian Railways is of an exceedingly varied and beautiful description, and the coast of Cardigan Bay, to which the line affords the most convenient access, offers great advantages for sea-bathing in the long reaches of firm, safe, and sandy beach, with which it abounds, and in its pure and bracing air. The mountain ranges of SNOWDON, CADER IDRIS, and PLYNLIMON, with their Rivers and Lakes, are also readily accessible from the various Watering-places, thus placing within the reach of visitors a delightful combination of the natural beauties of sea and land.

The Valley of the Wye, through which the line to Brecon runs, also possesses great attractions for Tourists and Anglers.

Arrangements are made during the Summer Months for the conveyance of Visitors by Coach to and from places of interest in the vicinity of the Coast Line at reduced charges, by which means, and also by the Festiniog, Talyllyn, and Corris miniature-gauge Railways, whose termini are on the Cambrian system, the following amongst other places can easily be visited by daily Excursions:—

Snowdon, Beddgelert, Tan-y-bwlch, Festiniog Slate Quarries, Cwmbychan Lake, Mawddach Estuary, Precipice Walk and Torrent Walk (Dolgelley), Talyllyn Lake, Corris, Llyfnant Valley, Rheidol Lake, Devil's Bridge, Maentwrog, Abersoch &c.

Special Tickets at Reduced Fares

Are also issued between Local Stations to TOURISTS, and for FISHING, PIC-NIC and OTHER PARTIES.

A Special Service of Express Trains

Is run, daily during the season, in connection with Fast trains on the London and North Western and other Railways, with Through Carriages from and to London, Liverpool, Manchester, Birmingham, Stafford, Shrewsbury, Hereford, Merthyr, Cardiff, Newport (Mon.) &c.

Through Carriages run daily throughout the year between London (Euston) and Aberystwith.

"PICTURESQUE WALES" (Illustrated).

The Official Guide Book to the Cambrian Railways, edited by Mr. GODFREY TURNER, price 6d., can be obtained at the Bookstalls, or on application to the Company's Offices or Stations; also of Messrs. W. J. Adams & Sons, 59, Fleet Street, London, E.C.

Time-tables, Guide-books, Tourist Programmes and full particulars of Trains, Fares, &c., may be obtained at any of the Company's Stations or Booking Offices, and at 34, James Street, Liverpool, or on application to the undersigned. Also from Mr. G. T. Purnell, 55, High Street, Croydon, and at the under-mentioned offices of Messrs. Henry Gaze & Sons, Excursion Tourist Agents—

LONDON—142, Strand. BIRMINGHAM—Stephenson Place, New Street Station.
DUBLIN—16, Suffolk Street. GLASGOW—34, Gordon Street.

COMPANY'S OFFICE, OSWESTRY. **J. CONACHER,**
Secretary and General Manager.

CALEDONIAN RAILWAY.

THE CALEDONIAN RAILWAY COMPANY have arranged a system of TOURS—over 100 in number—by Rail, Steamer (on Sea, River and Loch), and Coach, comprehending almost every place of interest either for scenery or historical associations throughout Scotland, including—

Edinburgh, Glasgow, Aberdeen, Dundee, Inverness, Gourock, Greenock, Paisley, Dumfries, Moffat, Peebles, Callander, Stirling, Perth, Crieff, Dunkeld, Oban, Inveraray,

The Trossachs, Loch-Katrine, Loch-Lomond, Loch-Eck, Loch-Earn, Loch-Tay, Loch-Awe, Caledonian Canal, Glencoe, Iona, Staffa, Skye, Balmoral, Braemar, Arran, Bute, The Firth of Clyde, The Falls of Clyde, Lowther Hills, &c.

☞ TOURISTS are recommended to procure a copy of the Caledonian Railway Company's "Tourist Guide," which contains descriptive notices of the Districts embraced in the Tours, Maps, Plans, &c. They can be had at any of the Company's Stations, and also at the chief Stations on the London and North-Western Railway. They are also supplied gratis to the chief Hotels, Hydropathics, Steamboats, &c., in Great Britain and Ireland.

Tickets for these Tours are issued at the Company's Booking Offices at all the chief Towns. The Tourist Season extends from JUNE to SEPTEMBER inclusive.

The CALEDONIAN RAILWAY, in conjunction with the LONDON AND NORTH-WESTERN RAILWAY, forms what is known as the

West Coast (Royal Mail) Route between
SCOTLAND AND ENGLAND.

London (Euston) and { Edinburgh (Princess Street) in 8½ hours.
{ Glasgow (Central) in 8¾ hours.

DIRECT TRAINS RUN FROM AND TO
Glasgow, Edinburgh, Androssan, Gourock, Greenock, Paisley, Stranraer, Stirling, Oban, Perth, Dundee, Aberdeen, Inverness, and other places in Scotland,
TO AND FROM
London (Euston), Birmingham, Liverpool, Manchester, Preston, Penrith (for Lake District), Leeds, Bradford, and other places in England.
Sleeping and Day Saloon Carriages. Through Guards and Conductors.

The Company's Trains from and to Edinburgh, Glasgow, Carlisle, &c., connect on the Clyde with the Caledonian S.S. Co.'s steamers; also with the "Columba," "Iona," "Lord of the Isles," "Ivanhoe," and other Steamers to and from Dunoon, Innellan, Rothesay, Largs, Millport, the Kyles of Bute, Arran, Campbeltown, Ardrishaig, Inveraray, LochGoil, Loch-Long, the West Highlands, &c.

There will be an express service between Glasgow (Central) and Androssan, in connection with steamers to and from Arran—90 minutes the whole distance.

Express service between Edinburgh and Glasgow, in 65 minutes; also from Edinburgh and Glasgow, Stirling, Oban, Perth, Dundee, Aberdeen, and the North, and *vice versâ*.

For particulars of Trains, Fares, &c., see the Company's Time Tables.

The Company's Line from Greenock to Gourock is now open and forms a direct and expeditious route in connection with steamboats to and from Dunoon, Kirn, Hunter's Quay, Holy Loch, Loch Long, Loch Goil, and the Watering Places in that district, the Western Highlands and Islands, and from and to Glasgow, Edinburgh, London, Liverpool, Manchester, Bristol, and other places in England and Scotland. Trains run alongside steamers.

The Caledonian Company's large and magnificent **CENTRAL STATION HOTEL, GLASGOW**, is under the Company's own Management.

Glasgow, 1890. JAMES THOMPSON, General Manager.

IRELAND.

Midland Great Western Railway.

CONNEMARA.

TOURIST TICKETS
From the principal Towns in ENGLAND & SCOTLAND, available for Two Months, for the
CONNEMARA
OR
CONNEMARA and KILLARNEY TOURS.
Issued at the Offices of the Railway and Steampacket Companies and Tourist Agencies.

CIRCULAR TOURS
From DUBLIN and BELFAST
TO THE
TOURIST, ANGLING, and SHOOTING RESORTS
IN THE
WEST OF IRELAND.
*** Reduced Fares for Parties of Two to Four Passengers.
Extra Coupons for extended Tours from Dublin, Broadstone Terminus, to the North and South of Ireland.

CONNEMARA.—Public Cars run during the season, passing through Leenaue, Kylemore, Letterfrack (for Renvyle), Clifden, Recess (for Glendalough), and Oughterard.

The Company's 1s. Illustrated Handbook to the West of Ireland,
Contains 16 full-paged toned Lithographs and numerous Woodcuts.

Apply to the Manager's Office, Broadstone, Dublin, where Programmes and all other information as to Fares, Routes, Conditions, etc., may be obtained.

VISITORS TO GLASGOW AND THE CLYDE

Should procure the

DICTIONARY OF THE CLYDE,

A Descriptive, Historic, and Statistical Guide
to the Towns, Villages, Watering Places, Mansions, Mountains, Islands, Lochs, Docks, Harbours, Shipping, Industries, Sports, Pastimes, Legends, and Scenic Features of the River from Source to Sea.

"Unquestionably the most concise, the most accurate, the most exhaustive, the handiest, and the cheapest of guide books."—*Industries.*

300 Pages. Price, **ONE SHILLING.** Five Maps.

To be had at Railway and River-boat Bookstalls; from MENZIES & Co., Glasgow and Edinburgh, SIMPKIN, MARSHALL, & Co., London, and all Booksellers.

Caithness, Orkney, and Shetland Steamers.

The North of Scot'and and Orkney and Shetland Steam Navigation Company's Steamships, "St. Rognvald," "St. Magnus," "St. Nicholas," "St. Clair," "St. Olaf," and "Queen," are intended to sail during the *SUMMER MONTHS* as under, but the arrangements are subject to alteration from month to month :—

From Leith in the morning, and from Aberdeen same afternoon or evening :
  To Lerwick every Wednesday and Friday.
  To Scalloway and West Side of Shetland every Monday.
  To Kirkwall every Wednesday and Friday.
  To Stromness every Monday.
  To St. Margaret's Hope every Monday.
  To Thurso every Monday.
  To Wick every Monday and Friday.
  To Stornoway, *during May and June*, every Monday.
Returning South :
  From Lerwick every Monday and Friday (or Saturday).
  From Scalloway every Wednesday evening.
  From Kirkwall every Tuesday and Saturday.
  From Stromness every Thursday.
  From St. Margaret's Hope every Thursday.
  From Stornoway every Wednesday evening.
  From Thurso every Thursday morning.
  From Wick every Tuesday forenoon and Thursday afternoon.

The Royal Mail Steamer "St. Olaf," from Stromness every week-day during April, May, June, July, August, and September at 3 p.m., touching at Scapa Pier (Kirkwall), thence to Scrabster Pier (Thurso), now calls going to Scrabster, and all afternoon sailings, summer and winter, landing Mail-bag by Boat at South Ronaldshay. From Scrabster Pier (Thurso), on receiving the Mails, about 8 p.m., and touching at Scapa Pier, thence to Stromness. Throughout the rest of the year, the "St. Olaf" leaves Stromness at 2 p.m. for Scrabster Pier, returning from Scrabster Pier about 7.30 p.m., touching at Scapa Pier going and returning.

PASSAGE FARES.

From Albert Dock, Leith.	1st Cabin.	2nd Cabin.	From Aberdeen.	1st Cabin.	2nd Cabin.
To Wick	18s.	9s. 0d.	To Wick	12s.	7s. 0d.
To Thurso	18s.	9s. 0d.	To Thurso	12s.	7s. 0d.
To St. Margaret's Hope	20s.	9s. 0d.	To St. Margaret's Hope	16s.	7s. 0d.
To Stromness	20s.	9s. 0d.	To Stromness	16s.	7s. 0d.
To Kirkwall	22s.	10s. 6d.	To Kirkwall	18s.	8s. 0d.
To Lerwick	26s.	10s. 6d.	To Lerwick	21s.	8s. 6d.
To Scalloway	26s.	10s. 6d.	To Scalloway	21s.	8s. 6d.
From Scalloway to places on West Side				5s.	2s. 6d.
From Lerwick to places in North Isles				6s.	3s. 0d.

☞ *Return Tickets available to return within three Calendar Months, are issued at the rate of a Single Fare and a half, with liberty to the holders to break the journey at any of the Ports of Call.*

Scrabster to Scapa and Stromness,   First Cabin, 6s.   Second Cabin, 3s.
Scapa to St. Margaret's Hope & Stromness ,, 2s.   ,,   1s.
St Margaret's Hope to Stromness   ,, 3s.   ,,   1s. 6d.
St. Margaret's Hope to Scrabster   ,, 4s.   ,,   2s.

Return Tickets issued to or from Orkney and Shetland by the other Vessels belonging to the Company, are NOT AVAILABLE by the Mail Steamer "St. Olaf" across the Pentland Firth. Return Tickets are issued for that passage only, at the usual rate.

First-class Hotel accommodation at Lerwick, Scalloway, Kirkwall, Stromness, Wick, and Thurso.

For further particulars, including days and hours of sailing, see Monthly Sailing Bills, which may be had on application to GEORGE HOURSTON, Agent, 64, Constitution Street, Leith   CHARLES MERRYLEES, Manager, Aberdeen.

SUMMER TOURS IN SCOTLAND

THE

ROYAL ROUTE.

GLASGOW and the HIGHLANDS
Viâ Crinan and Caledonian Canals.

ROYAL MAIL STEAMERS

Columba	Glencoe	Clansman	Loanda
Iona	Lochawe	Flowerdale	Gladiator
Fusilier	Lochness	Clydesdale	Pelican
Chevalier	Lochiel	Cavalier	Falcon
Grenadier	Linnet	Staffa	Udea
Gondolier	Fingal	Ethel	Texa
Pioneer	Islay	Handa	Countess
Glengarry	Claymore	Mabel	Margaret

Inveraray Castle

THE ROYAL MAIL SWIFT PASSENGER STEAMER
'COLUMBA' or 'IONA'

Sails daily from May till October, from Glasgow at 7 a.m., and from Greenock at 8.50, Prince's Pier about 9, Gourock Pier about 9.20, and Dunoon about 9.35, in connection with Express Trains from London and the South, Edinburgh, Glasgow, &c., for Kyles of Bute, Tarbert, and Ardrishaig, conveying passengers for Oban, Glencoe, Inverness, Lochawe, Loch Lomond, Loch Katrine, the Trossachs, Staffa and Iona, Mull, Skye, Gairloch, Lochinver, Stornoway, Thurso, &c.

A WHOLE DAY'S SAIL BY THE "COLUMBA" OR "IONA."
From Glasgow to Ardrishaig and Back (180 miles.)

CABIN FARE 6s.   Breakfast, Dinner and Tea, in Cabin, 6s.
FORE CABIN FARE, 3s. 6d.   do. do. do. in Fore-Cabin, 3s. 6d.

TOURS TO THE WEST HIGHLANDS (occupying about a week)
By STEAMSHIP
'CLAYMORE' or 'CLANSMAN,'

Viâ Mull of Kintyre, going and returning through the Sounds of Jura, Mull, and Skye, calling at Oban, Tobermory, Portree, STORNOWAY, and intermediate places.

Cabin Return Fare with superior sleeping accommodation,
or including meals.

The Route is through scenery rich in historical interest and unequalled for grandeur and variety. These vessels leave Glasgow every Monday and Thursday about 12 noon, and Greenock about 6 p.m., returning from Stornoway every Monday and Wednesday.

The Steam-Ship 'CAVALIER'

will leave Glasgow every Monday at 11 a.m. and Greenock at 4 p.m., for Inverness and Back (viâ Mull of Kintyre), leaving Inverness every Thursday morning; Cabin Fare for the Trip, with First-class Sleeping Accommodation, or including Meals.

Official Guide Book, 6d.

Time Bill, Map and List of Fares, sent free on application to the Owner

DAVID MACBRAYNE, 119, Hope Street, Glasgow.

North British Steam Packet Company.
LOCH LOMOND,
QUEEN OF SCOTTISH LAKES.

Splendid Saloon Steamers sail daily from Balloch Pier in direct connection with North British Trains from Edinburgh, Glasgow, &c.

Grand CIRCULAR TOUR of LOCH LOMOND and LOCH LONG.

For further information and hours of sailings apply to North British Railway Station Agents, or to

99, Main Street. Alexandria, N.B.

Derbyshire.

DOVEDALE.
PEVERIL OF THE PEAK HOTEL,

Pleasantly situated close to this beautiful valley.

TESTIFIED CUISINE,
    NICE APARTMENTS,
        HOME COMFORTS,
            MODERATE TARIFFS,
                AND **GOOD FISHING.**

CARRIAGES by order meet trains at Ashbourne, North Staffordshire Railway.

G. POYSER, Proprietor.

Postal Address:—Thorpe, near ASHBOURNE.
Nearest Telegraph at Ashbourne, 4 miles.

Derbyshire.

ASHBOURNE.

(*The nearest Railway Station to DOVEDALE.*)

GREEN MAN AND BLACK'S HEAD
HOTEL,

(Family and Commercial Posting House.)

OMNIBUSES to and from **EVERY TRAIN.**

BILLIARDS.

Extract from Boswell's "Life of Dr. Johnson," September, 1771:—

"After breakfast I departed and pursued my journey northwards. I took my post chaise from the GREEN MAN, a very good Inn at Ashbourne, the Mistress of which, a mighty civil gentlewoman, courtseying very low, presented me with an Engraving of the sign of her house, to which she had subjoined in her own handwriting an address in such singular simplicity of style, that I have preserved it, pasted upon one of the boards of my original Journal at this time, and shall here insert it for the amusement of my readers:—

"M. Killingleys duly waits upon Mr. Boswell, is exceedingly obliged to him for this favor; whenever he comes this way, hopes for a continuance of the same; would Mr. Boswell name the house to his extensive acquaintance, it would be a singular favor conferred on one who has it not in her power to make any other return but her most grateful thanks and sincerest prayers for his happiness in time and in a blessed eternity."

FANNY WALLIS, Proprietress.

Derbyshire.

Shortest Telegraphic Address:—"**Crescent Hotel, Buxton.**"

CRESCENT HOTEL,
BUXTON.

FIRST-CLASS for Families and Gentlemen. Best situation. Forms wing of the Crescent. Due South aspect. Close to Railway Stations. Covered Colonnade to Baths, Wells and Gardens. Dining, Drawing, Billiard, Smoke, and Reading Rooms. The Dining Saloon is acknowledged to be one of the finest rooms in the kingdom. Suites of apartments for Families. Rooms on ground floor level if required.

TABLE D'HOTE AT SEPARATE TABLES.
EXCELLENT CUISINE.   CHOICE WINES.   BILLIARDS.

JOHN SMILTER, *Proprietor.*

BUXTON.
THE GEORGE FAMILY HOTEL,

A First-class House, adjoining the Baths and Pavilion Gardens; near the Church and Railway Station; Suites of Rooms, without staircases, for Invalids; Public Dining and Drawing Rooms; Private Sitting Rooms; Billiard, Reading, and Smoke Rooms. Every convenience pertaining to a good modern Hotel. Moderate Terms. The House is detached, and has a splendid situation; well sheltered. In connection with NEW BATH HOTEL, Matlock Bath. For Terms apply to

MILL & TYACK, Proprietors.

BUXTON.
1, Hartington Terrace.

Superior and select apartments, every comfort and excellent cooking. Elevated situation nearly 1,100 feet above the sea level, and south-west aspect. At the south end of the **Broad Walk**, close to the Pavilion and Gardens, and five minutes walk from the Baths.

Train or coach to Chatsworth, Haddon Hall, Matlock, Dove Dale, Castleton, and the romantic scenery of the Peak of Derbyshire. Express trains to London 4¼ hours, Manchester 40 minutes.

Personally recommended by the author of the "Thorough Guide" Series.

ADDRESS: **Mrs. A. A. BRADBURY**,
1, Hartington Terrace, West Street, Buxton.

Derbyshire—Devonshire.

MATLOCK BATH.
TYACK'S NEW BATH HOTEL,
Recently enlarged and newly furnished.

A first class family house, with every comfort and modern improvement. Beautifully situated amidst its own charming grounds of twelve acres, from whence the most lovely views in Derbyshire can be seen. Very large Dining room, Drawing room, Billiard room, and private Sitting rooms. A large Swimming Bath in the hotel, and Hot Baths. Fishing. Lawn Tennis. A 'Bus to meet each train. Terms strictly moderate.

T. Tyack, Proprietor.

THE OLDEST, LARGEST & PRINCIPAL HOTEL in the TOWN.
NEW INN FAMILY HOTEL,
BIDEFORD,
Family, Commercial, and General Posting House.
HENRY ASCOTT, Proprietor.

11 miles from Clovelly; pleasantly situated in the most central part of the town, and commanding very extensive views. Booking Office for Coaches to Clovelly and Bude.

TANTON'S HOTEL,
BIDEFORD.
Large and Well-Appointed
COFFEE, COMMERCIAL AND BILLIARD ROOMS.
HOT & COLD BATHS.
Posting in all its Branches.
OMNIBUSES MEET EVERY TRAIN.

W. GIDDIE, Proprietor.

Devonshire.

CENTRAL FOR THE WHOLE OF NORTH DEVON,
Including WESTWARD HO! CLOVELLY, HARTLAND,
BUDE, ILFRACOMBE, and LYNTON.

Four-in-hand Coaches in the Season to above places.

| Adjoining Railway Station. | **ROYAL HOTEL, BIDEFORD.** | Overlooking the River TORRIDGE and OLD BRIDGE. |

THE MOST MODERN HOTEL IN THE WEST OF ENGLAND.

| Every Luxury and Comfort | **CONTINENTAL COURTYARD.** | Ventilation and Sanitary Arrangements Perfect. |

Superbly Furnished and lofty Rooms, Hot and Cold Baths, Elegant Billiard Saloon (Two Tables).

COMPLETELY SHELTERED FROM E. & N.E. WINDS.

Delightful summer and winter resort, one of the mildest and healthiest in the Kingdom.

Specially Reduced Winter Tariff.

| First class horses and carriages of every description always ready. | **Save OMNIBUS and PORTERAGE.** | Finest Stabling and Lock-up Coachhouse in Devonshire. |

For situation the Royal is probably unequalled in the North of Devon, and from its size and the admirable way in which it is fitted out must be regarded as one of the best Hotels in the West of England. It stands amid the interesting spots and charming scenery made notorious by "Westward Ho!" and is within easy distance of the many romantic nooks with which the North Devon coast abounds. A portion of the house was built in the year 1688 by an old merchant prince, and contains a magnificent oak staircase and drawing room, which are objects of admiration and interest. The ceiling of the latter has the reputation of being one of the grandest in the country. The work comprises festoons of flowers, fruit, and foliage in high relief, and was the workmanship of Italian artists specially commissioned two hundred years ago. In this room also Charles Kingsley wrote a portion of "Westward Ho!" and on one of the panels hangs a portrait (said to be from the brush of Vandyke) of John Strange, the great grandfather of Rose Salterne (the fickle "Rose of the Torridge"), immortalised by Kingsley in "Westward Ho!"—*Vide Public Press.*

BIDEFORD.—Chiefly remarkable for having a first-rate hotel.—*Punch, Oct. 5th,* 1889.

Devonshire.

POPLE'S
NEW LONDON HOTEL
EXETER.

RE-FURNISHED AND RE-DECORATED.
For Families and Gentlemen.

This first-class Hotel has long stood pre-eminent, and is patronised by the leading County families. Adjoining Northernhay Park and within three minutes' walk of the Cathedral.

TABLE D'HOTE.   NIGHT PORTER.
Large Covered Continental Courtyard.
POSTING ESTABLISHMENT.
Omnibuses and Cabs meet all Trains.

Also Proprietor of the Globe Hotel, Newton Abbot.

Telegrams to "POPLE, EXETER."

PORLOCK.
PORLOCK WEIR HOTEL (Anchor)
(Viâ Minehead, Somersetshire).

This Hotel is situated on the shore of Porlock Bay, close by the sea, and in the rich and lovely Vale of Porlock. It is in the centre of the Stag and Fox-Hunting country, and at the foot of Exmoor, whose wild and beautiful recesses are most conveniently visited from it. Every comfort ensured.

Fishing and Shooting. Good Stabling; Post-Horses and Carriages. Hotel 'bus to principal Trains.

J. P. GODDARD Proprietor.

** *The Proprietor has also a Private Lodging House.*

Devon—Cornwall.

Lynmouth, North Devon.

LYNDALE
AND
TORS PARK HOTEL
(Under the same management),

First Class, with every convenience for Families and Tourists, is most beautifully situated on an eminence, with all front rooms commanding the grandest uninterrupted views of the Harbour, Bristol Channel, Woods and Hills, and the best Landscape Scenery in the North of Devon; also overlooking the East and West Lyns, and within three minutes' walk to the Beach; standing in its own very extensive grounds. Good Trout and Salmon Fishing. Lawn Tennis. Cheap Boarding terms. Write for Tariff with Photo' showing position of Hotels.

WILLIAM BEVAN, Proprietor.

Lighted with Electric Light, and fitted with all recent improvements. All Coaches stop outside the Hotels to take up and put down Passengers.

PENZANCE.
SEA-SIDE.—THE QUEEN'S.
(On the Esplanade. Facing due South).

Patronized by Her Majesty the Queen of Holland.

THIS Hotel is the Principal and Largest, and is most comfortably furnished. It has a frontage of over 170 feet, all the rooms of which overlook the Bay and St. Michael's Mount. For Families, Ladies and Gentlemen only. Apartments *en suite.*

Penzance stands unrivalled for the quiet beauty and variety of its scenery, whilst the mildness and equability of its climate are admirably adapted to invalids. Ladies' Drawing, Reading, Coffee, Smoking and Billiard Rooms. Hot and Cold Baths. Table d'Hôte. An Omnibus meets every train. Posting in all its branches. Yachts, &c.

ALEX. H. HORA, Proprietor.

Devonshire.
VALLEY OF ROCKS HOTEL.
Fitted with Electric Light, and all the most modern conveniences.

"The position of the splendid new **Valley of Rocks Hotel** is absolutely unequalled and unparalleled in the South of England."—*Daily Telegraph*, April 7th, 1890.

COMMANDS UNRIVALLED VIEWS.

Salmon and Trout Fishing. Billiards. Post Horses, Carriages. Luxurious suites of Private Apartments, elegant Salle à manger, Ladies' Drawing Room, range in a long front facing the Sea.

Best routes to Lynton, G.W.R., book to Minehead, where on and after June 1st, **Valley of Rocks Coach** meets trains leaving Minehead 1 p.m., and Paddington, 9 a.m., or L. & S.W.R. viâ Barnstaple, where Mail Coach meets train. Coaches to and from Ilfracombe.

Carriages meet trains at Minehead, Barnstaple, and Ilfracombe on receipt of telegram to "Hotel, Lynton."

Proprietors:
The Lynton & Lynmouth Hotel & Property Company, Ld.

JOHN HEYWOOD, *Resident Director.*

Telegraphic Address, "HOTEL, LYNTON."

LYNTON, NORTH DEVON.

ROYAL CASTLE FAMILY HOTEL.

PATRONISED by the English and Continental Royal Families. First-class Hotel, especially favourite and attractive. Table d'hôte. Reading and Drawing Rooms. New Smoking and Billiard Pavilions, all facing the Sea. Magnificent Views and Ornamental Grounds of Twelve Acres.

Private Hotel Attached,

THOMAS BAKER, Proprietor.

THE FOUNTAIN BATHS
(MATLOCK BATH).

LARGE SWIMMING BATH

68 degrees Fahrenheit.

600,000 gallons of clear spring water flow through this Bath daily. Swimming taught

HOT BATHS, SHOWER & DOUCHE BATHS.

For further information apply to W. E. HOWE, the Library, Matlock Bath.

Devonshire—Somerset.

COACHING.
LYNTON, LYNMOUTH, and BARNSTAPLE.

THE WELL-APPOINTED FAST
FOUR-HORSE COACH
"TANTIVY"

(CARRYING THE MAILS), RUNS DAILY THROUGHOUT THE YEAR (Sundays excepted), in connection with the Trains of L. & S. W. Railway, passing through some of the finest Scenery in Devonshire.

Up.		Down.	
Lynton ... ... dep.	8 0 a.m.	Waterloo ... ... dep.	9 0 a.m.
Barnstaple ... ... arr.	10 55 „	Barnstaple ... ... arr.	3 21 p.m.
„ ... ... dep.	11 3 „	„ ... ... dep.	3 40 „
Waterloo ... ... arr.	5 17 „	Lynton ... ... arr.	6 30 „

also convenient for train leaving Paddington 9 a.m., arriving at Lynton 6.30 p.m.

AN ADDITIONAL COACH

will run daily (Sundays excepted) during the months of July, August, and September between Lynton, Lynmouth, and Barnstaple, in connection with the London and South Western Trains, as under, being convenient for Great Western Trains also.

Up.		Down.	
Lynton ... ... dep.	12 0 noon	Waterloo ... ... dep.	11 0 a.m.
Barnstaple ... ... arr.	3 0 p.m.	Barnstaple ... ... arr.	4 43 p.m.
„ ... ... dep.	3 21 „	„ ... ... dep.	4 50 „
Waterloo ... ... arr.	10 10 „	Lynton ... ... arr.	7 40 „

LYNTON, BIDEFORD, CLOVELLY, WESTWARD HO! BUDE, AND NORTH CORNWALL.

Up.			Down.		
Lynton	dep. 8 0 a.m.	12 0 noon	Bude ... dep.	9 45 a.m.	9 45 a.
Barnstaple	„ 11 8 „	3 26 p.m.	Clovelly „	12 15 p.m.	12 15 p
Bideford	„ 11 31 „	3 46 „	Bideford „	2 53 „	2 53 „
Clovelly	arr. 1 0 p.m.	5 15 „	Barnstaple „	3 40 „	5 0 „
Bude ...	„ 8 0 „	8 0 „	Lynton arr.	6 30 „	7 40 „

THROUGH TICKETS issued at all L. & S. W. Railway Stations.
Booking Office, opposite VALLEY of ROCKS HOTEL, LYNTON.

JONES BROS., House Agents,
Proprietors, Lynton.

PLYMOUTH.
GRAND HOTEL (on the Hoe).
The only Hotel with Sea View.
Mail Steamers anchor in sight.

Also, at **IVY BRIDGE** (11 miles from Plymouth),

The London Hotel,
Hunting, Fishing, Beautiful Scenery.

JAMES BOHN, *Proprietor*.

Devon.

DUCHY HOTEL, PRINCETOWN,
DARTMOOR.

This **First Class Family Hotel** is situated in the very centre of Dartmoor, and is one of the **highest hotels** in the country, being about 1,400 feet above the sea-level.

Visitors to Dartmoor will do well to make this their headquarters, Dartmeet, Post Bridge, Wistman's Wood, Crockern Tor, Mis Tor, and various other places of interest being situated within easy distances.

Good Trout and Salmon Fishing may be obtained from March 1st to September 31st in the East and West Darts and tributaries, licenses for which may be obtained at this Hotel.

Good Snipe and other shooting may also be had.

Several Packs of Foxhounds and Harriers meet in the neighbourhood.

"DUCHY HOUSE,"

recently built to meet the increased demand for accommodation, is within two minutes' walk from the Duchy Hotel.

A First-Class Boarding and Lodging House,

containing all the most modern improvements and conveniences. Private Sitting Rooms.

This will be found to be a most suitable house for private families staying any length of time.

Good Posting. Excellent Dairy.

Tariff and Boarding Terms on application.

MARTHA ROWE, Proprietress (for 40 years.)

English Lakes.

THE
WINDERMERE WATERHEAD
HOTEL, AMBLESIDE.

(ADJOINING STEAM BOAT PIER. TERMINUS OF THE FURNESS & MIDLAND RAILWAY SYSTEMS.)

MICHAEL TAYLOR, Proprietor of the SALUTATION and QUEEN'S Hotels (both of which will be carried on by him as heretofore) has taken over the above first-class Hotel (recently enlarged and re-furnished), which will be conducted on a liberal and popular tariff.

Taylor's FOUR-IN-HAND COACHES run from the three Hotels to Keswick, Coniston, Ullswater, and the Langdales daily during the season, Sundays excepted. Boats, Fishing Tackle, &c.

A. HOULDIN,
Bookseller, Stationer, and Dealer in Fancy Goods,
LAKE ROAD,
AMBLESIDE.
—:o:—

Frith's Photographs of the Lake District. London, Liverpool, Manchester and other Papers supplied.

CROWN HOTEL, CONISTON.

Within three minutes' walk of the Railway Station and five from the Lake.

Choice Wines and Spirits, &c.
Post Horses and Conveyances.
BOATS ON THE LAKE.
BILLIARDS.
Conveyances to meet the Trains.

JAS. DOVE, Proprietor.

English Lakes.

CONISTON LAKE.
TYSON'S
WATERHEAD HOTEL.

Tel. Address: "Waterhead, Coniston."

This first-class Establishment is one of the most delightfully situated Hotels in the district. It stands in its own pleasure grounds, which are tastefully laid out, and has a large private frontage to the Lake, with shaded and beautiful walks leading to the Landing-stage of the "Gondola."

CROQUET AND TENNIS LAWN.
BOATS, BILLIARDS.

Postal Telegraph Station at Coniston.

Open and closed Carriages. Post Horses.

An Omnibus meets all Trains.

JOSEPH TYSON, Proprietor.

WOOLPACK INN,
ESKDALE.

Postal Address: —Eskdale, Boot, viâ Carnforth.
Telegraphic Address: —Woolpack, Ravenglass.

This ancient Inn has been recently enlarged and fitted up with Hot and Cold Baths, also refurnished for the accommodation of Tourists and Visitors. It is centrally situated in the beautiful valley of Eskdale between Scawfell, Scawfell Pikes, Bowfell, and Harter Fell. Esk Falls and Stanley Gill, the finest scene of its kind in the country, are within easy reach.

One mile from Boot Station. Conveyances kept.

Dixon Sharpe, Proprietor.

English Lakes.

DUNGEON GHYLL NEW HOTEL,
GREAT LANGDALE,
Near AMBLESIDE,

The nearest Hotel to Dungeon Ghyll and the Langdale Pikes.

Most conveniently situated for the a-cent of Scawfell and Bowfell; or for crossing the Passes to Wastwater, Borrowdale, &c. The best guides, conveyances, and mountain ponies may be had at the Hotel; also all information respecting mountains and mountain passes. **JOS. YOUDELL, Proprietor.**

Board and Lodging (except in August) 35s. a week.

This Hotel holds the Official Appointment of the GENERAL TOURIST'S CLUB. It is also Head-quarters of the C. T. C.

GRASMERE.

The very heart of the Lake District, the most Central Place from which to make Excursions to all the other Lakes and Mountains.

THE PRINCE OF WALES
LAKE HOTEL,

Patronised by

H.R.H. THE PRINCE OF WALES, PRINCE ARTHUR,
and the Nobility.

Beautifully situated on the margin of the Lake.

BILLIARDS, LAWN TENNIS, BOATING, ETC.

POSTING IN ALL ITS BRANCHES.

Char-a-bancs or Coaches to Ullswater, Coniston, Langdales, and Keswick during the season. Omnibuses meet the Steamboats at Waterhead.

Mrs. BROWN, Proprietress.

English Lakes.

(The Home of Pedestrians.—Central point of the Lake District.)

COWPERTHWAITE'S
ROTHAY HOTEL,
GRASMERE.

Delightfully situated in its own grounds of several acres, on the banks of the Rothay, and the nearest hotel to the resting-place of Wordsworth and Hartley Coleridge in Grasmere Churchyard.

This Hotel is under entirely new management and has been refurnished and redecorated.

Its position in the very heart of the loveliest scenery of English Lakeland, and on the coach-route from Windermere to Keswick, renders it an unsurpassed head-quarters from which to make **excursions in all directions.** The places conveniently visited from it by *carriage* include Rydal (the home of Wordsworth), Ambleside, Windermere, Coniston, the Langdales, Thirlmere, Keswick, and Patterdale (Ullswater); there are direct *pony-tracks* to Easedale Tarn, Borrowdale, Derwentwater, Ullswater, and the tops of Helvellyn and Fairfield; while the *pedestrian* has the greatest possible choice of routes.

Omnibuses to and from the Hotel every half-hour in connection with Windermere Steamers.

Special Note.—Public Coaches to Keswick, Coniston, Ullswater, the Langdales and Windermere.

PONIES AND GUIDES.
Lawn Tennis. Billiards. Boating, Fishing.

Parties, coming to the Hotel or to other places in the village can have conveyances to meet them at Windermere, Ambleside (Waterhead), or Keswick on application.

Telegraph: "Rothay Hotel, Grasmere."

J. COWPERTHWAITE, Proprietor.
Late of Mr. Fraser's Loch Awe Hotel, Argyleshire.

English Lakes.

THE KESWICK HOTEL.
(Lighted by electricity.)

This Hotel is pleasantly situated on an eminence overlooking the new Fitz Park, and commanding views of unsurpassed loveliness, including the principal mountains of the District, and is within a few minutes' walk from

Derwentwater. It is connected with the Railway Station by a covered way; porters attend all the trains, and the guests virtually alight at and depart from the Hotel. Spacious COFFEE and DRAWING ROOMS; also, lately added, a commodious and well supplied READING ROOM and a RECREATION ROOM. The Kitchen is supervised by an experienced Chef.

WILLIAM WILSON, Lessee.

English Lakes.

LAKE DERWENTWATER.

QUEEN'S HOTEL,
KESWICK.

This Hotel is the principal and largest in the town, is entirely under new management, and will be found replete with every comfort, having been redecorated and refurnished throughout.

Extensive and uninterrupted views of Skiddaw, Saddleback, Lake Derwentwater, and the surrounding scenery. Billiards, Hot and Cold Baths, and every accommodation required in a First Class Hotel.

Head Quarters for the Cyclist Touring Club.
COACHES TO ALL PARTS OF THE LAKE DISTRICT.
Posting in all its Branches.
An Omnibus and Porters meet all Trains at the Station Door.
PARTIES BOARDED BY WEEK OR MONTH.

R. BOWNASS, Proprietor.

KESWICK, CUMBERLAND.

JEFFERY'S "BLENCATHRA" HOTEL.
First-Class Temperance Commercial House.

This Old-Established Leading Temperance Hotel is situated close to the Station, and commands extensive and uninterrupted views of the charming scenery of the Lake District. Ladies' Public Drawing-room. Fine Coffee and Commercial Rooms. Hot and Cold Baths. Posting in all Departments. 'Bus meets all Trains. Telegrams to be addressed to

JEFFERY, Blencathra, Keswick.

English Lakes.

DERWENTWATER LAKE.
THE ROYAL OAK HOTEL, KESWICK.

Telegraphic Address :—ROYAL OAK, KESWICK."

Patronised by
The Late Queen Dowager.
H.R.H.
The Prince of Wales.
The King of Saxony.
The Grand Duke Constantine of Russia, &c., &c.

An Omnibus and Porters meet the Trains at the Station Door.

A Coach to Buttermere every morning at 10.

E. BOWDEN, Proprietor.

DERWENTWATER, KESWICK.
THE BORROWDALE HOTEL.

This Hotel is situate at the **head of Derwentwater** and commands unequalled views of the Lake and Mountain Scenery of this romantic district. Special Boarding arrangements.

'BUS FROM KESWICK STATION, 6d.

POSTING.

MOUNTAIN PONIES, BOATS, FISHING TACKLE, ETC.

Postal Address: "Borrowdale Hotel, Keswick."
Telegraphic: "Askew's 'Bus, Keswick."

W. ASKEW, Proprietor.

THE TOWER, PORTINSCALE.

(One Mile from Keswick.)

One of the most charmingly situated **Private Boarding and Lodging Houses** in the Lake District. Stands in its own Grounds. Commands views of the whole of Derwentwater, Bassenthwaite Lake, the Vale of Keswick, and the surrounding mountains. Ten minutes' walk from Crosthwaite Church, five from the Lake.

Derwentwater Hotel 'Bus meets the trains and coaches to and from all parts in connection with the Tower.

J. CARTMELL, Lessee.

Postal Address: PORTINSCALE, KESWICK.
Telegraphic Address: PORTINSCALE.

English Lakes.

BOATS. PONIES.
LAWN TENNIS.

DERWENTWATER HOTEL, Portinscale, Keswick.

Beautifully situated in its own grounds which slope down to the Lake, and surrounded on all sides by delightful walks and driving excursions.

Tel. Address (Office on the premises): "Harker, Portinscale, Keswick."

Mr. & Mrs. HARKER, Proprietors.
(Mrs. HARKER late M. E. BOWNASS of the Ullswater Hotel.)

Close to the Church.
COACHES TO ALL PARTS

English Lakes.

Tariff on Application.
TABLE D'HOTE 7 P.M.

Conveyances to all Parts of the District.
BILLIARDS, BOATS, &c.

ULLSWATER HOTEL, Patterdale. Penrith.

Is one of the largest and best situated first-class Hotels in the district for Families and Tourists, delightfully placed on the shores of Ullswater, within a few yards of the Steam Yacht pier, and commands most charming and varied views of the Lake and of the wild secluded glens and lofty rugged heights with which this picturesque and beautiful neighbourhood is surrounded. Helvellyn and Aira Force are in close proximity. The Steam Yacht and Coaches start from the front of the Hotel several times a-day.

M. BOWNASS, Proprietress.

Tel. Address: "Bownass, Patterdale."

English Lakes.

HOWTOWN HOTEL.

POSTAL ADDRESS—POOLEY BRIDGE, PENRITH.

Howtown is situated by the side of the beautiful bay at the end of the first reach of Ullswater. It is 4 miles from Pooley Bridge (nearest *Tel. Off.*), 6 from Patterdale, 9 from Penrith Station, 5 from the majestic "High Street," and 1½ hours' walk from Haweswater.

Good fishing may be enjoyed in the Lake close by. Pleasure boats and Guides. Steam-yacht calls 3 times a day both ways.

Parties taken in to Board and Lodge on reasonable terms.

Mrs. FARRER, Proprietress.

LOW WOOD HOTEL,
WINDERMERE.

ONE OF THE OLDEST ESTABLISHED HOTELS IN THE LAKE DISTRICT.

Beautifully situated close to, and overlooking, the finest expanse of Windermere Lake, with the loftiest cluster of English mountains, including Scawfell, Bowfell, the Langdale Pikes, and the Coniston Old Man, in the background; also within a few minutes' walk of the famous Troutbeck Road view of Windermere.

Centrally situated for excursions, on the high road from Windermere to Keswick, and easily accessible from all parts of the district.

Steamboat pier, at which all steamers call, opposite the door. Coaches and omnibuses to and from Windermere Station (3 miles) for every train.

May, 1890.

JOHN LOGAN, Proprietor.

English Lakes.

RIGG'S WINDERMERE HOTEL,
WINDERMERE,

(Nearest First Class Hotel in the Lake District to the "West Coast" route to Scotland.)

At this establishment Families and Tourists will meet with every accommodation. The Hotel is most beautifully situated on an eminence, commanding views of the Lake, Mountain, and Landscape Scenery, which are unsurpassed by any in the Lake District; and also within a convenient distance of the Windermere Railway Station. Spacious Coffee and Drawing Rooms, Private Drawing Rooms, also Billiard and Smoking Rooms. Postal and Telegraph arrangements excellent. Tariff, with full information, forwarded upon application.

The Royal Mail Four-Horse Stage Coaches run from this Hotel and the Windermere Railway Station daily (Sundays excepted), to and from Ambleside, Rydal, Grasmere Lake, Grasmere, Wythburn, Thirlmere, and Keswick-on-Derwentwater. For times of arrival and departure see London and North Western Railway Time Tables at all their Stations. Private Carriages or Omnibuses can be secured to meet the Trains at Windermere to convey families to other parts of the Lake District.

Tel. Address: "Rigg, Hotel, Windermere."

MAY, 1890.   JOHN RIGG, Proprietor.

WINDERMERE HYDROPATHIC.

The only Hydropathic in the Lake District.

Affords every convenience for pleasure and health seekers. Panoramic Views of Lake, Wood and Mountain. Four-in-hand Coaches start from the House daily. The largest Dining and Drawing Rooms in the district. Bedrooms unusually capacious and well ventilated.

Massage and Pumiline preparations in connection with Turkish and other Baths.

Illustrated Prospectus.   Address: THE MANAGER.

English Lakes.

OLD ENGLAND HOTEL,
BOWNESS-ON-WINDERMERE,
(Telegraphic Address: " Old England, Windermere.")
Within a hundred yards of the steamboat pier.

A First-class Hotel, patronised by the Nobility and best English and American families.

The Grounds extend to the Lake, with private Boat-Landings.

Billiards, Hot and Cold Baths, Lawn Tennis, &c.

Head Quarters of the Royal Windermere Yacht Club.

Four-in-Hand Coaches daily throughout the season to Coniston, Keswick, Ullswater, and the district generally.

Omnibuses attend all Trains at Windermere Station; also, at the steamboat pier, the boats from Lake Side (terminus of the Midland and Furness route) and Ambleside.

TARIFF ON APPLICATION.

Mrs. RICHARDS, Proprietress.

THE ROYAL HOTEL
BOWNESS-ON-WINDERMERE,
IS THE OLDEST ESTABLISHED HOTEL IN THE LAKE DISTRICT.

A Coffee Room is set apart for Ladies and Parties.

Coaches to all parts of the District.

Private Conveyances of every Description

Tel. Address: " Royal, Bowness, Windermere."

English Lakes.

CROWN HOTEL,
BOWNESS-ON-WINDERMERE.

Delightfully situated, immediately overlooking the Lake. Coaching and Posting to all parts daily.

Omnibuses and Servants attend all Trains and Steamers.

Tariff on Application.

F. GARNETT, Proprietress.

Telegrams: CROWN, WINDERMERE.

WASTWATER HOTEL,
WASDALE.

GREATLY ENLARGED.

Postal Address:—" Wasdale, Gosforth, viâ Carnforth."

Situated 1 mile above the head of the famous Wastwater, at the foot of the loftiest cluster of mountains in England, including Scawfell Pike, Scawfell, Great Gable, and the Pillar, and approached by the most romantic pony-tracks in the kingdom from all parts of the Lake District; also by road from Drigg (13 *miles*) and Seascale stations on the Furness Railway. Five miles by pony-track from Boot Station.

Conveyances, Guides, and Mountain Ponies.

English Lakes.

WINDERMERE.

LAKESIDE HOTEL
(*under new management*).

Postal Address: "near Ulverston"; *Telegraphic,* "Walker, Hotel, Newby Bridge."

Opposite Steamboat Pier and Railway Terminus
(Furness and Midland).
Fast Service of Trains from all parts; direct from St. Pancras.
COMMANDS A FINE VIEW UP THE LAKE.
Acknowledged to be the most artistic entrance to the District.

Boats.   Billiards.   Lawn Tennis.   Good Fishing.

Taylor B. Walker, Proprietor.

To open for the 1890 *season.*

THE "MORTAL MAN,"
TROUTBECK, WINDERMERE,

3½ miles from Windermere Station, 4 from Ambleside, 10 from Ullswater.

This well-known Inn has been greatly enlarged and converted into a comfortable

TOURIST HOTEL.

It is situated in the beautiful valley of Troutbeck on the coach route between Windermere and Ullswater, and commands a charming view of the Valley and Lake.

Wm. HAYTON, Proprietor.

English Lakes.

J. HOLLAND, House Agent,
Lake View Villas, Board & Lodging Houses,
BOWNESS-ON-WINDERMERE.

With or without Attendance, Linen and Plate.

Elevated Site, Fine Views of Lake and Mountains. Terraced Gardens. Three minutes' walk to the Lake.

Ireland.

Ardara, Co. Donegal.
NESBITT ARMS HOTEL.

The above Hotel, having been rebuilt and furnished in the most modern style, will be found most comfortable for Tourists visiting the Donegal Highlands.

Splendid Fishing and Charming Scenery in the Neighbourhood.

TERMS MODERATE.

N. McNELIS, Proprietor.

Ireland.

GRESHAM HOTEL, DUBLIN.

One of the largest, best appointed, and most comfortable Hotels in Ireland.

SITUATED IN SACKVILLE STREET.
Special Dining & Drawing Rooms for Ladies & Families.
Suites of Apartments.   First-class Cuisine.   Moderate Tariff.
Sanitary Certificate from Sir Chas. Cameron.

Connemara, Ireland.
(OPENED 1883.)

RENVYLE HOUSE HOTEL,

5 miles from Letterfrack; 14 from Clifden; 32 from Westport. Good Sea Bathing. Good Seal and Mixed Shooting. Good brown Trout and Sea Fishing. The situation of this Hotel is the finest in the country, close to the Sea, with Sea and Mountain Views, delightful in Spring, Summer and Autumn; it is mild in Winter, though there are fresh breezes from the sea. Renvyle should be full all the year.

PONY TRAPS, CARS, BOATS, & PONIES ON HIRE.
Two Lawn Tennis Grounds.

THE QUARTERLY REVIEW, April, 1887, says:—"At Renvyle is perhaps the purest and most fragrant air in Ireland or the British Isles."
"One of the loveliest places in the British Isles."—*Star*.
"We hope to come again, and shall certainly send our friends."—SYDNEY BUXTON, Esq., M.P., 15, Eaton Place, London.

TERMS: 10s. per day; £3. per week.
MRS. BLAKE, Renvyle, Letterfrack, Galway.

GIANT'S CAUSEWAY.

KANE'S ROYAL HOTEL.

Lately Renovated and Refitted with Bath-rooms, Hot and Cold Water, two large Coffee rooms, two Ladies' Drawing-rooms, Private Sitting-rooms.

Breakfast and Luncheon from 1s.; Dinner, 1s. 6d. to 2s. 6d. Bedroom for one person, 2s.; for two occupying one room, 3s. *No charge for attendance.* Weekly Terms on application to Mrs. KANE.

POSTING IN ALL ITS BRANCHES
At the lowest Terms to Carrick-a-Rede and back, on daily Car, 2s., or a party; same Terms.

This hotel is opposition to Causeway Hotel. Car and Porter attend all trams on public road.

Ireland.
GIANT'S CAUSEWAY.

CAUSEWAY HOTEL.

The only Hotel in Ireland which is lighted with Electric Light. A first-class Hotel, recently enlarged, and replete with every comfort, with Reception Room, Coffee Room, and Public Drawing Room, and accommodation for 70 guests. It is beautifully situated, overlooking the Atlantic, and within a few minutes' walk of the far-famed Giant's Causeway.

THE ELECTRIC TRAMWAY

runs from Portrush Railway Station direct to the Hotel Grounds, a distance of 8 miles. Everybody should travel by the Electric Cars (the great wonder of the age), and stay at the Causeway Hotel, where the charges will be found moderate.

Charming Views, Walks and Drives. Asphalte and Grass Tennis Courts.
Refreshment Kiosk & Electric Holophote.
GUIDES, BOATS AND POSTING AT FIXED CHARGES.
Posta and Telegraph Address—"The Manager, Causeway Hotel, Bushmills."

Ireland.
Killarney.
GRAHAM'S HOTEL,
NEW STREET
(Near POST OFFICE, opposite PRESBYTERIAN CHAPEL).

Tourists visiting Killarney will find this Hotel clean, comfortable, and home-like.

Tariff, Single Bed, 1s. 9d.; Double, 2s. Dinners 2s. 6d.; Tea 1s.

Our own Cars run daily to the Gap of Dunloe, Muckross, &c., and our own Boats ply every day on the Lakes with parties from the Hotel.

Write for Graham's "Programme of Tours" for two or three days, Post Free. Coupons for this Hotel can be obtained at Gaze's Dublin Office.

THE ROYAL BAY VIEW HOTEL,
(TOURIST AND COMMERCIAL),

KILLYBEGS, Co. DONEGAL.

Recently erected with all modern improvements, Hot and Cold Water, Plunge and Shower Baths.

POSTING IN ALL ITS BRANCHES.

Good Trout Fishing on the Lakes. The harbour is perfectly safe for Bathing, Boating, and Fishing.

Places of Interest in the District.

St. Catherine's Well, The Lighthouse, McSwine's Bay, St. Mary's Church, Niall Mor Tombstone, Fintragh, Caves of Muckross, Slieve League, the One Man's Pass and Bunglass, the Martello Towers, Tor Mor, Glen Gesh, and the Caves of Moghery.

Ireland—North Wales.

KILLALOE, CO. CLARE.
(One of Ireland's brightest beauty-spots.)

Good Salmon, Peel, and Trout fishing; Comfortable Accommodation with moderate charges at the

ROYAL HOTEL,

Within a few hours of Dublin by direct line.

Good Trout, Pike, and Perch fishing (*free*) on the lovely Lough Derg, the home of the famous Gillaroo Trout. May-fly fishing with natural fly attracts many regular visitors. A "second rise" frequently occurs in August. Peel fishing is at its best in June. Visitors have the privilege of some excellent salmon fishing free. No other Hotel of same name.

Miss Hurley, Proprietress.

BETTWS-Y-COED.

ROYAL OAK HOTEL

Tel. Address: "Oak, Bettws-y-Coed."

This celebrated Hotel has an unrivalled situation, and is very suitable as a centre from which the most beautiful scenery in North Wales may be visited.

Private Road to Station.

Omnibus meets all Trains

The Coaches for Llanberis, Beddgelert, Bangor, &c, start daily from this Hotel.

Posting. Lawn Tennis. Billiards. First-class Stabling.

EDWARD PULLAN, Proprietor.

North Wales.

THE GEORGE HOTEL,
BANGOR FERRY.

Bangor is the best centre for visiting all the best scenery in Snowdonia, etc.

The position of the Hotel is unrivalled, standing in its own extensive grounds on the banks of the Menai Straits, overlooking the famous Tubular and Suspension Bridges.

OMNIBUS MEETS TRAINS AT BANGOR STATION.

LAWN TENNIS, BOATS, BILLIARDS, POSTING, &c.

Tel. Address: "George Hotel, Bangor."

W. DUDLEY DANCE, Manager.

JUNCTION HOTEL, near CONWAY.

Within five minutes' walk of Conway Castle, immediately opposite Llandudno Junction Station and within ten minutes Train to Llandudno. Families, Tourists, and Commercial Gentlemen will find every comfort at this Hotel. Charges Moderate. Excellent Coffee and Private Sitting Rooms. With good view of Castle, River, and Town of Conway. Posting. Choicest Wines, Spirits, and Cigars.

C. JONES, Proprietress.

THE
VICTORIA HOTEL,
MENAI BRIDGE.

First-rate accommodation and reasonable charges. Omnibuses to and from Bangor Station four times daily. The Packets to and from Liverpool land passengers within two minutes' walk of the hotel. A first-class Billiard Table. Posting, Sea Bathing, Hot and Cold Baths, etc.

Special Winter Tariff on application.

C. HUMPHREYS, *Proprietress.*

Scotland.

ABERFOYLE.
BAILIE NICOL JARVIE HOTEL.

Tourists and Families will find every comfort at this Hotel, which has recently been enlarged. It is situated amidst enchanting scenery on the banks of the River Forth, at the *Starting Point* of the *New Road* to the Trossachs and Loch Katrine, over which Coaches are run daily during the summer. Boats on Loch Ard and Loch Chon for Fishing and Pleasure Parties. Tennis Lawn.

Railway Station, Post and Telegraph Offices within two minutes walk of the Hotel.

POSTING IN ALL ITS BRANCHES.

JAMES BLAIR,—Proprietor.

BLAIR ATHOLE.
ATHOLE ARMS HOTEL
(ADJOINING THE STATION).

Tel. Address : " Hotel, Blairathole."

Now one of the largest and best-appointed Hotels in the Highlands. Situation unrivalled as a central point from which to visit the scenery of the Perthshire Highlands, such as Killiecrankie, the Queen's View of Loch Tummel, Lochs Tay and Rannoch, Glen Tilt and Braemar, the Falls of Bruar, Garry, Tummel and Fender, Dunkeld, &c.

This is also the most convenient resting place for breaking the long railway journey to and from the North of Scotland.

Posting Department extensive and complete. Guides and Ponies for Braemar or Mountain Excursions.

D. MACDONALD & SONS,
Proprietors.

Scotland.

BRAEMAR.

THE
INVERCAULD ARMS,

In connection with the Invercauld Arms Hotel, Ballater.

THE FINEST HOTEL SITUATION IN SCOTLAND.

Recently Re-erected after Plans by J. T. WIMPERIS, *Esq., Sackville Street, London.*

Magnificent Dining Hall,

Elegant Ladies' Drawing Room,
AND
Numerous Suites of Apartments.

POSTING IN ALL ITS BRANCHES.

By appointment Posting Master to the Queen.

☞ **Coaches during the Season to Blairgowrie, Dunkeld, and Ballater.**

EXCELLENT SALMON FISHING
In connection with the Hotel.

Letters and Telegrams punctually attended to.

Tel. Address: "Invercauld Arms, Braemar."

A. McGREGOR.

Scotland.

DUNKELD.
FISHER'S
ROYAL HOTEL,

Under the Patronage of the Royal Family.

MR. FISHER begs to state that the additions and alterations to this large first-class Establishment are now completed; and, having been redecorated and refurnished in an elegant style, it will be found equal to any in the North of Scotland. A Large and Elegant Dining Saloon, with Ladies' Drawing Room (*en suite*). Private suites of Apartments, and Spacious Billiard and Smoking Saloon.

The only COACH for BRAEMAR and BALMORAL, via BLAIRGOWRIE, starts from the Hotel, where seats for the above can only be secured. Telegrams for Apartments, Coach Seats, or carriages punctually attended to. Omnibuses from the Hotel attend the different Trains.

LAURENSON & CO.,
Manufacturers of Shetland Goods
OF ALL DESCRIPTIONS,
LERWICK.

TO TOURISTS.

House of **West Hall** and Lodge of **Houllmawater** TO LET during summer.

West Hall House is about 1½ miles distant from Lerwick, and in close proximity to a beautiful white sea-beach, thus forming a nice quiet seaside resort.

Houllmawater Lodge is situated about 20 miles from Lerwick on the road to Walls, and is closely surrounded with a number of good fishing lochs. It has 3 rooms furnished and should make an excellent resort for a small party during the summer months.

Terms very moderate.

For further particulars apply to

GANSON BROTHERS, Lerwick.

Scotland.

EDINBURGH.

Nearly opposite the General Post Office, and only a few minutes' walk from General Railway Terminus.

Special terms for board during Winter Months.

DARLING'S
REGENT TEMPERANCE HOTEL,
20, WATERLOO PLACE, PRINCES STREET.

Edinburgh.

THE
WINDSOR HOTEL.
FIRST CLASS HOTEL FOR FAMILIES & GENTLEMEN.
100, PRINCES STREET,
OPPOSITE THE CASTLE.

A. M. THIEM, Proprietor.

BADDELEY'S Map of Loch Lomond, Trossachs, etc.,
By BARTHOLOMEW.
Half-inch to the mile, 6d.; by Post, 6½d.

London :— DULAU & Co., 37, Soho Square, W
Glasgow :—T. MURRAY & SON.

Scotland.

WATERLOO HOTEL,
Waterloo Place, Princes Street,
EDINBURGH.

J. GRIEVE, *Proprietor.*

EDINBURGH.
COCKBURN HOTEL,
Adjoining the WAVERLEY STATION.

Bed and Attendance from 2s. 6d. Tariff equally moderate.

JOHN MACPHERSON, Proprietor.

NOTE.—Within 10 minutes of Exhibition grounds.
No Spirituous Liquors.

Edinburgh.

LONDON HOTEL,
ST. ANDREW SQUARE.

Visitors to the International Electrical Exhibition will find this hotel most convenient. It is very central, quiet and comfortable.

Wines and Cuisine excellent.
CHARGES MODERATE.

J. J. MEPHIUS, Proprietor.

ROXBURGHE HOTEL,
CHARLOTTE SQUARE, EDINBURGH.

FIRST-CLASS FAMILY HOTEL.

In connection with the above is Christie's Private Hotel. Apartments *en suite*, and Board on moderate terms.

J. CHRISTIE, Proprietor.

Edinburgh.

CLARENDON HOTEL,
The Most economical First-Class Hotel in Scotland.
104 to 106, PRINCES STREET
(*Facing the Castle and Princes Gardens*).

THE FINEST SITE IN EDINBURGH.
ENGLISH MANAGEMENT.

GEO. ELLIS, Proprietor.

Scotland.

GLASGOW.
PHILP'S COCKBURN HOTEL,
141, BATH STREET.

PASSENGER ELEVATOR.

BILLIARD ROOMS.

Turkish & other Baths.

100 Rooms.

High Class Temperance House.

Bed and Attendance from 2s. 6d.

NOTICE—As the Proprietor *does not fee* the Cabmen, intending Visitors will please to see that they are at "Philp's Hotel, 141, Bath St.," before paying fare.

In connection with
PHILP'S COCKBURN HOUSE,
6, MONTAGUE PLACE, RUSSELL SQUARE,
LONDON.

TO TOURISTS, ANGLERS, AND ARTISTS.
THE GLENAFFRIC HOTEL,
CANNICH, STRATHGLASS, N.B.

This Hotel is beautifully situated on the river Cannich, and in one of the most romantic Glens in Scotland; is under New Management, and has recently undergone thorough repair, newly furnished throughout, and a fresh supply of water by gravitation added. Parties patronising this house will receive every attention and comfort, with cleanliness and moderate charges.

NEW CIRCULAR ROUTE.—Can be approached from Inverness by train to Beauly and drive of seventeen miles (one of the finest in the North, passing Beaufort Castle, Falls of Kilmorack, The Druim, Eilean Aigas, and Erchless Castle): or, by steamer from Inverness, Banavie, or Oban to Temple Pier, Loch Ness, thence a drive of fourteen miles through Glenurquhart and Corremonie. This route forms a Circular Tour unequalled in the Highlands.

Splendid Salmon and Trout Fishing for 2 miles on the River Cannich. Families and Gentlemen boarded by the week. Posting.

JOHN MACPHERSON, Proprietor.

Scotland.

GLENELG HOTEL,
STROME FERRY.

This Hotel, which has been rebuilt, is situated in one of the most beautiful parts of the West Coast of Scotland, easy of access by daily steamer from Oban, and quite near the island of Skye. The scenery all round is magnificent.

The Hotel is one of the most comfortable in the North of Scotland, and is under the personal superintendence of the lessee. The Bedrooms are large, airy, and comfortable, and the Coffee Room affords excellent accommodation. The cooking is good, and the Wines and Spirits have been selected with great care. Gentlemen staying at the GLENELG HOTEL have the privilege of SALMON and SEA-TROUT FISHING FREE on the Glenelg River; also GROUSE, BLACK GAME, and HARE SHOOTING, by the week or month, at a Moderate Charge. The Sea Fishing is about the best on the West Coast.

Boats and Boatmen.   Billiards.   Hot, Cold, and Shower Baths.

Among places of interest near are The Pictish Towers of Glenbeg, Cup Marked Stones, Glenbeg Water Falls, Loch Duich, Loch Hourn, Glenshiel, Falls of Glomach, Shiel Hotel, &c. *Telegraphic Address*, 'Glenelg Hotel, Lochalsh.'

DONALD MACDONALD MACKINTOSH, Lessee.

INVERNESS.

WAVERLEY HOTEL, INVERNESS.

Unsurpassed for Situation and Comfort

Combined with Moderate Charges.

One Minute's walk from the Railway Station.

Porter of the Hotel attends all Trains,

And an Omnibus runs in connection with the Caledonian Canal Steamers.

D. DAVIDSON,
PROPRIETOR.

Scotland.

ROYAL HOTEL,
INVERNESS.

The Proprietor of the above Hotel can with confidence solicit the patronage of all those visiting the Capital of the Highlands.

The ROYAL is conveniently situated, and is the only one *immediately opposite*, and within a *few yards* of the Railway Station entrance.

The Public Rooms, Private Sitting Rooms, and Bedrooms are large, lofty, and furnished throughout in the handsomest manner possible, and no expense has been spared to make this Hotel one of the best, as it is one of the quietest and most comfortable in Scotland.

Bed and Attendance from 3/-.
TARIFF EQUALLY MODERATE.

TABLE D'HÔTE DAILY.

The Hotel Porters await the arrival of all trains.

An Omnibus attends all the Canal Steamers.

J. S. CHRISTIE,
Proprietor.

Scotland.

INVERNESS.

VICTORIA HOTEL.

THE ONLY FIRST CLASS HOTEL FACING THE RIVER AND CASTLE.

Parties boarded by the week on Special Terms.
The Nearest Hotel to Canal Steamers.

JOHN BLACK.

Scotland.

LOCH AWE HOTEL.

(Under the same Management as the Dalmally Hotel, Loch Awe.)

This large and magnificently situated Hotel, at the foot of Ben Cruachan, and commanding a full view of the upper reaches of Loch Awe, with its beautiful islands, and Kilchurn Castle, has been fitted up with all the most modern improvements. The Loch Awe Station of the Callander and Oban Railway, and the Pier which forms the terminus of all the steamer routes, adjoin the grounds.

The Hotel Steamer "COUNTESS OF BREADALBANE" sails daily in connection with the beautiful drives through the Pass of Melfort and Glen Nant, and also to the Falls of Cruachan in the Pass of Brander.

Splendid Saloon Steamer "Mona" on Hire with Excursion Parties

Numerous Daily Excursions of Great Interest and Beauty.

Special arrangements made with families and large parties. Boats and boatmen in attendance.

Salmon and Trout Fishing on the Loch, Free.

Address:—D. FRASER, Loch Awe Hotel, Loch Awe.

DALMALLY HOTEL

(connected by Telephone with Loch Awe Hotel, 2½ m. distant),

is in the beautiful valley of the Orchy, half-a-mile from Dalmally Station. It has been much enlarged, and a handsome Dining Hall has been added.

THE CHALET.— On a fine site close to the Hotel there is erected a commodious Villa, which is used in connection with the Hotel, and where families can enjoy all the privacy of a home.

The Dalmally, Lochlomond (Tarbet), and Inveraray Coaches arrive at, and depart from this Hotel daily, and Tourists are booked to Dalmally by the splendid Steamer "Lord of the Isles."

LAWN TENNIS.

The Salmon-fishing in the Orchy, free to visitors at the Hotel, is amongst the best near the West Coast.

The following is a favourite route to the Highlands: Train to Greenock or Gourock; steamer "Lord of the Isles" to Inveraray; coach to Dalmally; train to Oban.

Tourists will find the above Hotels most convenient for breaking the journey to and from Oban and the Western Highlands, and most desirable starting-places for the excursions to Staffa and Iona, Glencoe, Loch Etive, Inveraray, Loch Awe, Falls of Orchy, &c., all of which can be made in a day.

D. FRASER, Proprietor.

Scotland.

PORTSONACHAN HOTEL,
LOCH AWE.

The proprietor of this well-known and favourite Hotel has had it enlarged, and it now contains spacious Dining Room, Smoking Room, Drawing Room, Private Sitting Rooms, and superior Bedroom accommodation.

The Hotel is delightfully situated, commanding views of Lake and Mountain Scenery which are unsurpassed in the west of Scotland.

Its Position is also very central, and many places of interest can be visited daily, including Oban, Inveraray, Loch Etive Head, Falls of Blairgour, Ford, and the Pass of Brander. All the steamers on the Lake call at the Hotel Pier, and the Hotel Steamer, besides visiting the various places of interest on the Loch, plies three times daily to and from Loch Awe Station in connection with trains from Oban and the South (*see Time-table below*). The Hotel can also be visited from Oban by the beautiful new route through Glen-Nant, originated by the proprietor.

The Fishing on Loch Awe is free, as also on several Hill Lakes, and first-class boats and experienced boatmen are reserved for the use of visitors. For fishing in connection with this hotel, see Sportsman's Guide, 1890.

A *Post Office* and a *Telegraph Office* have now been established in the Hotel, and letters are received and despatched three times daily during the season.

Letters and Telegrams receive prompt attention.

Postal Address :—　　　　　Telegraphic Address :—
PORTSONACHAN HOTEL,　　CAMERON, PORTSONACHAN.
LOCHAWE,
PORTSONACHAN, ARGYLLSHIRE, N.B.

STEAMER SAILINGS.		HOTEL TARIFF.	
Approximate.		Breakfast	2/6
("KILCHURN CASTLE.")		Lunch, from	1/0
Leave	Leave	Dinner	3/6
Portsonachan.	Lochawe Station.	Tea (plain)	1/6
*8.0 a.m.	†9.30 a.m.	Bedroom, from	2/6
12.40 p.m.	1.50 p.m.	Attendance	1/6
4.0 p.m.	5.20 p.m.	Fishing boat...per day	1/6

THOMAS CAMERON, Proprietor.

*Up to 1st July, 10 a.m.　　† Up to 1st July, 11.30 a.m.

Scotland.

Free Trout, Salmon, & Salmo-Ferox Fishing on Loch Awe.

TAYCREGGAN HOTEL,
NORTH PORTSONACHAN.

First-Class Hotel for Families and Anglers, close to Loch Awe at Portsonachan, half-an-hour's sail from Loch Awe Station, and one hour's drive from Taynuilt Station. Replete with every convenience. Is the *nearest* First-Class Hotel to Loch Awe, Loch Avich, Loch Nant, and ten other Hill Lochs, all Free to Visitors and mostly within easy walking distance, and some of which have been stocked with Loch Leven Trout and can only be fished by staying at this Hotel. All Steamers call at the Hotel Pier. A coach in connection with the steamer, 'Countess of Breadalbane,' leaves the Hotel daily in the season, running through Glen Nant. Passengers booked for Taynuilt, Oban, Head of Loch Etive and Loch Awe *vid* Pass of Brander.

Baths. Good Boats. Best Fishing Tackle. Post Horses.

Families Boarded.   Lawn Tennis.

Telegraphic Address: 'Taycreggan, Portsonachan, ¼ m.

A. & A. MUNRO.

THE TARBET HOTEL,
LOCH LOMOND,

Has recently undergone considerable alterations with extensive additions, and commands the best view of Ben Lomond.

Coaches to and from Inverary, Loch Awe, and Oban daily.

BOARDING ON MODERATE TERMS.

Small Boats on the Lake.   Fishing free.

Telegraphic Address:—Tarbet Hotel, Lochlomond.

A. H. MACPHERSON, Proprietor.

MOULIN HOTEL, PITLOCHRY,

One mile from and 150 feet above

PITLOCHRY STATION.

Enlarged and Refurnished.

BATH ROOM.   POSTING.
Beautiful Situation.   Invigorating Air.

Reduced Terms till August 1st.

Mrs. McDIARMID, Proprietress.

Scotland.

OBAN.
BOYD'S PRINTING OFFICE,
54, 56, & 58, GEORGE STREET.

The Leading Establishment in the Highlands, for the supply of all kinds of Books, Stationery, Fancy Goods, Charts, Maps, Guide Books, Photographs, Artists' Drawing Materials, &c., &c.

CHEAP ALBUM OF BONA-FIDE PHOTOGRAPHS,
In Scarlet and Gold Binding,
Contains 12 views for 1/-; Size, 4½×3 inches.
2 of Oban 1 Sunset from Oban (or Shepherd's Hat), Dunollie; Dunstaffnage and Gylen Castles; Blairgour Fall; Kilchurn Castle, Lochawe; Brander and Melfort Passes; Iona Cathedral; Fingal's Cave, Staffa.

Visitors should purchase BOYD's
Shilling Guide to Oban and Neighbourhood,
by
M. J. B. BADDELEY, Editor of "Thorough Guide" Series.
Plan of Oban and 4 Maps by BARTHOLOMEW.
Post Free.

Monthly Time Table and Diary, 1d.

Agent for Houses and Apartments to let in Oban and West Highlands. Printed Lists on application.

Villa on Isle of Kerrera, opposite Oban, to let.

CIRCULATING LIBRARY.

THOMAS BOYD,
Printer, Publisher, Bookseller,
Stationer & News-Agent.
(Facing the Bay.)

Scotland.

Great Western Hotel, OBAN.

LARGEST AND LEADING HOTEL IN THE WEST HIGHLANDS.

Beautifully situated on the Esplanade,
Close to the Pier
and
within five minutes' walk of the Railway Station.

An Omnibus conveys visitors to and from the hotel free of charge.

OBAN

ROYAL HOTEL.

(First-Class. New Management.)

Beautifully situated close to Railway Station and Steamboat Pier, commanding splendid views of marine and mountain scenery. Every Home Comfort. Moderate Charges. Billiards. Ladies' Drawing Room. Private Parlours. Boarding by arrangement. Trout and Salmon Angling.

JOHN McKENZIE, Proprietor.

(From Trossachs Hotel).

Scotland.

OBAN.
KING'S ARMS HOTEL.

This old-established Hotel has just been Rebuilt and Enlarged.

Has a commanding Sea View; is adjacent to the Railway Station and Steamboat Wharf; and possesses home comforts, combined with Moderate Charges.

Ladies' Drawing Room. Billiard, Smoking, and Bath Rooms.

Parties Boarded on moderate terms.

Table d'Hôte Daily.

Boots waits the arrival of Trains and Steamers.
Bus not necessary.   C.T.C. Headquarters.

ALEXANDER M'TAVISH, Proprietor.

ST. FILLANS.
DRUMMOND ARMS HOTEL,
ST. FILLANS, BY CRIEFF.

This commodious Hotel, beautifully situated at the foot of Lochearn, is well adapted for Families and Tourists.

St. Fillans is one of the loveliest places to be met with anywhere.

BOATS FOR FISHING
AND
CARRIAGES FOR HIRE.

Caledonian Coaches pass daily during the summer months.

Telegraphic Address :—Davie, St. Fillans.

A. DAVIE.

Scotland.

CUILFAIL HOTEL
KILMELFORD by LOCHGILPHEAD.
JOHN M'FADYEN.

Daily communication between GLASGOW and HERE by Steamer Via Ardrishaig, thence Coach; or by Rail to Oban, thence Coach.

Trout Fishing Boats kept & Steady Boatmen. | Telegraphic Office. Kilmartin, 14 Miles.
Luncheon & Tea always ready on arrival of Coaches from Oban & Loch Awe. | Telegrams by Post Daily at 3 P.M.

PASS OF MELFORT, near OBAN.
FIRST-CLASS TROUT FISHING.
Season—1st of April to end of September.

Gentlemen residing at Cuilfail Hotel have the privilege of fishing on several first-rate Lochs, some of which are annually stocked by the Hotel-keeper with the famous Loch Leven and Fontinalis, or Great American Brook Trout, from the Howieton Fishery, Stirling, which has greatly improved the Trout fishing Mr. M'Fadyen has boats and steady boatmen for the use of Anglers. Ther is excellent Deep-Sea Fishing, and delightful Sea Bathing. The scenery around is magnificent. The famous Pass of Melfort, which is very grand, is within a few minutes' walk of the Hotel; altogether a very healthy, charming place.

A handsome new Billiard Room (30 ft by 22 ft.) has this Spring been added to the Hotel, on the ground floor, the old Billiard Room having been converted into Bedrooms.

Lawn Tennis, Hot and Cold Baths, and all conveniences connected with Hotels.

Families can be boarded by the Week or Month.

POSTAL DELIVERY DAILY.

Gentlemen should write beforehand so as to secure rooms.
Luncheons always ready on arrival of Coaches to and from Oban, Ford, and Loch Awe.

CHARGES STRICTLY MODERATE.
POSTING IN ALL ITS BRANCHES.

ROUTE:—Per Caledonian Railway to Oban, thence per Coach daily; or by Steamer 'Columba' from Glasgow, Greenock or Gourock to Ardrishaig, thence per Royal Mail Coach daily, through magnificent Highland Scenery.

Address:—**JOHN M'FADYEN**, Cuilfail Hotel, Kilmelford, Argyllshire, N.B.   TELEGRAPH OFFICE:—KILMARTIN, N.B.
Telegrams by Post daily at 3 p.m., 14 miles.

Scotland.

PHILP'S
GLENBURN HYDROPATHIC ESTABLISHMENT,
ROTHESAY,

Recently Purchased from the Representatives of the late Dr. PATERSON by Mr. A. PHILP, of the COCKBURN HOTELS *EDINBURGH and GLASGOW.*

Rothesay, with its lovely Bay, is already famous as a Winter, and Spring Residence for those who suffer from the east winds, so prevalent in this country. Mr. PHILP, being sole proprietor, and unfettered by colleagues, as in most similar Establishments managed by Limited Companies, will be always anxious to adopt any improvement calculated to secure the greater Comfort and Enjoyment of the Visitors to Glenburn. He will also bring to bear in the Management and General Arrangement of the Establishment his long and successful experience in providing for the Travelling Public.

Resident Physician—Dr. PHILP, formerly of the Conishead Priory.

Prospectuses may be had on application to "The Manager," or at PHILP'S COCKBURN HOTEL, 141, BATH STREET, GLASGOW.
Also at the well-known
COCKBURN HOTEL, EDINBURGH.

ISLE OF SKYE.
BROADFORD HOTEL.

The best starting place for the Cuchullins, Loch Scavaig, and Loch Coruisk, which are seen to greatest advantage when approached from the sea.

Good Sea, River, and Loch fishing; also Boats free of charge. Parties boarded at moderate terms. All Steamers between Oban, Strome Ferry, Portree, Gairloch, Stornoway, &c., call here daily.

POSTING.   POST AND TELEGRAPH OFFICE.

J. ROSS, Lessee.

KYLEAKIN HOTEL.

This Hotel is situated in the Sound of Skye, amongst some of the grandest scenery of the Highlands, and is a suitable starting-point for the Cuchullins and other parts of Skye. One of Mr. David Macbrayne's swift line of Steamers calls daily during the Season, either going or returning between Oban and Gairloch, Ross-shire; also "Claymore" or "Clansman," twice a week between Glasgow and Stornoway.

Good Fishing and very suitable Bathing places in the vicinity. Often frequented by Artists. Every attention given to Sportsmen, Tourists, &c.

CHARGES MODERATE.

Mrs. TURNER, Lessee.

SKYE.
SLIGACHAN HOTEL.
NEAREST HOUSE TO LOCH CORUISK.

Beautifully situated at the foot of the Coolin Hills. Parties living in the hotel have the privilege of good Sea-Trout Fishing on the river Sligachan; also good Loch and Sea Fishing.

BOATS FREE OF CHARGE.
BOATMEN, 4s. per Day.

Parties landing at Coruisk can have Ponies or Guides sent to meet them at Camasunary, or the hill above Coruisk, by sending letter or telegram addressed "Sligachan, viâ Portree, per post" the day previous. Posting.

W. SHARP, Lessee.

Shetland.

THE
GRAND HOTEL,
LERWICK.

Under new management.

This large first-class Hotel is now open under entirely new management, and will be found by Tourists and others visiting Shetland one of the most comfortable and best appointed Hotels in the North.

Large and Spacious Coffee Room.

SPLENDID BILLIARD ROOM.

PRIVATE PARLOURS.

Hot and Cold Baths.

BOATING.   FISHING.   SEA BATHING.

Address :—THE MANAGER.

. Telegrams to GRAND HOTEL, LERWICK.

Scotland.

SPA HOTEL,
STRATHPEFFER, N.B.

The Oldest Established and Leading Hotel.
RECENTLY ENLARGED.
Replete with every Comfort.
Best Situation (400 feet above sea-level).
Magnificent Dining Room, Drawing Room, Conservato.ies,
Library, Smoking and Billiard Rooms, &c.
Bowling and Tennis Greens.
LADIES' AND GENTLEMEN'S BATHROOMS.
DOUCHE ROOM.
Excellent Salmon Angling, also Trout-fishing in several Lochs.
TERMS MODERATE.
A. WALLACE, PROPRIETOR.

www.ingramcontent.com/pod-product-compliance
Lightning Source LLC
Chambersburg PA
CBHW031901220426
43663CB00006B/722